Scott Foresman·Addison Wesley

enVisionMATH™

D0880693

Scott Foresman·Addison Wesley

enVisionMATH
Illinois

Authors

Randall I. Charles
Professor Emeritus
Department of Mathematics
San Jose State University
San Jose, California

Janet H. Caldwell
Professor of Mathematics
Rowan University
Glassboro, New Jersey

Mary Cavanagh
Mathematics Consultant
San Diego County Office of Education
San Diego, California

Dinah Chancellor
Mathematics Consultant with Carroll ISD
Southlake, Texas
Mathematics Specialist with Venus ISD
Venus, Texas

Juanita V. Copley
Professor
College of Education
University of Houston
Houston, Texas

Warren D. Crown
Associate Dean for Academic Affairs
Graduate School of Education
Rutgers University
New Brunswick, New Jersey

Francis (Skip) Fennell
Professor of Education
McDaniel College
Westminster, Maryland

Alma B. Ramirez
Sr. Research Associate
Math Pathways and Pitfalls WestEd
Oakland, California

Kay B. Sammons
Coordinator of Elementary Mathematics
Howard County Public Schools
Ellicott City, Maryland

Jane F. Schielack
Professor of Mathematics
Associate Dean for Assessment and
Pre K-12 Education, College of Science
Texas A&M University
College Station, Texas

William Tate
Edward Mallinckrodt Distinguished
University Professor in Arts & Sciences
Washington University
St. Louis, Missouri

John A. Van de Walle
Professor Emeritus, Mathematics Education
Virginia Commonwealth University
Richmond, Virginia

Consulting Mathematicians

Edward J. Barbeau
Professor of Mathematics
University of Toronto
Toronto, Canada

Sybilla Beckmann
Professor of Mathematics
Department of Mathematics
University of Georgia
Athens, Georgia

David Bressoud
DeWitt Wallace Professor of Mathematics
Macalester College
Saint Paul, Minnesota

Gary Lippman
Professor of Mathematics and Computer Science
California State University East Bay
Hayward, California

PEARSON
Scott Foresman

Editorial Offices: Glenview, Illinois • Parsippany, New Jersey • New York, New York
Sales Offices: Boston, Massachusetts • Duluth, Georgia • Glenview, Illinois
Coppell, Texas • Sacramento, California • Mesa, Arizona

Consulting Authors

Charles R. Allan
Mathematics Education Consultant
(Retired)
Michigan Department of Education
Lansing, Michigan

Verónica Galván Carlan
Private Consultant Mathematics
Harlingen, Texas

Stuart J. Murphy
Visual Learning Specialist
Boston, Massachusetts

Jeanne Ramos
Secondary Mathematics Coordinator
Los Angeles Unified School District
Los Angeles, California

ELL Consultants/Reviewers

Jim Cummins
Professor
The University of Toronto
Toronto, Canada

Alma B. Ramirez
Sr. Research Associate
Math Pathways and Pitfalls WestEd
Oakland, California

National Math Development Team

Cindy Bumbales
Teacher
Lake in the Hills, IL

Ann Hottovy
Teacher
Hampshire, IL

Deborah Ives
Supervisor of Mathematics
Ridgewood, NJ

Lisa Jasumback
Math Curriculum Supervisor
Farmington, UT

Rebecca Johnson
Teacher
Canonsburg, PA

Jo Lynn Miller
Math Specialist
Salt Lake City, UT

Patricia Morrison
Elementary Mathematics Specialist K-5
Upper Marlboro, MD

Patricia Horrigan Rourke
Mathematics Coordinator
Holliston, MA

Elise Sabaski
Teacher
Gladstone, MO

Math Advisory Board

John F. Campbell
Teacher
Upton, MA

Enrique Franco
Coordinator Elementary Math
Los Angeles, CA

Gladys Garrison
Teacher
Minot AFB, ND

Pat Glubka
Instructional Resource Teacher
Brookfield, UT

Shari Goodman
Math Specialist
Salt Lake City, UT

Cathy Massett
Math Facilitator
Cobb County SD, GA

Mary Modene
Math Facilitator
Belleville, IL

Kimya Moyo
Math Manager
Cincinnati, OH

Denise Redington
Teacher
Chicago, IL

Arlene Rosowski
Supervisor of Mathematics
Buffalo, NY

Darlene Teague
Director of Core Data
Kansas City, MO

Debbie Thompson
Elementary Math Teaching Specialist
Wichita, KS

Michele Whiston
Supervisor
Curriculum, Instruction, and Assessment
Mobile County, AL

Scott Foresman-Addison Wesley
enVisionMATH™
Illinois

ISBN-13: 978-0-328-33056-0
ISBN-10: 0-328-33056-6

Copyright © 2009 Pearson Education, Inc.
All rights reserved. Printed in the United States of America. This publication is protected by Copyright, and permission should be obtained from the publisher prior to any prohibited reproduction, storage in a retrieval system, or transmission in any form by any means, electronic, mechanical, photocopying, recording, or otherwise. For information regarding permission(s), write to: Permissions Department, Scott Foresman, 1900 East Lake Avenue, Glenview, Illinois 60025.

2 3 4 5 6 7 8 9 10 V042 12 11 10 09 08

Many of the designations used by manufacturers and sellers to distinguish their products are claimed as trademarks. Where those designations appear in this book, and Scott Foresman was aware of a trademark claim, the designations have been printed with initial capitals and in cases of multiple usage have also been marked with either ® or ™ where they first appear.

enVisionMATH is trademarked in the U.S. and/or foreign countries of Pearson Education, Inc. or its affiliate(s).

Topic Titles

Contents

Illinois Mathematics Performance Descriptors and Illinois Mathematics Assessment Framework Objectives for each Topic are listed throughout these Contents pages.

MATH STRAND COLORS

Number and Operations

Algebra

Geometry

Measurement

Data Analysis and Probability

Problem Solving

Mathematical Processes, which include problem solving, reasoning, communication, connections, and representations, are infused throughout all lessons.

Topic 1 — Numeration

Performance Descriptors
6A.Stage D.1., 8A.Stage D.5.
Assessment Framework Objectives
6.4.01, 6.4.05, 6.4.11, 6.4.16, 8.4.04

Topic 2 — Adding and Subtracting Whole Numbers

Performance Descriptors
6C.Stage D.1., 8C.Stage D.1.
Assessment Framework Objectives
6.4.10, 6.4.14, 6.4.16, 8.4.05, 8.4.06

enVisionMATH™ Illinois

enVisionMATH Illinois

Problem Solving Using
Number and Operations

Sedimentary Rock in Illinois

Illinois has about 80 thousand cubic miles of sedimentary rock. A cubic mile is a cube that is one mile long on each side. Much of this rock formed at a time when the land was covered by shallow seas and huge swamps. About $\frac{1}{2}$ of Illinois' sedimentary rock is limestone. About $\frac{1}{4}$ is sandstone. Illinois also has coal that formed from the remains of plants that lived long ago.

Illinois State Reptile

The painted turtle became the Illinois State Reptile in 2005. Painted turtles are often found in calm, shallow bodies of water. They often sun themselves on logs, and they eat fish. An adult painted turtle weighs about 13 ounces. A female painted turtle can lay 2 to 3 sets of eggs each year. Each set has 8 to 9 eggs.

Directions: Write your answers to questions 1–20 on a separate sheet of paper.

Flying Pumpkins

Every year the city of Morton holds a pumpkin-tossing contest. People throw pumpkins as far as they can. They even shoot them from air cannons. In 2001 it was reported that the Q36 air cannon threw a pumpkin 4,860 feet! In 2006 the longest throw by a person was reported as $49\frac{3}{4}$ feet.

1

Which correctly compares the amount of limestone and sandstone in Illinois?

A $\frac{1}{2} < \frac{1}{4}$.
More limestone.

B $\frac{1}{2} < \frac{1}{4}$.
More sandstone.

C $\frac{1}{2} > \frac{1}{4}$.
More limestone.

D $\frac{1}{2} > \frac{1}{4}$.
More sandstone.

2

A painted turtle can be $\frac{1}{2}$ foot long. Write a fraction that is equivalent to $\frac{1}{2}$.

3

A painted turtle laid 3 sets of eggs in one year. Each set contained 8 eggs. What was the total number of eggs?

4

What is the total weight of five adult painted turtles?

A About 50 ounces **C** About 80 ounces
B About 65 ounces **D** About 95 ounces

5

A person threw a pumpkin $49\frac{3}{4}$ feet. Which is equivalent to $49\frac{3}{4}$?

A $49\frac{2}{3}$ **C** $49\frac{9}{12}$

B $49\frac{4}{5}$ **D** $49\frac{9}{10}$

6

An air cannon threw a pumpkin 4,860 feet. Which is another way to write 4,860?

A $4 + 8 + 6 + 0$ **C** $400 + 80 + 6 + 0$
B $40 + 80 + 60$ **D** $4000 + 800 + 60$

enVisionMATH Illinois

Problem Solving Using
Geometry

Home of General Ulysses S. Grant · · · · · · · · · · · · · · · ·

After the Civil War was over, General Ulysses S. Grant returned to Galena. The city celebrated. People were so pleased by Grant's return that they bought him a house. Grant was elected President of the United States in 1868. Today people can tour Grant's home. Visitors see how the inside of the home might have looked in the 1860s.

7

Look at one of the windows in the photograph of Grant's home. What is the shape of the window?

A Rectangle   **C** Oval
B Circle   **D** Square

8

What are the map coordinates of Grant's home?

A (4, D)   **C** (4, B)
B (3, E)   **D** (3, D)

9

What are the map coordinates of the location where Decatur Street crosses the Galena River?

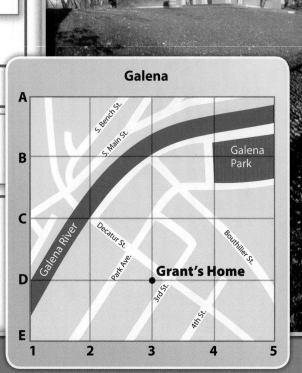

Galena

Problem Solving Using
Measurement

Great Plains Prairie Postage Stamps

Much of Illinois was once covered with prairie. In some places, prairie grass may have been 10 feet high. Pioneers compared the Great Plains prairie to an ocean of grass. Sheets of postage stamps showing plants and animals of the Great Plains prairie were released in 2001. Each sheet contained 10 stamps. A sheet was about 9 inches wide and 7 inches high.

©2001 USPS

N A T U R E   O F

Popeye Statue

The man who created Popeye was born in the city of Chester. Some people believe many of the characters in Popeye were based on people who lived in the city. Today a 6-foot statue of Popeye stands in one of Chester's parks. The city has a Popeye Picnic every year.

10

Which is the best estimate of the perimeter of a sheet of prairie postage stamps?

   A 16 inches   **C** 28 inches

   B 22 inches   **D** 32 inches

11

Which shows how to find the approximate area of a sheet of prairie postage stamps?

   A 9×7 **C** $9 \div 7$

   B $9 + 7$ **D** $9 - 7$

12

How tall is the Popeye statue in yards? Explain your answer.

enVisionMATH Illinois

Problem Solving Using
Data Analysis and
Probability

Children's Museum of Illinois

Decatur is the home of the Children's Museum of Illinois. Museum visitors can explore all kinds of fun things. They can even use a 3-D virtual-reality system to experience snowboarding or play soccer. The exhibits change over time. In 2006 an exhibit allowed visitors to make giant bubbles that were bigger than they were.

13

Use the graph below. How likely is it that a giant bubble made in 2006 at the Children's Museum of Illinois could be at least 60 inches in height?

A Certain   **C** Unlikely

B Likely   **D** Impossible

14

Look at the graph showing the heights of giant bubbles. What is the median height?

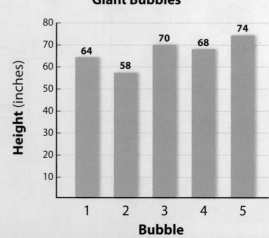

Giant Bubbles

Illinois State Fossil

Illinois has its own state fossil—the Tully Monster! Tully Monsters once swam in the ocean that covered much of the land that later became Illinois. They had sharp teeth, and they probably ate other animals. They are extinct now. Tully Monsters were named after Francis Tully, who took some of their fossils to the Field Museum of Natural History in Chicago in 1958.

Lincoln Pennies

Abraham Lincoln was born in 1809. When he was a young man, he moved to Illinois. He was elected President of the United States in 1860. In 1909 the Lincoln penny was made to celebrate the 100th anniversary of Lincoln's birth. The design on the backs of Lincoln pennies used to show two stalks of wheat. In 1959 the design was changed to show the Lincoln Memorial.

Pennies in Students' Pockets

Student	Number of Pennies
Maria	卌
Lisa	||
Joon	卌 ||||
Reggie	||||
Sue	卌 ||

15

How likely would it be to find a Tully Monster living in Illinois today?

A Certain   **C** Unlikely

B Likely   **D** Impossible

16

Look at the tally chart showing the number of pennies in students' pockets. What is the total number of pennies?

A 19   **C** 27

B 22   **D** 31

17

How many more pennies does Joon have than Sue? Explain how you know.

18

A penny that is tossed can land on heads or tails. If a 2006 penny is tossed many times, how often should it land on tails?

A $\frac{1}{2}$ of the time   **C** $\frac{1}{4}$ of the time

B $\frac{1}{3}$ of the time   **D** $\frac{1}{5}$ of the time

Problem Solving Using
Algebra

Dragonflies

Illinois is home to many types of dragonflies. That's good news for people because dragonflies eat mosquitoes and black flies. Some dragonflies can flap their wings more than 30 times per second. They may reach a speed as fast as 88 feet per second while flying! Dragonflies see very well. Their eyes cover much of their heads.

19

A dragonfly flapped its wings 30 times each second while it was flying. It flapped its wings a total of 180 times. In the number sentence below, what value for Δ shows the number of seconds the dragonfly flew?

$$30 \times \Delta = 180$$

A 5   **C** 7
B 6   **D** 8

20

A dragonfly flies 80 feet per second for 5 seconds. Write a number sentence to show the number of feet the dragonfly has flown.

Problem-Solving Handbook

Scott Foresman·Addison Wesley
enVisionMATH™

Problem-Solving Handbook

Use this Problem-Solving Handbook throughout the year to help you solve problems.

Don't give up!

Everybody can be a good problem solver!

There's almost always more than one way to solve a problem!

Don't trust key words.

Pictures help me understand!

Explaining helps me understand!

Problem-Solving Process

Read and Understand

? What am I trying to find?
- Tell what the question is asking.

? What do I know?
- Tell the problem in my own words.
- Identify key facts and details.

Plan and Solve

? What strategy or strategies should I try?

? Can I show the problem?
- Try drawing a picture.
- Try making a list, table, or graph.
- Try acting it out or using objects.

? How will I solve the problem?

? What is the answer?
- Tell the answer in a complete sentence.

Strategies
- Show What You Know
  - Draw a Picture
  - Make an Organized List
  - Make a Table
  - Make a Graph
  - Act It Out/ Use Objects
- Look for a Pattern
- Try, Check, Revise
- Write an Equation
- Use Reasoning
- Work Backward
- Solve a Simpler Problem

Look Back and Check

? Did I check my work?
- Compare my work to the information in the problem.
- Be sure all calculations are correct.

? Is my answer reasonable?
- Estimate to see if my answer makes sense.
- Make sure the question was answered.

Using Bar Diagrams

Use a bar diagram to show how what you know and what you want to find are related. Then choose an operation to solve the problem.

Problem 1

Carrie helps at the family flower store in the summer. She keeps a record of how many flower bouquets she sells. How many bouquets did she sell on Monday and Wednesday?

Carrie's Sales

Days	Bouquets Sold
Monday	19
Tuesday	22
Wednesday	24
Thursday	33
Friday	41

Bar Diagram

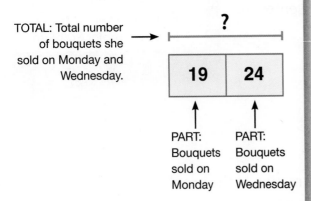

TOTAL: Total number of bouquets she sold on Monday and Wednesday.

PART: Bouquets sold on Monday

PART: Bouquets sold on Wednesday

19 + 24 = ▨

 Think I can add to find the total.

Problem 2

Kim is saving to buy a sweatshirt from the college her brother attends. She has $18. How much more money does she need to buy the sweatshirt?

Bar Diagram

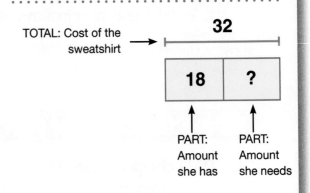

TOTAL: Cost of the sweatshirt

PART: Amount she has

PART: Amount she needs

32 − 18 = ▨

 Think I can subtract to find the missing part.

Pictures help me understand!

Don't trust key words!

Tickets to a movie on Saturday cost only $5 each no matter what age you are. What is the cost of tickets for a family of four?

Bar Diagram

TOTAL: Total cost of the tickets → **?**

| 5 | 5 | 5 | 5 |

↑ PART: Cost of each ticket

$$4 \times 5 = \blacksquare$$

Think I can multiply because the parts are equal.

Thirty students traveled in 3 vans to the zoo. The same numbers of students were in each van. How many students were in each van?

Bar Diagram

TOTAL: Total number of students → **30**

| ? | ? | ? |

↑ PART: Number in each van

$$30 \div 3 = \blacksquare$$

Think I can divide to find how many are in each part.

Problem-Solving Strategies

Strategy	Example	When I Use It
Draw a Picture	The race was 5 kilometers. Markers were at the starting line and the finish line. Markers showed each kilometer of the race. Find the number of markers used.	Try drawing a picture when it helps you visualize the problem or when the relationships such as joining or separating are involved.
Make a Table	Phil and Marcy spent all day Saturday at the fair. Phil rode 3 rides each half hour and Marcy rode 2 rides each half hour. How many rides had Marcy ridden when Phil rode 24 rides?	Try making a table when: • there are 2 or more quantities, • amounts change using a pattern.
Look for a Pattern	The house numbers on Forest Road change in a planned way. Describe the pattern. Tell what the next two house numbers should be.	Look for a pattern when something repeats in a predictable way.

Draw a Picture example diagram:

Start Line ———————————— Finish Line

Start Line — 1 km — 2 km — 3 km — 4 km — Finish Line

Make a Table example:

Rides for Phil	3	6	9	12	15	18	21	24
Rides for Marcy	2	4	6	8	10	12	14	16

Look for a Pattern house numbers: 3 6 10 15 ? ?

Strategy	Example	When I Use It
Make an Organized List	How many ways can you make change for a quarter using dimes and nickels?	Make an organized list when asked to find combinations of two or more items.

1 quarter =
1 dime + 1 dime + 1 nickel
1 dime + 1 nickel + 1 nickel + 1 nickel
1 nickel + 1 nickel + 1 nickel + 1 nickel + 1 nickel

Try, Check, Revise	Suzanne spent $27, not including tax, on dog supplies. She bought two of one item and one of another item. What did she buy? $8 + $8 + $15 = $31 $7 + $7 + $12 = $26 $6 + $6 + $15 = $27	Use Try, Check, Revise when quantities are being combined to find a total, but you don't know which quantities.

Dog Supplies Sale!
Leash.................................$8
Collar................................$6
Bowls $7
Medium Beds....................$15
Toys $12

Write an Equation	Maria's new CD player can hold 6 discs at a time. If she has 204 CDs, how many times can the player be filled without repeating a CD? Find $204 \div 6 = n$.	Write an equation when the story describes a situation that uses an operation or operations.

Everybody can be a good problem solver!

Even More Strategies

Strategy	Example	When I Use It
Act It Out	How many ways can 3 students shake each other's hand?	Think about acting out a problem when the numbers are small and there is action in the problem you can do.
Use Reasoning	Beth collected some shells, rocks, and beach glass. **Beth's Collection** 2 rocks 3 times as many shells as rocks 12 objects in all How many of each object are in the collection?	Use reasoning when you can use known information to reason out unknown information.
Work Backward	Tracy has band practice at 10:15 A.M. It takes her 20 minutes to get from home to practice and 5 minutes to warm up. What time should she leave home to get to practice on time? Time Tracy leaves home **?** ← 20 minutes ← Time warm up starts ← 5 minutes ← Time practice starts **10:15**	Try working backward when: • you know the end result of a series of steps, • you want to know what happened at the beginning.

> I can think about when to use each strategy.

Strategy	Example	When I Use It

Solve a Simpler Problem 	Each side of each triangle in the figure at the left is one centimeter. If there are 12 triangles in a row, what is the perimeter of the figure?
	
	 I can look at 1 triangle, then 2 triangles, then 3 triangles.
	
	     perimeter = 3 cm
	
	     perimeter = 4 cm
	
	     perimeter = 5 cm
		Try solving a simpler problem when you can create a simpler case that is easier to solve.

Make a Graph	Mary was in a jump rope contest. How did her number of jumps change over the five days of the contest? 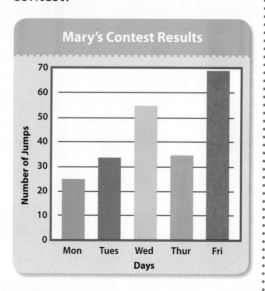	Make a graph when: • data for an event are given, • the question can be answered by reading the graph.

Writing to Explain

Here is a good math explanation.

Writing to Explain What happens to the area of the rectangle if the lengths of its sides are doubled?

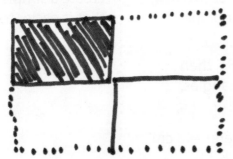

■ = $\frac{1}{4}$ of the whole rectangle

The area of the new rectangle is 4 times the area of the original rectangle.

Tips for Writing Good Math Explanations....

A good explanation should be:
- correct
- simple
- complete
- easy to understand

Math explanations can use:
- words
- pictures
- numbers
- symbols

This is another good math explanation.

Explaining helps me understand!

Writing to Explain Use blocks to show 13 × 24. Draw a picture of what you did with the blocks.

First we made a row of 24 using 2 tens and 4 ones. Then we made more rows until we had 13 rows. Then we said 13 rows of 2 tens is 13 × 2 tens = 26 tens or 260. Then we said 13 rows of 4 ones is 13 × 4 = 52. Then we added the parts. 260 + 52 = 312   So, 13 × 24 = 312.

Problem-Solving Recording Sheet

Name ___Jane___

Teaching Tool
1

Problem-Solving Recording Sheet

Problem:
On June 14, 1777, the Continental Congress approved the design of a national flag. The 1777 flag had 13 stars, one for each colony. Today's flag has 50 stars, one for each state. How many stars were added to the flag since 1777?

Find?

Number of stars added to the flag

Know?

Original flag
13 stars

Today's flag
50 stars

Strategies?

Show the Problem
- ☑ Draw a Picture
- ☐ Make an Organized List
- ☐ Make a Table
- ☐ Make a Graph
- ☐ Act It Out/Use Objects

- ☐ Look for a Pattern
- ☐ Try, Check, Revise
- ☑ Write an Equation
- ☐ Use Reasoning
- ☐ Work Backwards
- ☐ Solve a Simpler Problem

Show the Problem?

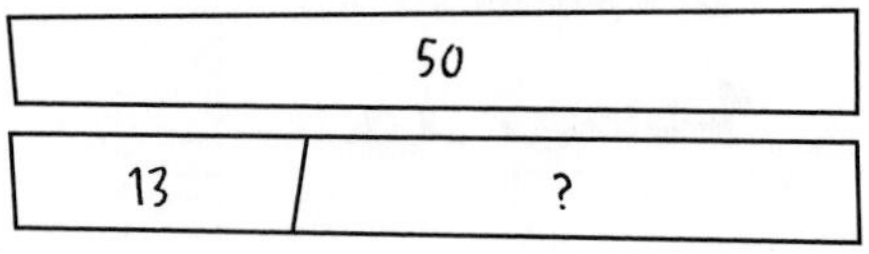

50

13	?

Solution?

I am comparing the two quantities.
I could add up from 13 to 50. I can also subtract 13 from 50. I'll subtract.

$$\begin{array}{r} 50 \\ -\ 13 \\ \hline 37 \end{array}$$

Answer?

There were 37 stars added to the flag from 1777 to today.

Check? Reasonable?

37 + 13 = 50 so I subtracted correctly.

50 − 13 is about 50 − 10 = 40
40 is close to 37. 37 is reasonable.

Teaching Tools • 1

Name _Benton_

Teaching Tool
1

Problem-Solving Recording Sheet

Problem:

Suppose your teacher told you to open your math book to the facing pages whose pages numbers add to 85. To which two pages would you open your book?

Find?

Two facing page numbers

Know?

Two pages.
Facing each other.
Sum is 85.

Strategies?

Show the Problem
☑ Draw a Picture
☐ Make an Organized List
☐ Make a Table
☐ Make a Graph
☐ Act It Out/Use Objects

☐ Look for a Pattern
☑ Try, Check, Revise
☑ Write an Equation
☐ Use Reasoning
☐ Work Backwards
☐ Solve a Simpler Problem

Show the Problem?

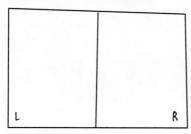

$L + R = 85$
L is 1 less than R

Solution?

I'll try some numbers in the middle.
40 + 41 = 81, too low
How about 46 and 47?
46 + 47 = 93, too high
Ok, now try 42 and 43.
42 + 43 = 85.

Answer?

The page numbers are 42 and 43.

Check? Reasonable?

I added correctly.
42 + 43 is about 40 + 40 = 80
80 is close to 85.
42 and 43 is reasonable.

Teaching Tools • 1

Topic 1

Numeration

1 "Baby," the snake, weighs 403 pounds. Is it the heaviest snake that is living in captivity? You will find out in Lesson 1-3.

2 About how many people visit the Brookfield Zoo each year? You will find out in Lesson 1-4.

3 The African continent has an area of 11,608,000 square miles. Is it the largest continent on Earth? You will find out in Lesson 1-3.

Review What You Know!

Vocabulary

Choose the best term from the box.

> • digits   • period
> • compare   • number line
> • even   • odd

1. A group of three digits in a number separated by a comma is a _?_.

2. A _?_ is a line that shows numbers in order using a scale.

3. The number 8 is an _?_ number.

4. The number 5 is an _?_ number.

Comparing Numbers

Compare each set of numbers using >, < or =.

5. 13 ◯ 10   6. 7 ◯ 7   7. 28 ◯ 29

8. 14 ◯ 5   9. 43 ◯ 34   10. 0 ◯ 1

11. 52 ◯ 52   12. 13 ◯ 65   13. 22 ◯ 33

Place Value

Tell if the underlined digit is in the ones, tens, or hundreds place.

14. 34<u>6</u>   15. <u>1</u>7   16. 9<u>2</u>1

17. <u>1</u>06   18. 3<u>3</u>   19. <u>4</u>7

20. <u>2</u>17   21. <u>3</u>20   22. 81<u>0</u>

23. 1,00<u>6</u>   24. <u>9</u>99   25. 1,4<u>0</u>5

26. **Writing to Explain** How does using commas to separate periods help you read large numbers?

4

How much gold is stored in Fort Knox? You will find out in Lesson 1-2.

Lesson

1-1

Understand It!
There are many ways to
represent a number.

Thousands

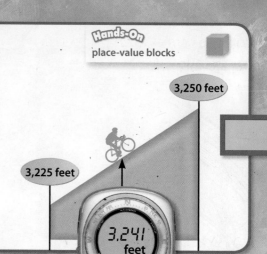

Hands-On
place-value blocks

3,250 feet

3,225 feet

3.241 feet

What are some ways to write numbers in the thousands?

Jill is 3,241 feet above sea level. There are different ways to represent 3,241.

Another Example How do you read and write numbers in the thousands?

Another bicycle racer is 5,260 feet above sea level. Write 5,260 in standard form, expanded form, and word form.

When writing a number in standard form, write only the digits: 5,260.

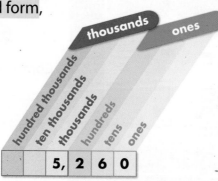

thousands   ones

hundred thousands | ten thousands | thousands | hundreds | tens | ones

| | | 5, | 2 | 6 | 0 |

Each group of 3 digits starting from the right forms a period.

A number in expanded form is written as the sum of the value of the digits: 5,000 + 200 + 60 + 0.

Use periods in the place-value chart to write 5,260 in word form: five thousand, two hundred sixty.

Explain It

1. Explain why the value of 5 in 5,264 is 5,000.

2. Is the expanded form for 5,260 the same as for 5,206?

You can represent numbers using place-value blocks.

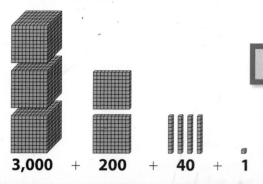

3,000 + **200** + **40** + **1**

You can represent numbers on a number line.

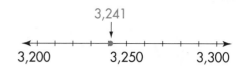

3,241
↓
3,200   3,250   3,300

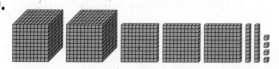
Guided Practice*

Do you know HOW?

In **1** through **4**, write the word form, and tell the value of the red digit in each number.

1. 15,324

2. 135,467

3. 921,382

4. 275,206

In **5** and **6**, write the expanded form.

5. 42,158

6. 63,308

Do you UNDERSTAND?

7. If Jill climbed 100 feet more, how many feet above sea level would she be?

8. What is the value of the 2 in 3,261? the 3? the 1?

9. Write one hundred one thousand, eleven in standard form.

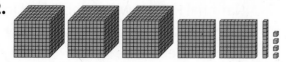
Independent Practice

Leveled Practice In **10** through **13**, write each number in standard form.

10.

11.

12.

13.

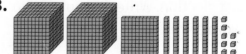

Animated Glossary, eTools
www.pearsonsuccessnet.com

*For another example, see Set A on page 24.

In **14** and **15**, write each number in standard form.

14. Eighty-three thousand, nine hundred two

15. Three hundred twenty-one thousand, two hundred nine

In **16** and **17**, write each number in expanded form.

16. Four hundred ninety-seven thousand, three hundred thirty-two

17. Twenty-one thousand, eight hundred seven

In **18** and **19**, write each number in word form.

18. 300,000 + 8,000 + 20 + 9

19.

20. Reasoning The pedometer below counts the number of steps you walk. It can show 5 digits. What is the greatest number it can show?

21. A town library has 124,763 books and 3,142 DVDs. This year, they bought 1,000 books and 2,000 DVDs. How many books does the library have now?

   A 5,142 books   **C** 125,763 books

   B 23,142 books   **D** 134,763 books

22. Number Sense Which digit is in the same place in all three numbers below? Name the place-value position.

   574,632   24,376   204,581

23. Reasoning What is the greatest 4-digit number you can write? What is the least 4-digit number?

24. A city counted 403,867 votes in the last election. Write this number in word form.

25. Yellowstone is the nation's first National Park. It was established in the year 1872. What is this number in expanded form?

Roman Numerals

The system of Roman numerals uses certain letters to represent different numbers. The chart below lists the letters the Romans used with the equivalent number.

I = 1   C = 100
V = 5   D = 500
X = 10   M = 1,000
L = 50

Most clocks with Roman numerals show the number 4 as IIII, not IV.

Examples:

To find the numbers not listed in the chart, add the values when the letters are the same.

$$III = 1 + 1 + 1$$
$$= 3$$

When a letter is to the right of a letter of greater value, add the values.

$$VIII = 5 + 3$$
$$= 8$$

When a letter is to the left of a letter of greater value, subtract the values.

$$IV = 5 - 1$$
$$= 4$$

When a letter is between two letters of greater value, subtract the smaller value from the larger value to its right.

$$XIX = 10 + 9$$
$$= 19$$

Practice

For **1** through **4**, write the time shown on each clock.

1.    **2.**    **3.**    **4.**

For **5** through **9**, find the value of each set of Roman numerals.

5. XXXIX   **6.** LX   **7.** XL   **8.** CXXXVI   **9.** MMIV

For **10** through **14**, write the Roman numeral for each number.

10. 23   **11.** 55   **12.** 611   **13.** 333   **14.** 1,666

Understand It!
Place value can be used to read and understand numbers in the millions.

Millions

What are some ways to write numbers in the millions?

From 2001 through 2005, 356,039,763 fans attended professional baseball games. Write the expanded form and word form for 356,039,763. Use a place-value chart to help.

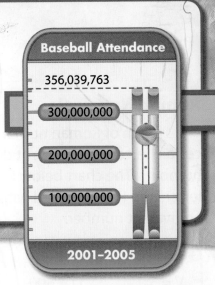

Baseball Attendance

356,039,763

300,000,000

200,000,000

100,000,000

2001–2005

Guided Practice*

Do you know HOW?

In **1** and **2**, write the number in word form. Then, tell the value of the red digit in each number.

1. 75,600,295

2. 249,104,330

In **3** through **6**, write the number in expanded form.

3. 6,173,253

4. 75,001,432

5. 16,107,320

6. 430,290,100

Do you UNDERSTAND?

7. What is the value of the 5 in 356,039,763?

8. What is the value of the 9 in 356,039,763?

9. Between 1996 and 2000, 335,365,504 fans attended games. Which digit is in the millions place in 335,365,504?

Independent Practice

In **10** through **12**, write each number in standard form.

10. 300,000,000 + 40,000,000 + 7,000,000 + 300,000 + 10,000 + 6,000 + 20 + 9

11. 900,000,000 + 20,000,000 + 6,000,000 + 20,000 + 4,000 + 10

12. 80,000,000 + 1,000,000 + 600,000 + 20,000 + 900 + 40 + 8

In **13** through **16**, write the number in word form. Then, tell the value of the red digit in each number.

13. 7,915,878

14. 23,341,552

15. 214,278,216

16. 334,290,652

For another example, see Set A on page 24.

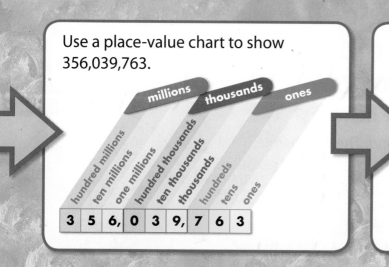

Use a place-value chart to show 356,039,763.

millions thousands ones

hundred millions | ten millions | one millions | hundred thousands | ten thousands | thousands | hundreds | tens | ones

| 3 | 5 | 6, | 0 | 3 | 9, | 7 | 6 | 3 |

There is a 3 in the hundred millions place. Its value is 300,000,000.

Expanded Form: 300,000,000 + 50,000,000 + 6,000,000 + 30,000 + 9,000 + 700 + 60 + 3

Word Form: Three hundred fifty-six million, thirty-nine thousand, seven hundred sixty-three

---

In **17** through **20**, write the number in expanded form. Then, tell the value of the red digit in each number.

17. 7,330,968   **18.** 30,290,447   **19.** 133,958,840   **20.** 309,603,114

Problem Solving

21. Writing to Explain Which number will take less time to write in expanded form, 800,000,000 or 267,423?

22. Write the expanded form of 123,456,789 and 987,654,321. Which digit has the same value in both numbers?

23. In 2005, seventy-four million, nine hundred fifteen thousand, two hundred sixty-eight fans attended baseball games. Which choice shows this number in standard form?

A 74,015,268   **C** 74,905,268

B 74,900,268   **D** 74,915,268

24. Write the standard form of a 9-digit number with a 5 in the millions place and a 9 in the tens place.

a Write a number that is ten million more than the number you chose.

b Write a number that is one million less than the number you chose.

25. Number Sense Fort Knox holds 147,300,000 ounces of gold. Write the number that is one million more.

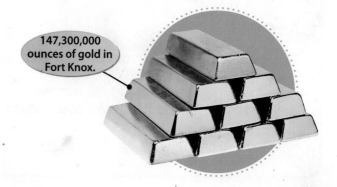

147,300,000 ounces of gold in Fort Knox.

Lesson
1-3

Understand It!
Place value and number lines can be used to compare and order whole numbers.

Comparing and Ordering Whole Numbers

How do you compare numbers?

Earth is not perfectly round. The North Pole is 6,356 kilometers from Earth's center. The equator is 6,378 kilometers from the center. Which is closer to the Earth's center: the North Pole or the equator?

North Pole 6,356 km from center

Equator 6,378 km from center

Earth's Center

Another Example **How do you order numbers?**

The areas of 3 continents on Earth are shown in the table at the right. Which shows the areas in order from **least** to **greatest**?

A 9,450,000; 4,010,000; 6,890,000

B 4,010,000; 9,450,000; 6,890,000

C 6,890,000; 9,450,000; 4,010,000

D 4,010,000; 6,890,000; 9,450,000

Continent	Areas (in square miles)
Europe	4,010,000
North America	9,450,000
South America	6,890,000

Step 1 Plot the numbers on a number line.

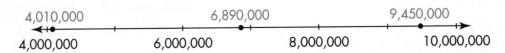

4,010,000 6,890,000 9,450,000

4,000,000 6,000,000 8,000,000 10,000,000

Step 2 Order the numbers. On a number line, numbers to the right are greater.

Reading from left to right: 4,010,000; 6,890,000; 9,450,000

The correct choice is **D**.

Explain It

1. Describe how you would order the continents' areas using place value.

2. **Reasonableness** How can you rule out choices A and C as the correct answer?

Step 1

Use place value to compare numbers.

Write the numbers, lining up places. Begin at the left and compare.

6,356
6,378

The thousands digit is the same in both numbers.

Step 2

Look at the next digit.

6,356
6,378

The hundreds digit also is the same in both numbers.

Step 3

The first place where the digits are different is the tens place. Compare.

6,356
6,378

5 tens < 7 tens, so 6,356 < 6,378.

The symbol > means is greater than, and the symbol < means is less than.

The North Pole is closer to Earth's center than the equator.

Guided Practice*

Do you know HOW?

In **1** through **4**, copy and complete by writing > or < for each ◯.

1. 2,643 ◯ 2,801   **2.** 6,519 ◯ 6,582

3. 785 ◯ 731   **4.** 6,703 ◯ 6,699

In **5** and **6**, order the numbers from least to greatest.

5. 7,502   6,793   6,723

6. 80,371   15,048   80,137

Do you UNDERSTAND?

7. Writing to Explain Why would you look at the hundreds place to order these numbers?

32,463   32,482   32,947

8. Compare the area of Europe and South America. Which is greater?

Independent Practice

In **9** through **16**, copy and complete by writing > or < for each ◯.

9. 221,495 ◯ 210,388

10. 52,744 ◯ 56,704

11. 138,752 ◯ 133,122

12. 4,937 ◯ 4,939

13. 22,873 ◯ 22,774

14. 1,912,706 ◯ 1,913,898

15. 412,632 ◯ 412,362

16. 999,999,999 ◯ 9,990,999

Leveled Practice In **17** through **20**, copy and complete the number lines. Then use the number lines to order the numbers from greatest to least.

17. 27,505   26,905   26,950

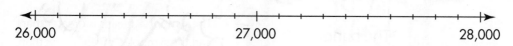

18. 3,422,100   3,422,700   3,422,000

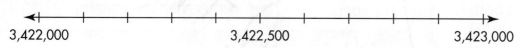

19. 7,502   7,622   7,523   7,852

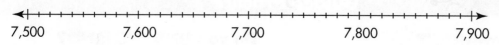

20. 3,030 3,033 3,003

In **21** through **28**, write the numbers in order from least to greatest.

21. 57,535 576,945 506,495

22. 18,764 18,761 13,490

23. 25,988 25,978 25,998

24. 87,837 37,838 878,393

25. 43,783 434,282 64,382

26. 723,433 72,324 72,432

27. 58,028 85,843 77,893

28. 274,849,551 283,940,039 23,485,903

Problem Solving

29. Estimation Aaron added 57 and 20 and said the answer is greater than 100. Is Aaron correct?

30. Number Sense Write three numbers that are greater than 780,000 but less than 781,000.

31. Reasoning Could you use only the millions period to order 462,409,524, 463,409,524, and 463,562,391?

32. Describe how to order 7,463, 74,633, and 74,366 from least to greatest.

33. The heaviest snake living in captivity is a Burmese Python named "Baby." An average Anaconda snake weighs 330 pounds. Which snake weighs more?

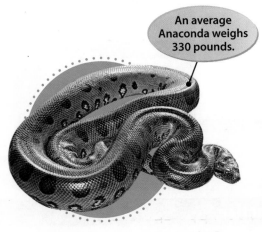

An average Anaconda weighs 330 pounds.

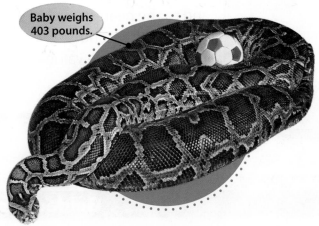

Baby weighs 403 pounds.

34. Which list of numbers is in order from least to greatest?

A	1,534	1,576	1,563
B	18,732	18,723	18,765
C	234,564	234,568	234,323
D	383,847	383,848	383,849

35. Asia and Africa are the two largest continents on Earth. Which continent is larger?

Continent	Land Area (square miles)
Africa	11,608,000
Asia	17,212,000

36. The chart below shows the number of game cards owned by the top collectors in one school. Which student had the most cards?

A Shani   **C** Ariel

B Lin   **D** Jorge

Collector	Number of cards
Shani	3,424
Ariel	3,443
Lin	2,354
Jorge	2,932

37. The Atlantic Ocean has an area of 33,420,000 square miles. This area is between which numbers?

A 33,400,000 and 33,440,000

B 33,000,000 and 33,040,000

C 33,100,000 and 33,419,000

D 33,430,000 and 33,500,000

Lesson

1-4

Understand It!
Place value can be used to round whole numbers.

Rounding Whole Numbers

How can you round numbers?

Round 293,655,404 to the nearest thousand and to the nearest hundred thousand. You can use place value to round numbers.

293, 655, 404

281, 421, 906

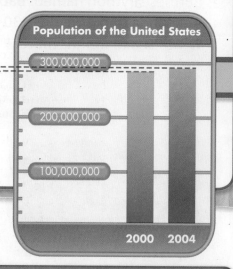

Population of the United States

300,000,000

200,000,000

100,000,000

2000   2004

Guided Practice*

Do you know HOW?

In **1** through **6**, round each number to the place of the underlined digit.

1. 128,955

2. 85,639

3. 9,924

4. 1,194,542

5. 160,656

6. 149,590

Do you UNDERSTAND?

7. Writing to Explain Explain how to round a number when 7 is the digit to the right of the rounding place.

8. In 2000, the population of the United States was 281,421,906. Round 281,421,906 to the nearest hundred thousand.

Independent Practice

Leveled Practice In **9** through **28**, round each number to the place of the underlined digit. You may use a number line to help you.

9. 493,295

☐☐☐,000

10. 39,230

☐☐,000

11. 77,292

☐☐,☐0

12. 54,846

☐0,000

13. 4,028

14. 6,668,365

15. 453,280

16. 17,909

17. 1,406

18. 55,560

19. 21,679

20. 3,417,547

21. 117,821

22. 75,254

23. 9,049

24. 1,666,821

25 2,420

26. 9,000,985

27. 9,511

28. 73,065

Round 293,655,404 to the nearest thousand.

thousands place

↓

293,65**5**,404

If the digit to the right of the rounding place is 5 or more, add 1 to the rounding digit. If it is less than 5, leave the rounding digit alone.

293,65**5**,000

Since 4 < 5, leave the rounding digit as is. Change the digits to the right of the rounding place to zeros.

So, 293,655,404 rounds to 293,655,000.

Round 293,655,404 to the nearest hundred thousand.

hundred thousands place

↓

293,**6**55,404

The digit to the right of the rounding place is 5.

293,**7**00,000

Since the digit is 5, round by adding 1 to the digit in the hundred thousands place.

So, 293,655,404 rounds to 293,700,000.

Problem Solving

For **29** and **30**, use the table at the right.

29. For each zoo in the chart, round the attendance to the nearest hundred thousand.

30. Reasoning Which zoo had the greatest number of visitors?

Zoo Attendance	
Nashville Zoo	513,561
Brookfield Zoo	1,872,544
Oregon Zoo	1,350,952

31. Number Sense Write four numbers that round to 700 when rounded to the nearest hundred.

32. Reasoning Write a number that when rounded to the nearest thousand and hundred will have a result that is the same.

33. Jonas read that about 1,760,000 people will graduate from high school in the next four years. Jonas thinks this number is rounded to the nearest ten thousand. What would the number be if it was rounded to the nearest hundred thousand?

34. Liz had attended class every day since she started school as a kindergartner. She said she had been in school for about 1,000 days. What could the actual number of school days be if she rounded to the nearest ten?

35. When rounded to the nearest ten thousand, which number would be rounded to 120,000?

　A 123,900　　**C** 128,770

　B 126,480　　**D** 130,000

36. A fruit market sold 3,849 apples, 3,498 oranges, and 3,894 pears in one day. Write these numbers in order from greatest to least.

Lesson
1-5

Understand It!
Place value can show the decimal value of money.

Hands-On
money

Using Money to Understand Decimals

How are decimals related to money?

A dime is one tenth of a dollar.

0.1

A penny is one hundredth of a dollar.

0.01

Guided Practice*

Do you know HOW?

In **1** and **2**, copy and complete.

1. $9.75 = ☐ dollars + ☐ dimes + ☐ pennies

9.75 = ☐ ones + ☐ tenths + ☐ hundredths

2. $3.62 = ☐ dollars + ☐ pennies

3.62 = ☐ ones + ☐ hundredths

Do you UNDERSTAND?

3. Writing to Explain How many hundredths are in one tenth? Explain using pennies and a dime.

4. How many pennies are equal to 6 dimes?

5. Gina's allowance is $2.50. How much is this in dollars and dimes?

 Tip *Remember, the number of dimes is the same as the number of tenths.*

Independent Practice

In **6** through **9**, copy and complete.

6. $5.83 = ☐ dollars + ☐ pennies

5.83 = ☐ ones + ☐ hundredths

7. $7.14 = ☐ dollars + ☐ pennies

7.14 = ☐ ones + ☐ hundredths

8. $2.19 = ☐ dollars + ☐ dime + ☐ pennies

2.19 = ☐ ones + ☐ tenth + ☐ hundredths

9. $3.24 = ☐ dollars + ☐ dimes + ☐ pennies

3.24 = ☐ ones + ☐ tenths + ☐ hundredths

DIGITAL
Animated Glossary, eTools
www.pearsonsuccessnet.com

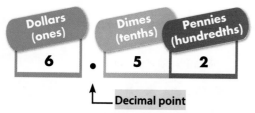

One Way

You can use a place-value chart to show the decimal value of money.

Dollars (ones)		Dimes (tenths)	Pennies (hundredths)
6	.	5	2

Decimal point

Read: six dollars *and* fifty-two cents.

Another Way

You can show $6.52 several ways.

$6.52 = 6 dollars + 5 dimes + 2 pennies
       = 6 ones + 5 tenths + 2 hundredths

$6.52 = 6 dollars + 52 pennies
       = 6 ones + 52 hundredths

In **10** through **13**, write the amount with a dollar sign and decimal point.

10. 6 dollars + 9 dimes + 3 pennies

11. 5 dollars + 8 pennies

12. 7 dollars + 3 dimes + 4 pennies

13. 4 dollars + 7 dimes

Problem Solving

14. Make a place-value chart to show the value of 5 dollars, 1 dime, and 3 pennies.

15. **Writing to Explain** Why do you only need to look at the number of dollars to know that $5.12 is greater than $4.82?

16. Pablo saves $1.20 each week. How much has he saved, in dollars and dimes, after one week? two weeks? three weeks?

17. **Number Sense** Which is more?

  a 4 dimes and 6 pennies or 6 dimes and 4 pennies?

  b 5 dimes or 45 pennies?

In **18** and **19**, use the information at the right.

18. How could you use only dollars, dimes, and pennies to buy the bubble blower?

19. How could you use only dollars, dimes, and pennies to buy the snow globe?

$9.29

$4.59

bubble blower   snow globe

20. Which is equal to 6 dollars, 3 dimes, and 4 pennies?

  A $3.46   **B** $3.64   **C** $6.34   **D** $6.43

Understand It!
Start with bills and coins that have the largest value, and count on from the cost to make change.

Counting Money and Making Change

Hands-On
money

How do you count money and make change?

Noreen has the bills and coins shown. How much money does she have?

Other Examples

Dimitri buys flowers for $17.65. He pays with a $20 bill. How much change does he get?

Count on from $17.65.

Cost   **Amount Paid**
$17.65 ⟶ $17.75 ⟶ $18.00 ⟶ $19.00 ⟶ $20.00

Dimitri's change is two $1 bills, 1 quarter, and 1 dime, or $2.35.

Guided Practice*

Do you know HOW?

Count the money.

1.

Find how much change you would receive if you paid with the bills shown.

2. Cost: $14.58

Do you UNDERSTAND?

3. Why do you start with the bills or coins that have the greatest value when counting money?

4. If Noreen found 7 more quarters, how much money would she have now?

5. **Reasoning** If you buy an item that costs $8.32, why would you pay with one $10 bill, 3 dimes, and 2 pennies?

eTools
www.pearsonsuccessnet.com

First count the bills. Start with the bill of greatest value.

 +  +  +  +

$10.00 $15.00 $16.00 $17.00 $18.00

Count the remaining coins. Start with the coin of greatest value.

+ + + + +

$18.25 $18.50 $18.60 $18.70 $18.75 $18.76

Write: $18.76   **Say:** eighteen dollars and seventy-six cents

Independent Practice

For **6** through **9**, count the money. Write each amount with a dollar sign and a decimal point.

6. three $1 bills, 2 quarters, 3 pennies

7. one $10 bill, two $5 bills, 4 dimes

8. two $1 bills, 3 quarters, 2 dimes, 1 nickel

9. four $1 bills, three quarters, 8 pennies

For **10** through **13**, list the coins and bills you would use to make change from the bills shown. Then write each amount with a dollar sign and a decimal point.

10. Cost: $25.24

11. Cost: $17.59

12. Cost: $46.85

13. Cost: $23.65

14. Writing to Explain Gina pays for an item that costs $6.23 with a $10 bill. What is the least number of coins and bills she could get as change? Explain.

15. Which number is 153,276,337 decreased by 100,000?

 A 153,176,337   **C** 154,214,337

 B 153,274,337   **D** 253,276,337

16. The 2005 U.S. Census listed the population of the state of New York as nineteen million, two hundred fifty-four thousand, six hundred-thirty. What is the population of New York in standard form?

17. A six digit number has a 4 in the thousands place and a 6 in the ones place. All other digits are two. What is this number in words?

Lesson
1-7

Understand It!
Learning how and
when to make an
organized list can help
solve problems.

Problem Solving

Make an Organized List

Arthur is tiling a bathroom wall. He has 520 wall tiles. He wants to arrange them in patterns of hundreds and tens.

Using only hundreds and tens blocks, how many ways can he make 520?

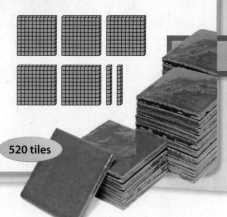

520 tiles

Guided Practice*

Do you know HOW?

Solve. Make an organized list to help you.

1. It costs Celia 50¢ admission to enter the aquarium. How many different ways can Celia pay the admission using only quarters, dimes, and nickels?

Do you UNDERSTAND?

2. What were the titles for the columns of your list in Problem 1?

3. **Write a Problem** Write a problem that you can solve using an organized list.

Independent Practice

Solve.

4. Using only hundreds blocks and tens blocks, list the ways to show 340.

5. Simon asked Margaret to guess a number. He gave these hints.
   - The number has 3 digits.
   - The digit in the 100s place is less than 2.
   - The digit in the 10s place is greater than 8.
   - The number is even.

   What are the possible numbers?

6. Make a list showing the ways you can make a dollar using only quarters, dimes, and nickels using no more than one nickel and no more than 9 dimes.

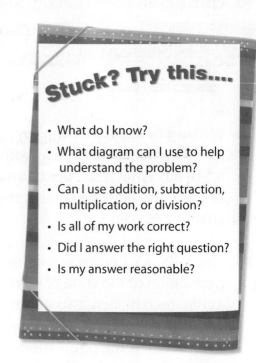

Stuck? Try this....

- What do I know?
- What diagram can I use to help understand the problem?
- Can I use addition, subtraction, multiplication, or division?
- Is all of my work correct?
- Did I answer the right question?
- Is my answer reasonable?

What do I know?	I can use only hundreds blocks and tens blocks.
What am I asked to find?	All of the combinations that show a total of 520

Record the combinations using an organized list.

Hundreds	5	4	3	2	1	0
Tens	2	12	22	32	42	52

There are 6 ways to make 520.

The answer is reasonable because the combinations have 5 or fewer hundreds blocks.

7. Lou's sandwiches are made with either wheat or white bread and have only one type of cheese— Swiss, Cheddar, American, or Mozzarella. How many different kinds of sandwiches can Lou make?

8. A magazine has a total of 24 articles and ads. There are 9 ads. How many articles are there?

24 articles and ads

9	?

9. Janie is making a bracelet. She has 1 red bead, 1 blue bead, and 1 white bead. How many possible ways can Janie arrange the beads?

10. Reasoning What two numbers have a sum of 12 and a difference of 4?

11. Alan has a cat, a goldfish, and a dog. He feeds them in a different order each day. How many different ways can he feed his pets?

12. Heather is writing a 3-digit number. She uses the digits 1, 5, and 9. What are the possible numbers she can write?

13. At the driving range, James wants to buy 200 golf balls. The golf balls are sold in buckets of 100, 50, and 10 golf balls. How many different ways can James buy 200 golf balls?

50 golf balls

100 golf balls

10 golf balls

1. Which of the following is another way to write the numeral 10,220? (1-1)

   A One thousand, two hundred twenty

   B Ten thousand, two hundred two

   C Ten thousand, two hundred twenty

   D Ten thousand, twenty-two

2. Florida has about sixteen million, three hundred thousand acres of forested land. Which of the following is another way to write this number? (1-2)

   A 16,300

   B 16,000,300

   C 16,030,000

   D 16,300,000

3. Which number is less than 4,329,349? (1-3)

   A 4,359,219

   B 4,329,391

   C 4,329,319

   D 4,359,291

4. What is the missing number? (1-5)

   $5.47 = 5$ dollars + ▨ dimes + 7 pennies

   $5.47 = 5$ ones + ▨ tenths + 7 hundredths

   A 4   **C** 7

   B 5   **D** 9

5. What number is best represented by point P on the number line? (1-1)

   A 378

   B 382

   C 388

   D 392

6. The table shows the areas of four states. Which of the four states has the least area? (1-3)

State	Area (sq. mi)
Montana	147,042
Oklahoma	68,898
Oregon	98,381
Wyoming	97,814

   A Montana

   B Oklahoma

   C Oregon

   D Wyoming

7. Betsy is making a flag. She can choose three colors from red, white, blue, and yellow. How many choices does Betsy have? (1-7)

   A 3

   B 4

   C 6

   D 24

8. A game costs $18.78. Jared gave the cashier a $20 bill. Which shows his change? (1-6)

  A 2 pennies, 2 nickels, 1 dime, 1 dollar

  B 2 pennies, 2 nickels, 1 dollar

  C 2 pennies, 2 dimes, 1 dollar

  D 2 pennies, 2 dimes, two $1 bills

9. What is 543,259,809 rounded to the nearest ten thousand? (1-4)

  A 540,000,000

  B 543,250,000

  C 543,259,810

  D 543,260,000

10. In 361,427,548, which digit is in the ten millions place? (1-2)

  A 1

  B 2

  C 4

  D 6

11. Carrie has 340 marbles to put in vases. She wants the vases to hold either 100 marbles or 10 marbles. Which is a way she can arrange the marbles? (1-7)

  A 34 hundreds

  B 3 hundreds 40 tens

  C 1 hundred 24 tens

  D 2 hundreds 24 tens

12. The U. S. Constitution contains 4,543 words, including the signatures. What is 4,543 rounded to the nearest hundred? (1-4)

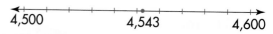

  A 4,000

  B 4,500

  C 4,540

  D 4,600

13. Jillian has the money shown below to spend on her mother's gift. How much money does Jillian have to spend? (1-6)

  A $15.76

  B $15.66

  C $15.71

  D $15.51

Set A, pages 4–6, 8–9

Use a place-value chart to write the expanded form and word form of 26,500.

Expanded form: 20,000 + 6,000 + 500

Word form:
twenty-six thousand, five hundred

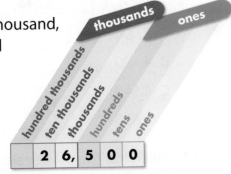

Remember that periods can help you read large numbers.

Use place-value charts to write each number in expanded form and word form.

1. 7,549   **2.** 27,961

3. 321,209   **4.** 3,454

5. 6,792,365   **6.** 15,164,612

Set B, pages 10–13

45,423 ◯ 44,897

Use place value to compare. Start comparing from the left. Look for the first digit that is different.

45,423   44,897

5 > 4

So, 45,423 > 44,897.

Remember that a number line can be used to compare numbers.

Write > or < for each ◯.

1. 11,961 ◯ 12,961

2. 735,291,000 ◯ 735,291,001

Order the numbers from greatest to least.

3. 22,981   14,762   21,046

Set C, pages 14–15

Round 346,764,802 to the nearest hundred thousand.

hundred thousands place
↓

346,<u>7</u>64,802   The digit to the right of the rounding place is 6.

346,800,000   Since 6 > 5, round by adding 1 to the digit in the hundred thousands place.

So, 346,764,802 rounds to 346,800,000.

Remember to look at the number to the right of the rounding place. Then change the digits to the right of the rounding place to zeros.

Round each number to the place of the underlined digit.

1. 166,742   **2.** 7<u>6</u>,532

3. <u>5</u>,861   **4.** 2,43<u>2</u>,741

5. <u>1</u>32,505   **6.** <u>2</u>57,931

Set D, pages 16–17

Write 4 dollars, 8 dimes, and 2 pennies with a dollar sign and a decimal point.

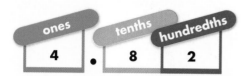

Read: four dollars and eighty-two cents

Write: $4.82

Remember that a dime is one tenth of a dollar, and a penny is one hundredth of a dollar.

Write each amount with a dollar sign and a decimal point.

1. 3 dollars + 4 pennies

2. 1 dollar + 5 dimes + 6 pennies

3. 9 dollars + 6 dimes

4. 4 dollars + 9 pennies

Set E, pages 18–19

Count on from the cost to make change.

Jill pays an $18.73 bill with $20. What is her change?

Adding two pennies makes $18.75.

Adding one quarter makes $19.00.

Adding one dollar makes $20.00.

The change is $1 + $0.25 + $0.02 = $1.27.

Remember that there is more than one right way to make change.

Calculate the change from a $10 bill.

1. $4.50   **2.** $8.90

3. $3.32   **4.** $4.11

5. $7.84   **6.** $5.49

Set F, pages 20–21

Using only hundreds and tens blocks, how many ways can you make 440?

What do I know?   I can use only hundreds blocks and tens blocks

What am I being asked to find?   All of the combinations that make a total of 440

Record the combinations using an organized list.

Hundreds	4	3	2	1	0
Tens	4	14	24	34	44

Remember that the way you organize a list can help you find all the possibilities in a problem.

Solve. Make an organized list to help you.

1. Troy collects plastic banks. He has three different plastic banks: a pig, a cow, and a frog. How many ways can he arrange his banks on a shelf?

Adding and Subtracting Whole Numbers

1

When was the Washington Monument completed? You will find out in Lesson 2-2.

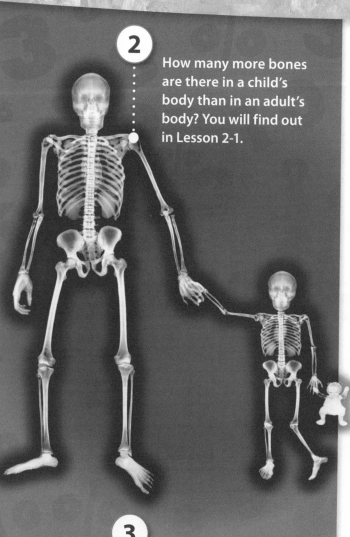

2 How many more bones are there in a child's body than in an adult's body? You will find out in Lesson 2-1.

3 The lunar rover set the surface speed record on the moon. Find out the rover's estimated speed in Lesson 2-4.

Review What You Know!

How many more bones are there in a child's body than in an adult's body? You will find out in Lesson 2-1.

The lunar rover set the surface speed record on the moon. Find out the rover's estimated speed in Lesson 2-4.

Vocabulary

Choose the best term from the box.

- rounding
- sum
- difference
- mental math
- tens
- regroup

1. In order to subtract 140 from 530, you need to _?_.

2. _?_ tells about how many or about how much.

3. When you subtract two numbers, the answer is the _?_.

4. When you add numbers together, you find the _?_.

Addition Facts

Find each sum.

5. 4 + 6   **6.** 7 + 5   **7.** 9 + 8

8. 14 + 5   **9.** 3 + 7   **10.** 37 + 7

11. 9 + 6   **12.** 6 + 5   **13.** 15 + 7

14. 3 + 8   **15.** 14 + 6   **16.** 25 + 5

Subtraction Facts

Find each difference.

17. 27 − 3   **18.** 6 − 4   **19.** 15 − 8

20. 11 − 8   **21.** 6 − 2   **22.** 17 − 8

23. 16 − 4   **24.** 20 − 5   **25.** 11 − 6

26. 14 − 6   **27.** 15 − 10   **28.** 13 − 7

29. Writing to Explain Why does 843 round to 840 rather than to 850?

Understand It!
Numbers can be broken apart and combined in many ways.

Using Mental Math to Add and Subtract

How can you use mental math to add and subtract?

Properties can sometimes help you add using mental math. How many years have Ms. Walston and Mr. Randall been teaching? What is the total number of years all of the teachers in the chart have been teaching?

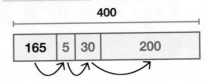

Teacher	Years Teaching
Ms. Walston	12
Mr. Roy	5
Mr. Randall	30

Other Examples

Add using mental math.

Find 135 + 48.

```
        ?
├───────────────┤
┌───────────┬───────┐
│    135    │  48   │
└───────────┴───────┘
```

Use breaking apart to find a ten.

Adding 5 to 135 is easy. Break apart 48.

```
        ?
├───────────────┤
┌───────────┬──┬────┐
│    135    │5 │ 43 │
└───────────┴──┴────┘
```

$135 + 5 = 140$
$140 + 43 = 183$
So, $135 + 48 = 183$.

Use compensation.

$135 + 48$
$135 + 50 = 185$

Think I added 2 too many, so I will subtract 2.

$185 - 2 = 183$
So, $135 + 48 = 183$.

Subtract using mental math.

Find 400 − 165.

Use counting on.

```
                      400
├──────────────────────────────────────┤
┌───────┬──┬──┬───────────┐
│  165  │5 │30│    200    │
└───────┴──┴──┴───────────┘
```

$165 + 5 = 170$
$170 + 30 = 200$
$200 + 200 = 400$

$5 + 30 + 200 = 235$
So, $400 - 165 = 235$.

Use compensation.

Find 260 − 17.

It is easy to subtract 20.

$260 - 20 = 240$

Think I subtracted 3 too many, so I will add 3.

$240 + 3 = 243$
So, $260 - 17 = 243$.

Commutative Property of Addition

You can <u>add two numbers in any order</u>.

42	
12	30

$12 + 30 = 30 + 12$

Ms. Walston and Mr. Randall have been teaching a combined total of 42 years.

Associative Property of Addition

You can <u>change the grouping of addends</u>.

47		
12	30	5

$(12 + 30) + 5 = 12 + (30 + 5)$

The total number of years the three teachers have been teaching is 47 years.

Identity Property of Addition

<u>Adding zero does not change the number</u>.

$12 + 0 = 12$

Guided Practice*

Do you know HOW?

In **1** through **6**, use mental math to add or subtract.

1. $86 + 25$

2. $497 + 0$

3. $566 - 359$

4. $169 - 48$

5. $239 + 509$

6. $(40 + 5) + 8$

Do you UNDERSTAND?

7. How could you use compensation to find $391 - 26$?

8. **Writing to Explain** Explain how you used mental math to find the answer to Exercise 4.

Independent Practice

Leveled Practice In **9** through **18**, use mental math to complete the calculation.

9. $400 - 227$

400			
227	3	70	100

10. $500 - 89$

500		
89	11	400

11. $906 - 289$

906			
289	11	600	6

12. $7,000 + 2,130$

?			
7,000	2,000	100	30

13. $583 + 317$

?			
583	7	10	300

14. $125 + 28$

?		
125	5	23

15. $1,700 - 315$

16. $2,000 + 4,996$

17. $438 - 129$

18. $0 + 284$

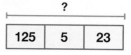

Animated Glossary
www.pearsonsuccessnet.com

DIGITAL

*For another example, see Set A on page 50.

For **19** through **21**, use the table to the right.

19. Which state has the greatest land area in square miles?

20. Which two states shown in the table have the smallest difference in land area?

21. Which two states shown in the table have the greatest difference in land area?

State	Total Square Miles
Alaska	571,951
Texas	261,797
California	155,959
Montana	145,552
New Mexico	121,356

22. Colin had 148 CDs in his collection. He traded 32 of them for 23 that he really wanted. How many CDs does Colin now have in his collection? Use mental math.

   A 106 CDs

   B 108 CDs

   C 116 CDs

   D 139 CDs

23. Ms. Gomez's class collected pencils for the community school supplies drive. Ethan's group brought in 143 pencils and Marcelina's group added 78 more. How many pencils did the groups contribute altogether?

   A 184 pencils   **C** 221 pencils

   B 204 pencils   **D** 245 pencils

24. Number Sense Is 881 − 262 more or less than 500? Explain how you can tell using mental math.

25. Writing to Explain How can you use mental math to subtract 158 − 29?

26. An adult human body has a total of 206 bones. There are 300 bones in a child's body because some of a child's bones fuse together as a child grows. How many more bones are in a child's body than in an adult's body?

300		
206	4	90

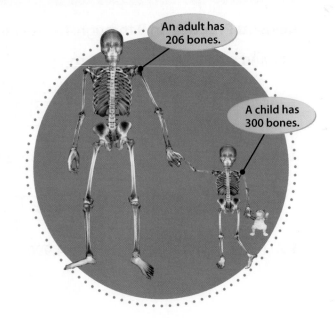

An adult has 206 bones.

A child has 300 bones.

27. Number Sense Write two numbers that have a 6 in the ones place and an 8 in the hundreds place.

Algebra Connections

Solving Number Sentences with Addition and Subtraction

A number sentence uses the equal sign (=) to show that two expressions have the same value.

Fill in the box in each number sentence with the number that makes the number sentence true. Check your answers.

Example: $8 + \boxed{} = 35$

Think *What number plus 8 equals 35?*

When solving an addition number sentence, use subtraction to identify the missing number.

What is 35 minus 8?

Subtract 8 from 35.   Now, add 8 and 27.

$35 - 8 = 27$ $8 + 27 = 35$

Copy and complete each number sentence.

1. $7 + \boxed{} = 31$

2. $\boxed{} + 6 = 21$

3. $26 - \boxed{} = 25$

4. $56 - \boxed{} = 38$

5. $\boxed{} - 47 = 12$

6. $66 + \boxed{} = 85$

7. $\boxed{} - 98 = 1$

8. $103 - \boxed{} = 72$

9. $10 + \boxed{} = 13$

10. $\boxed{} - 8 = 12$

11. $1 + \boxed{} = 7$

12. $744 - \boxed{} = 327$

. . . .

For **13** through **16**, copy and complete the number sentence below each problem. Use it to help explain your answer.

13. Cheryl made 8 free-throw shots. She shot a total of 10 free-throw shots. How many free-throw shots did she miss?

$8 + \boxed{} = 10$

14. George delivered 118 newspapers in two days. He delivered 57 newspapers the first day. How many newspapers did George deliver the second day?

$57 + \boxed{} = 118$

15. 7 rabbits less than a certain number of rabbits is 13 rabbits. What is the missing number?

$\boxed{} - 7 = 13$

16. The cost of an apple is 39¢. Robert had 25¢ in his pocket. How much more money did Robert need to purchase the apple?

$25 + \boxed{} = 39$

Understand It!
To estimate, change
numbers to ones that are
easy to add and subtract.

Estimating Sums and Differences of Whole Numbers

How can you estimate sums and differences of whole numbers?

The Empire State Building was completed in 1931. From ground to tip, it measures 1,250 feet. At the top of the building is a lightning rod which measures 204 feet. Estimate the total height of the structure.

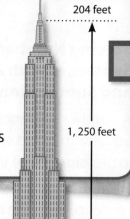

204 feet

1, 250 feet

Guided Practice*

Do you know HOW?

In **1** through **6**, estimate each sum or difference.

1. $\begin{array}{r} 563 \rightarrow 00 \\ + 375 \rightarrow 00 \\ \hline \end{array}$

2. $\begin{array}{r} 288 \rightarrow 0 \\ - 171 \rightarrow 0 \\ \hline \end{array}$

3. 645 + 253

4. 262 − 132

5. 952 − 402

6. 398 + 121

Do you UNDERSTAND?

7. **Writing to Explain** In the first example above, why can't you round both numbers to the nearest thousand?

8. The Statue of Liberty was completed in 1886. About how many years later was the Empire State Building completed than the Statue of Liberty?

Independent Practice

In **9** through **16**, estimate by rounding to the nearest ten.

9. $\begin{array}{r} 542 \\ + 27 \\ \hline \end{array}$

10. $\begin{array}{r} 281 \\ - 172 \\ \hline \end{array}$

11. $\begin{array}{r} 5,323 \\ - 2,611 \\ \hline \end{array}$

12. $\begin{array}{r} 6,324 \\ + 3,842 \\ \hline \end{array}$

13. 738 + 741

14. 895 − 305

15. 755 − 344

16. 586 + 278

In **17** through **24**, estimate by rounding to the nearest hundred.

17. $\begin{array}{r} 368 \\ + 137 \\ \hline \end{array}$

18. $\begin{array}{r} 918 \\ + 391 \\ \hline \end{array}$

19. $\begin{array}{r} 5,317 \\ + 1,734 \\ \hline \end{array}$

20. $\begin{array}{r} 778 \\ + 95 \\ \hline \end{array}$

21. 423 + 196

22. 891 + 223

23. 1,724 − 731

24. 551 − 249

For another example, see Set B on page 50.

Round each number to the nearest hundred.

The total height is about 1,500 feet.

$$
\begin{array}{r}
1{,}250 \longrightarrow 1{,}300 \\
+ \quad 204 \longrightarrow + \quad 200 \\
\hline
1{,}500
\end{array}
$$

The answer is reasonable because the total height is greater than the height of the Empire State Building.

The Washington Monument was completed in 1884. About how many years after was the Empire State Building completed?

$$
\begin{array}{r}
1{,}931 \longrightarrow 1{,}930 \\
- 1{,}884 \longrightarrow - 1{,}880 \\
\hline
50
\end{array}
$$

Round each number to the nearest ten. Show rounding to subtract.

The Empire State Building was completed about 50 years later.

Problem Solving

25. Kala bought a board game for $24.75. She paid with a $20 bill and a $10 bill. What bills and coins did Kala get back in change?

26. Theo was born in the year 2004. One of his older sisters was born in 1992. Rounding to the nearest ten, about how many years younger is Theo?

27. This year, 35,658 people ran in a marathon. Last year, 8,683 fewer people ran. About how many people ran last year?

28. During swimming practice, Juan swam 15 laps and Ted swam 9 laps. How many more laps did Juan swim than Ted?

29. The table below shows the number of students per grade. Estimate the total number of students in Grades 3, 4, and 5. About how many students are in Grades 4 and 5?

Grade	Number of Students
3	145
4	152
5	144
6	149

Data

30. Alex sold 86 tickets to a school talent show on Thursday and 103 tickets on Friday. About how many tickets to the talent show did Alex sell altogether?

A About 100

B About 200

C About 300

D About 400

Understand It!
Some problems have extra information and some do not have enough information to solve them.

Missing or Extra Information

Kendra had $7. She bought a sandwich, a drink, and an apple at the cafeteria. She spent a total of $3 on the sandwich and the drink.

How much money did Kendra have left?

> A drink and a sandwich cost $3.

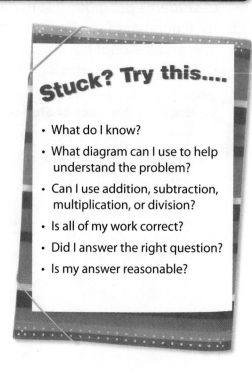

Guided Practice*

Do you know HOW?

1. At the zoo, Julie saw 18 penguins. She saw 8 Adelie penguins. The rest of the penguins she saw were Rockhopper penguins. She learned that Rockhopper penguins grow to be about 5 to 8 pounds. How many Rockhopper penguins did Julie see?

Do you UNDERSTAND?

2. What information was not needed in Problem 1?

3. **Write a Problem** Write a problem that contains too much or too little information.

Independent Practice

Decide if each problem has extra information or not enough information. Tell any information that is not needed or that is missing. Solve if you have enough information.

4. Carmin spent 30 minutes completing his homework after school. Then he played soccer. What information do you need to find how many minutes Carmin spent completing his homework and playing soccer altogether?

5. June only has quarters and pennies in her coin collection. She has 85 coins in all. What would you need to know to find out how many quarters June has in her collection?

Stuck? Try this....

- What do I know?
- What diagram can I use to help understand the problem?
- Can I use addition, subtraction, multiplication, or division?
- Is all of my work correct?
- Did I answer the right question?
- Is my answer reasonable?

Read & Understand

What do I know?

Kendra had $7. She bought a sandwich, a drink, and an apple. The sandwich and the drink was $3.

What am I asked to find?

The amount of money Kendra had left

Plan

Draw a diagram to show what you know and want to find.

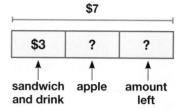

$7

| $3 | ? | ? |

sandwich and drink · apple · amount left

Think Is there missing information needed to solve the problem?

Is there any extra information not needed to solve the problem?

6. Kayla ate two tacos and an apple for lunch. The tacos had 260 calories. How many calories did Kayla eat for lunch?

7. There are 35 sopranos in the school choir. The 40 remaining choir members are altos. How many students are in the school choir?

8. There are 328 places for activity photographs in the yearbook. The yearbook club has decided to make most of the photographs black and white. How many color photographs will be in the yearbook?

9. A notebook costs $2.68 and a pen costs $1.79. Does Jasmine have enough money to buy a notebook and two pens?

10. The tallest steel roller coaster is in Jackson, New Jersey. It is 456 feet tall. The tallest wooden roller coaster is in Cincinnati, Ohio. The roller coaster is 7,032 feet long. How much taller is the steel roller coaster than the wooden roller coaster? Choose the letter that contains the information that is needed to solve the problem.

A The tallest steel roller coaster travels at 128 miles per hour.

B The tallest steel roller coaster is 3,118 feet long.

C The tallest wooden roller coaster travels at 78.3 miles per hour.

D The tallest wooden roller coaster is 218 feet tall.

11. Mrs. Song bought school supplies for her two children, Jason and Kevin. Jason is two years older than Kevin and is in the fourth grade. She spent $38 for Kevin's supplies and $46 for Jason's supplies. If she paid with a $100 bill, how much change did she get back?

$100 for school supplies		
$38	$46	?

Understand It!
Add numbers by adding ones, then tens, then hundreds, and then thousands.

Adding Whole Numbers

How do you add whole numbers?

If an artificial coral reef grew 257 inches last year and 567 inches this year, how much did it grow in all?

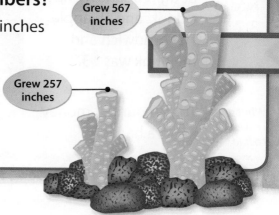

Grew 567 inches

Grew 257 inches

?	
257	567

Estimate: 300 + 600 = 900

Another Example **How do you add more than two numbers?**

Find the sum.
9,348 + 102 + 5,802 + 1,933

A 17,185   **C** 16,175

B 17,175   **D** 15,175

Estimate: 9,000 + 100 + 6,000 + 2,000 = 17,100

Step 1

Add the ones. Regroup if necessary.

```
   1
 9,348
   102
 5,802
+1,933
─────
     5
```

Step 2

Add the tens. Regroup if necessary.

```
   1
 9,348
   102
 5,802
+1,933
─────
    85
```

Step 3

Add the hundreds, regroup, and then add the thousands.

```
  2 1
 9,348
   102
 5,802
+1,933
──────
17,185
```

The correct answer is **A**.

Explain It

1. How are the ones regrouped in the example above?

2. **Reasonableness** In Step 3 above, how can you tell that the answer is reasonable?

Step 1	**Step 2**	**Step 3**

Step 1

Add 257 + 567.

Add the ones. Regroup if necessary.

$$\begin{array}{r} {}^{1} \\ 257 \\ +\ 567 \\ \hline 4 \end{array}$$

Step 2

Add the tens. Regroup if necessary.

$$\begin{array}{r} {}^{1\,1} \\ 257 \\ +\ 567 \\ \hline 24 \end{array}$$

Step 3

Add the hundreds. Regroup if necessary.

$$\begin{array}{r} {}^{1\,1} \\ 257 \\ +\ 567 \\ \hline 824 \end{array}$$

The reef grew 824 inches in all.

Other Examples

Adding larger numbers

Add 36,424 + 24,842.

Estimate:
36,000 + 25,000 = 61,000

$$\begin{array}{r} {}^{1\,1} \\ 36{,}424 \\ +\ 24{,}842 \\ \hline 61{,}266 \end{array}$$

The sum is reasonable because it is close to the estimate of 61,000.

Adding more than two numbers

Add 130,283 + 263,823 + 396,538.

Estimate:
130,000 + 264,000 + 397,000 = 791,000

$$\begin{array}{r} {}^{1\,1\,1\,1\,1} \\ 130{,}283 \\ 263{,}823 \\ +\ 396{,}538 \\ \hline 790{,}644 \end{array}$$

The sum is reasonable because it is close to the estimate of 791,000.

Guided Practice*

Do you know HOW?

In **1** through **6**, find each sum.

1. 821 + 4,543   **2.** 14,926 + 3,832

3. 1,321 + 2,246   **4.** 24,593 + 16,861

5.
$$\begin{array}{r} 3{,}258 \\ +\ 1{,}761 \\ \hline \end{array}$$

6.
$$\begin{array}{r} 16{,}018 \\ +\ 135 \\ \hline \end{array}$$

Do you UNDERSTAND?

7. When adding 36,424 and 24,842 above, why is there no regrouping in the final step?

8. Volunteer teams identified 73 fish species, 30 corals, and 71 other invertebrates on the reef. How many species of fish, coral, and invertebrates were found in all?

*For another example, see Set D on page 51.

In **9** through **24**, find each sum.

9. 78	**10.** 617	**11.** 873	**12.** 38,911
+ 421	+ 14,312	+ 4,893	+ 45,681

13. 327
  + 886

14. 295	**15.** 3,751	**16.** 623	**17.** 4,231
+ 805	+ 4,736	+ 2,815	+ 76,118

18. 265
  + 8,496

19. 9,634 + 2,958   **20.** 4,673 + 262   **21.** 7,845 + 509 + 3,746

22. 526 + 276 +1,086   **23.** 2,868 + 865   **24.** 15,891 + 527 + 1,086

Problem Solving

25. In 1972, the Apollo 16 lunar rover set the current lunar speed record at 11 miles per hour. In order to break free from Earth's orbit, Apollo missions had to go 24,989 miles per hour faster than the record speed of the lunar rover. How fast did the Apollo rockets travel?

26. There were 10,453 items checked out of the public library one week. The next week, 12,975 items were checked out. A week later, 9,634 items were checked out. How many items were checked out in three weeks?

27. Sandy read 235 pages of a book. She had 192 more pages to read before she was done. How many pages were there in the book?

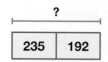

?	
235	192

28. Cheryl and Jason collect baseball cards. Cheryl has 315 cards, and Jason has 186 cards. How many cards do they have altogether?

?	
315	186

29. Number Sense The sum of 86, 68, and 38 is 192. What do you also know about the sum of 68, 38, and 86?

30. Estimation Maria added 45,273 and 35,687. Will her answer be greater or less than 80,000?

31. The population of New City is 23,945. Eastdale has a population of 12,774. What is the total population of the two communities?

  A 35,719   **B** 36,619   **C** 36,719   **D** 37,619

Mixed Problem Solving

Some Facts About Natural Regions in the United States	
The Alaska Range	The highest peak in this mountain range is Mount McKinley, reaching 20,320 feet. Southwest of this mountain is Mount Foraker, which reaches 17,400 feet.
Crater Lake	The elevation of this lake is 6,178 feet. It is the deepest lake in the United States with the lowest point at 1,949 feet above sea level.
Death Valley	Death Valley is the lowest point in the United States at 282 feet below sea level.

1. Estimate how much higher Mount McKinley is than Mount Foraker.

2. Estimate the depth of Crater Lake.

3. Mount McKinley is the highest point in the United States. Death Valley is the lowest point in the United States. Estimate the difference between the highest point and the lowest point in the United States.

4. The deepest point of the Pacific Ocean is 36,198 feet below sea level, located in a region called the Marianas Trench. Estimate the difference between the deepest points of the Pacific Ocean and Death Valley.

5. Alaska was purchased from Russia in 1867. How many years after the Louisiana Purchase was Alaska purchased?

6. Including interest, the United States paid a total of $23,213,568 for the Louisiana Territory. Round 23,213,568 to the nearest million.

7. The Louisiana Purchase almost doubled the size of the United States. Approximately how large was the United States after the purchase?

8. When was the 200th anniversary of the Louisiana Purchase?

Some History of the Louisiana Purchase
The United States purchased Louisiana from France in 1803. The Louisiana Territory belonged to Spain before France.
The price for the land was about 3 cents per acre. The total cost was $15,000,000.
Approximately 828,000 square miles of land was purchased.

? square miles	
828,000	828,000

Understand It!
Subtract numbers by subtracting ones, then tens, then hundreds, and then thousands.

Subtracting Whole Numbers

How do you subtract numbers?

Brenda has a total of 221 songs in her computer. Her sister, Susan, has a total of 186 songs in her computer. How many more songs does Brenda have in her computer than Susan?

Choose an Operation Subtract to find how many more songs.

221

186   ?

Guided Practice*

Do you know HOW?

In **1** through **4**, subtract.

1.   527
       − 338

2.   716
       − 254

3.   139
       − 86

4.   1,268
       − 429

Do you UNDERSTAND?

5. In the example at the top, why was the 0 in the hundreds place not written in the answer?

6. Brenda would like to have 275 songs on her computer by next year. How many more songs does she need to download?

Independent Practice

In **7** through **26**, subtract.

7.   336
       − 259

8.   693
       − 150

9.   881
       − 79

10.   479
        − 88

11.   1,931
        − 509

12.   1,673
        − 849

13.   2,173
        − 108

14.   8,617
        − 3,909

15. 552 − 228

16. 3,711 − 1,683

17. 217 − 166

18. 562 − 199

19. 7,475 − 5,130

20. 5,831 − 1,156

21. 9,385 − 720

22. 1,111 − 589

23. 8,476 − 2,185

24. 6,251 − 964

25. 7,374 − 1,246

26. 8,327 − 3,796

DIGITAL   Animated Glossary
www.pearsonsuccessnet.com

For another example, see Set E on page 51.

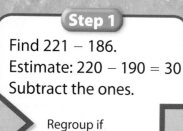

Step 1

Find 221 − 186.
Estimate: 220 − 190 = 30
Subtract the ones.

Regroup if necessary.

$$\begin{array}{r} {\scriptstyle 1\ 11} \\ 22\!\!\!/1 \\ -\ 186 \\ \hline 5 \end{array}$$

Step 2

Subtract the tens.
Subtract the hundreds.

Regroup if necessary.

$$\begin{array}{r} {\scriptstyle 1\ 11\ 11} \\ 22\!\!\!/1 \\ -\ 186 \\ \hline 35 \end{array}$$

Step 3

Operations that undo each other are inverse operations. Addition and subtraction have an inverse relationship.

$$\begin{array}{r} {\scriptstyle 1\ 1} \\ 186 \\ +\ 35 \\ \hline 221 \end{array}$$ Add to check your answer.

The answer checks.

Problem Solving

27. A crayon company makes 17,491 green crayons and 15,063 red crayons. How many more green crayons are made than red crayons?

  A 2,428   **C** 10,456

  B 3,463   **D** 32,554

28. Angela hiked a trail that climbed 526 feet. Raul hiked a trail that climbed 319 feet. How many more feet did Angela climb than Raul?

526 feet	
319	?

29. Jermaine and Linda collected aluminum cans for one month. Look at the chart below to see how many aluminum cans each student collected.

  a Who collected more cans?

  b Find the difference between the number of cans collected.

30. Mount Kilimanjaro is a mountain in Africa. A group of mountain climbers begin their descent from the peak. On Monday, the mountain climbers descended 3,499 feet. On Tuesday, they descended another 5,262 feet. How many feet have the mountain climbers descended?

Data	Jermaine	1,353 cans
	Linda	1,328 cans

31. Mike's team scored 63 points in the first half of a basketball game. His team won the game by a score of 124 to103. How many points did his team score in the second half?

Mount Kilimanjaro is 19,341 feet high.

Subtracting Across Zeros

How do you subtract across zeros?

An airplane flight to Chicago has seats for 300 passengers. The airline sold 278 tickets for the flight. How many seats are still available for the flight?

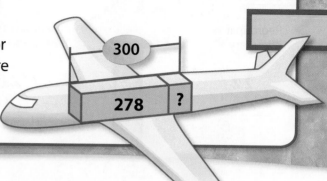

300

278 ?

Guided Practice*

Do you know HOW?

In **1** through **6**, subtract.

1.   600
    − 177

2. 1,086
   − 728

3. 810 − 638

4. 3,304 − 1,137

5. 1,001 − 868

6. 4,000 − 1,698

Do you UNDERSTAND?

7. How would you check if the answer in the example above is correct?

8. One passenger flew from New York to Phoenix. The flight was 2,145 miles. Another passenger flew from Boston to Seattle. The flight was 2,496 miles. How many more miles was the flight to Seattle?

Independent Practice

In **9** through **28**, subtract.

9.   902
   − 883

10.   502
    − 380

11. 3,000
   − 673

12.   5,604
   − 1,717

13. 1,830
   − 722

14.   7,006
   − 3,529

15. 1,902
   − 903

16.   6,008
   − 4,879

17. 450 − 313

18. 5,025 − 178

19. 406 − 381

20. 1,001 − 35

21. 6,090 − 5,130

22. 2,700 − 1,699

23. 10,807 − 4,373

24. 504 − 319

25. 3,000 − 1,047

26. 5,001 − 368

27. 700 − 520

28. 900 − 406

For another example, see Set E on page 51.

One Way

Find 300 − 278.

Estimate: 300 − 280 = 20

Regroup hundreds to tens and tens to ones.

$$\overset{\overset{9}{2\ \cancel{10}\ 10}}{\cancel{3}\ \cancel{0}\ \cancel{0}}$$ 3 hundreds =
− 2 7 8   2 hundreds + 9 tens +
   ‾‾‾‾‾‾
   2 2   10 ones

There are 22 seats available for the flight.

Another Way

Find 300 − 278.

Estimate: 300 − 280 = 20

Think of 300 as 30 tens and 0 ones.

$$\overset{29\ \ 10}{\cancel{3}\cancel{0}\ \cancel{0}}$$ 30 tens + 0 ones =
− 2 7 8   29 tens + 10 ones
   ‾‾‾‾‾‾
   2 2

There are 22 seats available for the flight.

Problem Solving

29. Shawn scored 10,830 points playing a video game. Miguel scored 9,645 points. How many more points did Shawn score than Miguel?

30. Writing to Explain Will the difference between 4,041 and 3,876 be greater or less than 1,000? Explain your answer.

31. Use the chart on the right. Music City sells CDs. Which of the following tells how many more Hip Hop CDs were sold than Latin CDs in April?

  A 887   **C** 7,090

  B 897   **D** 13,293

CDs Sold in April	
Music style	CDs sold in April
Rock	4,008
Hip Hop	7,090
Country	5,063
Latin	6,203

32. William drove from Atlanta, Georgia, to Portland, Oregon. The round trip was 5,601 miles. He traveled 2,603 miles to get to Portland, Oregon, but he decided to take a different route back. How many miles did he travel to get back to Atlanta?

33. On Thursday, 10,296 people attended a college basketball home game. The following week, 12,000 people attended an away game. How many more people attended the away game than the home game?

12,000 people in all

10,296	?

34. In a dart game, Casey scored 42 points, and Maggie scored 28 points. Jesse scored fewer points than Casey but more points than Maggie. Which is a possible score for Jesse?

  A 50 points   **C** 34 points

  B 46 points   **D** 26 points

Lesson
2-7

Understand It!
Learning how and when
to draw a picture can help
you solve problems.

Problem Solving

Draw a Picture and Write an Equation

The mass of a human brain is how much greater than the mass of a chimpanzee brain?

Average Masses of Brains	
House cat	30 grams
Chimpanzee	420 grams
Human	1,350 grams
Dolphin	1,500 grams

The human brain has a mass of 1,350 grams.

Guided Practice*

Do you know HOW?

Solve. Draw a picture to help you.

1. In one week, Sandy earned $36 from her babysitting job. She got $15 more for doing her chores. How much money did Sandy earn?

? in all

$36	$15

Do you UNDERSTAND?

2. How can you show that 930 grams is a reasonable answer for the question asked above?

3. **Write a Problem** Write a problem using the table at the top.

Independent Practice

Solve. Draw a picture to help you.

4. Four cities are on the same road that runs east to west. Fleming is west of Bridgewater, but east of Clinton. Union is between Fleming and Bridgewater. It is 21 miles from Fleming to Union. It is 55 miles from Clinton to Union. How far is it from Clinton to Fleming?

5. Scott and his friends walk to school together. Scott leaves his home at 7:00 A.M. He meets Johnny and Zach at the end of the block. Next, they meet Paul, Tim, and Pete. Dan and Torey join them one block before the school. How many friends walk to school altogether?

Stuck? Try this....

- What do I know?
- What diagram can I use to help understand the problem?
- Can I use addition, subtraction, multiplication, or division?
- Is all of my work correct?
- Did I answer the right question?
- Is my answer reasonable?

*For another example, see Set F on page 51.

What do I know? The average mass of a chimpanzee brain is 420 grams. The average mass of a human brain is 1,350 grams.

What am I asked to find? The difference between the masses

Draw a picture.

1,350 grams	
420 grams	?

Write an equation. Use subtraction to solve.

$$1,350 - 420 = \boxed{}$$

The human brain has a mass that is 930 grams more than the chimpanzee brain.

---

6. The American Kennel Club recognizes 17 breeds of herding dogs and 26 breeds of terriers. Draw a picture that could help find the total number of herding dogs and terriers.

7. Using the information in Exercise 6, write an equation to find how many more breeds of terriers than herding dogs there are.

For **8** through **10**, use the table to the right.

8. There are about 200 more animals in the Minnesota Zoo than in the Phoenix Zoo. About how many species of animals are in the Minnesota Zoo?

9. About how many more species are in the Indianapolis Zoo than the Phoenix Zoo?

10. How can you find the number of species of animals at the San Francisco Zoo?

Data	Name of Zoo	Approximate Number of Animals
	Phoenix	200
	Minnesota	
	San Francisco	
	Indianapolis	360
	Total Animals	1,210

11. A parking lot had a total of 243 cars in one day. By 6:00 A.M., there were 67 cars in the lot. In the next hour, 13 more cars joined these. How many more cars would come to the lot by the end of the day?

243 cars in all

67	13	?

12. A shoe store sold 162 pairs of shoes. The goal was to sell 345 pairs. How many pairs of shoes did they **NOT** sell?

345 pairs of shoes

162	?

For **13** and **14**, use the table at the right.

13. What equation can you write to help find the cost of the shoes and socks together?

14. What equation can you write to help find the difference between the cost of the shirt and the shorts?

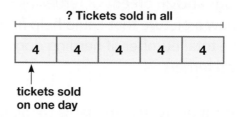

Cost of Gym Clothes

Data		
Shirt	:	$12
Shorts	:	$19
Shoes	:	$42
Socks	:	$2
Hat	:	$15

15. Byron spent $7.75 on popcorn and a drink at the movie theater. The popcorn was $4.25. How much was the cost of the drink?

$7.75 in all

$4.25	?

16. Each school day, Mikaela sold the same number of tickets to the school play. On Monday, she sold 4 tickets. How many tickets did she sell all together in 5 days?

? Tickets sold in all

4	4	4	4	4

tickets sold
on one day

17. Writing to Explain Ken makes 2 nametags in the time it takes Mary to make 5 nametags. When Mary has made 15 nametags, how many has Ken made?

18. Mr. Lee had 62 pencils at the beginning of the school year. At the end of the school year, he had 8 pencils left. How many pencils were given out during the year?

62 pencils in all

8	?

Think About the Process

19. Carlene bought a book for $13.58. She paid with a $10 bill and a $5 bill. Which expression would find the amount of change Carlene would receive?

A $15 − $13.58   **C** $10 + $5

B $15 − $1.42   **D** $13.58 + $1.42

20. Terrence rode 15 rides before lunch at the county fair. He rode 13 rides after lunch. Each ride requires 3 tickets. Which expression represents the number of rides he rode during the day?

A 15 − 13   **C** 15 − 3

B 15 + 13   **D** 13 − 3

Subtracting Decimals

Use 🔧 tools Place-Value Blocks to subtract $0.82 - 0.57$.

Step 1 Go to the Place-Value Blocks eTool.
Select a two-part workspace.

Step 2 ↗ Using the arrow tool, select a flat place-value block, and click in the top workspace to display one flat.

One

In the Select Unit Block drop-down menu, select Flat to let this block represent one.

🔨 Use the hammer tool to break it into parts. Notice each strip is part of a flat.

Step 3 Select and break one of the strips. Notice that there are 10 small blocks in a strip and 100 small blocks in a flat.

Step 4 Show 0.82 with the place-value blocks. 🖌 Use the erase tool to erase any blocks you don't need.

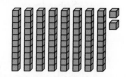

Step 5 🔨 Use the hammer tool to break one tenth strip into 10 hundredths. 🖌 Use the erase tool to take away 0.57 by erasing 7 hundredths and then 5 tenths. Move them to the lower workspace. Look at the blocks that are left to find the difference.
$0.82 - 0.57 = 0.25$.

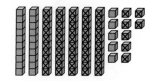

Practice

Solve.

1. $0.64 - 0.14$ **2.** $0.27 - 0.13$ **3.** $0.89 - 0.72$ **4.** $0.93 - 0.27$

5. $0.86 - 0.71$ **6.** $0.38 - 0.19$ **7.** $0.11 - 0.08$ **8.** $0.35 - 0.21$

9. $0.56 - 0.19$ **10.** $0.74 - 0.49$ **11.** $0.71 - 0.58$ **12.** $0.85 - 0.38$

1. Joe got 34,867 points playing a video game, and Carlos got 29,978 points. How many more points did Joe get than Carlos? (2-5)

   A 14,889

   B 4,999

   C 4,989

   D 4,889

2. The table shows tickets sold to the school play.

Tickets Sold	
Thursday	320
Friday	282
Saturday	375

Which is the best estimate of the total tickets sold? (2-2)

   A 1,100

   B 1,000

   C 900

   D 800

3. David bought a 3-ring binder for $4.49, a package of pencils for $1.19, and two packages of paper. What information is needed to find the total amount David spent before tax? (2-3)

   A The cost of a package of paper

   B The cost of a package of erasers

   C The color of the binder

   D How much money David gave the clerk

4. Manuel has 60 minutes to get to karate class. If it takes him 27 minutes to ride his bike to class and 10 minutes to change into his karate uniform, how much time does he have before he must leave his house? (2-7)

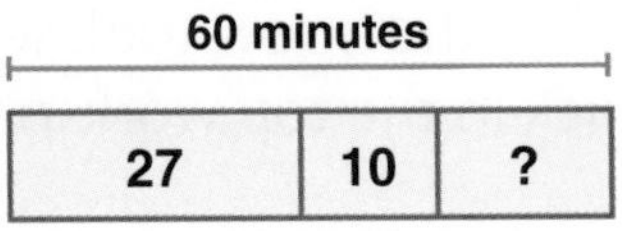

60 minutes		
27	10	?

   A 20

   B 21

   C 23

   D 97

5. To advertise for the school fun fair, 325 flyers were printed on Wednesday, 468 flyers were printed on Thursday, and 815 flyers were printed on Friday. How many flyers were printed in all? (2-4)

   A 1,620

   B 1,608

   C 1,508

   D 1,600

6. Garrett drove 239 miles on Saturday and 149 miles on Sunday. To find $239 + 149$, Garrett made a multiple of ten, as shown below. What is the missing number? (2-1)

$239 + 149 = 240 + \boxed{} = 388$

   A 129

   B 130

   C 147

   D 148

7. A musical group made 8,000 copies of a CD. So far, they have sold 6,280 copies. How many copies are left? (2-6)

A 2,720

B 2,280

C 1,820

D 1,720

8. In April, 5,326 books were checked out of the library. In May, 3,294 books were checked out. How many books were checked out in all? (2-4)

A 8,620

B 8,610

C 8,520

D 8,510

9. What number makes the number sentence true? (2-1)

$28 + 79 = \boxed{} + 28$

A 59

B 69

C 79

D 89

10. Betty had 719 pennies in her piggy bank. If she gave her sister 239 pennies, how many pennies did Betty have left? (2-5)

A 519

B 500

C 480

D 408

11. The last total solar eclipse seen in Dallas was in 1623. The next one will not be seen until 2024. Which number sentence shows the best way to estimate the number of years between the eclipses? (2-2)

A $2020 - 1630 = 390$

B $2030 - 1620 = 410$

C $2020 - 1620 = 400$

D $2020 - 1600 = 420$

12. Daria's book has 323 pages. She has read 141 pages. Which diagram models how to find the number of pages she has left to read? (2-7)

A
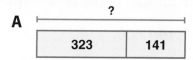

B
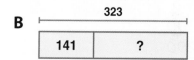

C
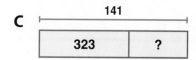

D
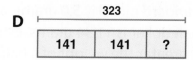

13. Find $5,000 - 2,898$. (2-6)

A 2,000

B 2,210

C 2,120

D 2,102

Set A, pages 28–30

Add 155 + 83. Use mental math.

Use the breaking apart method.
Adding 5 to 155 is easy.

Break apart 83 into 5 and 78.

155 + 5 = 160

160 + 78 = 238

So, 155 + 83 = 238.

Remember that when you use compensation, you must adjust the sum or difference.

1. 53 + 88   **2.** 372 + 226

3. 5,342 + 1,826   **4.** 283 − 169

5. 676 − 521   **6.** 1,089 − 961

Set B, pages 32–33

Estimate   1,579
          + 1,248

Round each number to the nearest hundred.

1,579 rounds to 1,600.

1,248 rounds to 1,200.

Add   1,600
       + 1,200
          2,800

Remember you can round numbers to the nearest hundred or thousand when estimating sums and differences.

1. 473 + 465   **2.** 8,352 − 3,421

3. 586 − 483   **4.** 4,094 + 246

5. 1,440 − 933   **6.** 748 − 392

7. 981 + 193   **8.** 725 + 635

Set C, pages 34–35

The standard weight of a penny is 2.50 grams, a standard nickel is 5.0 grams, and a standard half dollar is 11.34 grams. Estimate how much greater the weight of a half dollar is than a nickel.

Use subtraction to solve.

11.34 rounds to 11.
11.0 − 5.0 = 6.0

The half dollar is about 6.0 grams heavier.

The weight of a penny was extra information.

Remember some problems do not have enough information to solve.

1. Todd read 35 pages of his book on Saturday. He read for 10 minutes on Sunday. How many pages did Todd read over the weekend?

2. Molly bought 150 sheets of paper. She put 50 sheets in her math folder, 25 sheets in her science folder, 25 sheets in her social studies folder, and 40 sheets in her reading folder. How many sheets did Molly have left?

Set D, pages 36–38

Add 359 + 723.

Estimate: 400 + 700 = 1,100

Add the ones.
Regroup if
necessary.

$$\begin{array}{r} 1 \\ 359 \\ + 723 \\ \hline 2 \end{array}$$

Add the tens.
Regroup if
necessary.

$$\begin{array}{r} 1 \\ 359 \\ + 723 \\ \hline 82 \end{array}$$

Add the
hundreds.

$$\begin{array}{r} 1 \\ 359 \\ + 723 \\ \hline 1,082 \end{array}$$

The answer is reasonable.

Remember to regroup if necessary
when adding whole numbers.

1. 215 + 8,823   **2.** 14,296 + 444

3. 2,417 + 3,573   **4.** 572 + 941

5.   32,834   **6.**   14,382
      + 17,384   + 9,243

Set E, pages 40–41 and 42–43

Find 831 − 796.

Estimate: 830 − 800 = 30

Subtract the
ones. Regroup
if necesary.

$$\begin{array}{r} {}^{2}\,{}^{11} \\ 8\cancel{3}\cancel{1} \\ - 796 \\ \hline 5 \end{array}$$

Subtract the
tens. Subtract
the hundreds.

$$\begin{array}{r} {}^{7}\,{}^{12}\,{}^{11} \\ \cancel{8}\cancel{3}\cancel{1} \\ - 796 \\ \hline 35 \end{array}$$

Add to check
your answer.

$$\begin{array}{r} {}^{1}\,{}^{1} \\ 796 \\ + 35 \\ \hline 831 \end{array}$$

The answer is reasonable.

Remember you may need to regroup
before you subtract.

1. 415 − 323   **2.** 4,978 − 2,766

3. 700 − 255   **4.** 4,508 − 2,613

5.   18,005   **6.**   601
      − 6,291   − 482

Set F, pages 44–46

Cathy spent $8 on lunch. She bought a
sandwich, a fruit cup, and a milk at the snack
bar. She spent a total of $6 on the sandwich
and milk. How much did the fruit cup cost?

What do I know?   Cathy had $8. Cathy bought
a sandwich, a milk, and a
fruit cup. Cathy spent $6 on
the sandwich and the milk.

*What am I being
asked to find?*   The amount of money
Cathy spent on the fruit cup

$8 − $6 = $2

Cathy spent $2 on the
fruit cup.

Remember to draw a picture to help
you solve a problem.

Draw a picture and write an equation
to solve.

1. Doug saw 5 Agile wallabies and
9 Rock wallabies at the zoo. How
many wallabies did Doug see?

2. Luz had collected a total of
393 tokens from the games at
Funland. To win a large stuffed
animal, 500 tokens were needed.
How many more tokens does
Luz need to win the large
stuffed animal?

Topic 3

Multiplication Meanings and Facts

1 How many years were in one full cycle of the Aztec calendar? You will find out in Lesson 3-4.

2 How many miles long is the Appalachian Trail? You will find out in Lesson 3-3.

3

How many rooms are in the White House? You will find out in Lesson 3-6.

Review What You Know!

Vocabulary

Choose the best term from the box.

> • breaking apart   • product
> • factor   • multiples

1. In the number sentence $8 \times 3 = 24$, 8 is a ? .

2. In the number sentence $2 \times 6 = 12$, 12 is the ? .

3. $191 + 67 = (191 + 9) + 58$ is an example of using the ? strategy.

4. To find ? of the number 3, multiply numbers by 3.

Skip Counting

Find the term that comes next in the pattern.

5. 2, 4, 6, 8, ▢   6. 20, 25, 30, 35, ▢

7. 6, 9, 12, 15, ▢   8. 8, 16, 24, 32, ▢

9. 7, 14, 21, 28, ▢   10. 11, 22, 33, 44, ▢

Multiplication

Copy each array and circle equal groups of 3.

11.

12. ▢ ▢ ▢
      ▢ ▢ ▢

13. **Writing to Explain** Henry is thinking of a whole number. He multiplies the number by 5, but the result is less than 5. What number is Henry thinking about? Explain.

Understand It!
When groups or rows are equal, multiply to find the total.

Meanings of Multiplication

How can multiplication be used when equal groups are combined?

4 rows of 3

How many ducks are there in 4 rows of 3? To find the total, multiply the number of equal groups by the number in each group. <u>Objects arranged in equal rows form an</u> array.

Another Example How can multiplication be used when you only know the number in one group?

Rudi and Eva collect plastic frogs. Rudi collected 5 frogs. Eva collected 3 times as many frogs. How many frogs did Eva collect?

   A 3 frogs

   B 5 frogs

   C 10 frogs

   D 15 frogs

Rudi's frogs   Eva's frogs

Eva collected 3 times as many frogs as Rudi.

Multiply by 3:

$3 \times 5 = 15$

Eva collected 15 frogs. The correct choice is **D**.

Explain It

1. Write an addition sentence that shows how many frogs Eva collected.

2. Draw an array of 16 frogs. Then, write a multiplication sentence describing the array.

There are 4 rows. Each row has 3 rubber ducks.

Repeated Addition: $3 + 3 + 3 + 3 = 12$
adding 4 rows of 3

Multiplication: $4 \times 3 = 12$

factors   product

The product is the answer to a multiplication problem. Factors are the numbers multiplied together to find the product.

The same rubber ducks can be arranged in another way.

Each group has 4 rubber ducks.

Repeated Addition: $4 + 4 + 4 = 12$

Multiplication: $3 \times 4 = 12$

There are 12 rubber ducks in all.

Guided Practice*

Do you know HOW?

In **1** and **2**, write an addition sentence and a multiplication sentence for each picture below.

1.

2.

Do you UNDERSTAND?

3. Beth saw 2 groups of 4 moths. Draw a picture to show 2 groups of 4. Then draw an array to show 2×4.

4. How could you use repeated addition to find the total number of objects in 3 groups of 2?

5. Martha has 5 rubber ducks. Jim has twice as many rubber ducks. How many rubber ducks does Jim have?

Independent Practice

Leveled Practice In **6** through **8**, write an addition sentence and a multiplication sentence for each picture.

6.

7.

8.

In **9** through **11**, write a multiplication sentence for each addition sentence.

9. $3 + 3 + 3 + 3 = 12$

10. $5 + 5 + 5 + 5 + 5 = 25$

11. $8 + 8 + 8 = 24$

Animated Glossary
www.pearsonsuccessnet.com

*For another example, see Set A on page 72.

12. Which number is three hundred three million, thiry-three thousand, three in standard form?

   A   300,333,003

   B   330,303,003

   C   300,303,033

   D   303,033,003

13. Reasoning Frank wrote 3 × 6 to describe the total number of paper clips shown. Alexa wrote 6 × 3. Who is correct? Explain.

14. Jacob, Hannah, and their grandmother visited the petting zoo. One scoop of animal food cost two dollars. How much did their grandmother pay to buy a scoop for each child?

15. Writing to Explain Without multiplying, how do you know that a 4 × 4 array will have more items than a 3 × 3 array?

16. Taylor helped his father with the grocery shopping. He bought three bags of cheese sticks. Each bag contained 8 cheese sticks. How many cheese sticks were there in all?

   A   3 cheese sticks

   B   16 cheese sticks

   C   24 cheese sticks

   D   30 cheese sticks

17. Sam is setting the table for a family dinner. He needs to put two forks at each place setting. Ten people will come for dinner. Write a multiplication sentence to show how many forks Sam needs.

18. **Think** About the Process Harry arranged the marbles in the pattern shown to the right. Which number sentence best represents Harry's arrangement of marbles?

   A   3 groups of 9 marbles   **C**   2 groups of 13 marbles

   B   4 groups of 5 marbles   **D**   4 groups of 7 marbles

19. Lisa has 2 rings. Tina has 4 times as many rings. How many rings does Tina have?

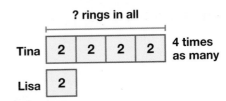

Mixed Problem Solving

National Animals	Facts
Australia: Kangaroo	Kangaroos move at a rate of about 18 feet per second for several hours.
Canada: Beaver	Adult male and female beavers can weigh over 55 pounds.
India: Bengal Tiger	A typical male Bengal Tiger can measure 72 inches long not including the length of its tail or 120 inches including its tail.
Thailand: Thai Elephant	On May 19, 1998, it was approved that March 13 would be marked as Thai Elephants Day.
United States: Bald Eagle	The Bald Eagle has been a symbol for the United States since June 20, 1782.
Botswana: Zebra	The life expectancy of a zebra can be 40 years.

1. How far can a kangaroo travel in 5 seconds?

? Distance a kangaroo can jump in 5 seconds

18	18	18	18	18

↑
Feet jumped per second

2. How long can the tail of a male Bengal Tiger be?

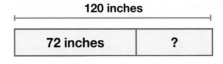

3. About how many beavers weigh the same as a 165 pound adult?

4. In what year will the 25th anniversary of Thai Elephants Day occur?

5. The Continental Congress adopted the Great Seal of the United States in 1782. The American Revolution started 7 years earlier. In what year did the American Revolution begin?

6. The largest of all zebras is the Grevy's zebra. A male Grevy's zebra, on average, weighs 431 kilograms. The average female Grevy's zebra weighs 386 kilograms. How much more does a male Grevy's zebra weigh than a female Grevy's zebra?

7. A Bald Eagle can lay 1 to 3 eggs a year. What is the largest number of eggs a Bald Eagle can lay in 8 years?

8. A female Bengal Tiger can measure about 60 inches in length. About how many inches longer is the male Bengal Tiger than the female Bengal Tiger?

Patterns for Facts

What are the patterns for multiples of 2, 5, and 9?

A multiple is the product of any two whole numbers.

○ multiples of 2

☐ multiples of 5

△ multiples of 9

1	②	3	④	[5]	⑥	7	⑧	△9	[⑩]
11	⑫	13	⑭	[15]	⑯	17	△⑱	19	[⑳]
21	㉒	23	㉔	[25]	㉖	△27	㉘	29	[㉚]
31	㉜	33	㉞	[35]	△㊱	37	㊳	39	[㊵]

Guided Practice*

Do you know HOW?

In **1** through **4**, skip count to find the number that comes next.

1. 2, 4, 6, 8, ▢   **2.** 20, 22, 24, ▢

3. 20, 25, 30, ▢   **4.** 36, 45, 54, ▢

In **5** through **8**, find the product.

5. 9×1 **6.** 2×8

7. 5×4 **8.** 4×2

Do you UNDERSTAND?

9. In the chart above, what pattern do you see for the numbers that have both red circles and green squares?

10. How do you know that 63 is not a multiple of 2? Explain using the pattern for multiples of 2.

11. Felix is sorting socks. He has 11 pairs of socks. How many socks does he have in all?

Independent Practice

In **12** through **15**, skip count to find the number that comes next.

12. 18, 27, 36, ▢   **13.** 12, 14, 16, ▢   **14.** 5, 10, 15, ▢   **15.** 88, 90, 92, ▢

In **16** through **30**, find each product.

16. 2×6 **17.** 5×3 **18.** 5×2 **19.** 5×8 **20.** 9×1

21. 2×7 **22.** 5×7 **23.** 9×3 **24.** 9×6 **25.** 2×4

26. 2×3 **27.** 5×9 **28.** 5×6 **29.** 4×7 **30.** 5×5

Animated Glossary
www.pearsonsuccessnet.com

DIGITAL

For another example, see Set B on page 72.

To find multiples of 2, skip count by 2s.

②, ④, ⑥, ⑧,
⑩, ⑫, ⑭, ⑯ ...

All multiples of 2 are even numbers.

To find multiples of 5, skip count by 5s.

5 , 10 , 15 , 20 ,
25 , 30 , 35 , 40 ...

All multiples of 5 have a 0 or 5 in the ones place.

To find multiples of 9, skip count by 9s.

9 , 18 , 27 , 36 ,
45 , 54 , 63 , 72 ...

The digits of multiples of 9 add to 9 or a multiple of 9.

For 99, for example, $9 + 9 = 18$, and 18 is a multiple of 9.

Problem Solving

31. How many arms do 9 starfish have

   a if each starfish has 6 arms?

   b if each starfish has 7 arms?

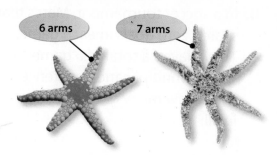

6 arms   7 arms

32. In wheelchair basketball, players use sports chairs that have 2 large wheels and 3 small wheels. If there are 5 players, how many

   a large wheels do the sports chairs have?

   b small wheels do the sports chairs have?

   c wheels do the sports chairs have in all?

33. Jody is working on her model train. She adds 9 pieces of track. Each piece of track is attached with 4 screws. How many screws does she need in all?

   A 18 screws   **C** 54 screws

   B 36 screws   **D** 72 screws

34. Geometry Each pentagon shown below has 5 sides. How many sides are there in all? Skip count by 5s to find the answer. Then, write the multiplication sentence.

35. Use the digits 3, 4, and 6 to make as many 3-digit numbers as you can. Put the numbers in order from least to greatest.

36. Which is equal to 7 dollars, 8 dimes, and 7 pennies?

   A $8.87   **C** $7.87

   B $8.78   **D** $7.78

Lesson

3-3

Understand It!
Multiplication properties can be used to remember basic facts.

Multiplication Properties

How can properties help you multiply?

Multiplication properties can help you remember basic facts.

Commutative Property of Multiplication
Two numbers can be multiplied in any order and the product will be the same.

3 groups of 2 (6 in all)

2 groups of 3 (6 in all)

$3 \times 2 = 2 \times 3$

Guided Practice*

Do you know HOW?

In **1** through **4**, find the product.

1. 0×5 **2.** 1×6

3. 1×0 **4.** 1×9

In **5** and **6**, copy and complete.

5. $4 \times 7 = 7 \times \square$

6. $6 \times 10 = \square \times 6$

Do you UNDERSTAND?

7. When you multiply any number by one, what is the product?

8. In a soccer tournament, Matt's team scored zero goals in each game. They played a total of 6 games. Write a multiplication sentence to show how many goals they scored in all.

Independent Practice

In **9** through **18**, find the product.

9. 1×5 **10.** 7×0 **11.** 3×9 **12.** 0×8 **13.** 0×3

14. 4×0 **15.** 9×4 **16.** 2×7 **17.** 5×6 **18.** 1×1

In **19** through **26**, find the missing number.

19. $4 \times 5 = \square \times 4$ **20.** $9 \times 12 = 12 \times \square$ **21.** $0 \times 6 = \square \times 0$ **22.** $9 \times 8 = \square \times 9$

23. $8 \times 11 = \square \times 8$ **24.** $1 \times 9 = \square \times 1$ **25.** $6 \times 4 = \square \times 6$ **26.** $7 \times 5 = \square \times 7$

DIGITAL   Animated Glossary
www.pearsonsuccessnet.com

Zero Property of Multiplication
The product of any number and zero is zero.

2 groups of 0

$2 \times 0 = 0$

Identity Property of Multiplication
The product of any number and one is that number.

1 group of 7

$1 \times 7 = 7$

Problem Solving

For **27** and **28**, use the table at the right.

27. Annie has 6 packages of tennis balls. How many packages of yellow ping-pong balls would Annie need to have so that she has an equal number of ping-pong balls and tennis balls?

28. If Annie and her three friends each bought 1 package of baseballs, how many baseballs do they have in all?

Type of Ball	Number in each Package
Baseball	1
Tennis Balls	3
Ping-Pong Balls	6

29. Writing to Explain How do you know that $23 \times 15 = 15 \times 23$ without finding the products?

30. The Appalachian Trail is 2,174 miles long. If Andy hiked the entire trail one time, how many miles did he hike?

31. Mrs. Grayson has 27 students in her class. She wants to rearrange the desks in equal groups. If the desks are in 9 groups of 3 desks now, what is another way that she could arrange the desks?

 Use a multiplication property.

   A 3 groups of 9 desks   **C** 5 groups of 6 desks

   B 2 groups of 13 desks   **D** 4 groups of 7 desks

Lesson
3-4
. . . .
Understand It!
Use known facts to
help find the products
for other facts.

3 and 4 as Factors
How can you break apart facts?

Darnel is replacing the wheels on
8 skateboards. Each skateboard has
4 wheels. How many wheels does
he need in all?

Use the Distributive Property to <u>break
apart facts to find the product</u>.

Each skateboard
has 4 wheels.

Guided Practice*

Do you know HOW?

In **1** through **4**, use breaking apart to
find each product.

1. $3 \times 4 = (1 \times 4) + (\boxed{} \times 4) = \boxed{}$

2. $4 \times 7 = (2 \times 7) + (\boxed{} \times 7) = \boxed{}$

3.   3
   $\times\,9$

4.   4
   $\times\,6$

Do you UNDERSTAND?

5. In Exercise 4, find 4×6 by breaking
apart the 6.

6. On Friday, Darnel received a box
of skateboard wheels from the
factory. The box contained 12 sets
of 4 wheels. How many wheels were
there in all?

Independent Practice

Leveled Practice In **7** through **20**, use breaking apart to find each product.

7. $9 \times 5 = (5 \times 5) + (\boxed{} \times 5) = \boxed{}$

8. $8 \times 3 = (4 \times 3) + (4 \times \boxed{}) = \boxed{}$

9. $3 \times 13 = (3 \times \boxed{}) + (3 \times 3) = \boxed{}$

10. $12 \times 4 = (\boxed{} \times 4) + (2 \times 4) = \boxed{}$

11.   6
   $\times\,3$

12.   0
   $\times\,4$

13.   6
   $\times\,4$

14.   8
   $\times\,4$

15.   5
   $\times\,4$

16. 3×5

17. 3×6

18. 4×7

19. 4×9

20. 3×7

DIGITAL
Animated Glossary
www.pearsonsuccessnet.com

For another example, see Set D on page 73.

Find 8 × 4. Break apart 4 into 2 + 2.

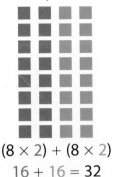

(8 × 2) + (8 × 2)

16 + 16 = 32

So, 8 × 4 = 32.

Darnel needs 32 wheels in all.

Find 8 × 4. Break apart 8 into 3 + 5.

3 × 4 = 12

5 × 4 = 20

12 + 20 = 32

So, 8 × 4 = 32.

Darnel needs 32 wheels in all.

Problem Solving

For **21** and **22**, use the table at the right.

21. In the Aztec calendar, each year has a number from 1 to 13. It also has one of 4 signs, as shown in the table. It takes 4 × 13 years to go through one complete cycle of years. How many years are in one cycle?

22. The year 2006 is the year 7-Rabbit in the Aztec calendar. What is the year 2010 in the Aztec calendar?

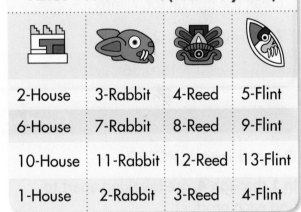

Aztec Year Names (first 16 years)

2-House	3-Rabbit	4-Reed	5-Flint
6-House	7-Rabbit	8-Reed	9-Flint
10-House	11-Rabbit	12-Reed	13-Flint
1-House	2-Rabbit	3-Reed	4-Flint

23. Writing to Explain Vicki scored 6 two-point baskets and 6 one-point free throws. Li scored 6 three-point baskets. Explain how you know each girl scored the same total.

24. In his last basketball game, Andrew scored 15 points. Which of the following is **NOT** a way he could have scored his points?

A 5 three-point shots

B 3 three-point shots in the first half and 2 three-point shots in the second half

C 3 two-point shots and 2 one-point free throws

D 5 two-point shots and 5 one-point free throws

Lesson
3-5

Understand It!
Use known facts to
break apart a fact.

6, 7, and 8 as Factors

Are there different ways to break apart a fact?

Mrs. White's class drew a map of their town. The map is 6 blocks by 6 blocks. How many square blocks are on the map?

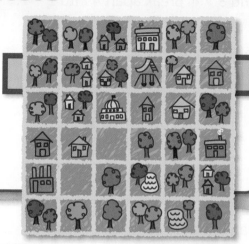

Other Examples

Find 7×8.
Break the first factor, 7, into $5 + 2$.

$7 \times 8 = (5 \times 8) + (2 \times 8)$

$40 + 16 = 56$

Find 8×8.
Break the first factor, 8, into $5 + 3$.

$8 \times 8 = (5 \times 8) + (3 \times 8)$

$40 + 24 = 64$

Guided Practice*

Do you know HOW?

In **1** through **4**, use breaking apart to find each product.

1. $6 \times 8 = (6 \times 4) + (6 \times \boxed{}) = \boxed{}$

2. $7 \times 3 = (7 \times 1) + (\boxed{} \times 2) = \boxed{}$

3. 7×9 **4.** 8×8

Do you UNDERSTAND?

5. Writing to Explain In the example at the top, how can $3 \times 6 = 18$ help you find 6×6?

6. Two streets are added to one side of the map, so it now covers an area of 8 blocks by 6 blocks. How many square blocks are on the map now?

Independent Practice

Leveled Practice In **7** through **20**, use breaking apart to find each product.

7. $9 \times 5 = (9 \times 1) + (9 \times \boxed{}) = \boxed{}$

8. $3 \times 5 = (2 \times \boxed{}) + (1 \times 5) = \boxed{}$

9. $7 \times 6 = (7 \times \boxed{}) + (7 \times 4) = \boxed{}$

10. $4 \times 8 = (4 \times 5) + (4 \times \boxed{}) = \boxed{}$

Find 6 × 6.

You can break apart the first factor or the second factor.

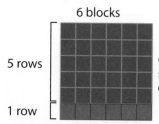

6 blocks

5 rows

1 row

6 rows of 6 is the same as 5 rows of 6 and 1 row of 6.

Break apart 6 into 5 + 1.

6 × 6 = (5 × 6) + (1 × 6)

30 + 6 = 36

So, 6 × 6 = 36.

There are 36 square blocks on the map.

---

11. 6 × 6   **12.** 7 × 5   **13.** 8 × 7   **14.** 4 × 6   **15.** 3 × 7

16. 9 × 3   **17.** 8 × 9   **18.** 4 × 4   **19.** 6 × 3   **20.** 7 × 7

Problem Solving

21. Tara said she multiplied 6 × 6 to help her find the product of 7 × 6. Draw a picture and explain what she means.

22. Betsy's school needs $2,000 to send the band to the state finals. So far, they have raised $465 in a fundraiser. How much more money do they need?

23. Joe, Vicki, and Tom took a hiking vacation. They traveled the distances shown in the table below. Who walked the farthest?

    A Joe   **C** Vicki

    B Tom   **D** They all walked the same distance.

24. For the chessboard shown below, write a multiplication sentence to find the total number of

    a red pieces.

    b squares with pieces.

    c squares on the board.

Hiker	Distance walked
Joe	9 miles each day for 8 days.
Vicki	8 miles each day for 4 days and 4 miles each day for 8 days.
Tom	7 miles each day for 5 days then 5 miles each day for 7 days.

Data

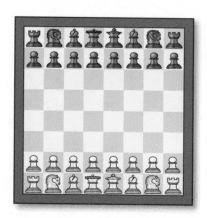

10, 11, and 12 as Factors

12 plants = 1 dozen

What are the patterns for multiples of 10, 11, and 12?

How many plants are in 3 dozen containers if there is one plant in each container?

Patterns can help you when multiplying by 10, 11, or 12.

Guided Practice*

Do you know HOW?

In **1** through **4**, use patterns to find each product.

1. 10×3

2. 11×4

3. 11×7

4. 10×5

Do you UNDERSTAND?

5. Writing to Explain How can you use 7×10 to help you find 7×12?

6. A flower shop ordered one gross of flower pots. A gross is 12 dozen. Use breaking apart to find out how many flower pots they ordered.

Independent Practice

Leveled Practice In **9** through **26**, use breaking apart and patterns to find each product.

7. $12 \times 6 = (10 \times 6) + (\times 6) = $

8. $12 \times 8 = (10 \times 8) + (2 \times) = $

9. $9 \times 11 = (9 \times) + (9 \times 1) = $

10. $11 \times 11 = (11 \times 10) + (\times 1) = $

11. 11×6

12. 12×2

13. 10×6

14. 4×11

15. 4×10

16. 12×4

17. 11×8

18. 10×8

19. 10×3

20. 7×12

21. 11×10

22. 10×10

23. 11×2

24. 12×5

25. 10×1

26. 12×10

*For another example, see Set F on page 73.

Multiples of 10	Multiples of 11	Multiples of 12
$10 \times 1 = 10$	$11 \times 1 = 11$	$12 \times 1 = 12$
$10 \times 2 = 20$	$11 \times 2 = 22$	$12 \times 2 = 24$
$10 \times 3 = 30$	$11 \times 3 = 33$	$12 \times 3 = 36$
$10 \times 4 = 40$	$11 \times 4 = 44$	$12 \times 4 = 48$
$10 \times 5 = 50$	$11 \times 5 = 55$	$12 \times 5 = 60$
⋮	⋮	⋮

Place a zero to the right of the number to create a new ones digit.

Multiply the factor that is not 11 by 10. Then add the factor to the product.

$$11 \times 6 = (10 \times 6) + 6$$

Break apart 12.

$$12 = 10 + 2$$

$$12 \times 3 = (10 \times 3) + (2 \times 3)$$

There are 36 plants in 3 dozen containers.

Problem Solving

27. A pet store has 55 guppies. On Friday, Saturday, and Sunday, the store sold 11 guppies each day. How many guppies are left?

28. Reasonableness Jillian said that the product of 11×12 is 1,212. Is this reasonable? Why or why not?

29. Roger has 3 dimes and 6 pennies. He wrote a multiplication sentence to show the total value. One factor was 12.

a What was the other factor?

b What is the product?

30. Think About the Process Mrs. Sanchez is installing new tile on her bathroom floor. If a 7×12 array of tiles fits perfectly, which expression shows how many tiles to use?

A $7 + 7 + 7 + 7 + 7 + 7 + 7$

B $(7 \times 10) - (7 \times 2)$

C $(7 \times 10) + (7 \times 2)$

D $(4 \times 10) + (3 \times 2)$

31. Use breaking apart to find the number of rooms in the White House.

$12 \times 11 = (12 \times \boxed{}) + (12 \times \boxed{}) = \boxed{}$

32. Steve, John, and Damon drove to a car race together. They each paid $34 for the day, including a $24 ticket and their portion of the parking fee. How much was the total parking fee?

A $10　　　**C** $40

B $30　　　**D** $60

Understand It!
Learning how and when to draw a picture can help you solve problems.

Draw a Picture and Write an Equation

A stegosaurus was 5 times as long as a velociraptor. If a velociraptor was 6 feet long, how long was a stegosaurus?

Stegosaurus: ? feet long

Velociraptor: 6 feet long

Guided Practice*

Do you know HOW?

Solve. Write an equation to help you.

1. Manuel has a collection of coins, all of which are nickels and quarters. He has 8 nickels and three times as many quarters.

   a How many quarters does he have?

   b How many coins does Manuel have in all?

Do you UNDERSTAND?

2. How did the picture in the example above help you to write an equation?

3. **Write a Problem** The length of an iguanodon is 28 feet. A velociraptor is 6 feet long. Use this information to write a problem you can solve by writing an equation. Then solve.

Independent Practice

Solve.

4. For the science fair, James decided to make a model of sauroposeidon, the tallest dinosaur ever discovered. He made his model 3 feet tall. The actual dinosaur was 20 times the height of James' model. How tall was sauroposeidon?

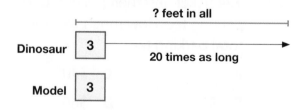

Dinosaur | 3 — ? feet in all — 20 times as long

Model | 3

Stuck? Try this....

- What do I know?
- What diagram can I use to help understand the problem?
- Can I use addition, subtraction, multiplication, or division?
- Is all of my work correct?
- Did I answer the right question?
- Is my answer reasonable?

*For another example, see Set G on page 73.

What do I know?

A velociraptor was 6 feet long. A stegosaurus was 5 times as long as a velociraptor.

What am I asked to find?

The length of a stegosaurus

Draw a picture.

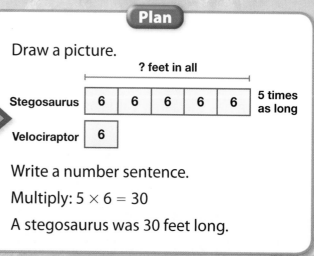

Write a number sentence.

Multiply: $5 \times 6 = 30$

A stegosaurus was 30 feet long.

---

5. Carmen's recipe calls for three times as many carrots as peas. If Carmen uses 2 cups of peas, how many cups of carrots will she use?

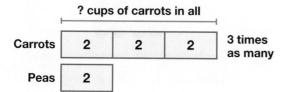

6. Rae's recipe calls for twice as many tomatoes as peppers. She uses 2 cups of peppers. How many cups of tomatoes and peppers will she use in all?

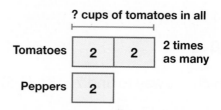

7. Marley, Jon, and Bart swim a relay race. Jon swims two more laps than Marley. Bart swims twice as many laps as Marley. If Marley swims 3 laps, how many laps do they swim altogether?

8. Jack's dog has a rectangular pen. The length is two feet longer than the width. The width is 6 feet. Write an equation to find the perimeter. What is the perimeter of the pen?

9. When Matilda was born, she was 20 inches tall. Matilda's mother is 3 times as tall as Matilda was at birth. Use the model below to find Matilda's mother's height.

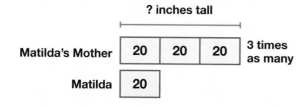

10. **Think** **About the Process** Four relay team members run an equal part of an 8-mile race. Which equation shows how far each member runs?

A $2 + 2 = 4$

B $4 \times 2 = 8$

C $4 + 4 + 4 + 4 = 16$

D $2 \times 2 = 4$

1. Which has the same value as 3×5? (3-1)

A $5 + 3$

B $5 + 5 + 5$

C $5 + 5 + 5 + 3$

D $3 + 3 + 3 + 3$

2. Grant made 4 flags for the school play. Each flag had 1 white star. How many white stars did Grant need? (3-3)

A 5

B 4

C 1

D 0

3. Which is a way to find 7×8? (3-5)

A $(7 \times 5) + (7 \times 2)$

B $(4 \times 8) + (3 \times 8)$

C $(7 \times 5) + (8 \times 1)$

D $(5 \times 8) + (2 \times 7)$

4. Each flower has 5 petals.

If Stephanie counted the petals in groups of 5, which list shows numbers she could have named? (3-2)

A 12, 15, 18, 30

B 15, 20, 34, 40

C 15, 20, 25, 30

D 10, 12, 14, 16

5. Elizabeth bought 3 packages of buttons. Each package had 12 buttons. Which number sentence can be used to find the total number of buttons Elizabeth bought? (3-6)

A $12 - 3 = \square$

B $3 + 12 = \square$

C $3 \times \square = 12$

D $3 \times 12 = \square$

6. Derrik arranged some balls on a table as shown.

Which number sentence best represents Derrik's arrangement? (3-1)

A $3 \times 4 = 12$

B $3 \times 5 = 15$

C $3 + 4 = 7$

D $12 - 4 = 8$

7. Gina made an invitation for each of her 10 friends. She used 11 stickers on each invitation. How many stickers did Gina use in all? (3-6)

A 100

B 101

C 110

D 111

8. Trevor's display case has 6 shelves. Each shelf displays 8 golf balls. Which number sentence shows how many golf balls are displayed in the case? (3-7)

? golf balls in all

8	8	8	8	8	8

↑
Golf balls on
each shelf

A $6 + 8 = 14$

B $6 - 3 = 3$

C $6 \times 8 = 48$

D $8 \times 8 = 64$

9. Sue collected 5 rocks. Angie collected 4 times as many rocks as Sue. Which of these shows the total number of rocks Angie collected? (3-1)

A The sum of 4 and 5

B The difference between 20 and 4

C The quotient of 20 and 4

D The product of 4 and 5

10. The Mendez family replaced tile on their kitchen counter. A 9×4 array of tiles fit the area. How many tiles did they use? (3-4)

A 13

B 27

C 34

D 36

11. Which number makes the number sentence true? (3-3)

$6 \times 2 = \boxed{} \times 6$

A 0

B 1

C 2

D 6

12. Which is a way to break apart 4×8? (3-4)

A $(4 \times 8) + (4 \times 8)$

B $(2 \times 5) + (2 \times 3)$

C $(2 \times 4) + (2 \times 4)$

D $(2 \times 8) + (2 \times 8)$

13. Before touring Kickapoo Cavern State Park, the 4th graders were put into 6 groups of 12 students. Which is a way to find 6×12? (3-6)

A $(3 \times 10) + (3 \times 2)$

B $(3 \times 6) + (3 \times 6)$

C $(6 \times 10) + (6 \times 2)$

D $(6 \times 12) + (6 \times 12)$

14. It takes Dave 7 minutes to paint one section of a fence. How many minutes would it take him to paint 3 sections? (3-5)

A 18

B 21

C 24

D 28

Set A, pages 54–56

Write an addition sentence and a multiplication sentence.

$5 + 5 + 5 = 15$

$3 \times 5 = 15$

Remember you can multiply when adding the same number over and over.

1.  2.

Set B, pages 58–59

Find 2×10.

When you multiply a number by 2, the product is always even.

$2 \times 10 = 20$

When you multiply a number by 5, the product always ends in 0 or 5.

$5 \times 2 = 10$

Remember you can solve some multiplication problems by using patterns of multiples.

1. 6×5	**2.** 9×8
3. 9×6	**4.** 2×3
5. 2×7	**6.** 5×7
7. 9×5	**8.** 2×5
9. 5×8	**10.** 9×3
11. 9×9	**12.** 5×3

Set C, pages 60–61

Find 9×0.

When you multiply any number by 0, the product is 0.

$9 \times 0 = 0$

When you multiply any number by 1, the product is the original number.

$6 \times 1 = 6$

Remember you can change the order of the factors when you multiply.

1. 10×0	**2.** 8×4
3. 4×8	**4.** 1×12
5. 1×11	**6.** 7×2
7. 1×5	**8.** 9×6
9. 7×1	**10.** 0×11
11. 0×100	**12.** 9×4

Set D, pages 62–63

Find 3 × 9 using breaking apart.

3 groups of 9 = 3 groups of 5 + 3 groups of 4

$$3 \times 9 = (3 \times 5) + (3 \times 4)$$

15 + 12

27

Remember you can use breaking apart to remember multiplication facts.

1. 3 × 8   **2.** 4 × 9

3. 4 × 2   **4.** 3 × 10

Set E, pages 64–65

What are two ways to break apart 8 × 7?

Break apart the first factor.

$$8 \times 7 = (4 \times 7) + (4 \times 7)$$

28 + 28

56

Break apart the second factor.

$$8 \times 7 = (8 \times 5) + (8 \times 2)$$

40 + 16

56

Remember you can break apart either factor to find a multiplication fact.

1. 12 × 6   **2.** 8 × 8

3. 9 × 8   **4.** 6 × 9

Set F, pages 66–67

Find 7 × 12 using breaking apart.

7 groups of 12 = 7 groups of 10 + 7 groups of 2

$$7 \times 12 = (7 \times 10) + (7 \times 2)$$

70 + 14

84

Remember you can use patterns or breaking apart to multiply.

1. 12 × 12   **2.** 9 × 9

3. 11 × 7   **4.** 10 × 6

Set G, pages 68–69

Marisol has 8 pennies in her collection. She has four times as many quarters as pennies. How many coins are in Marisol's collection?

? quarters in all

| quarters | 8 | 8 | 8 | 8 | 4 times as many |

| pennies | 8 |

4 × 8 = 32 quarters

Add 8 pennies to find how many coins are in Marisol's collection.

32 + 8 = 40 coins in all

Remember you can draw a picture to help you write an equation.

Draw a picture and write an equation to solve.

1. The length of Mel's basement is 10 times the length of a broom. The length of a broom is 3 feet. What is the length of the basement?

Division Meanings and Facts

1

When did people start riding carousels in the United States? You will find out in Lesson 4-4.

2 Gouramis go to the surface of a fish tank to breathe air directly. How many gouramis can you keep in a 15-gallon tank? You will find out in Lesson 4-1.

3 How many years will it take the U.S. Mint to release all of the 50 state quarters? You will find out in Lesson 4-2.

Review What You Know!

Vocabulary

Choose the best term from the box.

> • divisor   • quotient
> • multiple   • product
> • factor   • division

1. In the number sentence $9 \times 5 = 45$, 45 is the ? .

2. The number you divide by is the ? .

3. The answer in a division problem is the ? .

Multiplication Facts

Find each product.

4. 5×3	**5.** 7×2	**6.** 6×8
7. 8×0	**8.** 1×4	**9.** 2×8
10. 5×7	**11.** 3×6	**12.** 4×4
13. 4×5	**14.** 4×8	**15.** 2×6

Addition and Subtraction Facts

Write a subtraction fact for each addition fact.

16. $8 + 8 = 16$ **17.** $4 + 7 = 11$

18. $6 + 6 = 12$ **19.** $9 + 5 = 14$

20. Write a subtraction fact for the array below.

★★★★★★★★
✕✕✕✕✕✕✕

21. Writing to Explain Explain how you could subtract $146 - 51$ using mental math.

Meanings of Division

When do you divide?

A museum wants to display a collection of 24 gems on four shelves, placing the same number of gems on each shelf. How many gems will be on each shelf?

Choose an Operation Think about sharing. Divide to find the number in each group.

24 gems on 4 shelves

Another Example How can you divide to find the number of groups?

Terri has 24 gems. She wants to display them on shelves. She decides to display 4 gems on each shelf. How many shelves does she need?

Choose an Operation Think about repeated subtraction. Divide to find the number of groups.

What You Show

To find the number of shelves, put 4 gems in each group. How many groups are there?

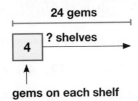

24 gems

4

? shelves

gems on each shelf

What You Write

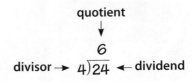

quotient

6

divisor → 4)24 ← dividend

Terri needs 6 shelves.

Explain It

1. How can repeated subtraction be used to find the number of shelves needed to hold 24 gems if each shelf holds 6 gems?

2. Explain what the quotient represents in each of the examples above.

What You Show

Think of sharing the gems equally among the 4 shelves. How many gems are on each shelf?

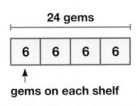

24 gems

| 6 | 6 | 6 | 6 |

gems on each shelf

What You Write

divisor

$$24 \div 4 = 6$$

dividend   quotient

Each shelf should have 6 gems.

Guided Practice*

Do you know HOW?

In **1** and **2**, draw pictures to help you divide.

1. You put 18 people into 3 rows. How many people are in each row?

2. Rocco is putting 14 drawings into 2 art binders. How many drawings are in each binder?

Do you UNDERSTAND?

3. Explain how you could use repeated addition to check the answer to the example above.

4. Sixteen players came to soccer practice. They formed four teams with the same number of players per team. How many players were on each team?

Independent Practice

Leveled Practice In **5** through **7**, copy and complete the diagrams to help you divide.

5. Kevin is arranging 12 chairs in 3 equal groups. How many chairs are in each group?

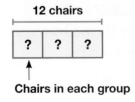

12 chairs

| ? | ? | ? |

Chairs in each group

6. Meg has 36 beads. Each bracelet has 9 beads. How many bracelets does she have?

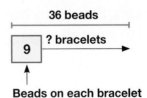

36 beads

? bracelets

9

Beads on each bracelet

7. A farmer has 15 fruit trees. He plants 3 trees in each row. How many rows are there?

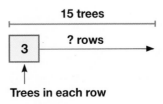

15 trees

? rows

3

Trees in each row

*For another example, see Set A on page 92.

Lesson 4-1

77

Independent Practice

In **8** through **11**, draw pictures to solve each problem.

8. Jeff puts 25 quarters into 5 equal groups. How many quarters are in each group?

9. Sally has 12 flower bulbs and divides them into 4 equal groups. How many flower bulbs are in each group?

10. Jena is making apple pies. She has 33 apples. She is putting 11 in each pie. How many pies will Jena make?

11. There are 30 stuffed bears in a gift shop arranged in 5 equal rows. How many bears are in each row?

Problem Solving

In **12** through **15**, use the table at the right.

12. How many students will be in each row for Mrs. Raymond's class photo?

13. How many more students will be in each row for Mr. Peterson's class than for Mr. Chen's class?

14. In which class will there be 7 students in each row?

Class Picture Day	
Each class must be arranged into three equal rows.	
Name of Teacher	**Number of Students**
Mrs. Raymond	24
Mr. Chen	18
Miss Clifford	21
Mr. Peterson	27

15. If 3 students were absent from Miss Clifford's class on picture day, how many fewer students would be in each row?

16. A fish store tells you that you need 3 gallons of water for each gourami. How many fish can you keep in a 15-gallon tank?

17. Ray collects toy cars. He stores them in special boxes that fit 6 cars each. He had a total of 48 cars. Today he got 12 more cars. How many boxes will Ray need to store all of his cars now?

    A 2 boxes

    B 6 boxes

    C 8 boxes

    D 10 boxes

18. **Think About the Process** The drama club collects 242 bottles and 320 cans in a fundraiser. Each is worth a nickel. However, 48 cans were rejected. Which expression shows how many nickels they raised?

    A $(242 + 320) - 48$

    B $242 + 320 + 48$

    C $(320 - 242) + 48$

    D $(320 - 242) - 48$

Algebra Connections

Properties and Number Sentences

Remember multiplication properties can be used to help you solve multiplication problems:

- Commutative Property
  $3 \times 2 = 2 \times 3$
- Associative Property
  $(5 \times 2) \times 4 = 5 \times (2 \times 4)$
- Identity Property
  $9 \times 1 = 9$
- Zero Property
  $8 \times 0 = 0$

Example: $(6 \times 4) \times 2 = \boxed{} \times (4 \times 2)$

Think The Associative Property of Multiplication means you can change the grouping of factors.

Since $(6 \times 4) \times 2 = \boxed{} \times (4 \times 2)$, the value of $\boxed{}$ must be 6.

Copy and complete. Check your answers.

1. $39 \times \boxed{} = 39$

2. $\boxed{} \times 12 = 12$

3. $(8 \times 5) \times 2 = \boxed{} \times (5 \times 2)$

4. $20 \times 4 = 4 \times \boxed{}$

5. $6 \times \boxed{} = 5 \times 6$

6. $0 = \boxed{} \times 9$

7. $\boxed{} \times 8 = 8 \times 9$

8. $1 \times \boxed{} = 24$

9. $\boxed{} \times 25 = 0$

10. $15 \times 3 = \boxed{} \times 15$

11. $16 \times \boxed{} = 16$

12. $(\boxed{} \times 4) \times 5 = 6 \times (4 \times 5)$

13. $12 \times 0 = \boxed{}$

14. $7 \times \boxed{} = 0$

15. $7 \times (1 \times \boxed{}) = (7 \times 1) \times 3$

For **16** through **18**, use the information in the table to find the answer.

16. Write two number sentences to represent the number of seats in 6 rows.

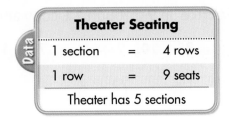

Theater Seating		
1 section	=	4 rows
1 row	=	9 seats
Theater has 5 sections		

17. No one is sitting in the last row of the theater that is otherwise filled. How many seats are being used?

18. How many rows of seats does the theater have?

Lesson
4-2

Understand It!
Multiplication and
division are related in
the same way that
addition and subtraction
are related.

Relating Multiplication and Division

Operations that undo each other are inverse operations. Multiplying by 3 and dividing by 3 are inverse operations.

Each trading card sheet has 3 rows with 2 pockets in each row. How many pockets are on each sheet?

3 rows of 2

Guided Practice*

Do you know HOW?

In **1** and **2**, copy and complete each fact family.

1. $8 \times \boxed{} = 32$

$32 \div \boxed{} = 4$

$32 \div \boxed{} = \boxed{}$

$\boxed{} \times \boxed{} = 32$

2. $6 \times 9 = \boxed{}$

$54 \div \boxed{} = 9$

$54 \div 9 = \boxed{}$

$9 \times \boxed{} = \boxed{}$

In **3** and **4**, write the fact family for each set of numbers.

3. 3, 6, 18

4. 5, 7, 35

Do you UNDERSTAND?

5. Why are there four number sentences in the example above?

6. Is $2 \times 6 = 12$ part of the fact family from the example above?

7. Why is $3 + 3 = 6$ **NOT** in the fact family of 2, 3, and 6?

8. If you know $7 \times 9 = 63$, what division facts do you know?

Independent Practice

Leveled Practice In **9** through **12**, copy and complete each fact family.

9. $5 \times \boxed{} = 35$

$35 \div 7 = \boxed{}$

$\boxed{} \times \boxed{} = 35$

$35 \div \boxed{} = \boxed{}$

10. $9 \times \boxed{} = 72$

$72 \div 8 = \boxed{}$

$\boxed{} \times \boxed{} = 72$

$72 \div \boxed{} = \boxed{}$

11. $3 \times \boxed{} = 18$

$18 \div 6 = \boxed{}$

$\boxed{} \times \boxed{} = 18$

$18 \div \boxed{} = \boxed{}$

12. $2 \times \boxed{} = 24$

$24 \div 12 = \boxed{}$

$\boxed{} \times \boxed{} = 24$

$24 \div \boxed{} = \boxed{}$

DIGITAL

Animated Glossary
www.pearsonsuccessnet.com

For another example, see Set B on page 92.

A **fact family** shows all the related multiplication and division facts for a set of numbers. You can use fact families to help you remember division facts.

This is the fact family for 2, 3, and 6:

$$2 \times 3 = 6 \qquad 6 \div 2 = 3$$
$$3 \times 2 = 6 \qquad 6 \div 3 = 2$$

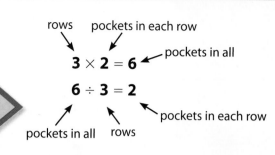

rows   pockets in each row

$$3 \times 2 = 6 \leftarrow \text{pockets in all}$$
$$6 \div 3 = 2$$

pockets in all   rows   pockets in each row

Each has 6 pockets.

In **13** through **24**, write a fact family for each set of numbers.

13. 7, 8, 56   **14.** 2, 8, 16   **15.** 6, 7, 42   **16.** 6, 6, 36

17. 3, 8, 24   **18.** 7, 10, 70   **19.** 6, 5, 30   **20.** 5, 8, 40

21. 4, 4, 16   **22.** 9, 3, 27   **23.** 1, 7, 7   **24.** 8, 6, 48

Problem Solving

25. Use the table at the right. How many years will it take to release all 50 state quarters? Write a division fact you can use to find this quotient.

United States State Quarters	
First quarters released	1999
Number of new quarters each year	5

26. In the fact family for the numbers 3, 7, 21, which term can **NOT** be used to describe 3 or 7?

  A Factor   **C** Product

  B Divisor   **D** Quotient

27. Josh practiced his drums two hours before dinner and three hours after dinner. How many hours did he practice in all?

  A 3 hours   **C** 5 hours

  B 4 hours   **D** 6 hours

28. Write the fact family that has 9 as a factor and 45 as a product.

29. Number Sense Why does the fact family for 64 and 8 have only two number sentences?

Understand It!
Thinking about multiplication can help when dividing with zero and one.

Special Quotients

Dividing by 1

How can you divide with 1 and 0?

A sandwich is cut into 8 pieces. How many people can have 1 piece each? Find 8 ÷ 1.

Think What number times 1 equals 8?

$1 \times 8 = 8$

So, $8 \div 1 = 8.$

1 group of 8

8 people can have 1 piece of sandwich

Rule: Any number divided by 1 is itself.

Guided Practice*

Do you know HOW?

In **1** through **8**, use multiplication facts to help you divide.

1. $9 \div 9$ **2.** $5 \div 1$

3. $0 \div 4$ **4.** $7 \div 1$

5. $3\overline{)0}$ **6.** $1\overline{)1}$

7. $1\overline{)2}$ **8.** $6\overline{)6}$

Do you UNDERSTAND?

9. What multiplication sentence can help you find $0 \div 8$?

10. What multiplication sentence can help you find $8 \div 8$?

11. Writing to Explain If none of the bread is left, how many pieces can 4 people have?

Independent Practice

In **12** through **15**, use multiplication facts to help you divide.

12. $1\overline{)3}$ **13.** $8\overline{)0}$ **14.** $2\overline{)0}$ **15.** $4\overline{)4}$

In **16** through **27**, copy and complete by writing >, <, or = for each ○.

16. $7 \div 7 \bigcirc 2 \div 2$ **17.** $0 \div 5 \bigcirc 3 \div 1$ **18.** $4 \div 1 \bigcirc 4 \div 4$

19. $6 \div 6 \bigcirc 0 \div 4$ **20.** $9 \div 1 \bigcirc 4 \div 1$ **21.** $3 \div 3 \bigcirc 6 \div 1$

22. $0 \div 3 \bigcirc 0 \div 8$ **23.** $0 \div 5 \bigcirc 5 \div 5$ **24.** $8 \div 1 \bigcirc 6 \div 1$

25. $0 \div 9 \bigcirc 0 \div 7$ **26.** $0 \div 1 \bigcirc 1 \div 1$ **27.** $7 \div 1 \bigcirc 0 \div 6$

*For another example, see Set C on page 93.

1 as a Quotient

To find $8 \div 8$, think 8 times what number equals 8?

$$8 \times 1 = 8$$

So, $8 \div 8 = 1$.

Rule: Any number (except 0) divided by itself is 1.

Dividing 0 by a Number

To find $0 \div 8$, think 8 times what number equals 0?

$$8 \times 0 = 0$$

So, $0 \div 8 = 0$.

Rule: 0 divided by any number (except 0) is 0.

Dividing by 0

To find $8 \div 0$, think 0 times what number equals 8?

There is no such number.

Rule: You cannot divide by 0.

Problem Solving

28. Three friends decided to buy lunch. Anne spent $3.42, Saul spent $4.41, and Ryan spent $4.24. Write these numbers from least to greatest.

29. Tony's family is driving 70 miles to a fair. They have already traveled 30 miles. They are traveling at a speed of 40 miles per hour. How many more hours will it take them to complete the rest of the trip?

30. On a trip to the beach, the Torrez family brought 5 beach balls for their 5 children.

    a If the beach balls are divided evenly, how many beach balls will each child get?

    b If the children give the 5 balls to 1 parent, how many balls will the parent have?

31. Algebra If $\square \div \triangle = 0$, what do you know about $\square$?

    A $\square$ cannot equal 0.

    B $\square$ must equal 0.

    C $\square$ must equal 1.

    D $\square$ must equal $\triangle$.

32. Write a Problem Write a word problem in which 5 is divided by 5 and another problem in which 5 is divided by 1.

33. In one season, a baseball team will practice 3 times a week. If there are 36 practices, how many weeks will the team practice in the season?

34. Number Sense Write a fact family for 3, 3, and 9.

Lesson
4-4

Understand It!
Thinking about
multiplication facts
can help you divide.

Using Multiplication Facts to Find Division Facts

How does multiplication help you divide?

Matt wants to buy 28 super bouncy balls to give as prizes. How many packs does Matt need to buy?

Choose an Operation Divide to find the number of equal groups.

7 balls in each pack

Guided Practice*

Do you know HOW?

In **1** through **6**, use multiplication facts to help you divide.

1. $27 \div 9$

2. $40 \div 5$

3. $24 \div 4$

4. $66 \div 6$

5. $9\overline{)63}$

6. $9\overline{)81}$

Do you UNDERSTAND?

7. What multiplication fact could you use to help you find $72 \div 9$?

8. Matt has 40 super bouncy balls to put in 10 bags. He puts the same number in each bag. What multiplication fact can you use to find the number of balls in each bag?

Independent Practice

Leveled Practice In **9** through **27**, use multiplication facts to help you find the quotient.

9. ▢ $\times 3 = 27$ $27 \div 3 =$ ▢

10. ▢ $\times 8 = 40$ $40 \div 8 =$ ▢

11. ▢ $\times 6 = 42$ $42 \div 6 =$ ▢

12. ▢ $\times 7 = 63$ $63 \div 7 =$ ▢

13. $7\overline{)49}$

14. $3\overline{)27}$

15. $6\overline{)48}$

16. $7\overline{)21}$

17. $4\overline{)16}$

18. $9\overline{)36}$

19. $5\overline{)15}$

20. $12\overline{)60}$

21. $6\overline{)36}$

22. $2\overline{)14}$

23. $3\overline{)24}$

24. $4\overline{)32}$

25. $2\overline{)18}$

26. $7\overline{)35}$

27. $7\overline{)56}$

For another example, see Set D on page 93.

How many groups of 7 are in 28?

$28 \div 7 = \square$

Change this to a multiplication sentence:

What number times 7 equals 28?

$\square \times 7 = 28$ $4 \times 7 = 28$

There are two ways to write division facts.

$$28 \div 7 = 4$$

or

$$\begin{array}{r} 4 \\ 7\overline{)28} \end{array}$$

Matt needs to buy 4 packs of bouncy balls.

Problem Solving

For **28** and **29**, use the table at the right.

28. On a field trip to the Alamo, Shana spends $24 in the gift shop. Which item can Shana buy the most of? Explain.

29. How many mini-flags can Shana buy if she uses all of her money?

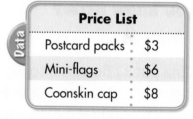

Price List	
Postcard packs	$3
Mini-flags	$6
Coonskin cap	$8

For **30**, use the diagram at the right.

30. People started riding carousels in the United States in 1835. The carousel drawing, at the right, has a total of 36 horses with an equal number of horses on each circle. Write a division fact you can use to find the number of horses on the outer circle.

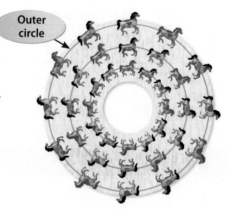

Outer circle

31. Carson plays a card word game. She gives the same number of cards to each of 4 players. If there are 20 cards in all, how many cards does each player get?

32. The total lunch bill for six people is $52. They add an $8 tip and split the bill evenly. How much is each person's equal share of the total bill?

A $6   C $10

B $8   D $12

4-5

Understand It!
Learning how and when to draw a picture and write an equation can help you solve problems.

Draw a Picture and Write an Equation

Ruben's scout troop is making 4 milk-jug birdfeeders. Each birdfeeder will use the same number of wooden dowels. If they have 24 dowels in all, how many dowels will be used for each feeder?

24 dowels

Guided Practice*

Do you know HOW?

Solve. Write an equation to help you.

1. Tina put 32 flowers into eight bouquets. How many flowers were in each bouquet if each had the same number of flowers?

32 flowers in all

?	?	?	?	?	?	?	?

↑
Flowers in each bouquet

Do you UNDERSTAND?

2. How did the picture in Problem 1 help you to write an equation?

3. How many birdfeeders could Ruben make with 36 dowels?

4. Write a Problem Write a problem about sharing items that you can solve by drawing a picture. Then solve.

Independent Practice

Solve.

5. Kylie bought a bag of 30 beads to make bracelets. Each bracelet requires 5 beads. How many bracelets can Kylie make?

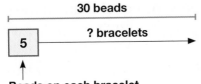

30 beads

| 5 | ? bracelets → |

↑
Beads on each bracelet

6. In Exercise 5, what equation can you write to answer the problem?

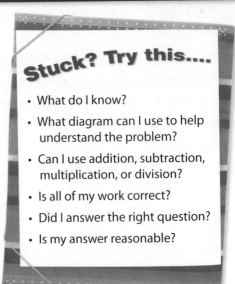

Stuck? Try this.....

- What do I know?
- What diagram can I use to help understand the problem?
- Can I use addition, subtraction, multiplication, or division?
- Is all of my work correct?
- Did I answer the right question?
- Is my answer reasonable?

For another example, see Set E on page 93.

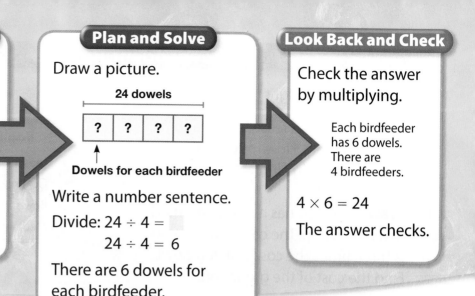

What do I know? There are 24 dowels. There are 4 birdfeeders. Each birdfeeder has the same number of dowels.

What am I asked to find? The number of dowels for each birdfeeder

Draw a picture.

24 dowels

| ? | ? | ? | ? |

Dowels for each birdfeeder

Write a number sentence.

Divide: 24 ÷ 4 =

24 ÷ 4 = 6

There are 6 dowels for each birdfeeder.

Check the answer by multiplying.

Each birdfeeder has 6 dowels. There are 4 birdfeeders.

$4 \times 6 = 24$

The answer checks.

---

7. Sheena is packing 18 paperweights in boxes. She packs them in 6 boxes with the same number of paperweights in each box. How many paperweights are in each box?

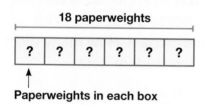

18 paperweights

| ? | ? | ? | ? | ? | ? |

Paperweights in each box

8. Jodi is bundling newspapers. She has 66 newspapers and puts 6 newspapers in each bundle. How many bundles does Jodi make?

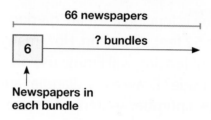

66 newspapers

| 6 | ? bundles →

Newspapers in each bundle

Use the bar graph at the right for **9** and **10**.

9. How much more money did Katie save in September than in October?

10. Katie used the money she saved in November and December to buy her mother a present. How much did she spend?

Katie's Savings September–December

11. Draw It Manny is going camping with friends. He packed 60 sandwiches. How many sandwiches can Manny and his friends eat each day if they go camping for 5 days and eat the same number of sandwiches each day?

12. Draw It Jenna bought 36 pencils to give to her friends before the first day of school. If each friend received 6 pencils, how many friends did Jenna buy pencils for?

Use the table at the right for **13** and **14**.

13. Everett bought a leash, collar, and bed at the sale. How much did Everett spend in all?

14. Draw It Everett has his dog groomed at the pet shop. The cost of grooming is three times the cost of a dog bowl. Find the cost of the grooming.

Dog Supplies Sale	
Leash	$8
Collar	$6
Bowls	$7
Medium Beds	$15

15. Rena has 16 scarves. If 4 of her scarves are blue and one half of her scarves are red, how many scarves are **NOT** red or blue?

16. Frank, Chuck, Bob, and Dan arranged their exercise mats in a row. Bob's mat is next to only one other mat. Dan is on the third mat. Chuck is not next to Dan. Who is on which mat?

17. Emma is fencing a square garden with 52 feet of fencing. How many feet of fencing will Emma use on each side? Draw a bar diagram and write a number sentence to solve the problem.

18. Oliver has 25 apple slices that he distributes to 5 students in his gymnastics class. How many slices does each student get?

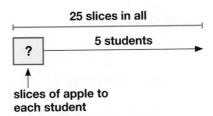

Think About the Process

19. Sandy spent $36 on pet toys. Each toy cost $12. Which number sentence can be used to find how many toys she bought?

    A $12 + 24 = $ ▨

    B $36 \div 12 = $ ▨

    C $6 \times 6 = $ ▨

    D $36 \div 6 = $ ▨

20. Three groups of 24 students each competed in the junior mathematics relay. What two simpler problems can you use to find the total number of students in the three groups?

    A $(3 + 24) - (12 + 4)$

    B $(3 \times 12) + (20 + 2)$

    C $(3 \times 20) + (3 \times 4)$

    D $(4 \times 12) + (32 + 4)$

Use Multiplication to Divide

Use 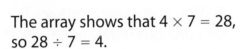 Counters.

Use multiplication to find 28 ÷ 7, 42 ÷ 7, and 72 ÷ 8.

Step 1 Go to the Counters eTool. Select the array workspace. ▦ Drag the resize button in the upper right corner of the rectangle to make a row that is 7 counters long. Drag the button up to increase the number of rows until there are 28 counters in all. The total number of counters is shown in the odometer at the bottom of the page.

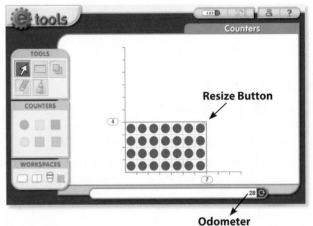

The array shows that $4 \times 7 = 28$, so $28 \div 7 = 4$.

Step 2 Increase the number of rows with 7 counters in each until there are 42 counters in all. The array shows that $6 \times 7 = 42$, so $42 \div 7 = 6$.

Step 3 Make an array with 8 counters in each row. Increase the number of rows until there are 72 counters in all. The array shows that $9 \times 8 = 72$, so $72 \div 8 = 9$.

Practice

Find the quotient by using multiplication.

1. 16 ÷ 2   **2.** 24 ÷ 4   **3.** 45 ÷ 5   **4.** 49 ÷ 7

5. 36 ÷ 6   **6.** 63 ÷ 9   **7.** 21 ÷ 3   **8.** 35 ÷ 5

9. 56 ÷ 7   **10.** 32 ÷ 8   **11.** 48 ÷ 6   **12.** 20 ÷ 5

13. 40 ÷ 8   **14.** 30 ÷ 6   **15.** 10 ÷ 2   **16.** 72 ÷ 9

17. 18 ÷ 9   **18.** 27 ÷ 3   **19.** 45 ÷ 9   **20.** 24 ÷ 8

21. 21 ÷ 7   **22.** 54 ÷ 9   **23.** 24 ÷ 12   **24.** 33 ÷ 11

1. Kent uses 8 nails to make each birdhouse. So far, he has used 24 nails. Which number sentence can be used to find the number of birdhouses he has made so far? (4-4)

   A $24 + 8 = 32$

   B $24 - 8 = 16$

   C $24 \times 8 = 192$

   D $24 \div 8 = 3$

2. Tammy made 10 friendship rings to share equally among 5 of her friends. How can she find how many rings to give each friend? (4-1)

   A Divide the number of rings by 5.

   B Add the number of rings 5 times.

   C Subtract the number of rings from 5.

   D Multiply the number of rings by 5.

3. Sierra bought 30 shells for her 6 hermit crabs. Which number sentence is **NOT** in the same fact family as the others? (4-2)

   A $6 \times 5 = 30$

   B $5 \times 6 = 30$

   C $30 \div 5 = 6$

   D $5 \times 30 = 150$

4. In which number sentence does 7 make the number sentence true? (4-4)

   A $35 \div \boxed{} = 7$

   B $28 \div \boxed{} = 4$

   C $48 \div \boxed{} = 8$

   D $20 \div \boxed{} = 5$

5. Three friends have 27 water balloons to share equally. How many water balloons will each friend get? (4-1)

   27 water balloons

?	?	?

   ↑
   Water balloons each friend gets

   A 9

   B 8

   C 6

   D 3

6. Which number sentence is in the same fact family as $63 \div 9 = \boxed{}$? (4-2)

   A $63 \times 9 = \boxed{}$

   B $\boxed{} \times 9 = 63$

   C $\boxed{} - 9 = 63$

   D $9 + \boxed{} = 63$

7. Which number makes the number sentence true? (4-4)

   $40 \div \boxed{} = 8$

   A 7

   B 6

   C 5

   D 4

8. Which number sentence is true? (4-3)

   A $4 \div 4 = 0$

   B $7 \div 1 = 1$

   C $2 \div 2 = 2$

   D $0 \div 8 = 0$

9. Which number makes both number sentences true? (4-4)

$$4 \times \boxed{} = 32$$

$$32 \div 4 = \boxed{}$$

A 9

B 8

C 7

D 6

10. Olivia has 48 daisies and 6 vases. Which number sentence shows how many daisies she can put in each vase if she puts the same number in each vase? (4-5)

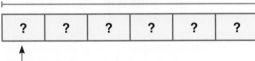

48 daisies

Daisies in each vase

A 48 − 6 = 42

B 48 + 6 = 54

C 48 ÷ 6 = 8

D 6 × 48 = 288

11. Which symbol makes the number sentence true? (4-3)

$$0 \div 9 \bigcirc 6 \div 6$$

A ×

B =

C <

D >

12. Mrs. Warren bought 3 packages of pencils for her students. Each package had 6 pencils. Which number sentence is in this fact family? (4-2)

A 2 × 3 = 6

B 6 − 3 = 3

C 3 + 6 = 9

D 18 ÷ 3 = 6

13. Mason bought a package of 20 wheels. Each model car needs 4 wheels. How many cars can he make? (4-1)

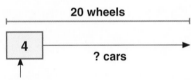

20 wheels

? cars

Wheels on each car

A 4

B 5

C 16

D 24

14. Mr. Nessels bought 14 apples to feed his horse. He wants to give the horse the same number of apples each day for 7 days. How many apples will the horse get each day? (4-4)

A 2

B 7

C 14

D 98

Set A, pages 76–78

Katherine is making 6 lunches. She has 30 carrot sticks. How many carrot sticks go in each lunch?

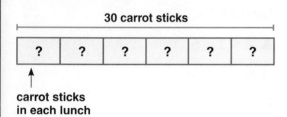

30 carrot sticks

| ? | ? | ? | ? | ? | ? |

↑
carrot sticks in each lunch

$30 \div 6 = 5$

There are 5 carrot sticks in each lunch when 30 carrot sticks are shared equally in 6 lunches.

Remember you can think about sharing or repeated subtraction to divide.

Use the diagram to help you divide.

1. There are 15 chairs in 3 groups. How many chairs are in each group?

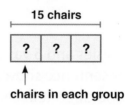

15 chairs

| ? | ? | ? |

↑
chairs in each group

2. The soccer club has 32 balls for 8 teams to share equally. How many balls will each team get?

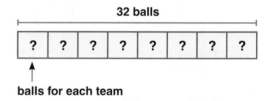

32 balls

| ? | ? | ? | ? | ? | ? | ? | ? |

↑
balls for each team

Set B, pages 80–81

Francine places 12 dolls on 3 shelves with the same number of dolls on each shelf.

shelves   dolls on each shelf
↓   ↓
$3 \times \boxed{} = 12$ ← dolls in all

Use the fact family for 3, 4, and 12 to find how many dolls are on each shelf.

$3 \times 4 = 12 \qquad 12 \div 3 = 4$

$4 \times 3 = 12 \qquad 12 \div 4 = 3$

There are 4 dolls on each shelf.

Remember a fact family shows all of the related facts for a set of numbers.

Copy and complete each fact family.

1. $5 \times \boxed{} = 40 \qquad \boxed{} \div 5 = 8$

$8 \times 5 = \boxed{} \qquad \boxed{} \div 8 = \boxed{}$

2. $7 \times 9 = \boxed{} \qquad \boxed{} \div 7 = 9$

$9 \times \boxed{} = 63 \qquad 63 \div \boxed{} = 7$

3. $6 \times 2 = \boxed{} \qquad \boxed{} \div 6 = 2$

$2 \times \boxed{} = 12 \qquad 12 \div \boxed{} = 6$

Set C, pages 82–83

Find 6 ÷ 6 and 6 ÷ 1.

Any number divided by itself, except 0, is 1.
So, 6 ÷ 6 = 1.

Any number divided by 1 is that number.
So, 6 ÷ 1 = 6.

Remember zero divided by any number is zero, but you cannot divide by zero.

Compare. Use >, <, or = for each ◯.

1. $8\overline{)8}$ ◯ $3\overline{)3}$ **2.** $1\overline{)7}$ ◯ $6\overline{)0}$

3. $1\overline{)7}$ ◯ $1\overline{)4}$ **4.** $2\overline{)0}$ ◯ $9\overline{)0}$

5. $1\overline{)8}$ ◯ $1\overline{)5}$ **6.** $2\overline{)0}$ ◯ $1\overline{)2}$

Set D, pages 84–85

Find 24 ÷ 4.

What number times
4 equals 24?

▨ × 4 = 24

6 × 4 = 24

So, 24 ÷ 4 = 6.

Remember to use multiplication facts to help you divide.

1. $5\overline{)30}$ **2.** $2\overline{)18}$

3. $7\overline{)28}$ **4.** $9\overline{)81}$

5. $8\overline{)56}$ **6.** $8\overline{)48}$

Set E, pages 86–88

What do I know? Mrs. Collins has 24 pairs of scissors. She puts the same number of each in 6 drawers. How many pairs of scissors are in each drawer?

What am I being asked to find? The number of scissors in each drawer

Draw a picture.

Divide to find the number of scissors in each drawer.

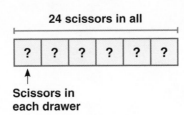

24 ÷ 6 = ▨

24 ÷ 6 = 4

There are 4 pairs of scissors in each drawer.

Remember to draw a picture to help you solve the problem.

Solve.

1. Winnie buys 20 bookmarks for herself and three of her friends. Each person received the same number of bookmarks. How many bookmarks did they each receive?

Multiplying by 1-Digit Numbers

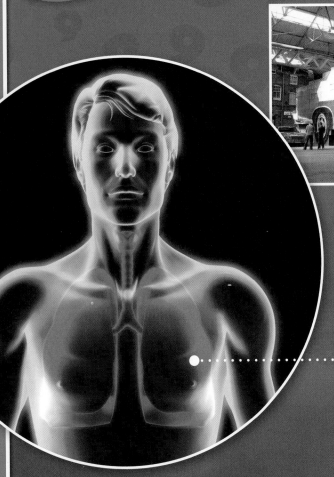

1 This sculpture is made out of boxes taped together. How many rolls of tape are needed to make one of these sculptures? You will find out in Lesson 5-6.

2 How many gallons of air does a student breathe each school day? You will find out in Lesson 5-1.

3 The Bald Eagle was named the United States national emblem in 1782. About how long is the wingspan of an adult female Bald Eagle? You will find out in Lesson 5-3.

4 How long was the longest blue whale? You will find out in Lesson 5-2.

Review What You Know!

Vocabulary

Choose the best term from the box.

> • product   • factor
> • array   • rounding

1. You multiply numbers to find a ? .

2. In the number sentence 8 × 6 = 48, 8 is a ? .

3. When you estimate to the nearest 10 or 100, you may use ? .

Multiplication Facts

Find each product.

4. 5 × 6   5. 7 × 3

6. 9 × 5   7. 6 × 8

8. 6 × 4   9. 12 × 3

10. 8 × 5   11. 9 × 9

Rounding

Round each number to the nearest ten.

12. 16   13. 82   14. 35

15. 52   16. 24   17. 96

18. 78   19. 472   20. 119

Round each number to the nearest hundred.

21. 868   22. 499   23. 625

24. 167   25. 772   26. 341

27. 1,372   28. 9,009   29. 919

30. **Writing to Explain** Explain how to round 743 to the hundreds place.

Understand It!
A pattern can help when multiplying by numbers like 40 and 300.

Multiplying by Multiples of 10 and 100

What is the rule when you multiply by multiples of 10 and 100?

You can use basic multiplication facts to multiply by multiples of 10 and 100. Find 3×50.

150 in all

Guided Practice*

Do you know HOW?

In **1** through **6**, use basic facts to help you multiply.

1. 7×70 **2.** 2×700

3. 3×20 **4.** 9×800

5. 6×10 **6.** 8×500

Do you UNDERSTAND?

7. How many zeros will be in the product for 5×200? Explain how you know.

8. Reasonableness Peter said the product of 4×500 is 2,000. Bob said it is 200. Who is correct?

Independent Practice

Leveled Practice In **9** through **32**, find each product.

9. $3 \times 7 =$ **10.** $6 \times 4 =$ **11.** $8 \times 5 =$ **12.** $2 \times 8 =$

$3 \times 70 =$ $6 \times 40 =$ $8 \times 50 =$ $2 \times 80 =$

$3 \times 700 =$ $6 \times 400 =$ $8 \times 500 =$ $2 \times 800 =$

13. 4×20 **14.** 7×40 **15.** 70×2 **16.** 8×60 **17.** 3×70

18. 5×500 **19.** 3×600 **20.** 9×700 **21.** 600×6 **22.** 100×9

23. 5×40 **24.** 200×6 **25.** 9×50 **26.** 900×4 **27.** 80×3

28. 8×70 **29.** 2×90 **30.** 300×4 **31.** 7×100 **32.** 800×5

For another example, see Set A on page 122.

Find 3 × 50.	Find 3 × 500.	When the product of a basic fact ends in zero, the answer will have an extra zero.
Multiply by the digit in the tens place.	Multiply by the digit in the hundreds place.	
Multiply: $3 \times 5 = 15$	Multiply: $3 \times 5 = 15$	$6 \times 5 = 30$
Write one zero after 15.	Write two zeros after 15.	$6 \times 50 = 300$
$3 \times 5\underline{0} = 15\underline{0}$	$3 \times 5\underline{00} = 1,5\underline{00}$	$6 \times 500 = 3,000$
So, $3 \times 50 = 150$.	So, $3 \times 500 = 1,500$.	

Problem Solving

In **33** and **34**, use the table to the right.

33. Tina visited Funland with her mom and a friend. They chose Plan C. How much did they save on the two children's tickets by buying combined tickets instead of buying separate tickets?

Funland Ticket Prices		
	Adult	Child
Plan A Waterpark	$30	$20
Plan B Amusement Park	$40	$30
Plan C Combined A + B	$60	$40

Data

34. Aimee's scout troop has 8 girls and 4 adults. How much did the troop pay for tickets to the amusement park?

35. A fourth grader breathes about 50 gallons of air per hour. Shana, a fourth grader, arrives at school at 8:00 A.M. and leaves at 3:00 P.M. How many gallons of air does she breathe at school?

36. Number Sense Without calculating the answer, tell which has the greater product, 4 × 80 or 8 × 400. Explain how you know.

37. Last year, the fourth graders at Summit School collected 500 cans of food for the food drive. This year's fourth graders want to collect two times as many cans. How many cans do this year's fourth graders hope to collect?

    A 250 cans   **C** 1,000 cans

    B 500 cans   **D** 10,000 cans

38. Ted, Jason, and Angelina are trying to raise 200 dollars for a local shelter. Ted raised 30 dollars. Jason raised 90 dollars. How much money does Angelina need to raise in order to reach their goal?

	$200	
Goal		

Amount raised	$30	$90	?

Using Mental Math to Multiply

What are some ways to multiply mentally?

Evan rode his bicycle for 18 miles each day for 3 days. How many miles did he ride his bicycle in all?

Find 3×18 mentally.

18 miles per day

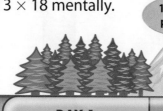

| DAY 1 | DAY 2 | DAY 3 |

Guided Practice*

Do you know HOW?

In **1** and **2**, use the breaking apart method to find each product mentally.

1. 6×37 **2.** 51×3

In **3** and **4**, use compatible numbers to find each product mentally.

3. 33×4 **4.** 9×83

Do you UNDERSTAND?

5. Explain how to use mental math to multiply 56×4.

6. How could place-value blocks be used to model the breaking apart method in the example at the top?

 You can draw place-value blocks to help you visualize the model.

Independent Practice

Leveled Practice In **7** through **20**, use mental math to find each product.

7. 4×36 Breaking apart: $(4 \times) + (4 \times) = $

8. 6×42 Breaking apart: $(6 \times) + (6 \times) = $

9. 5×17 Compatible numbers: $5 \times = 100$ $ - 15 = $

10. 7×29 Compatible numbers: $7 \times = 210$ $ - 7 = $

11. 7×28 **12.** 61×8 **13.** 14×5 **14.** 64×3 **15.** 2×58

16. 4×23 **17.** 3×27 **18.** 44×6 **19.** 5×35 **20.** 9×52

DIGITAL

Animated Glossary
www.pearsonsuccessnet.com

One Way

Find 3 × 18.

Break apart 18 into 10 and 8.

Think of 3 × 18 as
(3 × 10) + (3 × 8).

30 + 24

Add to find the total.
30 + 24 = 54

So, 3 × 18 = 54.

Another Way

Compatible numbers are numbers that are easy to work with mentally. Substitute a number for 18 that is easy to multiply by 3.

3 × 18
↓
3 × 20 = 60

Now adjust. Subtract 2 groups of 3.

60 – 6 = 54   So, 3 × 18 = 54.

Evan rode his bicycle 54 miles in all.

Problem Solving

For **21** and **22**, use the table to the right.

21. To raise money, the high school band members sold items shown in the table. Use mental math to find how much money the band raised in all.

Item	Cost	Number Sold
Caps	$9	36
Mugs	$7	44
Pennants	$8	52

22. How much more do 10 caps cost than 10 pennants?

23. Writing to Explain Ashley and 3 friends bought tickets to a musical. The cost of each ticket was 43 dollars per person. How much did the tickets cost in all? Explain how you found the answer.

? Total Cost

$43	$43	$43	$43

↑ Cost per person

24. **Think** About the Process Helen walked 5 miles every day for 37 days. Which choice shows how to find how many miles Helen walked?

A 35 × 5

B (40 × 5) + (3 × 5)

C (30 × 5) + (7 × 5)

D (30 × 5) – (3 × 5)

25. The height of one scuba diver is about 6 feet. The longest blue whale on record was about 18 scuba divers in length. Use breaking apart to estimate the length of the blue whale.

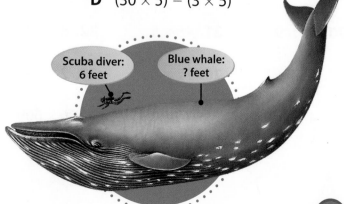

Scuba diver: 6 feet

Blue whale: ? feet

Understand It!
To estimate round factors to numbers you can multiply mentally.

Using Rounding to Estimate

How can you use rounding to estimate when you multiply?

Hoover School is holding a Read-a-thon. Any student who raises more than $500 earns a prize. Hector has pledges totaling $4 per page read. Alan has pledges totaling $3 per page read. Both want to know if they will earn a prize.

Hector reads 153 pages.

Alan reads 115 pages.

Guided Practice*

Do you know HOW?

In **1** through **8**, estimate each product.

1. 6×125
2. 39×5
3. 538×3
4. 7×314
5. 2×97
6. 4×261
7. 63×6
8. 9×48

Do you UNDERSTAND?

9. Is the estimate in Exercise 1 more or less than the actual answer? Explain how you know.

10. Alan collects pledges for 70 more pages. Estimate to see if he will now get a prize.

Independent Practice

Leveled Practice In **11** through **34**, estimate each product.

11. 7×34 is close to $7 \times$ ▪.
12. 6×291 is close to $6 \times$ ▪.
13. 41×9 is close to ▪ $\times 9$.
14. 814×3 is close to ▪ $\times 3$.

15. 117×4
16. 3×86
17. 9×476
18. 34×6
19. 7×77

20. 52×9
21. 46×5
22. 3×287
23. 6×131
24. 602×9

25. 354×2
26. 77×8
27. 2×863
28. 44×8
29. 303×5

30. 486×7
31. 719×5
32. 6×609
33. 249×4
34. 54×8

For another example, see Set C on page 123.

Estimate 4 × 153 using rounding.

4 × 153
Round 153 to 150.
4 × 150 = 600

Two 150s is 300. Four 150s is 600.
So, 4 × 153 is about 600.

Hector raised more than 500 dollars.

He has earned a prize.

Estimate 3 × 115 using rounding.

3 × 115
Round 115 to 100.
3 × 100 = 300

Alan has raised about 300 dollars.
This is not enough to earn a prize.

Problem Solving

35. Sam and his 2 brothers want to fly to San Antonio. One airline offers a round trip fare of $319. Another airline has a round trip fare of $389. About how much will Sam and his brothers save by buying the less expensive fare?

36. An adult female Bald Eagle has a wingspan that is about 7 feet long. If there are 12 inches in a foot, how long would you estimate a female Bald Eagle's wingspan is in inches?

37. Reasonableness Ellie estimates that the product of 211 and 6 is 1,800. Is this estimate reasonable? Why or why not?

38. Number Sense Which has more pencils, 3 packs with 40 pencils or 40 packs with 3 pencils? Explain.

39. The students at Spring Elementary voted on a school mascot. The bar graph at the right shows the results of the vote.

Which mascot has about 4 times as many votes as the unicorn?

A Lion   **C** Dragon

B Owl   **D** Bear

40. Which mascot had the least amount of votes?

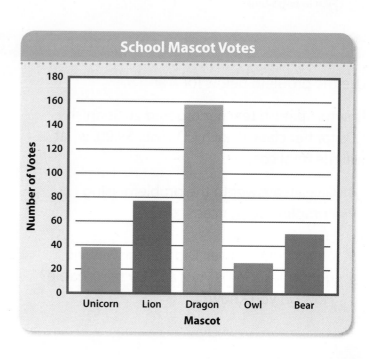

Understand It!
Deciding if an answer is reasonable can help you solve problems.

Problem Solving

Reasonableness

Karen glued sequins onto her project. She used 7 rows with 28 sequins in each row. How many sequins did Karen glue in all?

After you solve a problem, check whether your answer is reasonable. Ask yourself: Did I answer the right question? Is the calculation reasonable?

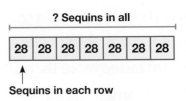

? Sequins in all

| 28 | 28 | 28 | 28 | 28 | 28 | 28 |

↑
Sequins in each row

Guided Practice*

Do you know HOW?

Solve and make an estimate to show that your answer is reasonable.

1. A fish store has 8 empty tanks. After a delivery, they put 40 fish in each tank. How many fish were in the delivery?

? Fish in all

| 40 | 40 | 40 | 40 | 40 | 40 | 40 | 40 |

↑
Fish in each tank

Do you UNDERSTAND?

2. In Problem 1, if your estimate was about 40 more than your actual answer, what would you do?

3. **Write a Problem** Write a problem about fish that would have an answer near 80. Then solve and use an estimate to show that your answer is reasonable.

Independent Practice

Use the problem below for **4** and **5**.

Dawn's Spanish teacher ordered 20 Spanish CDs for her class. If each CD costs $9.00, what will the total cost be?

4. Give an answer to the problem using complete sentences.

5. Check your answer. Did you answer the right question? Is your answer reasonable? How do you know?

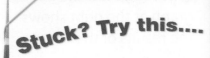

Stuck? Try this....

- What do I know?
- What diagram can I use to help understand the problem?
- Can I use addition, subtraction, multiplication, or division?
- Is all of my work correct?
- Did I answer the right question?
- Is my answer reasonable?

For another example, see Set D on page 123.

Reasonable	Not reasonable
There were 196 sequins in all.	There were 140 sequins in all.
Estimate: $7 \times 30 = 210$	Estimate: $7 \times 20 = 140$
The answer is reasonable because 210 is close to 196.	The answer is not reasonable because 140 is not close to 196.
The right question was answered and the calculation is reasonable.	The right question was answered, but the calculation is not reasonable.

For **6** through **9**, use the chart at the right and the information below.

A plane increases its height at a rate of 400 feet per second.

6. How high will the plane be after 5 seconds?

7. What number sentence can you use to solve Problem 6?

8. Did you answer the right question?

9. Is your answer reasonable? How do you know?

Elapsed Seconds	Increase in Height	Height
1 sec	400 ft	400 ft
2 sec	400 ft	800 ft
3 sec	400 ft	1,200 ft
4 sec	400 ft	1,600 ft
5 sec	400 ft	2,000 ft
6 sec	400 ft	2,400 ft

For **10** through **12**, use the chart.

10. About how much money does an American family spend in 8 weeks to feed a child who is 11 years old?

11. In four weeks, about how much more money does a family spend to feed a child who is 8 years old than a child who is 3 years old?

12. Is your answer for Problem 11 reasonable? How do you know?

Money Spent by an American Family to Feed a Child	
Age of Child	Weekly Amount
1–2 years	$27
3–5 years	$31
6–8 years	$42
9–11 years	$49

For **13** through **16**, use the chart at the right.

13. How many stickers does Mr. Richardson have on rolls?

14. How many more stickers on sheets does Mr. Richardson have than stickers in boxes?

15. Is your calculation for Problem 14 reasonable? How do you know?

16. How many stickers does Mr. Richardson have in all?

Mr. Richardson's Stickers

Each ♥ = 10 stickers

17. The distance from Bethany's home to New York City is 180 miles. After Bethany drove 95 miles, she said she had traveled over half the distance. Is Bethany correct?

180 miles to New York

95 miles	?

18. On her way from New York City, Bethany stopped for a break after driving 116 miles. How many miles does she have left to drive home?

180 miles to home

116 miles	?

Think About the Process

19. Which of the following uses the Distributive Property to solve the equation 4×9?

   A $4 \times 9 = (3 \times 3) + (1 \times 6)$

   B $4 \times 9 = (4 \times 9) + (4 \times 9)$

   C $4 \times 9 = (2 \times 9) + (2 \times 9)$

   D $4 \times 9 = (2 \times 3) + (2 \times 6)$

20. Louisa solved the equation $m - 16 = 54$ and got $m = 38$. Which statement best explains why Louisa's answer is **NOT** reasonable?

   A Louisa subtracted incorrectly.

   B Louisa forgot to regroup.

   C Louisa should have added.

   D Louisa forgot that 16 is less than 38.

Multiplying with Mental Math

Use  e tools Place-Value Blocks.

Explain how to use compatible numbers to find 4×28.

Step 1 Go to the Place-Value Blocks eTool. Select the two-part workspace. 30 is the closest number to 28 that is easy to multiply. Click on the horizontal long block. Then click in the top workspace to show 4 rows with 3 longs in each row, or 4×30.

Step 2 Click on the hammer tool icon. Then click on the last long in each row to break each into ten ones. Use the arrow tool to select two ones from the first group, and move them to the bottom workspace. Do the same for the last two ones in each row.

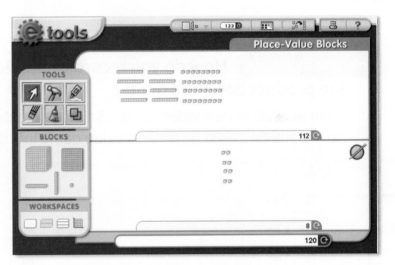

To find 4×28, find $4 \times 30 = 120$ and subtract $4 \times 2 = 8$.

So, $120 - 8 = 112$.

Practice

Use compatible numbers to find each product mentally.

1. 3×19	**2.** 4×18	**3.** 2×67	**4.** 6×29
5. 4×38	**6.** 3×47	**7.** 3×29	**8.** 4×49
9. 2×49	**10.** 3×58	**11.** 4×39	**12.** 2×39
13. 3×27	**14.** 3×28	**15.** 4×47	**16.** 2×48
17. 4×37	**18.** 4×48	**19.** 3×57	**20.** 3×68
21. 2×47	**22.** 3×38	**23.** 4×67	**24.** 4×58

Understand It! To find a product of two numbers, build an array and break it into two simpler parts.

Using an Expanded Algorithm

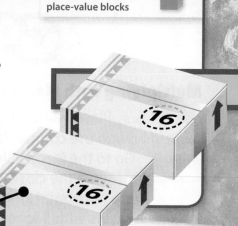

How can you record multiplication?

A store ordered 2 boxes of video games. How many games did the store order?

Choose an Operation Multiply to join equal groups.

Each box contains 16 video games.

Another Example How do you record multiplication when the product has three digits?

Gene played his new video game 23 times each day for 5 days. How many times did he play his video game in 5 days?

A 18

B 28

C 115

D 145

Choose an Operation Since 5 equal groups of 23 are being joined, you will multiply. Find 5×23.

What You Show

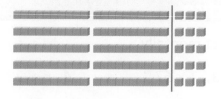

What You Write

$$
\begin{array}{r}
23 \\
\times \quad 5 \\
\hline
15 \\
+ \ 100 \\
\hline
115 \\
\end{array}
$$

Gene played his video game 115 times in 5 days. The correct choice is **C**.

Explain It

1. Explain how the partial products, 15 and 100, were found in the work above.

2. Reasonableness How can an estimate help you eliminate choices above?

What You Show

Build an array to show 2 × 16.

$2 \times 10 = 20$ $2 \times 6 = 12$

$20 + 12 = \mathbf{32}$

What You Write

Here is one way to record multiplication.

$$
\begin{array}{r}
16 \\
\times \quad 2 \\
\hline
12 \quad \leftarrow \text{Partial} \\
+ \ 20 \quad \leftarrow \text{Products} \\
\hline
32
\end{array}
$$

The store ordered 32 games.

Guided Practice*

Do you know HOW?

In **1** and **2**, use place-value blocks or draw pictures to build an array for each. Copy and complete the calculation.

1. $2 \times 34 = $ ▢

$$
\begin{array}{r}
34 \\
\times \quad 2 \\
\hline
▢ \\
+ \ ▢▢ \\
\hline
▢▢
\end{array}
$$

2. $3 \times 18 = $ ▢

$$
\begin{array}{r}
18 \\
\times \quad 3 \\
\hline
▢▢ \\
+ \ ▢▢ \\
\hline
▢▢
\end{array}
$$

Do you UNDERSTAND?

Use the array and the calculation shown for Problem 3.

$$
\begin{array}{r}
14 \\
\times \quad 3 \\
\hline
12 \\
+ \ 30 \\
\hline
42
\end{array}
$$

3. What calculation was used to give the partial product 12? 30? What is the product of 3×14?

Independent Practice

Leveled Practice In **4** and **5**, use place-value blocks or draw pictures to build an array for each. Copy and complete the calculation.

4.

$$
\begin{array}{r}
27 \\
\times \quad 3 \\
\hline
▢▢ \\
+ \ ▢▢ \\
\hline
▢▢
\end{array}
$$

5.

$$
\begin{array}{r}
22 \\
\times \quad 4 \\
\hline
▢▢ \\
+ \ ▢▢ \\
\hline
▢▢
\end{array}
$$

eTools
www.pearsonsuccessnet.com

*For another example, see Set E on page 124.

Lesson 5-5   **107**

Independent Practice

Leveled Practice In **6** through **15**, copy and complete the calculation. Draw a picture to help.

6. 26
     × 5

  +

7. 19
     × 3

  +

8. 24
     × 2

  +

9. 21
     × 4

  +

10. 24
      × 3

  +

11. 22
      × 8

12. 17
      × 3

13. 24
      × 8

14. 16
      × 5

15. 23
      × 7

Problem Solving

16. Geometry The sides of each of the shapes below are the same whole-number length. Which figure has a perimeter of 64 units? How long is each side?

17. Algebra Copy and complete each number sentence.

a ☐ × 14 = A where A is greater than 100.

b ☐ × 24 = B where B is less than 100.

18. Large tables in the library have 8 chairs and small tables have 4 chairs. How many students can sit at 3 large tables and 5 small tables if each seat is filled?

    A 20 students   **C** 44 students

    B 36 students   **D** 52 students

19. Estimation Emma wants to put 3 smiley stickers on each of her note cards. Use estimation to decide if a roll of smileys has enough stickers for 42 note cards.

Type of Sticker	Number of Stickers per Roll
★	50
🐕	75
🙂	100
🌸	125

100 stickers

20. Writing to Explain Tim called 3 × 20 and 3 × 4 *simple calculations*. Explain what he meant.

Algebra Connections

Simplifying Number Expressions

In order to simplify a number expression you must follow the order of operations.

First, complete the operations inside the parentheses.

Then multiply and divide in order from left to right.

Then add and subtract in order from left to right.

Example: $(5 + 3) \times 4$

Start with the operation inside the parentheses. What is 5 + 3?

$5 + 3 = 8$

Then, multiply 8 × 4.

$8 \times 4 = 32$

So, $(5 + 3) \times 4 = 32$.

Simplify. Follow the order of operations.

1. $4 \times 8 - 6$

2. $12 + 8 \div 4$

3. $5 \times (8 - 2)$

4. $35 + (4 \times 6) - 7$

5. $7 \times 5 + 9$

6. $8 + 18 \div 3$

7. $6 + 4 + (12 \div 2)$

8. $(8 - 2) \div 3$

9. $(9 + 8) \times 2$

10. $10 + 4 \div (9 - 7)$

11. $(54 \div 9) + (6 \times 6)$

12. $(16 - 4) + (16 - 4)$

13. $(21 - 3) + 7$

14. $9 + 9 \div 3 \times 3$

15. $2 \div 2 + 2 - 1$

16. $3 \times 3 \div 3 + 6 - 3$

17. $5 + 4 \times 3 + 2 - 1$

18. $6 \div 3 \times 2 + 7 - 5$

For **19** through **24**, write the expression represented by each problem and then simplify the expression.

19. There are 2 teachers and 6 rows of 4 students in a classroom.

20. Three cartons of a dozen eggs each, with 4 eggs broken in each carton

21. Two groups of 10 students are in a room. Four students leave the room.

22. Six rows of 5 small toys and 1 row of 7 large toys

23. 4 baskets of 10 apples, with 2 bruised apples in each basket

24. Five groups of 4 tulips and 2 roses in each group.

Understand It! To find a product like 26 × 3, break it into simpler problems.

Multiplying 2-Digit by 1-Digit Numbers

What is a common way to record multiplication?

How many T-shirts with the saying, *and your point is...* are in 3 boxes?

Choose an Operation Multiply to join equal groups.

Saying on T-shirt	Number of T-shirts per Box
Trust Me	30 T-shirts
and your point is...	26 T-shirts
I'm the princess that's why 👑	24 T-shirts
because I said so	12 T-shirts

Another Example **Does the common way to record multiplication work for larger products?**

Mrs. Stockton ordered 8 boxes of T-shirts with the saying, *I'm the princess that's why.* How many of the T-shirts did she order?

Choose an Operation Since you are joining 8 groups of 24, you will multiply. Find 8 × 24.

Step 1
Multiply the ones.
Regroup if necessary.

$$\begin{array}{r} 3 \\ 24 \\ \times 8 \\ \hline 2 \end{array}$$

8 × 4 = 32 ones
Regroup 32 ones as 3 tens 2 ones

Step 2
Multiply the tens.
Add any extra tens.

$$\begin{array}{r} 3 \\ 24 \\ \times 8 \\ \hline 192 \end{array}$$

8 × 2 tens = 16 tens
16 tens + 3 tens = 19 tens
or 1 hundred 9 tens

Mrs. Stockton ordered 192 T-shirts.

Explain It

1. **Reasonableness** How can you use estimation to decide if 192 is a reasonable answer?

2. In the example above, is it 8 × 2 or 8 × 20? Explain.

Remember, one way to multiply is to find partial products.

$$\begin{array}{r} 26 \\ \times\ \ 3 \\ \hline 18 \\ +\ \ 60 \\ \hline 78 \end{array}$$

← Partial Products

A shortcut for the partial products method is shown at the right.

Step 1

Multiply the ones. Regroup if necessary.

$$\begin{array}{r} ^1\ \\ 26 \\ \times\ \ 3 \\ \hline 8 \end{array}$$

Step 2

Multiply the tens. Add any extra tens.

$$\begin{array}{r} ^1\ \\ 26 \\ \times\ \ 3 \\ \hline 78 \end{array}$$

There are 78 T-shirts in 3 boxes.

Guided Practice*

Do you know HOW?

Find each product. Estimate to check reasonableness.

1. $\begin{array}{r} 15 \\ \times\ 5 \\ \hline \end{array}$

2. $\begin{array}{r} 28 \\ \times\ 3 \\ \hline \end{array}$

3. $\begin{array}{r} 34 \\ \times\ 7 \\ \hline \end{array}$

4. $\begin{array}{r} 43 \\ \times\ 4 \\ \hline \end{array}$

5. 5×70

6. 5×78

7. 3×24

8. 3×79

Do you UNDERSTAND?

9. Explain how you would estimate the answer in Exercise 3.

10. Carrie bought 8 boxes of T-shirts with the saying *Because I said so.* How many T-shirts did Carrie buy?

11. **Writing to Explain** Explain how the answer to Exercise 5 can be used to find the answer to Exercise 6.

Independent Practice

In **12** through **19**, find each product. Estimate to check reasonableness.

12. $\begin{array}{r} 12 \\ \times\ 6 \\ \hline \end{array}$

13. $\begin{array}{r} 18 \\ \times\ 7 \\ \hline \end{array}$

14. $\begin{array}{r} 72 \\ \times\ 5 \\ \hline \end{array}$

15. $\begin{array}{r} 49 \\ \times\ 8 \\ \hline \end{array}$

16. $\begin{array}{r} 31 \\ \times\ 4 \\ \hline \end{array}$

17. $\begin{array}{r} 52 \\ \times\ 6 \\ \hline \end{array}$

18. $\begin{array}{r} 79 \\ \times\ 7 \\ \hline \end{array}$

19. $\begin{array}{r} 87 \\ \times\ 7 \\ \hline \end{array}$

Independent Practice

In **20** through **27**, find each product.
Estimate to check reasonableness.

20. 9 × 23   **21.** 6 × 51   **22.** 4 × 29   **23.** 8 × 42

24. 3 × 64   **25.** 5 × 56   **26.** 6 × 83   **27.** 4 × 47

Problem Solving

28. Use the diagram to the right. How many floors does the Tower have if it has 5 times as many floors as a 15-story office building?

   A 60   **B** 75   **C** 105   **D** 1,010

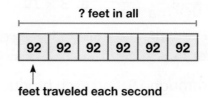

29. Estimation It takes 286 rolls of tape to make a car sculpture made of boxes. What is this number rounded to the nearest hundred?

   A 200   **C** 300

   B 280   **D** 380

30. **Think** **About the Process** Katie made 24 rag dolls. She gave away 8 of them as gifts. Which expression gives the number of rag dolls Katie had left?

   A 24 + 8   **C** 24 − 8

   B 24 × 8   **D** 24 ÷ 8

31. A skateboard speed record of almost 63 miles per hour (about 92 feet per second) was set in 1998. At that speed, about how many feet would the skateboarder travel in 6 seconds?

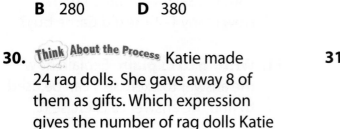

? feet in all

| 92 | 92 | 92 | 92 | 92 | 92 |

↑
feet traveled each second

For **32** and **33**, use the table to the right.

32. What is the average length fingernails will grow in one year?

   A 60 mm   **C** 40 mm

   B 50 mm   **D** 5 mm

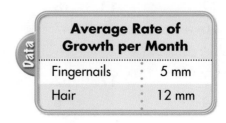

Average Rate of Growth per Month	
Fingernails	5 mm
Hair	12 mm

33. How much longer will hair grow than fingernails in one year?

Algebra Connections

Multiplication and Number Sentences

Remember that a number sentence has two numbers or expressions connected by <, >, or =. Estimation or reasoning can help you tell if the left side or right side is greater.

Copy and complete. Write <, >, or = in the circle. Check your answers.

 Remember

$>$ is greater than $<$ is less than $=$ is equal to

> **Example:** $7 \times 52 \bigcirc 7 \times 60$
>
> **Think** *Is 7 groups of 52 more than 7 groups of 60?*
>
> Since 52 is less than 60, the left side is less. Write "$<$".
>
> $7 \times 52 \overset{<}{\bigcirc} 7 \times 60$

1. $5 \times 71 \bigcirc 5 \times 70$ 2. $8 \times 30 \bigcirc 8 \times 35$ 3. $2 \times 90 \bigcirc 89 + 89$

4. $4 \times 56 \bigcirc 200$ 5. $6 \times 37 \bigcirc 37 \times 6$ 6. $190 \bigcirc 9 \times 25$

7. $3 \times 33 \bigcirc 100$ 8. $80 \bigcirc 4 \times 19$ 9. $10 \times 10 \bigcirc 9 \times 8$

10. $1 \times 67 \bigcirc 1 + 67$ 11. $2 + 34 \bigcirc 2 \times 34$ 12. $6 \times 18 \bigcirc 7 \times 20$

For **13** and **14**, copy and complete the number sentence below each problem. Use it to help explain your answer.

13. A red tray holds 7 rows of oranges with 8 oranges in each row. A blue tray holds 8 rows of oranges with 5 oranges in each row. Which tray holds more oranges?

    ___ × ___ ◯ ___ × ___

14. Look at the hats below. Mr. Fox bought 2 brown hats. Mrs. Lee bought 3 green hats. Who paid more for their hats?

    ___ × ___ ◯ ___ × ___

15. **Write a Problem** Write a problem using one of the number sentences in Exercises 1 to 6.

Understand It! To find a product like 264 × 3, break apart 264 using place value.

Multiplying 3-Digit by 1-Digit Numbers

How do you multiply larger numbers?

Juan guessed that the large bottle had 3 times as many pennies as the small bottle. What was Juan's guess?

Choose an Operation Multiply to find "3 times as many."

264 pennies

Guided Practice*

Do you know HOW?

In **1** through **4**, find each product. Estimate to decide if the answer is reasonable.

1. 519
    × 4

2. 337
    × 2

3. 181 × 9

4. 6 × 268

Do you UNDERSTAND?

5. **Number Sense** In the example at the top, 3 × 6 tens is how many tens?

6. Sue guessed the large bottle had 8 times as many pennies as the small bottle. What was Sue's guess?

Independent Practice

In **7** through **22**, find each product. Estimate to check reasonableness.

7. 423
    × 2

8. 506
    × 4

9. 821
    × 3

10. 159
     × 5

11. 624
     × 7

12. 124
     × 6

13. 281
     × 9

14. 114
     × 7

15. 2 × 256

16. 3 × 300

17. 3 × 649

18. 5 × 410

19. 2 × 125

20. 3 × 310

21. 4 × 265

22. 5 × 412

For another example, see Set G on page 125.

Step 1

Multiply the ones.
Regroup if needed.

$$\begin{array}{r} \overset{1}{26}4 \\ \times\ \ 3 \\ \hline 2 \end{array}$$

3 × 4 ones = 12 ones
or 1 ten 2 ones

Step 2

Multiply the tens.
Add any extra tens.
Regroup if needed.

$$\begin{array}{r} \overset{1\ 1}{26}4 \\ \times\ \ 3 \\ \hline 92 \end{array}$$

(3 × 6 tens) + 1 ten = 19 tens
or 1 hundred 9 tens

Step 3

Multiply the hundreds.
Add any extra hundreds.

$$\begin{array}{r} \overset{1\ 1}{264} \\ \times\ \ 3 \\ \hline 792 \end{array}$$

(3 × 2 hundreds) + 1 hundred
= 7 hundreds

Juan's guess was 792 pennies.

Problem Solving

In **23** through **25**, find the weight of the animal.

23. Horse

24. Rhino

25. Elephant

Elephant:
Weighs 9 times as
much as the bear

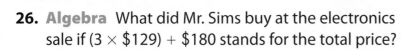

Horse:
Weighs 2 times as
much as the bear

Bear:
Weighs
836 pounds

Rhino:
Weighs 5 times as
much as the bear

26. Algebra What did Mr. Sims buy at the electronics
sale if (3 × $129) + $180 stands for the total price?

27. Number Sense Which costs more—2 laptop computers
or 4 picture phones? Use number sense to decide.

28. **Think** **About the Process** Which tells how to find the total
cost of a laptop computer and 5 digital cameras?

    A 5 × $420 × $295   **C** $420 + $295 + 5

    B (5 × $420) + $295   **D** $420 + (5 × $295)

Electronics Sale	
Digital Camera	$295
Laptop Computer	$420
DVD Player	$129
Picture Phone	$180

Lesson 5-8

Understand It! Learning how and when to draw a picture and write an equation can help when solving problems.

Problem Solving

Draw a Picture and Write an Equation

Pocket bikes are a lot smaller than cars but many can go 35 miles per hour. The length of the family car in the table to the right is 5 times the length of the pocket bike. How long is the family car?

	Pocket Bike Model 235	Family Car
Height (seat)	19 inches	?
Length	38 inches	?
Weight	39 pounds	3,164 lbs

Guided Practice*

Do you know HOW?

Solve.

1. Fran paid $8 a week for gasoline for her Superbike. How much did she pay for gasoline for 6 weeks?

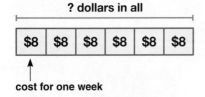

? dollars in all

| $8 | $8 | $8 | $8 | $8 | $8 |

↑ cost for one week

Do you UNDERSTAND?

2. What operation was needed to solve Problem 1? Tell why.

3. **Write a Problem** Write a problem that you can solve by

   a adding.

   b multiplying.

Independent Practice

Solve. Tell the operation or operations used.

4. Police officers walk about 1,632 miles per year. Mail carriers walk about 1,056 miles per year. About how many more miles does a police officer walk in a year than a mail carrier?

1,632 miles per year

| 1,056 | ? |

$1,632 - 1,056 = ?$

5. On David's map, each half inch represents 13 miles. The airport is 2 inches from the state park. How many miles is this?

Stuck? Try this....

- What do I know?
- What diagram can I use to help understand the problem?
- Can I use addition, subtraction, multiplication, or division?
- Is all of my work correct?
- Did I answer the right question?
- Is my answer reasonable?

116 *For another example, see Set H on page 125.*

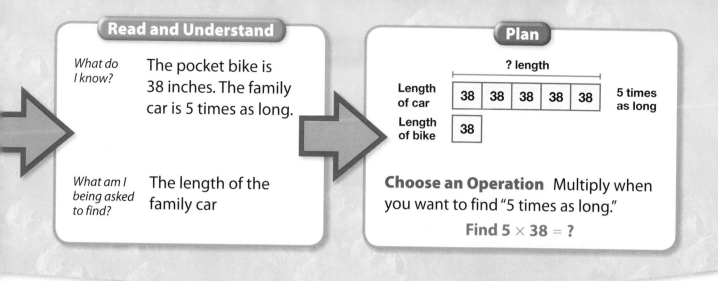

Read and Understand

What do I know? The pocket bike is 38 inches. The family car is 5 times as long.

What am I being asked to find? The length of the family car

Plan

? length

| Length of car | 38 | 38 | 38 | 38 | 38 | 5 times as long |

| Length of bike | 38 |

Choose an Operation Multiply when you want to find "5 times as long."

Find 5 × 38 = ?

---

6. In 1990, a high-school class in Indiana made a very large yo-yo. It weighed 6 times as much as a student who weighed 136 pounds. What was the weight of the yo-yo?

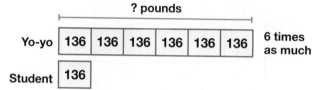

? pounds

| Yo-yo | 136 | 136 | 136 | 136 | 136 | 136 | 6 times as much |

| Student | 136 |

7. Yo-yos first appeared in the United States in 1866, but the name "yo-yo" was first used 50 years later. It is probably from a Filipino word for "come-come" or "to return." In what year did the toy get the "yo-yo" name?

? year

| 1866 | 50 |

8. What is the distance around (perimeter) the playground shown to the right?

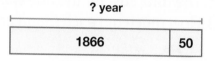

9. If the length of this park at the right was increased by 10 feet, what is the new perimeter?

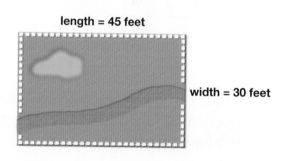

length = 45 feet

width = 30 feet

10. At a large dog show, there were 45 entries for each of the breeds in the chart at the right. What is the total number of dogs in this show?

11. A chihuahua weighs 6 pounds. A Great Pyrenees weighs 17 times as much. What is the weight of the Great Pyrenees dog?

Breed of Dog

Hound

Working

Terrier

Gundog

Pastoral

Utility

Toy

Great Pyrenees Weighs 17 times as much

Chihuahua Weighs 6 pounds

12. What would the total cost be for 3 round-trip tickets to Hawaii?

(Tip) *The prices in the table are one way!*

13. How much less does a one-way ticket to Orlando cost than a one-way ticket to Chicago?

$296	
$189	?

Destination	One-Way Price
Chicago	$296
New York	$239
Los Angeles	$349
Orlando	$189
Hawaii	$625

14. Use the data to the right. How much more is a ton of dimes worth than a ton of pennies?

15. Four friends shared the cost of a boat ride. The total cost for the ride was $28. How much did each friend pay?

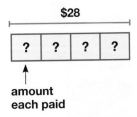

$28

?	?	?	?

↑
amount each paid

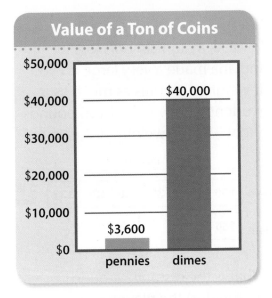

Value of a Ton of Coins

16. A food cart on an airplane has 6 slots. Each slot holds 2 food trays. How many trays are in 8 food carts?

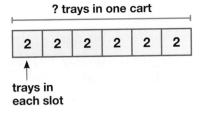

? trays in one cart

2	2	2	2	2	2

↑
trays in each slot

Think About the Process

17. A Super Pocket Bike costs 5 times as much as a 10-speed bicycle. If the bicycle costs $150, which expression gives the cost of the Super Pocket Bike?

　A 150 − 5　　**C** 150 + 5

　B 150 × 5　　**D** 150 ÷ 5

18. Tickets for a movie cost $8 for an adult and $6 for a child. Wally is buying 2 adult tickets and 1 child ticket. Which expression can be used to find the total?

　A 8 + 6 + 2 + 1　　**C** 8 + 6

　B (2 × 8) + (2 × 6)　　**D** (2 × 8) + 6

Operations on a Calculator

Jamie made 4 trips between Foster and Andersonville this summer. Each trip was 379 miles. How many miles were the 4 trips in all?

In September, Jamie traveled 379 miles from Andersonville to Foster, 244 miles from Foster to Leyton, and 137 miles from Leyton back to Andersonville. How many miles did Jamie travel in September?

Step 1 Draw a picture and choose an operation for the first question.

? miles in all

379	379	379	379

Multiply 4 × 379.

Step 2 Press: 4 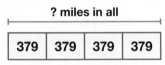 × 379 $\boxed{\text{ENTER} =}$

Display: $\boxed{1516}$

Jamie's four trips were 1,516 miles in all.

Step 1 Draw a picture and choose an operation for the second question.

? miles in all

379	244	137

Add 379 + 244 + 137.

Step 2 Press: 379 $\boxed{+}$ 244 $\boxed{+}$ 137 $\boxed{\text{ENTER} =}$

Display: $\boxed{760}$

Jamie traveled 760 miles in September.

Practice

For each problem, draw a picture, choose an operation, and solve.

1. How much farther did Jamie travel from Andersonville to Foster than from Foster to Leyton?

2. How many miles would Jamie travel if she went from Andersonville to Leyton and back to Andersonville?

1. Mrs. Ortiz can make 50 sopapillas out of one batch of dough. If she makes 4 batches of dough, how many sopapillas can she make? (5-1)

   A 8

   B 20

   C 200

   D 2,000

2. Mrs. Henderson bought 4 boxes of facial tissues. Each box has 174 tissues. Which number sentence shows the best way to use rounding to estimate the total number of tissues? (5-3)

   A $4 + 100 = 104$

   B $4 + 200 = 204$

   C $4 \times 100 = 400$

   D $4 \times 200 = 800$

3. Which shows one way to use breaking apart to find 7×32? (5-2)

   A $210 + 14 = 224$

   B $210 + 7 = 217$

   C $210 + 21 = 231$

   D $7 + 32 = 39$

4. A gallon of paint can cover about 400 square feet of wall space. How many square feet of wall space will 3 gallons cover? (5-1)

   A 12

   B 120

   C 1,200

   D 12,000

5. A bike trail is 8 miles long. Ed rode around the trail 18 times. To find 18×8, Ed used compatible numbers and multiplied $20 \times 8 = 160$. What should Ed do next? (5-2)

   A $160 - 8 = 152$

   B $160 + 8 = 168$

   C $160 + 16 = 176$

   D $160 - 16 = 144$

6. Susanna's school has 5 grades with an average of 48 students in each grade. Which is a reasonable number of students in Susanna's school? (5-4)

   A 205, because 5×48 is about $5 \times 40 = 200$.

   B 240, because 5×48 is about $5 \times 50 = 250$.

   C 285, because 5×48 is about $5 \times 60 = 300$.

   D 315, because 5×48 is about $6 \times 50 = 300$.

7. Each movie theater has 278 seats. Which number sentence can be used to find the number of seats in 3 movie theaters? (5-8)

   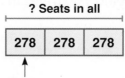

   A 3×278

   B $278 + 278$

   C $278 + 3$

   D $278 - 3$

8. A factory produced 275 cars in a week. At this rate, how many cars would the factory produce in 4 weeks? (5-7)

A 880 cars

B 1,000 cars

C 1,100 cars

D 8,300 cars

9. Nia has 48 paper clips in 5 piles. How many paper clips are there in all? (5-6)

A 340 paper clips

B 240 paper clips

C 140 paper clips

D 60 paper clips

10. Part of the calculation for 3 × 26 is shown below. What partial product should replace ▓▓ ? (5-5)

A 8

B 18

C 20

D 60

$$
\begin{array}{r}
26 \\
\times\ \ 3 \\
\hline
\blacksquare\blacksquare \\
+\ 60 \\
\hline
78
\end{array}
$$

11. Blane earned 230 points playing a video game. Jane earned 7 times as many points as Blane. How many points did Jane earn? (5-7)

A 1,610 points

B 1,421 points

C 1,410 points

D 161 points

12. Ivan gets $22 a week for completing his chores. Which is the best estimate for the amount of money Ivan would have if he saved all his chore money for 6 weeks? (5-3)

A $120

B $180

C $200

D $1,200

13. Ray cut 6 pieces of rope. Each piece was between 67 and 84 inches long. Which could be the total length of the 6 pieces of rope? (5-6)

A 360 inches

B 390 inches

C 480 inches

D 540 inches

14. There are 52 weeks in a year. If Jean turned 9 today, which is the best estimate of the number of weeks Jean has been alive? (5-3)

A 300

B 350

C 400

D 450

15. Ali ran for 19 minutes 7 days in a row. How many minutes did Ali run? (5-6)

A 26 minutes

B 70 minutes

C 106 minutes

D 133 minutes

Set A, pages 96–97

Use basic multiplication facts to multiply by multiples of 10 and 100.

For a multiple of 10, multiply by the digit in the tens place. Then, write one zero in the product.

Find 4×60 → Multiply $4 \times 6 = 24$.

Write one zero after 24.

$\quad 4 \times 60 = 240$

So, $4 \times 60 = 240$.

For a multiple of 100, multiply by the digit in the hundreds place. Then, write two zeros in the product.

Find 4×600 → Multiply $4 \times 6 = 24$.

Write two zeros after 24.

$\quad 4 \times 600 = 2,400$

So, $4 \times 600 = 2,400$.

Remember when the product of a basic fact has a zero, the answer will have an extra zero.

Write the basic fact. Then find the product.

1. 8×60	**2.** 3×40
3. 6×50	**4.** 5×300
5. 700×4	**6.** 2×900
7. 300×7	**8.** 80×8
9. 100×4	**10.** 30×6
11. 20×9	**12.** 9×800
13. 5×70	**14.** 2×70
15. 300×3	**16.** 40×9
17. 7×70	**18.** 500×4

Set B, pages 98–99

One way to multiply mentally is to use compatible numbers.

Find 2×27.

Subtract 2 from 27 to make 25.

$2 \times 25 = 50$

Now adjust. Add 2 groups of 2.

$50 + 4 = 54$

So, $2 \times 27 = 54$.

Remember to check your answer for reasonableness.

Find each product.

1. 6×13	**2.** 3×46
3. 7×63	**4.** 9×24
5. 5×87	**6.** 6×14
7. 2×72	**8.** 28×6
9. 61×9	**10.** 49×4
11. 47×6	**12.** 81×8
13. 5×72	**14.** 76×4

Set C, pages 100–101

Estimate 9 × 83.

Round 83 to 80.

9 × 83

↓

9 × 80

9 × 80 = 720

9 × 83 is about 720.

Remember when both rounded numbers are less than the factors they replace, their product will also be less than the product of the factors.

Estimate each product.

1. 8 × 76	**2.** 493 × 3
3. 96 × 5	**4.** 678 × 6
5. 707 × 4	**6.** 42 × 9
7. 148 × 3	**8.** 719 × 9
9. 5 × 299	**10.** 6 × 109
11. 4 × 253	**12.** 287 × 3

Set D, pages 102–104

Ty is making centerpieces for the tables at a banquet. There will be 12 tables with a centerpiece at each table. Each centerpiece needs 5 sheets of construction paper.

What do I know? — There are 12 tables at the banquet. Each centerpiece needs 5 sheets of construction paper.

What am I being asked to find? — The number of sheets of construction paper that will be needed to make all the centerpieces

? sheets in all

Number of sheets of construction paper

12 × 5 = 60

Estimate to determine if the answer is reasonable.

12 rounds to 10.

10 × 5 = 50

The answer is reasonable because 50 is close to 60.

Remember to check if your answer is reasonable.

Solve.

1. Mitchell earns 8 dollars per hour delivering newspapers. How much will Mitchell earn if he works for 10 hours?

? dollars in all

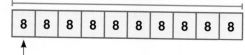

dollars earned per hour

2. Joan needs envelopes. Each pack costs $4. How much will Joan pay for 9 packs of envelopes?

? dollars in all

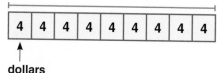

dollars per pack

Set E, pages 106-108

Find 4 × 12.

Use blocks or draw a picture to build an array.

```
   12
 ×  4
    8
 + 40
   48
```

4 × 10 = 40   4 × 2 = 8

40 + 8 = **48**

Find 6 × 22.

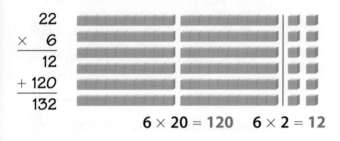

```
   22
 ×  6
   12
 + 120
  132
```

6 × 20 = 120   6 × 2 = 12

120 + 12 = **132**

Remember to check that your picture accurately shows the numbers that are being multiplied.

1. 28 × 6		**2.** 28 × 3	
3. 75 × 5		**4.** 53 × 4	
5. 88 × 2		**6.** 21 × 6	
7. 12 × 8		**8.** 45 × 5	
9. 42 × 7		**10.** 37 × 3	

Set F, pages 110–112

Find 5 × 13.

Step 1

Multiply the ones. Regroup if necessary.

```
  1
 13
× 5
  5
```

Step 2

Multiply the tens. Add any extra tens.

```
  1
 13
× 5
 65
```

Find 8 × 24.

Step 1

Multiply the ones. Regroup if necessary.

```
  3
 24
× 8
  2
```

Step 2

Multiply the tens. Add any extra tens.

```
  3
 24
× 8
192
```

Remember that you can use an array to help you multiply. Check your answer with an estimate.

1. 18 × 2		**2.** 48 × 5	
3. 33 × 6		**4.** 97 × 7	
5. 62 × 4		**6.** 25 × 8	
7. 45 × 8		**8.** 88 × 4	
9. 72 × 6		**10.** 54 × 7	

Set G, pages 114–115

Find 768 × 6.

Step 1

Multiply the ones. Regroup if necessary.

$$
\begin{array}{r}
{\scriptstyle 4} \\
768 \\
\times 6 \\
\hline
8
\end{array}
$$

Step 2

Multiply the tens. Add any extra tens. Regroup if necessary.

$$
\begin{array}{r}
{\scriptstyle 4\;4} \\
768 \\
\times 6 \\
\hline
08
\end{array}
$$

Step 3

Multiply the hundreds. Add any extra hundreds.

$$
\begin{array}{r}
{\scriptstyle 4\;4} \\
768 \\
\times 6 \\
\hline
4{,}608
\end{array}
$$

Remember to check your answer with an estimate.

1. $\begin{array}{r} 239 \\ \times 4 \\ \hline \end{array}$

2. $\begin{array}{r} 148 \\ \times 5 \\ \hline \end{array}$

3. $\begin{array}{r} 233 \\ \times 6 \\ \hline \end{array}$

4. $\begin{array}{r} 907 \\ \times 7 \\ \hline \end{array}$

5. $\begin{array}{r} 261 \\ \times 4 \\ \hline \end{array}$

6. $\begin{array}{r} 250 \\ \times 8 \\ \hline \end{array}$

Set H, pages 116–118

An orchard has 3 times as many apple trees as cherry trees. If there are 52 cherry trees, how many apple trees are there?

What do I know?   There are 52 cherry trees. There are 3 times as many apple trees.

What am I being asked to find?   The number of apple trees

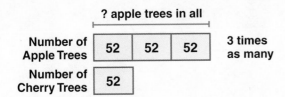

Choose an Operation Multiply when you want to find "times as many."

3 × 52 = 156

There are 156 apple trees.

Remember to draw a picture to help you solve a problem.

1. There are 24 hours in one day. How many hours are in one week?

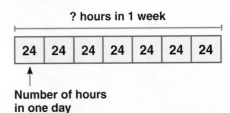

2. An office ordered 6 copy machines. Each machine weighed 108 pounds. Find the total weight of the order.

3. Celia has four weeks to save $58 for her vacation. In her first week, she saved $10, the second week $21, and the third week $17. How much more does she need to save?

Patterns and Expressions

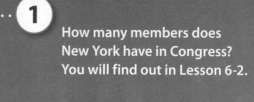

1 How many members does New York have in Congress? You will find out in Lesson 6-2.

2 Kudzu is the world's fastest growing plant. How fast can this weed grow? You will find out in Lesson 6-3.

Review What You Know!

Choose the best term from the box.

> • expression   • factors
> • ordered pair   • multiple

1. A _?_ is the product of a whole number and any other whole number.

2. A(n) _?_ may include numbers and at least one operation.

3. A(n) _?_ is a pair of numbers used to name a point on a coordinate grid.

4. _?_ are numbers multiplied together to find a product.

Patterns

For each set of numbers, find the missing number.

5. 2, ▩ , 4, 5, 6

6. ▩ , 10, 15, 20

7. 3, 6, 9, ▩

8. 4, 8, ▩ , 16

9. 17, ▩ , 35, 44

10. 50, 39, ▩ , 17

Multiplication

Solve.

11. 5 × 6   **12.** 120 × 4   **13.** 35 × 2

14. 9 × 8   **15.** 14 × 3   **16.** 132 × 5

17. In baseball, there are 6 outs in 1 full inning. Would you multiply or divide to find the number of outs in 2 innings?

18. Writing to Explain How would you describe the pattern for multiples of 2? multiples of 5?

3 In a leap year, one day is added to February. What will be the fifth leap year after the year 2000? You will find out in Lesson 6-1.

Variables and Expressions

How can you use expressions with variables?

A variable is a symbol that stands for a number.

A Tae Kwon Do class has 23 people. If *n* more people sign up, how many people will be taking the class?

n	23 + n
3	
5	
7	

Other Examples

An algebraic expression is a mathematical phrase that contains numbers or variables and at least one operation.

Word form	Expression
add 5	n + 5
multiply by 2	n × 2

Guided Practice*

Do you know HOW?

In **1** through **3**, copy and complete the table.

c	c + 8
1. 4	
2. 9	
3. 13	

Do you UNDERSTAND?

4. Writing to Explain Could you use the variable *k* instead of *n* to represent more students signing up for the Tae Kwon Do class?

5. If *n* is 12, how many people will be taking the Tae Kwon Do class?

Independent Practice

For **6** through **8**, copy and complete the table for each problem.

6.

d	d + 30
3	
7	
12	

7.

g	5 × g
6	
9	
15	

8.

m	m ÷ 10
350	
240	
120	

Animated Glossary
www.pearsonsuccessnet.com

*For another example, see Set A on page 138.

Use the expression, $23 + n$, to find the missing numbers.

$23 + n$

$23 + 3 = 26$

n	$23 + n$
3	$23 + 3$
5	$23 + 5$
7	$23 + 7$

If 3 more people sign up, there will be 26 people in the class.

If 5 more people sign up, there will be 28 people in the class.

If 7 more people sign up, there will be 30 people in the class.

For **9** through **12**, fill in the missing numbers.

9.

z	24	56	72	88
$z \div 8$	3		9	11

10.

t	43	134	245	339
$t + 47$	90	181		386

11.

y	387	201	65	26
$y - 13$	374	188		

12.

x	5	7	10	20
$x \times 12$	60	84		

Problem Solving

13. The year 2020 will be the fifth leap year after the year 2000. Name the years between 2000 and 2020 that are leap years.

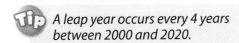
A leap year occurs every 4 years between 2000 and 2020.

14. Which expression represents how many seconds are in 5 minutes?

A $s + 5$

B $s \div 5$

C $s \times 5$

D $s - 5$

15. A Ferris wheel has 12 cars. The operator needs to keep 2, 4, or 6 cars empty. Make a table to show how many people can ride if each car holds 4 people.

16. Write an expression to represent the cost of parking a car for n hours in a lot that charges $7.00 per hour. Find the cost of parking the car for 3 hours.

17. Reasonableness Edgar used $10 \times d$ to represent the number of pennies in d dollars. Is this reasonable?

18. Reasoning How could you make $36.32 with exactly 4 bills and 4 coins?

Addition and Subtraction Expressions

Understand It!
A rule can help when writing expressions.

How can you find a rule and write an expression?

What is a rule for the table?
How can you use a rule to write an expression and find the sale price when the regular price is $18?

Let *p* stand for the regular price.

Regular price (p)	$21	$20	$19	$18
Sale price	$16	$15	$14	

Guided Practice*

Do you know HOW?

For **1** and **2**, use the table below.

Total number of test questions (q)	20	30	40	50
Number of multiple-choice questions	10	20	30	

1. What is a rule for the table in words? in symbols?

2. How many multiple-choice questions would be on a 50-question test?

Do you UNDERSTAND?

3. **Writing to Explain** How could you use place-value blocks to find a rule in the table to the left?

4. Tony earns $7 and saves $2. When he earns $49, he saves $44. When he earns $10, he saves $5. Write an expression for the amount he saves.

   Tip *Make a table to help you find a rule.*

5. In the example at the top, what is the sale price when the regular price is $30?

Independent Practice

Leveled Practice For **6** through **11**, find a rule.

6.
n	3	4	5
n +	7	8	9

7.
b	31	42	55
b −	23	34	47

8.
q	0	2	8
q +	15	17	23

9.
p	3	4	5
p +	68	69	70

10.
x	18	21	26
x −	5	8	13

11.
r	112	96	62
r −	73	57	23

For another example, see Set B on page 138.

<table>
<tr><td>

Subtract to find the sale price.

For a regular price of $21:

21 − 5 = 16

For a regular price of $20:

20 − 5 = 15

For a regular price of $19:

19 − 5 = 14

A rule is subtract 5.
So, the expression is *p* − 5.

</td><td>

Use the expression *p* − 5 to find the missing value when *p* = 18.

Subtract 5 from the regular price, *p*.

Regular price (p)	$21	$20	$19	$18
Sale price	$16	$15	$14	$18 − 5

When the regular price is $18, the sale price is $13.

</td></tr>
</table>

For **12** through **15**, copy and complete each table, and find a rule.

12.

n	15	18	20	27
n + ▢	58	61	63	▢

13.

u	212	199	190	188
u − ▢	177	164	155	▢

14.

c	31	54	60	64
c − ▢	5	28	34	▢

15.

a	589	485	400	362
a − ▢	575	471	386	▢

Problem Solving

For **16** and **17**, use the table at the right.

16. The United States Congress includes 2 senators from each state plus members of the House of Representatives. The number of representatives, *r*, is based on the state's population. Write a rule for the total number of members each state has in Congress.

17. How many members in Congress does each state in the table have?

Data

Number of Members in the United States Congress

State	House	Senate
Pennsylvania	19	2
Missouri	9	2
Hawaii	2	2
New York	29	2

18. Reasoning Don, Wanda, and Stu each play softball, basketball, or football. Each person plays only one sport. Wanda doesn't play football. Don doesn't play softball. Stu doesn't play basketball or softball. What sport does each person play?

19. Writing to Explain Chang has driven 1,372 miles. If the total mileage for his trip is 2,800 miles, how many miles does Chang have left to drive? Explain.

Multiplication and Division Expressions

How can you find a rule and write an expression?

What is a rule for the table?
How can Josie use a rule to
write an expression and find
the number of cards in 4 boxes?
Let *b* equal the number of boxes.

Number of boxes (b)	1	2	3	4
Number of note cards	15	30	45	

Guided Practice*

Do you know HOW?

For **1** and **2**, use the table below.

Number of tickets (t)	2	4	6	8
Total Price	$60	$120	$180	

1. What is a rule for the table in words? in symbols?

2. How much would 8 tickets cost?

Do you UNDERSTAND?

3. **Writing to Explain** How could you use place-value blocks to describe a rule in the table to the left?

4. How could you find the price of 1 ticket using the information from Problems 1 and 2?

5. In the example above, how many note cards are in 13 boxes?

Independent Practice

Leveled Practice For **6** through **8**, find a rule.

6.
n	3	8	10
n ×	18	48	60

7.
p	2	4	8
p ÷	1	2	4

8.
t	2	3	4
× t	16	24	32

For **9** through **12**, copy and complete each table, and find a rule.

9.
e	4	8	12	16
e ÷	1	2	3	

10.
j	7	9	11	16
× j	98	126	154	

11.
w	5	7	8	10
× w	35	49	56	

12.
s	60	80	85	90
s ÷	12	16	17	

*For another example, see Set C on page 139.

Multiply to find the number of cards.

For 1 box:
$1 \times 15 = 15$

For 2 boxes:
$2 \times 15 = 30$

For 3 boxes:
$3 \times 15 = 45$

A rule is multiply by 15. So, the expression is $b \times 15$.

Use the expression $b \times 15$ to find the missing value when $b = 4$.

$b \times 15 = 4 \times 15$

Number of boxes (b)	1	2	3	4
Number of note cards	15	30	45	4×15

There are 60 note cards in 4 boxes.

Problem Solving

For **13** and **14**, use the table at the right.

The Baker family is deciding which type of television to purchase for the family room.

13. How much more does a 50-inch Plasma cost than a 34-inch Flat Screen?

14. How much less does a 26-inch LCD cost than a 50-inch Plasma?

Type of Television	Cost
50-inch Plasma	$2800.00
34-inch Flat Screen	$900.00
26-inch LCD	$500.00

15. There are 60 minutes in one hour and 7 days in one week. About how many minutes are in a week?

   A About 1,500 minutes

   B About 6,000 minutes

   C About 10,000 minutes

   D About 42,000 minutes

16. Cami bought a book for $12.52 and a bookmark for $1.19. How much change would she get if she paid with a $20 bill?

   A $6.19

   B $6.29

   C $9.29

   D $13.71

For **17**, use the table at the right.

17. Kudzu is the world's fastest growing weed. Copy and complete the table to the right to find a rule for the growth rate of kudzu. What is a rule in words?

Day	1	2	3	4	5	6
Inches	12	24				72

Lesson
6-4

Understand It!
Learning how and when
to use reasoning can help
you solve problems.

Problem Solving

Use Objects and Reasoning

Hands-On
Cubes

Annette's shell collection has snail shells, yellow shells, and red shells. Use cubes to show the objects and solve the problem.

How many of each type of shell are in Annette's collection?

Annette's Collection

- 2 snail shells
- 3 times as many yellow shells as red shells
- 6 shells in all

2 snail shells

Guided Practice*

Do you know HOW?

Solve.

1. Patty made a picnic lunch for her friends. She made 6 sandwiches. Three of the sandwiches were turkey. There is 1 fewer chicken sandwich than roast beef. How many of each type of sandwich are there?

Do you UNDERSTAND?

2. **Reasonableness** Is your answer to Problem 1 reasonable? What number sentence can you write to check?

3. **Write a Problem** Write a problem that uses the following information:
   - 5 shirts in all
   - 2 blue shirts
   - 1 more yellow shirt than red shirts

Independent Practice

Solve. Use objects to help.

4. Margo takes juice boxes to the park. She brings apple, orange, and grape juice boxes. There are 9 juice boxes in all. There is 1 more apple juice box than grape. There are 2 grape juice boxes. How many of each type of juice box are there?

5. Jamie brings dried fruit, pretzels, and carrots to the clubhouse. There are 4 packages of dried fruit. There is 1 fewer package of pretzels than carrots. There are 7 packages of snacks in all. How many of each type of snack are there?

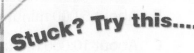
Stuck? Try this....

- What do I know?
- What diagram can I use to help understand the problem?
- Can I use addition, subtraction, multiplication, or division?
- Is all of my work correct?
- Did I answer the right question?
- Is my answer reasonable?

Read and Understand

Use objects to show what you know. Use reasoning to make conclusions.

There are 6 shells in all.
There are 2 snail shells.

That leaves a total of 4 yellow shells and red shells.

Plan

There are 4 yellow shells and red shells.

There are 3 times as many yellow shells as red shells.

There have to be 2 snail shells, 3 yellow shells, and 1 red shell.

$2 + 3 + 1 = 6$

So, the answer is reasonable.

---

6. Mark is saving his allowance for a new bike. The bike he wants will cost him $240. He can save $30 each week. How many weeks will Mark need to save his allowance to be able to buy the bike?

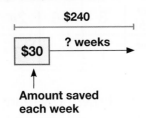

$240

$30 | ? weeks →

↑
Amount saved each week

7. Leah's garden has 11 rows. There are 4 rows of tomatoes. There is 1 more row of cucumbers than tomatoes. The rest of the rows are peppers. How many rows of each type of vegetable are in Leah's garden?

8. There are 14 campers in Group 1. Six campers are boating, and $\frac{1}{2}$ as many campers are doing arts and crafts as boating. How many campers are in each activity?

9. There are 13 campers in Group 2. There are 4 campers playing tennis and one camper fishing. There are twice as many campers swimming as playing tennis. How many campers from Group 2 are in each activity?

10. One more camper was added to Group 1, and each camper did a different activity. There are now 8 campers boating, and $\frac{1}{2}$ as many campers doing archery than boating. How many campers from Group 1 are in each activity?

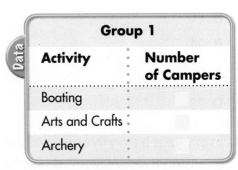

Data

Group 1	
Activity	**Number of Campers**
Boating	
Arts and Crafts	
Archery	

Data

Group 2	
Activity	**Number of Campers**
Swimming	
Tennis	
Fishing	

eTools
www.pearsonsuccessnet.com

1. There are 24 dancers in Joy's recital. If *n* represents the number of jazz dancers, which expression represents the number of other types of dancers? (6-1)

A $24 + n$

B $24 - n$

C $24 \times n$

D $24 \div n$

2. Based on the pattern in the table, how many runs will Shanna's softball team have for the season if they score 6 runs in their game? (6-2)

Shanna's Softball Team

Runs Scored in Game	1	3	4	6
Total for Season	16	18	19	

A 20

B 21

C 22

D 23

3. Every year a dog lives is like 7 years a human lives. Which is a way to find the number of human years that are like 9 dog years? (6-3)

Dog Years	1	2	3	4
Human Years	7	14	21	28

A Subtract 7 from 9

B Add 7 and 9

C Divide 9 by 7

D Multiply 9 by 7

4. What is a rule for the table? (6-2)

Regular Price (p)	$157	$145	$133	$121
Price with the Coupon	$145	$133	$121	$109

A $p + 13$

B $p - 13$

C $p + 12$

D $p - 12$

5. Mr. Robinson used the table below to calculate how many adults are needed to help on the 4th grade trip to the observatory.

Number of Students (s)	8	16	24	32
Number of Adults	1	2	3	4

Which rule shows how many adults are needed for *s* students? (6-3)

A $s - 7$

B $8 \times s$

C $s \div 8$

D $8 + s$

6. Tennis balls are sold 3 to a canister. Vera and Tia bought 12 canisters all together. Tia bought twice as many canisters as Vera. How many canisters did Vera buy? (6-4)

A 12

B 8

C 4

D 3

7. Al participated in a reading contest. He read for the same amount of minutes each night for 2 weeks. The table shows the running total of how many minutes he read.

Number of Days	3	7	10	14
Total Minutes Read	60	140	200	280

Using the pattern in the table, how would the teacher be able to tell how many minutes Al read each night? (6-3)

A Multiply Number of Days by Total Minutes Read

B Subtract the number in Total Minutes Read from Number of Days

C Divide the Total Minutes Read by the Number of Days

D Add all the numbers in Total Minutes Read and divide by 4

8. Which number completes the table? (6-1)

w	72	60	48	42
$w \div 6$	12	10	▮	7

A 8

B 9

C 42

D 288

9. What is a rule for the table? (6-2)

d	7	11	17	21
▮	42	46	52	56

A $d + 35$

B $d + 4$

C $d + d + d + d + d + d$

D $d - 35$

10. The table shows how many solar lights were installed along a sidewalk.

Number of Yards of Sidewalk	Number of Solar Lights
100	20
200	40
250	50
300	▮

How can the number of solar lights installed in 900 yards of sidewalk be found? (6-3)

A Multiply 5 by 300

B Divide 300 by 5

C Add 300 to 5

D Subtract 300 from 5

11. Corrina has $138. After babysitting, she will have $138 + x$, where x equals the amount she earns. If x is $25, how much money will she have? (6-1)

A $138

B $153

C $158

D $163

Set A, pages 128–129

Each car on a ride holds 8 children. For
c children, *c* ÷ 8 cars will be full on the ride.
How many cars will be full if there are
16, 24, or 40 children?

Find the value of *c* ÷ 8 for each value of *c*.

c	c ÷ 8
16	2
24	3
40	5

If there are 16 children, 2 cars will be full.

If there are 24 children, 3 cars will be full.

If there are 40 children, 5 cars will be full.

Remember to find unknown
values, you replace the variable
with known values.

1.
e	16	25	36
20 + e			

2.
h	14	16	18
h × 4			

3.
n	112	56	28
n − 14			

4.
f	18	36	42
f ÷ 6			

Set B, pages 130–131

Look at the table below. Start with the number
in the first column. What rule tells you how to
find the number in the second column?

Regular price (p)	Sale price
$43	$41
$45	$43
$46	$44
$47	

43 − 2 = 41
45 − 2 = 43
46 − 2 = 44

A rule is subtract 2, or *p* − 2.

Use a rule to find the missing
number in the table.

47 − 2 = 45

When the regular price is $47,
the sale price is $45.

Remember to ask "What is a rule?"

Copy and complete each table and
find a rule.

1.
n	☐ − n
3	12
5	10
8	7
12	

2.
x	☐ + x
34	100
0	66
8	74
13	

3.
t	4	6	8	13
t − ☐		4	6	11

4.
r	80	48	27	13
r + ☐	88	56	35	

Set C, pages 132–133

Look at the table below. What rule tells you how to find each number in the second column?

Hours worked (h)	Wage
2	$10
4	$20
6	$30
8	

Think

$2 \times 5 = 10$
$4 \times 5 = 20$
$6 \times 5 = 30$

A rule is multiply by 5, or $h \times 5$.

Use a rule to find the missing number in the table.

$8 \times 5 = 40$

Remember a rule must work with all of the numbers in the table.

1.
n	2	6	8	10
▢ × n	6	18	24	▢

2.
r	3	7	8	11
r × ▢	12	28	▢	44

3.
e	80	70	60	50
e ÷ ▢	8	7	▢	5

4.
s	55	40	35	15
s ÷ ▢	11	8	▢	3

Set D, pages 134–135

Janet collects rocks. Her collection has black rocks, white rocks, and brown rocks. Use cubes to show the objects and solve the problem.

Janet's collection:

2 black rocks

2 times as many brown rocks as white rocks

14 objects in all

What do I know? The collection has black, white, and brown rocks. There are 2 times as many brown rocks as white rocks. There are 14 objects in all.

What am I asked to find? The number of black rocks, brown rocks, and white rocks in Janet's collection

There are 2 black rocks, 4 white rocks, and 8 brown rocks.

$2 + 4 + 8 = 14$, so the answer is reasonable.

Remember you can make a list, use objects, and use reasoning to solve a problem.

1. Six friends play on three different teams: Orioles, Cardinals, and Blue Jays. There are an equal number of players on each team. Two of the friends play on the Cardinals. The names of the remaining friends are Fedor, Lisa, John, and Ashton. Fedor is on the Orioles. John is on the same team as Lisa. Ashton is not on the Blue Jays. What team is Lisa on?

Multiplying by 2-Digit Numbers

1 In 1858, a telegraph cable connected Europe and America for the first time. How long was the cable? You will find out in Lesson 7-2.

2 The Pike's Peak Cog Railway is the highest cog railway in the world. How long is the train ride to the top? You will find out in Lesson 7-4.

3 The *Queen Mary 2* is as tall as a 23-story building! How many feet high is this above the water? You will find out in Lesson 7-5.

Review What You Know!

Vocabulary

Choose the best term from the box.

- rounding
- compatible
- Commutative Property
- Distributive Property

1. _?_ numbers are easy to compute mentally.

2. Breaking apart problems into two simpler problems is an example of the _?_ of Multiplication.

3. You can use _?_ when you do not need an exact answer.

Estimating Sums

Estimate each sum.

4. 16 + 13   **5.** 688 + 95

6. 1,511 + 269   **7.** 3,246 + 6,243

8. 283 + 178   **9.** 1,999 + 421

Multiplying by 1-Digit Numbers

Find each product.

10. 53 × 9   **11.** 172 × 7

12. 512 × 6   **13.** 711 × 4

14. 215 × 3   **15.** 914 × 5

Partial Products

16. Writing to Explain Explain why the array shown below represents 3 × 21.

Using Mental Math to Multiply 2-Digit Numbers

How can you multiply by multiples of 10 and 100?

How many adults under 65 visit the Sunny Day Amusement Park in 10 days? How many children visit the park in 100 days? How many adults 65 and over visit the park in 200 days?

Average Number of Visitors Each Day

TICKET

KEEP THIS COUPON

Adults under 65:
400

Adults 65 and over:
50

Children:
800

Guided Practice*

Do you know HOW?

In **1** through **8**, use basic facts and patterns to find the product.

1. 30 × 100

2. 50 × 1,000

3. 25 × 10

4. 60 × 200

5. 20 × 20

6. 40 × 100

7. 400 × 50

8. 80 × 500

Do you UNDERSTAND?

9. When you multiply 60 × 500, how many zeros are in the product?

10. In cold weather, fewer people go to Sunny Day Amusement Park. November has 30 days. If the park sells 300 tickets each day in November, how many would they sell for the whole month?

Independent Practice

For **11** through **34**, multiply using mental math.

11. 30 × 10

12. 100 × 60

13. 50 × 10

14. 80 × 40

15. 20 × 1,000

16. 70 × 900

17. 40 × 20

18. 500 × 30

19. 250 × 40

20. 20 × 40

21. 300 × 40

22. 60 × 90

23. 70 × 800

24. 30 × 80

25. 60 × 500

26. 700 × 30

27. 600 × 50

28. 30 × 900

29. 25 × 400

30. 30 × 600

31. 400 × 30

32. 800 × 30

33. 500 × 80

34. 600 × 90

For another example, see Set A on page 160.

Adults under 65 in 10 Days

To multiply 400 × 10, use a pattern.

$$4 \times 10 = 40$$
$$40 \times 10 = 400$$
$$400 \times 10 = 4{,}000$$

4,000 adults under 65 visit the park in 10 days.

Children in 100 Days

The number of zeros in the product is the total number of zeros in both factors.

$$800 \times 100 = 80{,}000$$

2 zeros 2 zeros   4 zeros

80,000 children visit the park in 100 days.

Adults 65 and over in 200 Days

If the product of a basic fact ends in zero, include that zero in the count.

$$5 \times 2 = 10$$
$$50 \times 200 = 10{,}000$$

10,000 adults 65 and over visit the park in 200 days.

Problem Solving

For **35** and **36**, use the table at the right.

35. What is the total distance traveled in one triathlon?

36. Susan has completed 10 triathlons. How far did she bicycle in the races?

Data

Parts of an Olympic-Distance Triathlon	
Swimming	1,500 meters
Running	10,000 meters
Bicycling	40,000 meters

37. Writing to Explain Explain why the product of 50 and 800 has four zeros when 50 has one zero and 800 has two zeros.

38. Esther had 5 coins and two dollar bills to buy a snack at school. She paid $1.40 for her snack. She had exactly one dollar left. How did Esther pay for her snack?

39. For every 30 minutes of television air time, about 8 of the minutes are given to TV commercials. If 90 minutes of television is aired, how many minutes of commercials will be played?

  A 8 minutes   **C** 38 minutes

  B 24 minutes   **D** 128 minutes

40. If in one year a city recorded a total of 97 rainy days, how many of the days did it **NOT** rain?

365 days in one year

97	?

Lesson

7-2

Understand It!
Use strategies
like rounding and
compatible numbers to
help mulitply mentally.

Estimating Products

What are some ways to estimate?

In 1991, NASA launched the Upper Atmosphere Research Satellite (UARS). It orbits Earth about 105 times each week. There are 52 weeks in one year.

About how many orbits does it make in one year?

Orbits Earth about 105 times each week

Guided Practice*

Do you know HOW?

In **1** and **2**, use rounding to estimate each product.

1. 203×37

2. 177×14

In **3** and **4**, use compatible numbers to estimate each product.

3. 24×37

4. 15×27

Do you UNDERSTAND?

5. Writing to Explain In the example above, why are the estimates not the same?

6. About how many times does UARS orbit Earth in 3 weeks?

Independent Practice

For **7** through **30**, use rounding or compatible numbers to estimate each product.

 You can round just one number or round both to make compatible numbers.

7. 32×83

8. 64×85

9. 31×46

10. 63×61

11. 42×703

12. 51×23

13. 27×41

14. 61×202

15. 62×20

16. 18×74

17. 12×89

18. 22×27

19. 79×43

20. 26×43

21. 346×18

22. 6×153

23. 602×43

24. 210×19

25. 79×79

26. 96×37

27. 840×49

28. 17×78

29. 35×45

30. 8×55

144

For another example, see Set B on page 160.

One Way

Use **rounding** to estimate the number of orbits in one year.

52 × 105

↓ Round 105 to 100.

52 × 100 = 5,200

UARS orbits Earth about 5,200 times each year.

Another Way

Use **compatible numbers** to estimate the number of orbits in one year.

Compatible numbers are easy to multiply.

52 × 105

↓ ↓ Change 52 to 55.
Change 105 to 100.

55 × 100 = 5,500

UARS orbits Earth about 5,500 times each year.

Problem Solving

31. A long-haul truck driver made 37 trips last year. If her average trip was 1,525 miles, about how far did she drive in all?

32. In one mission, an American astronaut spent more than 236 hours in space. About how many minutes did he spend in space?

 There are 60 minutes in 1 hour.

33. Estimate to decide which has a greater product, 39 × 21 or 32 × 32. Explain.

34. The Mars Orbiter circles the planet Mars every 25 hours. About how many hours does it take to make 125 orbits?

35. Use the diagram below. In 1858, two ships connected a telegraph cable across the Atlantic Ocean for the first time. One ship laid out 1,016 miles of cable. The other ship laid out 1,010 miles of cable. Estimate the total distance of cable used.

36. **Think About the Process** About 57 baseballs are used in a professional baseball game. What is the best way to estimate how many baseballs are used in a season of 162 games?

A 6 × 100   **C** 60 × 1,000

B 60 × 160   **D** 200 × 200

|← 1,010 miles →|← 1,016 miles →|

Understand It!
Arrays can be used
to break a problem
like 12 × 25 into four
simpler problems.

Arrays and an Expanded Algorithm

How can you multiply using an array?

There are 13 bobble-head dogs in each row of the carnival booth. There are 24 equal rows. How many dogs are there?

Choose an Operation
Multiply to join equal groups.

13 dogs per row

Hands-On
grid paper

Another Example **What is another way to show the partial products?**

There are 37 rows with 26 seats set up at the ring at the dog show. How many seats are there?

Estimate 40 × 25 = 1,000

Step 1 Draw a table. Separate each factor into tens and ones. (30 + 7) × (20 + 6)

	30	7
20		
6		

Step 2 Multiply to find the partial products.

	30	7
20	600	140
6	180	42

Step 3 Add the partial products to find the total.

```
    42
   180
   140
 + 600
  ─────
   962
```

26 × 37 = 962
There are 962 seats at the dog show ring.

Explain It

1. How is breaking apart the problem 37 × 26 like solving four simpler problems?

2. **Reasonableness** Explain why the answer 962 is reasonable.

Step 1

Find 24 × 13.

Draw an array for 24 × 13.

Add each part of the array to find the product.

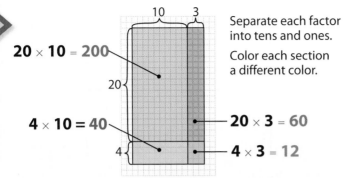

10   3

Separate each factor into tens and ones.

Color each section a different color.

20 × 10 = 200

20

4 × 10 = 40

4

20 × 3 = 60

4 × 3 = 12

Step 2

Find the number of squares in each rectangle.

```
   12
   40  ⎫ partial
   60  ⎭ products
+ 200
 ————
  312
```

In the booth, there are 312 bobble-head dogs.

Guided Practice*

Do you know HOW?

In **1** and **2**, copy and complete the calculation by finding the partial products.

1.
```
   13
 × 17
 ————
```

2. 24 × 16

```
        20    4
   10 ┌─────┬─────┐
      │     │     │
    6 ├─────┼─────┤
      └─────┴─────┘
```

Do you UNDERSTAND?

3. In the example at the top, what four simpler multiplication problems were used to find 24 × 13?

4. At the dog show, the first 2 rows are reserved. How many people can sit in the remaining 35 rows?

 There are 26 seats per row.

Independent Practice

Leveled Practice Use grid paper to draw a rectangle. Then copy and complete the calculations.

 You can solve the simpler problems in any order.

5.

```
   21
 × 14
 ————
```

6.

```
   12
 × 14
 ————
```

eTools
www.pearsonsuccessnet.com

DIGITAL

For another example, see Set C on page 160.

Leveled Practice For **7** and **8**, use grid paper to draw a rectangle. Then copy and complete the calculations.

7.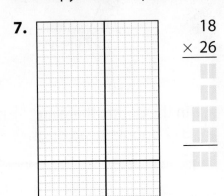

18
× 26
___

8.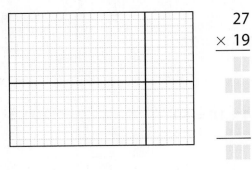

27
× 19
___

In **9** through **16**, copy and find the partial products. Then find the total.

9. 25 × 18

	20	5
10		
8		

10. 28 × 12

	20	8
10		
2		

11. 68 × 17

	60	8
10		
7		

12. 16
× 11
___

13. 21
× 31
___

14. 38
× 12
___

15. 29
× 17
___

16. 43
× 19
___

In **17** through **31**, find the products. Use partial products to help. Estimate to check for reasonableness.

17. 31
× 13

18. 21
× 33

19. 27
× 16

20. 59
× 41

21. 18
× 23

22. 28
× 29

23. 24
× 36

24. 43
× 39

25. 76
× 54

26. 88
× 22

27. 41
× 12

28. 38
× 27

29. 58
× 19

30. 29
× 15

31. 73
× 47

32. Writing to Explain Why is the product of 15 × 32 equal to the sum of 10 × 32 and 5 × 32?

33. The flagpole in front of City Hall in Luis' town is 35 feet tall. How many inches tall is the flagpole?

 *12 inches = 1 foot*

34. The prices at Nolan's Novelties store are shown at the right. If 27 boxes of neon keychains and 35 boxes of glow-in-the-dark pens were purchased, what is the total cost?

Item	Price per box
Neon key chains	$15
Glow-in-the-dark pens	$10

35. The Hollywood Bowl can seat almost 18,000 people. Section G2 has 22 rows of benches that can seat 18 people. How many seats are in this section?

36. Algebra Elijah has *n* customers in his lawn-mowing business. He mows each lawn once a week. Which expression shows how many lawns he mows in 12 weeks?

A $n + 12$ **C** $12 - n$

B $n \times 12$ **D** $12 \div n$

For **37** and **38**, use the diagram to the right.

37. Maggie is making a balloon game for the school fair. Kids will throw darts to try to pop the balloons. How many balloons are needed to set up the game?

38. Think About the Process Maggie knows that she will have to completely refill the balloon board about 15 times a day. Which expression shows how to find the number of balloons she will need?

A 15×13 **C** $15 \times (13 \times 14)$

B 15×14 **D** $15 \times (13 + 14)$

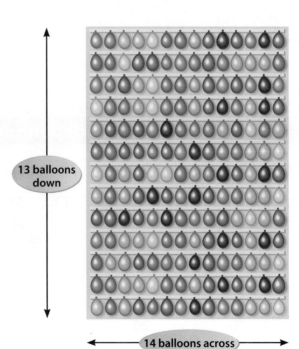

13 balloons down

14 balloons across

Multiplying 2-Digit Numbers by Multiples of Ten

28 rocks per kit

How can you find the product?

Mr. Jeffrey buys 20 rock identification kits for his science classes. If each kit has 28 rocks, how many rocks are there in all?

Choose an Operation
Multiply to find the number of rocks.

Guided Practice*

Do you know HOW?

In **1** through **6**, multiply to find each product.

1.   12
    × 20
    ▊▊ 0

2.   21
    × 30
    ▊▊ 0

3. 35 × 20

4. 63 × 20

5. 27 × 60

6. 66 × 40

Do you UNDERSTAND?

7. **Writing to Explain** Why is there a zero in the ones place when you multiply by 20 in the example above?

8. What simpler multiplication problem can you solve to find 38 × 70?

9. Each year, Mr. Jeffrey's school orders 100 rock kits. How many rocks are in all of the kits?

Independent Practice

Leveled Practice In **10** through **30**, multiply to find each product.

10.   12
    × 30
    ▊▊ 0

11.   24
    × 10
    ▊▊ 0

12.   33
    × 20
    ▊▊ 0

13.   71
    × 30
    ▊,▊ 0

14.   63
    × 40
    ▊,▊ 0

15. 18 × 10

16. 20 × 51

17. 32 × 30

18. 40 × 22

19. 24 × 40

20. 34 × 50

21. 40 × 73

22. 88 × 30

23. 75 × 40

24. 22 × 60

25. 13 × 50

26. 60 × 23

27. 32 × 20

28. 82 × 80

29. 62 × 60

30. 52 × 50

*For another example, see Set D on page 160.

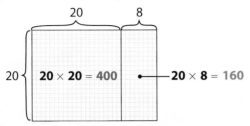

One Way

Find 20 × 28.

Break 28 into tens and ones: **28 = 20 + 8.**

Use a grid to find the partial products.

```
        20          8
   ┌──────────┬──────────┐
20 │ 20 × 20  │          │
   │  = 400   │ ●────── 20 × 8 = 160
   └──────────┴──────────┘
```

Add the partial products to find the total.
400 + 160 = 560

Another Way

Find 20 × 28.

Multiply 2 tens × 28.

```
   1
   28
 × 20
 ───
  560
```

Record a 0 in the ones place of the answer. This shows how many tens are in the answer.

There are 560 rocks in all.

Problem Solving

31. Number Sense Rex's class raised frogs from tadpoles. The class has 21 students, and each raised 6 tadpoles. All but 6 of the tadpoles grew to be frogs. Write a number sentence to show how many frogs the class has.

32. How many fossil kits with 12 samples each have the same number of fossils as 30 fossil kits with 8 samples each?

   A 20 fossil kits   **C** 200 fossil kits

   B 24 fossil kits   **D** 240 fossil kits

33. A ride on the Pike's Peak Cog Railway takes 75 minutes. If the train's average speed is 100 feet per minute, how long is the Pike's Peak Cog Railway?

34. In the United States, students spend about 900 hours per year in school. How many hours would a student spend in 12 years of school?

35. A roller coaster runs rides 50 times an hour and reaches speeds of 70 miles per hour. If each ride takes 8 rows of 4 people, how many people ride each hour?

   A 160 people

   B 1,500 people

   C 1,600 people

   D 2,240 people

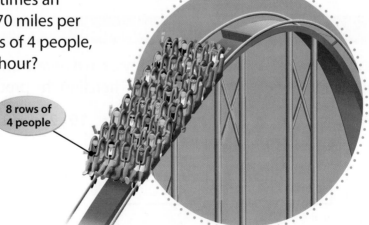

8 rows of 4 people

Understand It!
Partial products can be found to solve a multiplication problem.

Multiplying 2-Digit by 2-Digit Numbers

What is a common way to record multiplication?

A ferry carried an average of 37 cars per trip on Saturday. If the ferry made 24 one-way trips, how many cars did it carry?

Choose an Operation Multiply to join equal groups.

37 cars per trip

Guided Practice*

Do you know HOW?

In **1** through **6**, draw a diagram and fill it in with partial products. Then find the product.

1. 41
   × 23

2. 63
   × 31

3. 12
   × 27

4. 23
   × 36

5. 42
   × 18

6. 92
   × 34

Do you UNDERSTAND?

7. In the example above, is 888 a reasonable answer for 37 × 24?

8. **Writing to Explain** The ferry made 36 one-way trips on Sunday and carried an average of 21 cars on each trip.

   a How many cars were ferried on Sunday?

   b On which day were more cars ferried, Saturday or Sunday? Explain.

Independent Practice

Leveled Practice For **9** and **10**, copy each diagram and show the calculations for each partial product. Then find the product.

9. 18 × 33

	30	3
10	30 × 10 = 300	
8		3 × 8 = 24

10. 22 × 46

	40	6
20		
2		

For another example, see Set E on page 161.

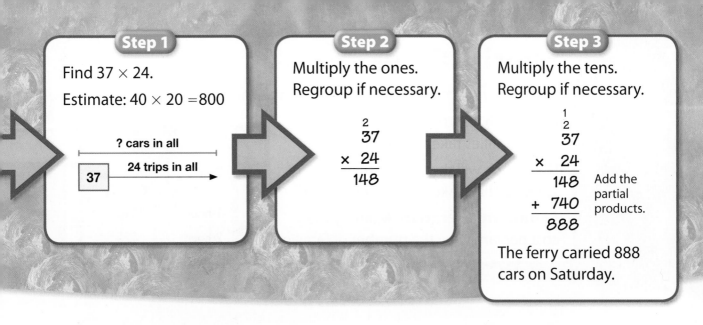

Step 1

Find 37 × 24.

Estimate: 40 × 20 = 800

? cars in all

37 | 24 trips in all →

Step 2

Multiply the ones.
Regroup if necessary.

$$\begin{array}{r} \overset{2}{37} \\ \times\ 24 \\ \hline 148 \end{array}$$

Step 3

Multiply the tens.
Regroup if necessary.

$$\begin{array}{r} \overset{1}{\overset{2}{37}} \\ \times\ 24 \\ \hline 148 \\ +\ 740 \\ \hline 888 \end{array}$$ Add the partial products.

The ferry carried 888 cars on Saturday.

In **11** through **20**, find the product.

11. 37
× 21

12. 54
× 37

13. 63
× 22

14. 34
× 41

15. 81
× 17

16. 56 × 31

17. 53 × 17

18. 81 × 46

19. 15 × 16

20. 17 × 21

21. Algebra Evaluate the expression $7 \times (15 + m)$ when $m = 31$.

  A 136   **C** 322

  B 232   **D** 682

22. Reasonableness Sara estimated 32 × 45 by using 30 × 40. How could Sara make a more accurate estimate?

23. Use the diagram to the right. The *Queen Mary 2's* height above the water is the same as a 23-story building. If a single story is 11 feet tall, how high above the water is the *Queen Mary 2*?

Each story is 11 feet tall.

23-story building   *Queen Mary 2*

24. Mr. Morris bought sketch pads for 24 of his students. Each pad contained 50 sheets. How many sheets of paper were there altogether?

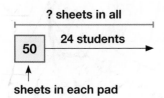

? sheets in all

50 | 24 students →

sheets in each pad

25. Geometry Jon's backyard is a rectangle that measures 32 feet by 44 feet. How many square feet is his backyard?

Tip *The area of a rectangle is length × width.*

Special Cases

How do you multiply greater numbers?

How much will the farm earn when 1,600 families take the one-hour tour?

How much will the farm earn when 2,000 families take the two-hour tour?

Choose an Operation Multiply the cost per family by the number of families.

Barrington Farm Tours	
Tours	**Cost per Family**
1-hour	$20
2-hour	$25

Guided Practice*

Do you know HOW?

In **1** through **6**, use mental math to find the product.

1. 100
     × 25

2. 200
     × 50

3. 3,000
     ×   30

4. 40,000
     ×   50

5. 30 × 600

6. 20 × 150

Do you UNDERSTAND?

7. Writing to Explain Why does the product of 25 × 2,000 have 4 zeros when 2,000 only has 3 zeros?

8. A school gets a special family pass of $20 for each of its 134 families. How much will the school families be charged altogether?

Independent Practice

In **9** through **28**, use mental math to find the product.

9.   240
      × 15

10.   440
       × 20

11. 9,000
       ×   60

12. 1,000
       ×   25

13.   170
       × 10

14. 1,500
       ×   40

15. 1,870
       ×   20

16. 20,000
       ×   40

17.   290
       × 20

18. 4,200
       ×   40

19. 5,000
       ×   70

20.   660
       × 40

21. 2,000
       ×   25

22. 1,200
       ×   80

23. 1,870
       ×   30

*For another example, see Set E on page 161.

Find 1,600 × 20.

Use mental math.

$$16 \times 2 = 32$$
$$1{,}600 \times 20 = 32{,}000$$

The farm will earn 32,000 from the 1-hour tours.

Find 2,000 × 25.

Use mental math.

$$25 \times 2 = 50$$
$$25 \times 2{,}000 = 50{,}000$$

The farm will earn $50,000 from the 2-hour tours.

24. $\begin{array}{r} 2{,}500 \\ \times\ \ \ \ 50 \\ \hline \end{array}$
25. $\begin{array}{r} 700 \\ \times\ \ 50 \\ \hline \end{array}$
26. $\begin{array}{r} 600 \\ \times\ \ 25 \\ \hline \end{array}$
27. $\begin{array}{r} 2{,}000 \\ \times\ \ \ \ 15 \\ \hline \end{array}$
28. $\begin{array}{r} 800 \\ \times\ \ 30 \\ \hline \end{array}$

Problem Solving

For **29** and **30**, use the table at the right.

29. In 2006, how many DVDs were rented in 52 weeks? How many DVDs were purchased in this same time?

30. In 2007, how many DVDs were rented? How many were purchased?

Videos-To-Go Sales Report (Weekly Averages)		
Year	DVDs Rented	DVDs Purchased
2006	100	800
2007	130	200

31. **Think About the Process** What are the partial products of 9 × 25?

   A $(9 \times 20) + (9 \times 5)$

   B $(9 \times 20) + (9 \times 25)$

   C $(20 \times 20) + (5 \times 5)$

   D $(3 \times 20) + (3 \times 5)$

32. A school buys 43 flat-screen computer monitors for $270 each. What is the total amount of the purchase?

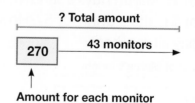

Amount for each monitor

33. **Algebra** What is the value of the expression $\$752 + (\$20 \times t)$ if $t = 125$?

Understand It!
A solution to one question can help you solve two-question problems.

Problem Solving

Two-Question Problems

Problem 1: Maya and Jose are preparing for a bike race. On Wednesday, they rode their bicycles 32 miles in the morning and 22 miles in the afternoon. How many miles did they ride in all?

Problem 2: Maya and Jose bicycled the same number of miles on Wednesday, Thursday, Friday, and Saturday. How far did they ride during the week?

Rode the same distance 4 days in a row

Guided Practice*

Do you know HOW?

Solve.

1. **Problem 1:** Julia used 3 rolls of film to take pictures on her vacation. There were 24 pictures on each roll. How many pictures did Julia take?

   Problem 2: It costs Julia 10¢ to print each picture. How much would it cost Julia to print every picture?

Do you UNDERSTAND?

2. Why do you need to know how many pictures Julia took to solve Problem 2?

3. **Write a Problem** Write a problem that uses the answer from Problem 1 below.

   Problem 1: Cal puts one vase on each of 5 tables. There are 6 flowers in each vase. How many flowers does Cal use?

Independent Practice

Solve. Use the answer from Problem 1 to solve Problem 2.

4. **Problem 1:** Martin buys a sandwich for $4, an apple for $1, and a drink for $2. How much did he pay altogether?

   ? Cost of Martin's lunch

$4	$1	$2

   Problem 2: How much change did Martin receive if he paid with a $20 bill?

   $20

Lunch	Change

Stuck? Try this....

- What do I know?
- What diagram can I use to help understand the problem?
- Can I use addition, subtraction, multiplication, or division?
- Is all of my work correct?
- Did I answer the right question?
- Is my answer reasonable?

For another example, see Set F on page 161.

Sometimes you have to answer one problem to solve another problem.

? miles bicycled on Wednesday

32	22

32 miles + 22 miles = 54 miles

Maya and Jose bicycled 54 miles on Wednesday.

Use the answer from Problem 1 to solve Problem 2.

? miles bicycled during the week

54	54	54	54

↑ Miles each day

4 × 54 miles = 216 miles

Maya and Jose rode 216 miles during the week.

---

5. **Problem 1:** Sally and Byron mow their neighbors' lawns in the summer. Sally mows 5 lawns each week. Byron mows three times as many lawns as Sally. How many lawns does Byron mow each week?

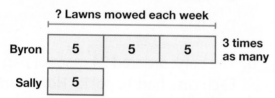

? Lawns mowed each week

| Byron | 5 | 5 | 5 | 3 times as many |
| Sally | 5 | | | |

Problem 2: Byron gets paid $20 for each lawn he mows. How much does Byron get paid each week?

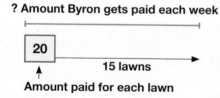

? Amount Byron gets paid each week

20

↑ Amount paid for each lawn

15 lawns

6. **Problem 1:** June's mom brought 3 bags of popcorn and 3 bottles of water to the park. How many bags of popcorn and bottles of water did June's mom take to the park?

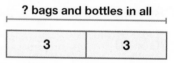

? bags and bottles in all

3	3

Problem 2: Each bag of popcorn that June's mom brought to the park contained 16 servings. How many servings of popcorn did June's mom bring to the park?

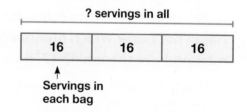

? servings in all

16	16	16

↑ Servings in each bag

7. **Problem 1:** Sydney made wooden penguins to sell at a fair. She used 5 pompoms and 4 beads for each penguin. How many pompoms and beads are there all together on each wooden penguin?

Problem 2: Sydney made 21 wooden penguins. How many pompoms and beads did she use for the wooden penguins altogether?

8. **Problem 1:** Dave plans to retile his porch floor. He wants to buy 25 black tiles and 23 white tiles. How many tiles will he buy in all?

Problem 2: Each tile he plans to use is one square foot. Each tile costs 2 dollars. How much money will it cost to retile his porch floor?

1. To find 30 × 700, Scott first found 3 × 7 = 21. How many zeros should Scott include in the product? (7-1)

   A 1

   B 2

   C 3

   D 4

2. There are 27 schools participating in the regional band competition. Each school brought 38 band members. Which shows the best way to estimate how many band members are in the competition? (7-2)

   A 20 × 30

   B 20 × 40

   C 25 × 40

   D 30 × 30

3. Telly has 15 pages in her coin collector's book. Each page has 32 coins. Telly is using the table below to calculate how many coins she has in her book. Which number is missing from the table? (7-3)

	10	5
30	300	
2	20	10

   A 15

   B 150

   C 315

   D 480

4. Which partial products can be used to find 35 × 64? (7-5)

   A 140 and 210

   B 140 and 2,100

   C 120 and 2,100

   D 140 and 1,800

5. There are 16 ounces in a pound. Which is the best estimate of the number of ounces a 97 pound dog weighs? (7-2)

   A 160

   B 900

   C 1,600

   D 9,000

6. The bank ordered 24 cases of paper. Each case had 10 packs. How many packs of paper did the bank order? (7-4)

   A 240

   B 250

   C 2,400

   D 2,500

7. Mr. Taylor installed 10 dozen tiles on his kitchen floor. Each tile cost $3. How much did Mr. Taylor spend, before tax? (7-7)

   A $390

   B $360

   C $300

   D $108

8. The school district bought 95 new microscopes. Each microscope cost $52. How much did the district spend? (7-5)

   A $4,940

   B $4,930

   C $4,240

   D $655

9. Which pair best completes the number sentence? (7-1)

   ◼ × 100 = ◼

   A 300 and 3,000

   B 30 and 30,000

   C 30 and 3,000

   D 30 and 300

10. Tom's goal is to learn 15 new words each day. At the end of day 40, how many new words will Tom have learned? (7-4)

   A 55

   B 400

   C 450

   D 600

11. An amusement park sold 500 adult admission tickets. Each adult ticket cost $30. What is the total cost of the adult tickets? (7-6)

   A $800

   B $1,500

   C $8,000

   D $15,000

12. What is 15×29? (7-3)

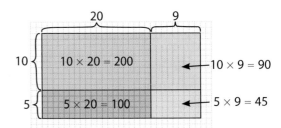

   A 535

   B 435

   C 390

   D 335

13. If 82 seats on a flight were sold for $89 each, about how much money did the airline make? (7-2)

   A $7,200

   B $8,200

   C $9,200

   D $11,000

14. Which shows one way to use partial products to find 60×78? (7-4)

   A $(30 \times 70) + (30 \times 8)$

   B $(60 \times 70) + (60 \times 80)$

   C $(60 \times 70) + (60 \times 78)$

   D $(60 \times 70) + (60 \times 8)$

15. There are 42 cases on display. Each case has 16 insects. How many insects are on display? (7-5)

   A 7

   B 26

   C 58

   D 672

Set A, pages 142–143

Use mental math to find 26 × 300.

You can think about the pattern.

26 × 3 = 78

26 × 30 = 780

26 × 300 = 7,800

Remember that when a product of a basic fact ends in zero, there is one more zero in the answer.

1. 4 × 10   **2.** 7 × 1,000

3. 80 × 600   **4.** 50 × 4,000

5. 3 × 900   **6.** 600 × 10

Set B, pages 144–145

Use rounding to estimate 16 × 24.

Round 24 to 20.

Round 16 to 20.

20 × 20 = 400

Remember you can also use compatible numbers to estimate.

1. 41 × 54   **2.** 79 × 32

3. 64 × 86   **4.** 32 × 71

Set C, pages 146–149

Find 14 × 12. Draw a 14 × 12 array.

Separate each factor into tens and ones. Color each section a different color. Add each part to find the product.

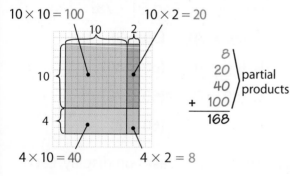

Remember you can solve the simpler problems in any order and the answer will remain the same.

Find the product. Use partial products to help.

1. 14 × 32   **2.** 64 × 12

3. 56 × 17   **4.** 72 × 15

5. 26 × 63   **6.** 47 × 27

Set D, pages 150–151

Find 16 × 30. Multiply 16 × 3 tens.

$$\begin{array}{r} \overset{1}{16} \\ \times\ 30 \\ \hline 480 \end{array}$$

The 0 in the ones places shows how many tens are in the answer.

Remember to record a 0 in the ones place of the answer.

1. 39 × 10   **2.** 56 × 30

3. 41 × 20   **4.** 60 × 13

Set E, pages 152–153 and 154–155

Find 19 × 14.

Multiply the ones.
Regroup if necessary.

$$\begin{array}{r} {\scriptstyle 3} \\ 19 \\ \times\ 14 \\ \hline 76 \end{array}$$

Multiply the tens.
Regroup if necessary.

$$\begin{array}{r} 19 \\ \times\ 14 \\ \hline 76 \\ +\ 190 \\ \hline 266 \end{array}$$

Remember to regroup if necessary.

1.
$$\begin{array}{r} 53 \\ \times\ 36 \\ \hline \end{array}$$

2.
$$\begin{array}{r} 23 \\ \times\ 18 \\ \hline \end{array}$$

3.
$$\begin{array}{r} 73 \\ \times\ 33 \\ \hline \end{array}$$

4.
$$\begin{array}{r} 31 \\ \times\ 74 \\ \hline \end{array}$$

5. 56 × 64

6. 39 × 82

7. 700 × 40

8. 420 × 20

9. 250 × 30

10. 6,000 × 15

Set F, pages 156–157

When you solve two-question problems, solve the first problem, and use that answer to help you solve the second problem.

Problem 1: It costs $3 for a ticket to the pool and $7 for a ticket to the water park. How much does it cost for 4 people to go to each?

Cost of 4 pool tickets:
4 × $3 = $12

Cost of 4 water park tickets:
4 × $7 = $28

Problem 2: How much more does it cost the group of 4 to go to the water park than to the pool?

28 − 12 = 16

It costs $16 more.

Remember to use the information from Problem 1 to answer Problem 2.

Solve.

Problem 1: Rose visited 14 cities on her vacation. She bought 3 souvenirs in each city to send to her friends. How many souvenirs did Rose buy on her vacation?

Problem 2: It costs Rose $2 to send each souvenir to her friends. How much did it cost Rose to send all of the souvenirs that she bought on vacation?

Dividing by 1-Digit Divisors

1 Where was the world's largest American flag displayed? You will find out in Lesson 8-6.

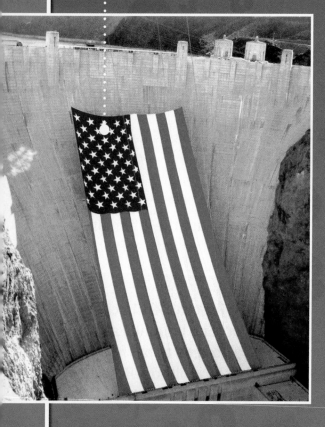

2 Selenium is an element found in certain materials, such as these selenite crystals. It is often used to conduct electricity. Some of the tallest selenite crystals are found in Chihuahua, Mexico. Find out how many times taller they are than a 4-foot-tall fourth grader in Lesson 8-5.

3 How many solar cells does it take to power a solar car? You will find out in Lesson 8-1.

4

How long does it take the International Space Station to orbit Earth one time? You will find out in Lesson 8-2.

Review What You Know!

Vocabulary

Choose the best term from the box.

- array
- compatible numbers
- factors
- partial product

1. An arrangement of objects in rows and columns is called a(n) ? .

2. When multiplying a two-digit number by a two-digit number, a ? is found by multiplying the first factor by the ones of the second factor.

3. Numbers that are easy to compute mentally are called ? .

Division Facts

Divide.

4. 15 ÷ 3   **5.** 64 ÷ 8   **6.** 72 ÷ 8

7. 35 ÷ 7   **8.** 12 ÷ 4   **9.** 45 ÷ 9

Multiplying by 10 and 100

Find each product.

10. 62 × 10   **11.** 24 × 100   **12.** 65 × 100

13. 14 × 10   **14.** 35 × 100   **15.** 59 × 10

Arrays

16. Write a multiplication problem for the array at the right.

17. **Writing to Explain** Is an array for 4 × 3 the same or different from the array shown above? Explain.

Lesson

8-1

Understand It!
Use basic facts and
place-value patterns
to find the quotient.

Using Mental Math to Divide

How can you use patterns to help you divide mentally?

Mr. Díaz ordered a supply of 320 pastels.
He needs to divide them equally among
four art classes. How many pastels
does each class get?

320 pastels

Choose an Operation
Division is used to make equal groups.

Guided Practice*

Do you know HOW?

In **1** and **2**, use patterns to find each
quotient.

1. $28 \div 7 =$ ▢
   $280 \div 7 =$ ▢
   $2,800 \div 7 =$ ▢
   $28,000 \div 7 =$ ▢

2. $64 \div 8 =$ ▢
   $640 \div 8 =$ ▢
   $6,400 \div 8 =$ ▢
   $64,000 \div 8 =$ ▢

Do you UNDERSTAND?

3. How is dividing 320 by 4 like
   dividing 32 by 4?

4. José orders 240 binders and divides
   them equally among the 4 classes.
   How many binders will each class
   get? What basic fact did you use?

Independent Practice

Leveled Practice In **5** through **8**, use patterns to find each quotient.

5. $36 \div 9 =$ ▢
   $360 \div 9 =$ ▢
   $3,600 \div 9 =$ ▢
   $36,000 \div 9 =$ ▢

6. $10 \div 2 =$ ▢
   $100 \div 2 =$ ▢
   $1,000 \div 2 =$ ▢
   $10,000 \div 2 =$ ▢

7. $45 \div 5 =$ ▢
   $450 \div 5 =$ ▢
   $4,500 \div 5 =$ ▢
   $45,000 \div 5 =$ ▢

8. $24 \div 8 =$ ▢
   $240 \div 8 =$ ▢
   $2,400 \div 8 =$ ▢
   $24,000 \div 8 =$ ▢

For **9** through **23**, use mental math to divide.

9. $200 \div 5$

10. $360 \div 4$

11. $540 \div 9$

12. $160 \div 4$

13. $160 \div 2$

14. $900 \div 3$

15. $320 \div 8$

16. $360 \div 6$

17. $180 \div 3$

18. $210 \div 7$

19. $720 \div 8$

20. $500 \div 5$

21. $350 \div 7$

22. $630 \div 9$

23. $480 \div 6$

*For another example, see Set A on page 190.

Find 320 ÷ 4.

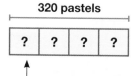

320 pastels

| ? | ? | ? | ? |

↑
pastels for each class

The basic fact is 32 ÷ 4 = 8.

32 tens ÷ 4 = 8 tens or 80.
320 ÷ 4 = 80

Each class will get 80 pastels.

Mr. Díaz wants to divide 400 erasers among 8 classes. How many erasers will each class get?

Find 400 ÷ 8.

The basic fact is 40 ÷ 8.

40 tens ÷ 8 = 5 tens or 50.
400 ÷ 8 = 50

Each class will get 50 erasers.

Problem Solving

24. Number Sense Selena used a basic fact to help solve 180 ÷ 6. What basic fact did Selena use?

25. There are 52 weeks in 1 year. How many years are equivalent to 520 weeks?

26. At the North American Solar Challenge, teams use up to 1,000 solar cells to design and build solar cars for a race. If there are 810 solar cells in rows of 9, how many solar cells are in each row?

9 rows of solar cells

27. A bakery produced 37 loaves of bread an hour. How many loaves were produced in 4 hours?

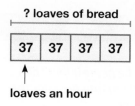

? loaves of bread

| 37 | 37 | 37 | 37 |

↑
loaves an hour

28. On Saturday afternoon, 350 people attended a play. The seating was arranged in 7 equal rows. How many people sat in each row? How do you know?

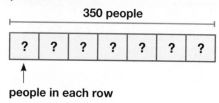

350 people

| ? | ? | ? | ? | ? | ? | ? |

↑
people in each row

29. Each row of seats in a stadium has 32 chairs. If the first 3 rows are completely filled, how many people are in the first 3 rows?

  A 9 people   **C** 96 people

  B 10 people   **D** 256 people

30. Writing to Explain If you know that 20 ÷ 5 = 4, how does that fact help you find 200 ÷ 5?

Lesson
8-2

Understand It!
There are different ways
to estimate quotients.

Estimating Quotients

When and how do you estimate quotients to solve problems?

700 rubber bands

Max wants to make 9 rubber-band balls. He bought a jar of 700 rubber bands. Estimate to find about how many rubber bands he can use for each ball.

Guided Practice*

Do you know HOW?

In **1** through **6**, estimate each quotient. Use multiplication or compatible numbers.

1. 48 ÷ 5

2. 235 ÷ 8

3. 547 ÷ 6

4. 192 ÷ 5

5. 662 ÷ 8

6. 362 ÷ 3

Do you UNDERSTAND?

7. Writing to Explain Is an estimate or exact answer needed for the problem below?

Max bought two jars of rubber bands for $4.65 each. How much did he spend?

8. Reasonableness Max decides to use the 700 rubber bands to make 8 balls. Is it reasonable to say that each ball would contain about 90 rubber bands?

Independent Practice

Leveled Practice In **9** through **28**, estimate the quotient.

 First round to the nearest ten. Then try multiples of ten that are near the rounded number.

9. 430 ÷ 9

10. 620 ÷ 7

11. 138 ÷ 5

12. 232 ÷ 6

13. 172 ÷ 3

14. 342 ÷ 8

15. 652 ÷ 6

16. 599 ÷ 9

17. 813 ÷ 8

18. 326 ÷ 4

19. 637 ÷ 6

20. 841 ÷ 2

21. 747 ÷ 8

22. 232 ÷ 9

23. 387 ÷ 4

24. 552 ÷ 7

25. 527 ÷ 5

26. 392 ÷ 2

27. 625 ÷ 3

28. 921 ÷ 3

Use compatible numbers.

What number close to 700 is easily divided by 9?

Try multiples of ten near 700.

   710 is not easily divided by 9.

   720 is 72 tens and can be divided by 9.

   $720 \div 9 = 80$

A good estimate is about 80 rubber bands for each ball.

A rounded solution is all that is needed. Max does not need to know the exact number of rubber bands to use for each ball.

Use multiplication.

9 times what number is about 700?

$9 \times 8 = 72,$
so $9 \times 80 = 720.$

$700 \div 9$ is about 80.

Problem Solving

Use the chart at the right for **29** and **30**.

29. Ada sold her mugs in 3 weeks. About how many did she sell each week?

30. Ben sold his mugs in 4 weeks. About how many did he sell each week?

Mugs Sold in Fundraiser
Each Mug = 50 mugs

Ada

Ben

31. Number Sense Tony's truck can safely carry 3,000 pounds. He has 21 televisions that he needs to deliver. Each television weighs 95 pounds.

  a Can Tony safely carry all of the televisions in his truck?

  b Is an exact answer needed or is an estimate needed? Explain.

32. Writing to Explain Copy and complete by filling in the circle with > or <. Without dividing, explain how you know which quotient is greater.

  $930 \div 4$ ◯ $762 \div 4$

33. The International Space Station takes 644 minutes to orbit Earth 7 times. About how long does each orbit take?

  A 80 minutes

  B 90 minutes

  C 95 minutes

  D 100 minutes

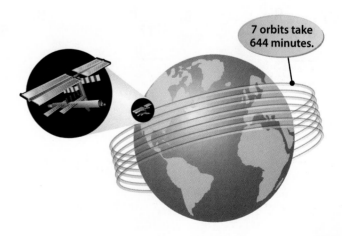

7 orbits take 644 minutes.

Lesson 8-3

Understand It!
Sometimes in division, there are some left over.

Dividing with Remainders

Hands-On
counters

What happens when some are left?

Maria has 20 pepper plants to place in 3 rows. She has to plant the same number in each row. How many plants will go in each row? How many are left over?

3 rows of plants

Guided Practice*

Do you know HOW?

In **1** through **4**, use counters or draw pictures. Tell how many items are in each group and how many are left over.

1. 26 pens
5 groups

2. 34 cars
7 boxes

3. 30 marbles
4 bags

4. 40 balls
6 bins

Do you UNDERSTAND?

5. Writing to Explain When you divide a number by 6, what remainders are possible?

6. Tia is planting her garden with 15 plants. She wants them planted in equal groups of 4. How many groups of 4 can she make? How many plants will she have left over?

Independent Practice

Leveled Practice In **7** through **14**, copy and then complete the calculations. Use counters or pictures to help.

 The remainder should always be less than the divisor.

7. 8)35 R

8. 3)17 R

9. 9)51 R

10. 5)48 R

11. 6)47 R

12. 7)65 R

13. 9)77 R

14. 4)30 R

DIGITAL Animated Glosssary, eTools
www.pearsonsuccessnet.com

168 *For another example, see Set C on page 191.*

Divide 20 counters among 3 rows.

$3 \times 6 = 18$ counters

The part that is left after dividing is called the remainder.

There are 2 counters left over. This is not enough for another row, so the remainder is 2.

Check your answer.

$$\begin{array}{r} 6\ \text{R}2 \\ 3\overline{)20} \\ -18 \\ \hline 2 \end{array}$$

Divide: 3 groups of 6 in 20
Multiply: $3 \times 6 = 18$
Subtract: $20 - 18 = 2$
Compare: $2 < 3$

$3 \times 6 = 18$, and $18 + 2 = 20$

Maria can plant 6 plants in each row. She will have 2 plants left over.

In **15** through **29**, divide. You may use counters or pictures to help.

15. $3\overline{)29}$ **16.** $7\overline{)41}$ **17.** $9\overline{)55}$ **18.** $8\overline{)62}$ **19.** $5\overline{)37}$

20. $7\overline{)45}$ **21.** $4\overline{)22}$ **22.** $6\overline{)28}$ **23.** $8\overline{)33}$ **24.** $8\overline{)75}$

25. $9\overline{)86}$ **26.** $6\overline{)34}$ **27.** $7\overline{)39}$ **28.** $5\overline{)23}$ **29.** $8\overline{)61}$

Problem Solving

30. Algebra If $69 \div 9 = n$ R6, what is the value of n?

31. How many craft sticks are left if 9 friends equally share a package of 85 craft sticks?

32. Write a division sentence with a quotient of 7 and remainder of 3.

33. Number Sense When you divide by 3, can the remainder be 5?

34. Reasonableness Carl's teacher took 27 photos on their class trip. She wants to arrange them on the wall in 4 equal rows. Carl said if she does this, she will have 7 photos left over. Is this reasonable?

35. Writing to Explain Jim has 46 compact discs. He wants to buy 5 cases that hold 8 discs. Explain why Jim needs to buy 6 cases to hold his 46 compact discs.

36. Think About the Process Jack helped Mrs. Sanchez pack 61 books in 7 boxes. Each box held 8 books. Which expression shows how to find how many books he had left?

A $61 - (7 + 8)$ **C** $61 + (7 \times 8)$
B $61 - (7 \times 8)$ **D** $61 + (7 + 8)$

37. At the school concert, there were 560 people seated in 8 rows. If there were no empty seats, how many people were in each row?

A 553 people **C** 70 people
B 480 people **D** 60 people

Lesson

8-4

. . . .

Understand It!
A quotient can be found
by using place value.

Connecting Models and Symbols

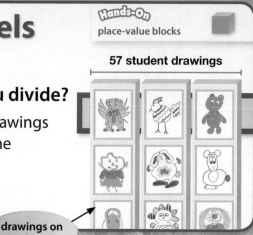

Hands-On
place-value blocks

How can place value help you divide?

Mrs. Lynch displayed 57 student drawings on 3 walls in her art classroom. If she divided the drawings equally, how many drawings are on each wall?

Estimate: $60 \div 3 = 20$

57 student drawings

drawings on each wall

Another Example How do you model remainders?

Helen has 55 postcards. As an art project, she plans to glue 4 postcards onto sheets of colored paper.

How many pieces of paper can she fill?

Step 1 Divide the tens.

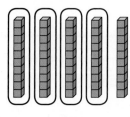

Division is used to find the number of equal groups.

$$\begin{array}{r} 1 \\ 4\overline{)55} \\ -4 \\ \hline 1 \end{array}$$

There is 1 ten in each group and 1 ten left over.

Step 2 Regroup the 1 ten as 10 ones and divide.

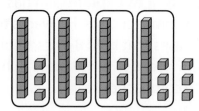

$$\begin{array}{r} 13\ R3 \\ 4\overline{)55} \\ -4 \\ \hline 15 \\ -12 \\ \hline 3 \end{array}$$

Trade the extra ten for ten ones.

The 1 ten and 5 ones make 15.

There are 3 ones in each group and 3 left over.

Helen will fill 13 pieces of colored paper.

Explain It

1. In the first step above, what does the 1 in the quotient represent?

2. **Reasonableness** How can you check that the answer is correct?

Use place-value blocks to show 57.	Trade the extra tens for ones.	Divide the ones.

Divide the tens into three equal groups.

$$\begin{array}{r} 1 \\ 3\overline{)57} \\ -3 \end{array}$$ 3 tens used

$$\begin{array}{r} 1 \\ 3\overline{)57} \\ -3 \\ \hline 27 \end{array}$$ 3 tens used
27 ones left

$$\begin{array}{r} 19 \\ 3\overline{)57} \\ -3 \\ \hline 27 \\ -27 \\ \hline 0 \end{array}$$ 27 ones used

There are 19 drawings on each wall.

Guided Practice*

Do you know HOW?

In **1** through **4**, use place-value blocks or draw pictures. Tell how many are in each group and how many are left over.

1. 76 magazines
5 boxes

2. 56 marbles
3 bags

3. 82 muffins
7 boxes

4. 72 photos
3 albums

Do you UNDERSTAND?

5. Describe another way to show 57 using place-value blocks.

6. Mrs. Lynch displayed 48 paintings in 3 sets. If each set had the same number of paintings, how many were in each set?

Independent Practice

Leveled Practice In **7** through **10**, use the model to complete each division sentence.

7. 71 ÷ ▢ = ▢ R2

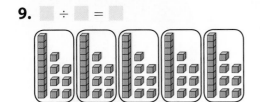

8. ▢ ÷ 4 = ▢

9. ▢ ÷ ▢ = ▢

10. ▢ ÷ ▢ = ▢ R ▢

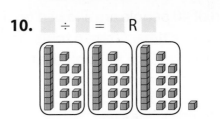

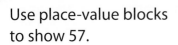

eTools
www.pearsonsuccessnet.com
DIGITAL

*For another example, see Set D on page 191.

Lesson 8-4

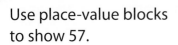

171

Independent Practice

In **11** through **30**, use place-value blocks or draw pictures to solve.

11. 3)46   **12.** 8)96   **13.** 4)55   **14.** 2)51   **15.** 5)89

16. 6)76   **17.** 7)36   **18.** 3)72   **19.** 2)63   **20.** 4)92

21. 3)44   **22.** 4)67   **23.** 6)85   **24.** 3)56   **25.** 5)97

26. 2)39   **27.** 4)31   **28.** 5)87   **29.** 7)82   **30.** 5)22

Problem Solving

31. Maya used place-value blocks to divide 87. She made groups of 17 with 2 left over. Use place-value blocks or draw pictures to determine how many groups Maya made.

32. Writing to Explain Harold has 64 toy cars in 4 equal boxes. To find the number in each box, he divided 64 by 4. How many tens did he regroup as ones?

33. **Think About the Process** Jake walks dogs and delivers papers to earn money. This month, he earned $52 delivering papers and $43 walking dogs. Each month, he puts half of his money into the bank. Which shows how much Jake saved this month?

    A $(52 + 43) + 2$ **C** $(52 + 43) \div 2$

    B $(52 + 43) \times 2$ **D** $(52 + 43) - 2$

34. Number Sense Tina has 50 berries. She wants to have some each day for lunch. How many berries can she have each day if she wants to eat them all in 5 days?

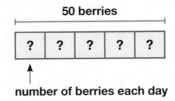

number of berries each day

35. The 4 fourth-grade classes from Jameson Elementary School took a trip to the United States Capitol. Each class had 24 students. At the Capitol, the students were divided into 6 equal groups. How many students were in each group?

36. A maximum of 40 people are allowed on a tour of the Capitol at one time. After 16 tours, how many people could have gone through the Capitol?

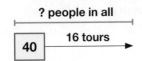

Enrichment

Dividing by Multiples of 10

Patterns can be used when dividing by multiples of 10. It is easy to divide mentally using basic facts and place-value patterns.

Examples:

$7\overline{)21} = 3$

$7\overline{)210} = 30$

$7\overline{)2,100} = 300$

$7\overline{)21,000} = 3,000$

As the number of zeros in the dividend increase, the number of zeros in the quotient increase by the same amount.

$4\overline{)20} = 5$

$40\overline{)200} = 5$

$400\overline{)2,000} = 5$

$4,000\overline{)20,000} = 5$

The number of zeros in the dividend and divisor increase by the same amount, and the quotient remains the same as in the basic fact.

Practice

For **1** through **12**, divide. Use mental math.

1. $30\overline{)90}$

2. $90\overline{)6,300}$

3. $2\overline{)8,000}$

4. $900\overline{)4,500}$

5. $80\overline{)560}$

6. $8\overline{)7,200}$

7. $200\overline{)1,400}$

8. $70\overline{)4,200}$

9. $7\overline{)350}$

10. $20\overline{)120}$

11. $70\overline{)2,800}$

12. $400\overline{)1,600}$

13. **Number Sense** Name another division problem with the same answer as $90\overline{)3,600}$.

14. **Number Sense** How is dividing 490 by 7 like dividing 49,000 by 700?

15. A science museum has 2,400 gemstones displayed equally in 30 cases. How many gemstones are in each case?

16. Ryan has a collection of 1,800 stickers. He wants to put them in equal groups into 20 sticker albums. How many stickers will be in each album?

Lesson

8-5

Understand It!
Find 2-digit quotients by breaking apart the problem and dividing tens, then ones.

Dividing 2-Digit by 1-Digit Numbers

What is a common way to record division?

At the school food drive, Al needs to put the same number of soup cans into four boxes. How many soup cans will go in each box?

Choose an Operation Divide to find the number in each group.

76 cans of soup in all

Another Example How do you divide with a remainder?

Al collects 58 cans of vegetables. He puts the same number of cans in four boxes. How many cans of vegetables will go in each box? How many cans will be left over?

A 14 cans, 2 cans left over

B 15 cans, 2 cans left over

C 16 cans, 2 cans left over

D 18 cans, 2 cans left over

Step 1

Divide the tens.

Regroup the remaining ten as 10 ones.

$$\begin{array}{r} 1 \\ 4\overline{)58} \\ -4 \\ \hline 1 \end{array}$$

Step 2

Divide the ones.

Subtract to find the remainder.

$$\begin{array}{r} 14 \\ 4\overline{)58} \\ -4 \\ \hline 18 \\ -16 \\ \hline 2 \end{array}$$

Step 3

Check: $14 \times 4 = 56$ and $56 + 2 = 58$.

There will be 14 cans of vegetables in each box and 2 cans left over.

The correct choice is **A**.

Explain It

1. **Reasonableness** How can you use estimation to decide if 14 cans is reasonable?

2. Why is multiplication used to check division?

Step 1

Divide the tens.

$$\begin{array}{r} 1 \\ 4\overline{)76} \\ -4 \\ \hline 3 \end{array}$$

Think There is **1** ten in each group and **3** tens left over.

Step 2

Divide the ones.

$$\begin{array}{r} 19 \\ 4\overline{)76} \\ -4 \\ \hline 36 \\ -36 \\ \hline 0 \end{array}$$

Think Trade the 3 tens for 30 ones.

30 ones and 6 ones make **36** ones.

There will be 19 soup cans in each box.

Step 3

Check by multiplying.

$$\begin{array}{r} 3 \\ 19 \\ \times\ 4 \\ \hline 76 \end{array}$$

The answer checks.

Guided Practice*

Do you know HOW?

In **1** and **2**, copy and complete each calculation.

1.
$$\begin{array}{r} 4 \\ 2\overline{)94} \\ -\ \blacksquare \\ \hline 4 \\ -1\blacksquare \\ \hline 0 \end{array}$$

2.
$$\begin{array}{r} 6R \\ 5\overline{)82} \\ -\ 5 \\ \hline \blacksquare\blacksquare \\ -\ \blacksquare\blacksquare \\ \hline \blacksquare \end{array}$$

Do you UNDERSTAND?

3. Explain how you would estimate the answer in Exercise 2.

4. Al collects 85 cans of fruit. He puts the same number of fruit cans in 4 boxes. Will he have any cans left over? If so, how many cans?

Independent Practice

Leveled Practice In **5** through **8**, copy and complete each calculation. Estimate to check reasonableness.

5.
$$\begin{array}{r} \blacksquare\blacksquare \\ 7\overline{)84} \\ -\ 7 \\ \hline 4 \\ -\ \blacksquare\blacksquare \\ \hline 0 \end{array}$$

6.
$$\begin{array}{r} 6 \\ 3\overline{)78} \\ -\ \blacksquare \\ \hline 8 \\ -1\blacksquare \\ \hline 0 \end{array}$$

7.
$$\begin{array}{r} \blacksquare\ R \\ 4\overline{)93} \\ -\ 8 \\ \hline \blacksquare\blacksquare \\ -1\blacksquare \\ \hline 1 \end{array}$$

8.
$$\begin{array}{r} 1\ R \\ 6\overline{)80} \\ -\ \blacksquare \\ \hline \blacksquare\blacksquare \\ -\ \blacksquare\blacksquare \\ \hline \blacksquare \end{array}$$

For **9** through **18**, find each quotient. Use multiplication to check.

9. $3\overline{)63}$ **10.** $7\overline{)88}$ **11.** $6\overline{)96}$ **12.** $4\overline{)52}$ **13.** $5\overline{)73}$

14. $5\overline{)93}$ **15.** $3\overline{)87}$ **16.** $4\overline{)72}$ **17.** $6\overline{)77}$ **18.** $2\overline{)37}$

For another example, see Set E on page 191.

In **19** through **28**, find each quotient. Use multiplication to check.

19. $3\overline{)46}$ **20.** $7\overline{)65}$ **21.** $8\overline{)27}$ **22.** $9\overline{)86}$ **23.** $4\overline{)66}$

24. $8\overline{)59}$ **25.** $4\overline{)92}$ **26.** $3\overline{)74}$ **27.** $5\overline{)68}$ **28.** $2\overline{)89}$

Problem Solving

29. Some of the tallest selenite crystals in a cave in Chihuahua, Mexico, are 50 feet tall. About how many times taller are the tallest crystals than a 4-foot-tall fourth grader?

30. Geometry Zelda has a piece of fabric that is 74 inches long. She wants to divide it into 2 equal pieces. What is the length of each piece?

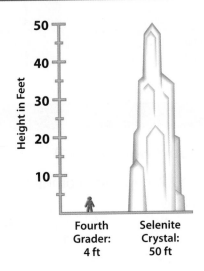

Height in Feet

Fourth Grader: 4 ft

Selenite Crystal: 50 ft

Use the recipe at the right for **31** and **32**.

31. How many ounces of Tasty Trail Mix are made following the recipe?

32. Maggie is making trail mix. She makes 4 batches of the recipe shown. Then she divides it into 3 equal sized bags. How many ounces are in each bag?

Tasty Trail Mix	
Granola	8 oz
Nuts	5 oz
Raisins	2 oz
Cranberries	3 oz

Data

33. Writing to Explain Why does $51 \div 4$ have two digits in the quotient, while $51 \div 6$ has only one digit in the quotient?

34. Write a Problem Write a problem that could be solved by dividing 78 by 5.

35. Estimation Paulo has 78 cattle on his ranch. He needs to divide them equally among 3 pastures. Which shows the best way to estimate the number of cattle in each pasture?

A $60 \div 3$ **C** $75 \div 3$

B $66 \div 3$ **D** $90 \div 3$

36. Every year, the city of San Marcos holds a Cinco de Mayo festival. If 60 students perform in 5 equal groups, how many students are in each group?

A 10 students   **C** 25 students

B 12 students   **D** 55 students

Enrichment

Venn Diagrams

A **Venn diagram** is a diagram that uses circles to show the relationships between groups of data. When the circles overlap, or **intersect**, the data belong to more than one group.

Example: Robin, Kevin, and Coreen are in the Math Club.

Sara, Callie, Mike, Brad, and Rachel are in the Science Club.

Gwen and Dan are in both clubs.

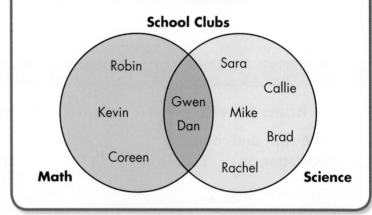

Practice

For **1** through **3**, use the Venn diagram to the right.

1. To which multiple does 24 belong?

2. Which numbers are multiples of both 3 and 5?

3. If you continued with the multiples, in which part of the Venn diagram would you place 48? 50? 60?

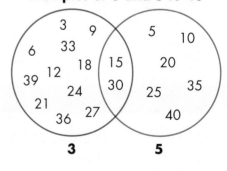

For **4** through **6**, use the Venn diagram to the right.

4. Which factors of 16 are also factors of 48?

5. Name the factors of 48 that are neither factors of 16 nor factors of 40.

6. Which numbers are factors of 16, 40, and 48?

7. Make a Venn diagram that uses two circles.

8. Make a Venn diagram that uses three circles.

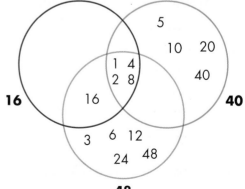

Dividing 3-Digit by 1-Digit Numbers

Understand It!
Larger numbers can be divided the same way as dividing smaller numbers.

How can you divide numbers in the hundreds?

A factory shipped 378 watches in 3 boxes. If the watches were equally divided, how many watches were there in each box?

Choose an Operation Divide to find the number in each group.

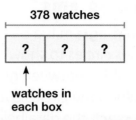

378 watches

| ? | ? | ? |

↑
watches in each box

Guided Practice*

Do you know HOW?

In **1** and **2**, copy and complete each calculation.

1.
```
   3
2)658
 -
 ───
 -
 ───
 -
 ───
```

2.
```
     R
4)954
 - 8
 ───
 -
 ───
 -
 ───
   2
```

Do you UNDERSTAND?

3. When you divide the hundreds in the first step above, what does the 1 in the quotient represent?

4. Jenny paid $195 to take violin lessons for 3 months. How much did 1 month of lessons cost?

$195

| ? | ? | ? |

↑ Cost for 1 month

Independent Practice

Leveled Practice In **5** through **13**, divide.
You may draw a picture to help you.

5.
```
   1
5)595
 -
 ───
 -
 ───
   4
 -
 ───
```

6.
```
2)832
 -
 ───
   3
 -
 ───
   2
 -
 ───
```

7.
```
   2   R
3)866
 -
 ───
 -
 ───
 -
 ───
```

8.
```
       R
4)575
 -
 ───
 -
 ───
 -
 ───
```

9. 4)952   10. 3)761   11. 5)615   12. 2)871   13. 3)638

Estimate:

$360 \div 3 = 120$

Divide the hundreds.

$$\begin{array}{r} 1 \\ 3\overline{)378} \\ -3 \\ \hline 7 \end{array}$$

Divide the tens.

$$\begin{array}{r} 12 \\ 3\overline{)378} \\ -3 \\ \hline 7 \\ -6 \\ \hline 1 \end{array}$$

Divide the ones.

$$\begin{array}{r} 126 \\ 3\overline{)378} \\ -3 \\ \hline 7 \\ -6 \\ \hline 18 \\ -18 \\ \hline 0 \end{array}$$

There are 126 watches in each box.

The answer is reasonable because 126 is close to 120.

Problem Solving

14. Geometry The largest United States flag ever created was displayed at the Hoover Dam. The flag measures 255 feet by 505 feet. How many feet longer is the flag than it is wide?

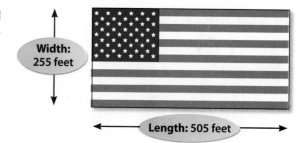

Width: 255 feet

Length: 505 feet

For **15** and **16**, use the table at the right.

15. There are 848 people getting on board the *Memphis Belle*. How many seats are needed for every person to sit?

16. Writing to Explain If 793 people are on the *Natchez Willie*, how many seats are needed for each person to sit?

Historic River Boat Tours

Natchez Willie	6 riders per seat
Memphis Belle	4 riders per seat

17. Algebra If $698 \div 4 = 174$ R ▢, what is the value of ▢?

18. The Galveston-Port Bolivar Ferry takes cars across Galveston Bay. One day, the ferry transported a total of 685 cars over a 5-hour period. If the ferry took the same number of cars each hour, how many cars did it take each hour?

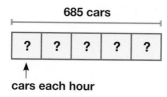

685 cars

?	?	?	?	?

↑ cars each hour

19. Theo bought a T-shirt for $21 and a pair of shorts for $16. He paid with two $20 bills. How much money did Theo get back?

A $1

B $2

C $3

D $4

Lesson
8-7

Understand It!
The first step to find
a quotient is deciding
where to start dividing.

Deciding Where to Start Dividing

What do you do when there aren't enough hundreds to divide?

Madison is making iguana key chains using pom-poms. She has 145 pink pom-poms. Are there enough pink pom-poms to make 36 key chains?

2 yellow pom-poms

4 pink pom-poms

7 blue pom-poms

31 green pom-poms

3 yards of plastic lace

4 pink pom-poms

Guided Practice*

Do you know HOW?

In **1** and **2**, copy and complete each calculation.

1.
```
     6
7)455
  -
     5
  -
```

2.
```
     R
5)319
  - 3
  -
```

Do you UNDERSTAND?

3. Madison has 365 blue pom-poms. How many key chains can she make?

4. Explain how an estimated quotient can help you decide where to start.

Independent Practice

Leveled Practice In **5** through **13**, divide. You may draw a picture to help you.

5.
```
6)444
 -
 -
```

6.
```
   1
3)588
 -
   8
 -
   8
 -
```

7.
```
   5 R
8)417
 -
 -
```

8.
```
     R
2)935
 - 8
 -
 -
```

9. 8)526

10. 5)690

11. 3)769

12. 4)923

13. 6)342

For another example, see Set G on page 192.

There are not enough hundreds to put one in each group.

Start by dividing the tens.

$$\begin{array}{r} 3 \\ 4\overline{)145} \\ -12 \\ \hline 25 \end{array}$$

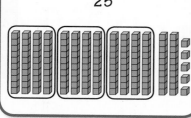

Divide the ones.

$$\begin{array}{r} 36 \text{ R1} \\ 4\overline{)145} \\ -12 \\ \hline 25 \\ -24 \\ \hline 1 \end{array}$$

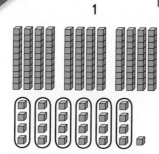

To check, multiply the quotient by the divisor and add the remainder.

$$\begin{array}{r} 2 \\ 36 \\ \times 4 \\ \hline 144 \end{array}$$

$144 + 1 = 145$

Madison has enough pink pom-poms to make 36 key chains.

In **14** through **23**, divide. Then check your answer.

14. $6\overline{)96}$ **15.** $5\overline{)295}$ **16.** $2\overline{)306}$ **17.** $9\overline{)517}$ **18.** $4\overline{)624}$

19. $7\overline{)430}$ **20.** $4\overline{)229}$ **21.** $5\overline{)655}$ **22.** $3\overline{)209}$ **23.** $6\overline{)438}$

Problem Solving

For **24** and **25**, use the bar graph at the right.

James is organizing his CDs. He plans to put them into stackable cubes that hold 8 CDs each.

24. How many cubes will James need for his entire collection?

25. If James decides to group his Rock and World music CDs together, how many cubes would he need for them?

26. Number Sense How can you tell without dividing that $479 \div 6$ will have a 2-digit quotient?

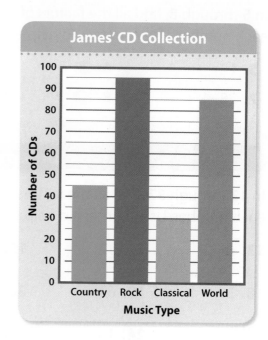

27. A family is going on a trip for 3 days. The total cost for the hotel is $336. They budgeted $100 a day for food. How much will each day of the trip cost?

    A $33   **B** $112   **C** $145   **D** $212

Lesson
8-8

Understand It!
Products can be broken down into many factors.

Factors

Hands-On
counters

How can you use multiplication to find all the factors of a number?

Jean has 16 action figures. She wants to arrange them in equal sized groupings around her room. What are the ways that Jean can arrange the action figures? Jean needs to think of all the factors of 16.

16 action figures

Guided Practice*

Do you know HOW?

In **1** through **4**, write each number as a product of two factors in two different ways.

1. 36   **2.** 42

3. 50   **4.** 64

In **5** through **8**, find all the factors of each number. Use counters to help.

5. 12   **6.** 20

7. 28   **8.** 54

Do you UNDERSTAND?

9. What factor does every even number have?

10. Writing to Explain Is 5 a factor of 16?

11. Jean got 2 more action figures. What are all the different equal groupings she can make now?

12. Jean's brother has 100 action figures. What are all of the factors for 100?

Independent Practice

In **13** through **32**, find all the factors of each number. Use counters to help.

Tip *For even numbers, remember 2 is always a factor.*

13. 6   **14.** 32   **15.** 45   **16.** 11   **17.** 36

18. 25   **19.** 63   **20.** 22   **21.** 51   **22.** 30

23. 14   **24.** 18   **25.** 27   **26.** 21   **27.** 40

28. 55   **29.** 39   **30.** 35   **31.** 29   **32.** 48

DIGITAL   eTools
www.pearsonsuccessnet.com

For another example, see Set H on page 192.

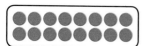

16 = 1 × 16

Jean can arrange
16 figures in 1 group
or
16 groups of 1 figure.

So, 1 and 16 are
factors of 16.

16 = 2 × 8

Jean can arrange
2 figures in 8 groups
or
2 groups of 8 figures.

So, 2 and 8 are
factors of 16.

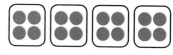

16 = 4 × 4

Jean can arrange
4 figures in 4 groups.

4 is a factor of 16.

The factors of 16 are
1, 2, 4, 8, and 16.

Problem Solving

33. As part of her science project, Shay is making a model of a California wind farm. She wants to put 24 turbines in her model. What arrays can she make using 24 turbines?

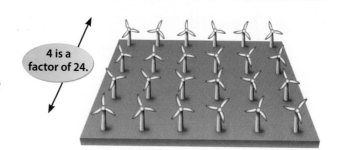

4 is a factor of 24.

34. Anita wants to include an array of 15 photos on her web site. Describe the arrays that she can make.

35. Which lists all the factors of 38?

   A 1, 38   **C** 1, 2, 38

   B 1, 2, 14, 38   **D** 1, 2, 19, 38

36. Number Sense Any number that has 9 as a factor also has 3 as a factor. Why is this?

37. Writing to Explain Which is greater, $\frac{3}{4}$ or 0.75?

38. The manatee is an endangered sea mammal. A mother manatee, pictured to the right, is three times as long as her baby. How long is the baby manatee?

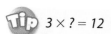 $3 \times ? = 12$

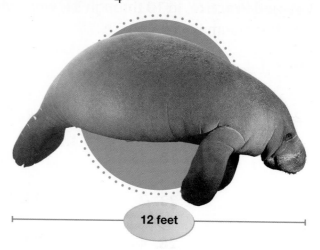

12 feet

Lesson
8-9

Understand It!
Knowing how many
factors a whole number
has can help tell if the
number is prime or
composite.

Prime and Composite Numbers

A prime number is a whole number greater than 1 that has exactly two factors, 1 and itself.

A composite number is a whole number greater than 1 that has more than two factors.

Data	Numbers	Factors
	2	1, 2
	3	1, 3
	4	1, 2, 4
	5	1, 5
	6	1, 2, 3, 6

Guided Practice*

Do you know HOW?

In **1** through **6**, tell whether each number is prime or composite.

1. 32

2. 41

3. 57

4. 21

5. 95

6. 103

Do you UNDERSTAND?

7. What is the only even prime number?

8. **Writing to Explain** Give an example of an odd number that is not prime. What makes it a composite number?

9. Roger has 47 cars. Can he group the cars in more than 2 ways?

Independent Practice

Leveled Practice In **10** through **31**, write whether each number is prime or composite.

10. 7 ⬚⬚⬚⬚⬚⬚

11. 9 ⬚⬚⬚⬚⬚⬚⬚⬚⬚   ⬚

12. 23

13. 33

14. 56

15. 67

16. 38

17. 58

18. 75

19. 101

20. 51

21. 300

22. 9

23. 2

24. 97

25. 1,900

26. 37

27. 11

28. 44

29. 1,204

30. 10

31. 59

DIGITAL
Animated Glossary
www.pearsonsuccessnet.com

For another example, see Set J on page 193.

Prime Numbers

The number 5 is a prime number. It has only two factors, 1 and itself.

$1 \times 5 = 5$

Composite Numbers

The number 6 is a composite number. Its factors are 1, 2, 3, and 6.

$1 \times 6 = 6$

$2 \times 3 = 6$

The number 1 is a special number. It is neither prime nor composite.

Problem Solving

For **32** and **33**, use the pictograph at the right.

32. Which type of flower did a prime number of people vote for?

33. How many votes are represented by the pictograph?

Favorite Flowers

Daffodils	
Daisies	
Tulips	

Key: Each flower icon equals 2 votes.

34. Which set of numbers below are all prime?

   A 1, 2, 7, 11, 25   **C** 3, 5, 13, 19

   B 1, 3, 5, 7, 9   **D** 15, 21, 27, 31

35. Writing to Explain Greta said that the product of two prime numbers must also be a prime number. Joan disagreed. Who is correct?

36. Use the following steps devised by the Greek mathematician Eratosthenes to create a list of prime numbers from 1 to 100. How many prime numbers are there between 1 and 100?

- Write all the numbers from 1 to 100.
- Draw a triangle around number 1; it is not prime nor composite.
- Circle 2 and cross out all other multiples of 2.
- Circle 3 and cross out all other multiples of 3.
- Circle 5, the next number that is not crossed out. Cross out other multiples of 5.
- Continue in the same way. When you have finished, the circled numbers are prime.

Understand It!
Identifying hidden questions can help you solve multiple-step problems.

Multiple-Step Problems

Justine and her father are going on a fishing trip. The prices for supplies, including tax, are shown in the table. Justine and her father have $25. They bought 2 box lunches, 2 bottles of water, 5 hooks, and 5 sinkers. How many pounds of bait can they buy?

Captain Bob's Price List	
Bait	$3 per pound
Hooks	60¢ each
Sinkers	40¢ each
Bottled water	$1 each
Box lunch	$6 each

Guided Practice*

Do you know HOW?

Solve.

1. Elsa babysits for the Smyth family. She earns $10 per hour on weekdays. She earns $15 per hour on the weekend. Last week, she worked 3 hours during the week and 4 hours on the weekend. How much did Elsa earn last week?

Do you UNDERSTAND?

2. What is the hidden question or questions?

3. **Write a Problem** Write a problem that contains a hidden question.

Independent Practice

Write the answer to the hidden question or questions. Then solve the problem. Write your answer in a complete sentence.

4. Gabriella buys lunch for herself and her friend. She buys 2 sandwiches and 2 drinks. Each sandwich costs $4. Each drink costs $1.50. How much did Gabriella spend on lunch?

5. Jamie is buying bowls for a school ice cream social. She buys 5 packages of red bowls, 3 packages of orange bowls, 4 packages of green bowls, and 7 packages of white bowls. Each package contains 8 bowls. How many bowls did she buy in all?

Stuck? Try this....

- What do I know?
- What diagram can I use to help understand the problem?
- Can I use addition, subtraction, multiplication, or division?
- Is all of my work correct?
- Did I answer the right question?
- Is my answer reasonable?

For another example, see Set K on page 193.

What do I know?

They bought:

2 lunches for $6 each
2 bottles of water for $1 each
5 hooks for 60¢ each
5 sinkers for 40¢ each

What am I asked to find?

The number of pounds of bait they can buy with the money they have left

Find the hidden question. How much money do Justine and her father have left?

The cost of lunches is	2 × $6	= $12
The cost of water is	2 × $1	= $2
The cost of hooks is	5 × 60¢	= $3
The cost of sinkers is	5 × 40¢	= $2
	The total is	$19

$25 − $19 = $6   They have $6 left.

Divide to find how many pounds of bait they can buy.

6 ÷ 3 = 2   They can buy 2 pounds of bait.

---

6. Kelly used 6 cups of apples, 4 cups of oranges, and 2 cups of grapes to make a fruit salad. She put an equal amount in each of 6 bowls. How many cups of fruit salad were in each bowl?

7. Muriel used the same recipe as Kelly to make her fruit salad. Muriel also added 1 cup of cherries and 1 cup of bananas. She put 2 cups of fruit salad into each bowl. How many bowls did Muriel need?

Use the data at the right for **8** through **11**.

8. The band needs to purchase 60 T-shirts. How much would it cost to purchase them from Shirt Shack?

9. How much would it cost the band to purchase 60 T-shirts from Just Jerseys?

10. How much more would it cost to buy 24 T-shirts at Just Jerseys than at Shirt Shack?

11. Writing to Explain Would it be less expensive to buy one shirt from Just Jerseys or Shirt Shack? Explain.

Data

Shirt Shack

Number of shirts	Price
10	$90
20	$180
50	$450

Data

Just Jerseys

Number of shirts	Price
8	$80
24	$240
48	$480

12. Each football practice is 45 minutes long. The team's next game is 6 practices away. How many minutes will they practice before the game?

  A 135 minutes   **C** 243 minutes

  B 270 minutes   **D** 2430 minutes

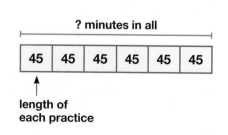

? minutes in all

45	45	45	45	45	45

length of each practice

1. A stadium has 30,000 seats and 6 main gates. How many seats are served by each gate if each gate serves the same number of seats? (8-1)

A 50

B 500

C 5,000

D 50,000

2. What is the quotient? (8-3)

A 3 R8

B 4 R2

C 4 R3

D 5 R2

3. Two boxes contain a total of 576 pencils. If each box has the same number of pencils, how many pencils are in each box? (8-6)

A 1,152

B 328

C 288

D 238

4. Tia has 15 metamorphic, 8 igneous, and 7 sedimentary rocks. She displays her rocks equally in 2 cases. Which shows how she found the number of rocks to put in each case? (8-10)

A 2 × 16

B 16 ÷ 2

C 2 × 30

D 30 ÷ 2

5. Nelly has 74 bricks to outline 5 different flower beds. How many bricks will she use for each flower bed if she uses the same number around each? (8-4)

A Each flower bed will use 10 bricks. There will be 4 left over.

B Each flower bed will use 13 bricks. There will be 9 left over.

C Each flower bed will use 14 bricks. There will be 0 left over.

D Each flower bed will use 14 bricks. There will be 4 left over.

6. What is 318 ÷ 4? (8-6)

A 78 R2

B 78

C 79 R2

D 79

7. Harold earned $196 by mowing 5 lawns. Which number sentence shows the best way to estimate the amount he earned for each lawn? (8-2)

A $200 ÷ 5 = $40

B $150 ÷ 5 = $30

C $200 ÷ 10 = $20

D 5 × $200 = $1,000

8. Eugenia bought 16 flowers. She used 3 flowers in each centerpiece. How many flowers were left over? (8-3)

A none

B 1 flower

C 2 flowers

D 6 flowers

9. Each costume requires 2 yards of material. How many costumes can Sara make out of 35 yards? How much material will she have left? (8-5)

A She can make 17 costumes with 1 yard left.

B She can make 17 costumes with 0 yards left.

C She can make 16 costumes with 3 yards left.

D She can make 16 costumes with 1 yard left.

10. Which shows all the factors of 24? (8-8)

A 1, 2, 3, 4, 6, 8, 12, 24

B 2, 3, 4, 6, 8, 12

C 1, 2, 3, 4, 12, 24

D 1, 2, 3, 4, 6, 12, 24

11. Which number is prime? (8-9)

A 88

B 65

C 51

D 17

12. Holly uses 7 sheets of tissue paper to make one flower. If she bought a package with 500 sheets of tissue paper, about how many tissue flowers will she be able to make? (8-2)

A 80

B 70

C 60

D 7

13. The baker made 52 rolls. He put an equal amount in each of the 4 baskets in the display case. How many rolls did he put in each basket? (8-5)

A 9

B 12

C 13

D 14

14. Which statement is true? (8-9)

A The only factors of 3 are 3 and 1.

B The only factors of 4 are 4 and 1.

C The only factors of 6 are 6 and 1.

D The only factors of 8 are 8 and 1.

15. What can you tell about 427 ÷ 7 just by looking at the problem? (8-7)

A It will have a three-digit quotient.

B It will have a two-digit quotient.

C It will have a one-digit quotient.

D It will have a remainder.

Set A, pages 164–165

A class shares 270 pens equally among 3 groups of students.

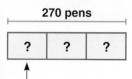

270 pens

| ? | ? | ? |

↑
Pens for each group of students

Find 270 ÷ 3.

The basic fact is 27 ÷ 3 = 9.
27 tens ÷ 3 = 9 tens or 90
So, 270 ÷ 3 = 90 pens.

Remember you can use patterns with zero to divide multiples of 10.

1. 250 ÷ 5   **2.** 81,000 ÷ 9

3. 3,200 ÷ 4   **4.** 42,000 ÷ 7

5. 1,000 ÷ 2   **6.** 240 ÷ 4

7. 450 ÷ 5   **8.** 72,000 ÷ 9

9. 3,600 ÷ 4   **10.** 49,000 ÷ 7

11. 2,000 ÷ 2   **12.** 280 ÷ 4

13. 2,100 ÷ 7   **14.** 56,000 ÷ 8

Set B, pages 166-167

Use estimation to find 42 ÷ 8.

What number close to 42 is easily divided by 8?

Try multiples of ten near 42:

40 is 4 tens and can be divided by 8.
40 ÷ 8 = 5

So, 42 ÷ 8 is about 5.

Use estimation to find 130 ÷ 7.

What number close to 130 is easily divided by 7?

Try multiples of ten near 130:

140 is 14 tens and can be divided by 7.
140 ÷ 7 = 20

So, 130 ÷ 7 is about 20.

Remember to try rounding the dividend to the nearest ten.

Estimate each quotient.

1. 718 ÷ 8   **2.** 156 ÷ 4

3. 482 ÷ 8   **4.** 28 ÷ 3

5. 843 ÷ 7   **6.** 321 ÷ 2

7. 428 ÷ 6   **8.** 811 ÷ 9

9. 561 ÷ 8   **10.** 723 ÷ 8

11. 632 ÷ 9   **12.** 362 ÷ 9

13. 57 ÷ 6   **14.** 122 ÷ 6

15. 251 ÷ 5   **16.** 362 ÷ 6

17. 494 ÷ 7   **18.** 93 ÷ 3

19. 331 ÷ 4   **20.** 174 ÷ 3

Set C, pages 168–169

Find 56 ÷ 9.

$$\begin{array}{r} 6 \text{ R2} \\ 9\overline{)56} \\ -\underline{54} \\ 2 \end{array}$$

Divide: 9 groups of 6 in 56
Multiply: 9 × 6 = 54
Subtract: 56 − 54 = 2
Compare: 2 < 9

Check: 9 × 6 = 54 and 54 + 2 = 56

56 ÷ 9 = 6 R2

Remember that you can use pictures to help.

1. 8$\overline{)41}$

2. 2$\overline{)15}$

3. 7$\overline{)59}$

4. 5$\overline{)22}$

5. 3$\overline{)28}$

6. 4$\overline{)27}$

7. 7$\overline{)69}$

8. 6$\overline{)47}$

Set D, pages 170–172

Tom divides 54 pennies equally among 4 stacks. How many pennies are in each stack? How many are left over?

Use place-value blocks.

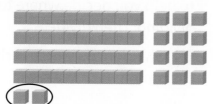

Each stack has 13 pennies.
Two pennies are left over.

Remember to divide the tens and then the ones.

Divide. You may use place-value blocks or pictures to help.

1. 38 CDs
5 stacks

2. 42 nickels
3 stacks

3. 62 dimes
4 stacks

4. 77 nickels
6 stacks

Set E, pages 174–176

Find 67 ÷ 4.

$$\begin{array}{r} 1 \\ 4\overline{)67} \\ -\underline{4} \\ 2 \end{array}$$

Divide.
Multiply.
Subtract.

$$\begin{array}{r} 16 \text{ R3} \\ 4\overline{)67} \\ -\underline{4}\downarrow \\ 27 \\ -\underline{24} \\ 3 \end{array}$$

Bring down the 7.
Divide.
Multiply.
Subtract.

Check:

$$\begin{array}{r} {}^{2}16 \\ \times\ \underline{4} \\ 64 \end{array} \qquad \begin{array}{r} 64 \\ +\ \underline{3} \\ 67 \end{array}$$

The answer checks.

Remember that the remainder must be less than the divisor.

Divide. Check your answer.

1. 43 ÷ 7

2. 33 ÷ 2

3. 19 ÷ 5

4. 53 ÷ 2

5. 86 ÷ 7

6. 85 ÷ 3

7. 94 ÷ 4

8. 47 ÷ 3

Set F, pages 178–179

Find 915 ÷ 6.

Estimate: 900 ÷ 6 = 150

The estimate is more than 100, so you can start dividing the hundreds.

```
      152 R3
  6)915      Divide the hundreds.
   - 6
     31      Divide the tens.
   - 30
     15      Divide the ones.
   - 12
      3      Include the remainder.
```

Remember to use an estimate to double-check your answers.

Divide. Check your answer.

1. 448 ÷ 4   **2.** 651 ÷ 5

3. 398 ÷ 3   **4.** 365 ÷ 3

5. 7)710   **6.** 5)572

7. 6)618   **8.** 7)814

Set G, pages 180–181

Find 566 ÷ 6.

```
      94 R2
  6)566      There are not enough
   - 0       hundreds to divide.
     56      Regroup the hundreds
   - 54      as tens and divide
     26      Bring down the ones
   - 24      and divide
      2
```

Remember to estimate the quotient to help you decide where to start dividing. Then divide.

Tell whether you will start dividing at the hundreds or the tens.

1. 710 ÷ 9   **2.** 601 ÷ 5

3. 398 ÷ 8   **4.** 429 ÷ 2

Set H, pages 182–183

Find the factors of 12.

Start with 1 group of 12.
12 = 1 × 12

Then 2 groups of 6.
12 = 2 × 6

Then 3 groups of 4.
12 = 3 × 4

Since the factor pairs have started to repeat, these are all the possible factors of 12: 1, 2, 3, 4, 6, 12.

Remember you can use counters to help find ways to multiply.

Write each number two different ways using multiplication.

1. 45   **2.** 40

3. 56   **4.** 63

5. 36   **6.** 16

Set J, pages 184–185

Is 49 prime or composite?

Find factors other than 1 and 49.

49 is composite because it is divisible by 7.

$49 = 7 \times 7$

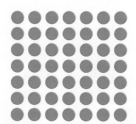

Remember that you can use an array to decide if a number is prime or composite.

Write whether each number is prime or composite.

1. 13   **2.** 25

3. 355   **4.** 2

5. 29   **6.** 2,232

Set K, pages 186–187

Answer the hidden question first. Then solve the problem.

Brett and his family spent $21 for admission to the county fair. They bought 2 adult passes for $6 each and 3 children's passes for $3 each. How much more money did Brett's family spend on adult passes than children's passes?

$6 \times 2 = \$12 \to$ Price of adult passes

$3 \times 3 = \$9 \to$ Price of children's passes

Brett's family spent $12 on adult passes and $9 on children passes.

Use the hidden question to solve the problem.

How much more money did Brett's family spend on adult passes than children passes?

$12 - \$9 = \$3

Brett's family spent $3 more on adult passes.

Remember to find a hidden question to help you solve the problem.

1. Angelique works at a store at the mall. She earns a wage of $8 an hour and earns $10 an hour if she works on weekends and holidays. Last week, she worked 24 hours during the week and 16 hours during the weekend. How much did Angelique earn last week?

2. Brendan takes violin and guitar lessons. Each day, he practices 40 minutes on the violin and 25 minutes on the guitar. How many minutes does he practice his instruments in 5 days?

Lines, Angles, and Shapes

1 The headquarters for the United States Department of Defense is named after the polygon it resembles. Which polygon does it look like? You will find out in Lesson 9-4.

2 There are 3 muscles in your neck that are critical for breathing and singing. They are named after a type of triangle that has a similar shape. What kind of triangle is it? You will find out in Lesson 9-5.

3 How could you use geometric terms to describe items on a map of Nevada? You will find out in Lesson 9-2.

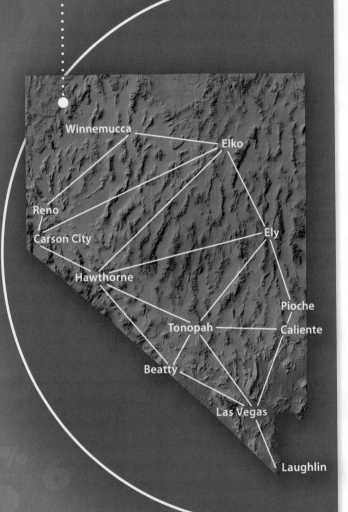

Winnemucca
Elko
Reno
Carson City
Ely
Hawthorne
Pioche
Tonopah
Caliente
Beatty
Las Vegas
Laughlin

Review What You Know!

Vocabulary

Choose the best term from the box.

> • triangle
> • plane figure
> • quadrilateral
> • line

1. A polygon with four sides is a ? .

2. A polygon with three sides is a ? .

3. A ? is a straight path of points that goes on forever in two directions.

4. A figure with only two dimensions is a ? .

Solids

Name what each figure looks like.

5.

6.

7.

8.

Addition

Solve.

9. 35 + 39   **10.** 72 + 109   **11.** 44 + 12

12. 145 + 238   **13.** 642 + 8   **14.** 99 + 41

15. 984 + 984   **16.** 22 + 888   **17.** 72 + 391

18. Writing to Explain To find the sum of 438 + 385, how many times will you need to regroup? Explain.

Understand It!
Geometric terms can be used to describe the location and position of things in our world.

Points, Lines, and Planes

What are some important geometric terms?

A point is an exact location in space.

•
Z

A line is a straight path of points that goes on and on in two directions.

A plane is an endless flat surface.

Guided Practice*

Do you know HOW?

For **1** through **4**, use the diagram at the right.

1. Name four points.

2. Name four lines.

3. Name two pairs of parallel lines.

4. Name two pairs of perpendicular lines.

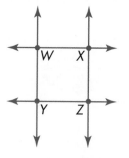

Do you UNDERSTAND?

5. What geometric term could you use to describe the top and bottom sides of a chalkboard? Why?

6. What geometric term could you use to describe a chalkboard?

7. What geometric term could you use to describe the tip of your pencil?

Independent Practice

In **8** through **14**, use geometric terms to describe what is shown.

8.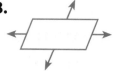

9.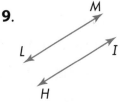

10.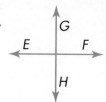

11. •
A

12.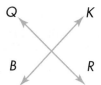

13.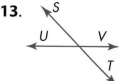

14.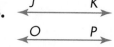

DIGITAL
Animated Glossary
www.pearsonsuccessnet.com

*For another example, see Set A on page 212.

Pairs of lines are given special names depending on their relationship.

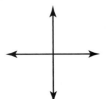

Parallel lines
never intersect.

Intersecting lines
pass through the
same point.

Perpendicular lines
are lines that form
square corners.

For **15** through **17**, describe each image shown using a geometric term.

15.

16.

17.

Problem Solving

18. Estimation Georgia purchased items to make dinner. She bought chicken for $5.29, salad items for $8.73, and rice for $1.99. Estimate how much Georgia spent in all.

19. I have 6 square faces and 8 vertices. What am I?

  A Cube   **C** Pyramid

  B Square   **D** Circle

For **20**, use the diagram at the right.

20. Reasoning Line *AB* is parallel to line *CD*, and line *CD* is perpendicular to line *EF*. What can you conclude about *AB* and *EF*?

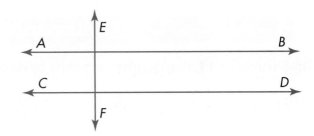

21. The web site of a company that sells sports equipment averages 850 visitors a day. How many visitors would the web site average in 7 days?

22. Which geometric term below best describes the surface of a desk?

  A Point   **C** Line

  B Plane   **D** Parallel

23. Writing to Explain If all perpendicular lines are also intersecting lines, are all intersecting lines also perpendicular? Explain.

24. If $40 \times 8 = 320$, how many zeros will there be in the product $4{,}000 \times 8$?

Understand It!
Geometric terms can be used to describe the location and position of things in our world.

Line Segments, Rays, and Angles

What geometric terms are used to describe parts of lines and types of angles?

A line segment is a part of a line with two endpoints.

G ●────────● R

A ray is a part of a line that has one endpoint and continues on forever in one direction.

N ●──────→ O

Guided Practice*

Do you know HOW?

In **1** through **4**, use geometric terms to describe what is shown.

1. ●────────●
P   X

2. P
Q ──── R

3. ●──────→
B   Y

4. L
M   N

Do you UNDERSTAND?

5. What geometric term describes a line that has only one endpoint?

6. What geometric term describes a line that has two endpoints?

7. Which geometric term describes what two edges of a book make when a corner is formed?

Independent Practice

In **8** through **11**, use geometric terms to describe what is shown.

8. H
O   S

9. ●────────●
B   D

10. ●──────→
X   Y

11. P
S   T

For **12** through **14**, use the figure shown to the right.

12. Name four line segments.

13. Name four rays.

14. Name 2 right angles.

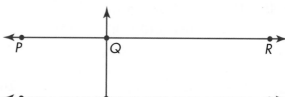

For another example, see Set B on page 212.

An angle <u>is a figure formed by two rays that have the same endpoint</u>.
Angles are given special names depending upon their size.

  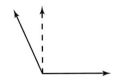 

A **right angle** is a square corner.

An **acute angle** is less than a right angle.

An **obtuse angle** is greater than a right angle.

A **straight angle** forms a straight line.

Problem Solving

15. Writing to Explain Is the figure shown below formed by two rays with a common endpoint? If so, is it an angle? Explain.

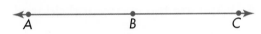

16. Which choice names the figure shown below?

G H

A Ray *GH*   **C** Ray *HG*

B Line *GH*   **D** Angle *GH*

17. What three capital letters can be written by drawing two parallel line segments and then one line segment that is perpendicular to the line segments you already drew?

18. Lexi said that two lines can both intersect a line and form perpendicular lines. Draw a picture to explain what she means.

For **19** through **21**, use the map of Nevada to the right. Which geometric term best fits each description?

19. The route between 2 cities

20. The cities

21. The north and west borders

22. Draw It Randy used 92 sticks to build a model project. Bryan used 3 times as many. Draw a diagram showing how many sticks Bryan used.

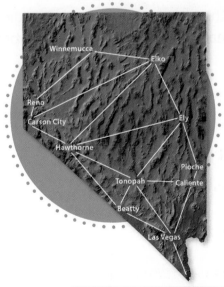

DIGITAL
Animated Glossary
www.pearsonsuccessnet.com

Understand It!
A protractor is used to measure angles.

Measuring Angles

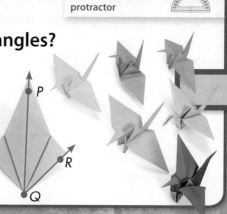

Hands-On
protractor

How do you measure and draw angles?

Angles are usually measured in units called degrees. The symbol ° indicates degrees. A protractor is a tool that is used to measure and draw angles.

A partially folded crane is shown at the right. Measure ∠PQR.

Guided Practice*

Do you know HOW?

For **1** and **2**, measure each angle.

1.
2.

For **3** and **4**, draw an angle with each measure.

3. 110°   **4.** 50°

Do you UNDERSTAND?

5. What is the angle measure of a straight line?

6. What are the vertex and sides of ∠PQR?

Independent Practice

For **7** through **14**, measure each angle. Tell if each angle is acute, right, or obtuse.

Tip *To measure an angle, you may need to trace it and extend its sides.*

7.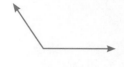
8.
9.
10.

11.
12.
13.
14.

DIGITAL
eTools, Animated Glossary
www.pearsonsuccessnet.com

For another example, see Set C on page 212.

Measure ∠PQR.

Place the protractor's center on the angle's vertex, Q. Place one side of the bottom edge on one side of the angle. Read the measure where the other side of the angle crosses the protractor. If the angle is acute, use the smaller number. If the angle is obtuse, use the larger number.

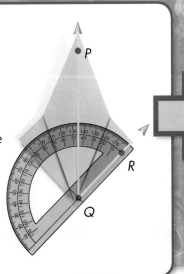

The measure of ∠PQR is 45°.

Draw an angle that measures 130°.

Draw a ray. Label the endpoint T. Place the protractor so that the middle of the bottom edge is over the endpoint of the ray. Place a point at 130°. Label it W. Draw ray TW.

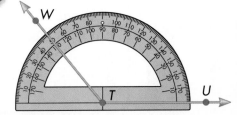

The measure of ∠WTU is 130°.

For **15** through **22**, draw an angle with each measure.

15. 140°   **16.** 180°   **17.** 20°   **18.** 65°

19. 45°   **20.** 115°   **21.** 90°   **22.** 155°

Problem Solving

23. Jorge is reading a book containing 3 chapters. The first chapter is 20 pages long. The second chapter is 36 pages long. There are 83 pages in the book. How many pages are in the third chapter?

24. Mariah made 5 three-point shots in her first game and 3 in her second game. She also made 4 two-point shots in each game and no one-point free throws in either game. How many total points did she score?

Use the diagram at the right for **25**.

25. Measure all of the angles created by the intersections of Main Street and Pleasant Street.

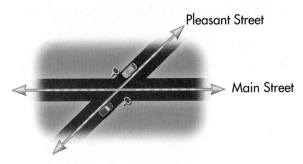

26. If ∠ABC is an obtuse angle, which of the following could **NOT** be its measure?

A 140°   **C** 105°

B 95°   **D** 90°

27. A newspaper stand orders 325 newspapers every day. How many newspapers will be ordered in the month of May?

Tip *There are 31 days in May.*

Lesson

9-4

Understand It!
Polygons are named by the number of sides they have.

Polygons

How do you identify polygons?

A polygon is a closed plane figure made up of line segments. Each line segment is a side. The point where two sides meet is called a vertex.

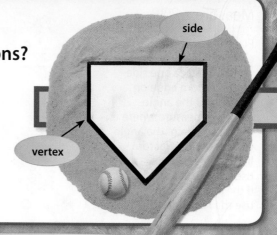

side

vertex

Guided Practice*

Do you know HOW?

Draw an example of each polygon. Write the number of sides and vertices it has.

1. pentagon
2. triangle

3. octagon
4. quadrilateral

Do you UNDERSTAND?

5. Is a circle a polygon? Why or why not?

6. Writing to Explain Does every hexagon have the same shape?

Independent Practice

In **7** through **18**, name each polygon if possible. Write the number of sides and vertices it has.

7.

8.

9.

10.

11.

12.

13.

14.

15.

16.

17.

18.

DIGITAL
Animated Glossary
www.pearsonsuccessnet.com

*For another example, see Set D on page 213.

Here are some examples of polygons.

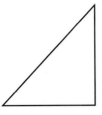  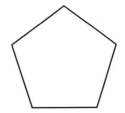 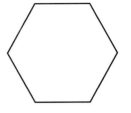 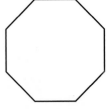

Triangle	Quadrilateral	Pentagon	Hexagon	Octagon
3 sides	4 sides	5 sides	6 sides	8 sides

Problem Solving

19. The building to the right is named for the polygon it looks like. What is the name of the polygon?

   A Quadrilateral   **C** Hexagon

   B Pentagon   **D** Octagon

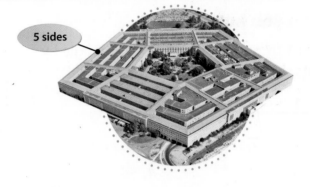

5 sides

20. What rule could be used to sort these polygons?

| Group A | |
| Group B | |

21. Draw It Tim and Peter both are on a swimming team. In one week, Tim swam 244 laps and Peter swam 196 laps. Draw a bar diagram to show how many more laps Tim swam than Peter.

22. Carla gathered a total of 124 seashells. How many seashells would she have if she gathered 4 times that amount?

23. Tasha is hosting a party for 216 people. If 6 people can sit at each table, how many tables will Tasha need to set up?

24. Writing to Explain What do you notice about the number of sides and the number of vertices a polygon has? How many vertices would a 20-sided polygon have?

25. Which polygon does **NOT** have at least 4 sides?

   A Octagon   **C** Quadrilateral

   B Hexagon   **D** Triangle

Lesson
9-5

Understand It!
Triangles can be classified by the lengths of their sides and by their angles.

Triangles

How can you classify triangles?

Triangles can be classified by their sides.

Equilateral Triangle
3 equal sides

Isosceles Triangle
2 equal sides

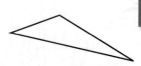

Scalene Triangle
0 equal sides

Guided Practice*

Do you know HOW?

In **1** through **4**, classify each triangle by its sides and then by its angles.

1. 　　**2.**

3. 　　**4.**

Do you UNDERSTAND?

5. Can a triangle have more than one obtuse angle? Explain.

6. Is it possible to draw a right isosceles triangle? If so, draw an example.

7. Can a triangle have more than one right angle? If so, draw an example.

Independent Practice

In **8** through **16**, classify each triangle by its sides and then by its angles.

8. 　　**9.** 　　**10.**

11. 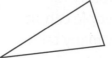　　**12.** 　　**13.**

14. 　　**15.** 　　**16.**

DIGITAL　Animated Glossary
www.pearsonsuccessnet.com

Triangles also can be classified by their angles.

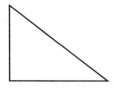

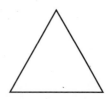

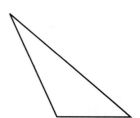

A right triangle <u>has one right angle</u>.

An acute triangle <u>has three acute angles</u>. All of its angles measure less than a right angle.

An obtuse triangle <u>has one obtuse angle</u>. One angle has a measure greater than right angle.

In **17** through **19**, classify each triangle by its sides and then by its angles.

17.

18.

19.

Problem Solving

20. Reasoning Use the diagram below. If the backyard is an equilateral triangle, what do you know about the lengths of the other two sides?

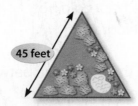

45 feet

21. If Chris uses a third line to make a triangle, what kind of triangle will it be?

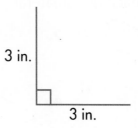

3 in.

3 in.

22. Writing to Explain Is an equilateral triangle always an isosceles triangle?

23. When you multiply any number by 1, what is the product?

Use the diagram at the right for **24**.

24. Which is the best name for this muscle group shown at the right?

A Right muscle group

B Scalene muscle group

C Isosceles muscle group

D Equilateral muscle group

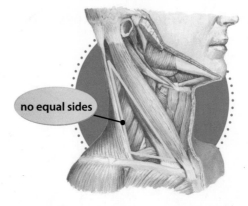

no equal sides

Understand It! Some quadrilaterals have special names depending on their angles and sides.

Quadrilaterals

How can you classify quadrilaterals?

Quadrilaterals can be classified by their angles or pairs of sides.

Square

Rectangle

Other Examples

A rhombus is a quadrilateral that has opposite sides that are parallel and all of its sides are the same length.

A trapezoid is a quadrilateral with only one pair of parallel sides.

Guided Practice*

Do you know HOW?

In **1** through **4**, write all the names you can use for each quadrilateral.

1.

2.

3.

4.

Do you UNDERSTAND?

5. What is true about all quadrilaterals?

6. Why is a trapezoid not a parallelogram?

7. What is the difference between a square and a rhombus?

Independent Practice

In **8** through **15**, write all the names you can use for each quadrilateral.

8.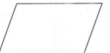

9.

10.

11.

DIGITAL
Animated Glossary
www.pearsonsuccessnet.com

*For another example, see Set E on page 213.

A **parallelogram** <u>has</u>
<u>2 pairs of parallel sides</u>.

A **rectangle** <u>has</u>
<u>4 right angles</u>. It is
also a parallelogram.

A **square** <u>has 4 right angles and</u>
<u>all sides are the same length</u>.
It is a parallelogram, rectangle,
and rhombus.

12.   13.  14.  15.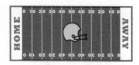

Problem Solving

16. A quadrilateral has two pairs of parallel sides and exactly 4 right angles. What quadrilateral is being described?

17. **Reasoning** Is it possible for a quadrilateral to be both a rhombus and a parallelogram?

18. **Algebra** What number comes next in the pattern?

   4, 16, 64, 256, ▢

19. **Writing to Explain** All the sides of an equilateral triangle are congruent. Is an equilateral triangle also a rhombus? Explain.

20. Valley Ridge Elementary has 108 fourth-grade students and 4 fourth-grade teachers. If split equally, how many students should be in each class?

21. If a theater can hold 235 people for one showing of a movie and they show the movie 5 times a day, how many people could view the movie in one day?

22. In math class, Mr. Meyer drew a quadrilateral on the board. It had just one set of parallel sides and no right angles. What shape was it?

   A Square   **C** Rectangle

   B Rhombus   **D** Trapezoid

23. Jamie went to exercise at a swimming pool. The length of the pool was 25 yards. If she swam a total of 6 laps, how many yards did Jamie swim?

   ? yards in all

25	25	25	25	25	25

   ↑
   Length of pool

Problem Solving

Make and Test Generalizations

What is true about all of these shapes?

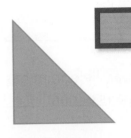

Guided Practice*

Do you know HOW?

1. Look at each group of three letters below. Give a generalization for each group of letters that does not apply to the other group of three letters.

| EFT | COS |

Do you UNDERSTAND?

2. **Writing to Explain** Is the generalization that every four sided polygon has at least one right angle correct? If not, draw a picture to show why not.

3. **Write a Problem** Select 3 items and make two correct generalizations about them.

Independent Practice

Solve.

4. Look at each group of numbers below. Compare the size of the factors to each product. What generalization can you make about factors and products for whole numbers?

   $6 \times 8 = 48$ $46 \times 5 = 230$ $1 \times 243 = 243$

5. Write the factors for 8, 16, and 20. What generalization can you make about all multiples of 4?

Stuck? Try this....

- What do I know?
- What diagram can I use to help understand the problem?
- Can I use addition, subtraction, multiplication, or division?
- Is all of my work correct?
- Did I answer the right question?
- Is my answer reasonable?

For another example, see Set F on page 213.

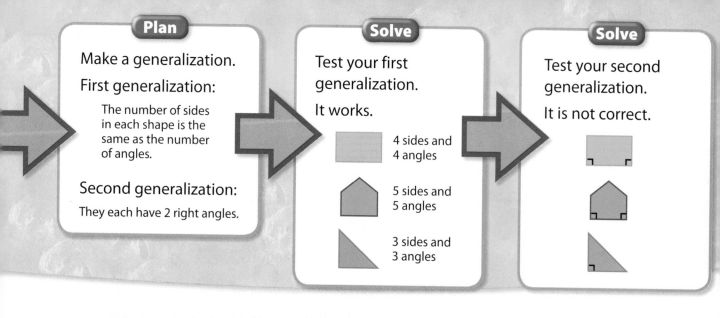

Make a generalization.

First generalization:

The number of sides in each shape is the same as the number of angles.

Second generalization:

They each have 2 right angles.

Solve

Test your first generalization.

It works.

4 sides and 4 angles

5 sides and 5 angles

3 sides and 3 angles

Solve

Test your second generalization.

It is not correct.

6. What generalization can you make about each of the polygons at the right?

   A   All sides of each polygon are the same length.

   B   All polygons have 5 sides.

   C   All polygons have 4 angles.

   D   All polygons have 3 angles.

7. The factors for 3 and 6 are shown in the table to the right. Jan concluded if you double a number, then you double the number of factors. Is Jan correct? Why or why not?

Number	3	6
Factors	1, 3	1, 2, 3, 6

8. How many sides does an octagon have? vertices?

9. How many acute angles can an isosceles triangle have?

10. Look at the pattern below. Draw the shape that would come next.

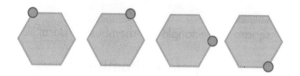

11. What generalization could be made about the triangles below?

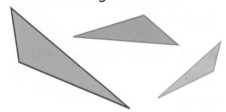

12. **Writing to Explain** Susan said that all squares are rectangles and therefore all rectangles are squares. Is Susan correct? Why or why not?

13. Michael lives on the 22nd floor of a 25 story building. If each floor is 12 feet in height, how many feet above ground level is Michael's apartment?

1. Which stick is parallel to stick *S*? (9-1)

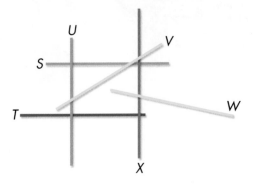

  A Stick *T*

  B Stick *U*

  C Stick *W*

  D Stick *X*

2. Which type of angle is angle *A*? (9-2)

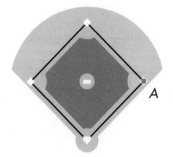

  A Acute

  B Obtuse

  C Right

  D Straight

3. Which triangle has no congruent sides? (9-5)

  A Isosceles

  B Scalene

  C Equilateral

  D Straight

4. Which polygon has more than 5 vertices? (9-4)

  A Pentagon

  B Quadrilateral

  C Triangle

  D Hexagon

5. Laney used drinking straws in art to form a figure that had perpendicular sides. Which could be her figure? (9-1)

  A

  B

  C

  D

6. Which statement is true about the quadrilaterals shown below? (9-6)

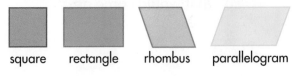

square   rectangle   rhombus   parallelogram

  A They are all rhombuses.

  B They are all squares.

  C They are all rectangles.

  D They are all parallelograms.

7. Which geometric term best describes the light that shines from a flashlight? (9-2)

A Point

B Ray

C Line segment

D Plane

8. Which geometric terms best describe the triangle below? (9-5)

A Isosceles; acute

B Isosceles; right

C Equilateral; obtuse

D Scalene; acute

9. Which quadrilateral has less than 2 pair of parallel sides? (9-6)

A Square

B Parallelogram

C Trapezoid

D Rhombus

10. Which polygon has 8 sides? (9-4)

A Pentagon

B Octagon

C Triangle

D Hexagon

11. Thomas chose these shapes.

He said the following shapes did not belong with the ones he chose.

Which is the best description of the shapes Thomas chose? (9-7)

A Polygons with more than 4 sides

B Polygons with parallel sides

C Polygons with all sides congruent

D Polygons with a right angle

12. What is the measure of the angle? (9-3)

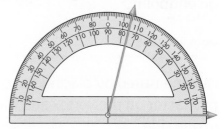

A 115°

B 85°

C 75°

D 65°

Set A, pages 196–197

Pairs of lines are given special names.

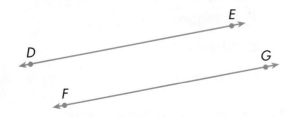

Line *DE* and line *FG* are parallel lines.

Remember that perpendicular lines intersect.

Match each term on the left with the correct image on the right.

1. _____ parallel lines   **a**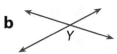

2. _____ point   **b**

3. _____ intersecting lines   **c**

Set B, pages 198–199

Geometric terms are used to describe figures.

A ray has one endpoint and continues on forever in one direction.

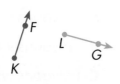

An angle is formed by two rays or line segments with a common endpoint.

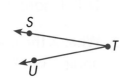

Remember that a line segment does not continue beyond its endpoints.

Use geometric terms to describe what is shown.

1. 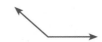   **2.**

3. 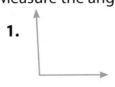   **4.**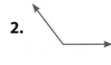

Set C, pages 200–201

Angles are measured by placing the center of the protractor on the vertex and the 0° mark on one side.

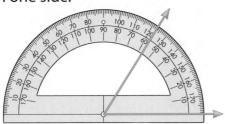

The measurement of the angle is 57°.

Remember that a straight line forms an angle of 180°.

Measure the angles.

1.   **2.**

3.   **4.**

Set D, pages 202–203

A polygon is a closed figure made up of line segments called sides. Each side meets at a point called a vertex.

side

vertex

Count the number of sides and vertices to identify the polygon.

The polygon is a hexagon.

Remember that polygons have the same number of sides and vertices.

Write the number of sides and vertices of each polygon.

1. octagon

2. square

3. triangle

4. trapezoid

Set E, pages 204–207

Triangles can be classified by their sides and angles.

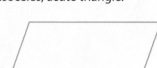

Two sides are the same length and all angles are acute. It is an isoceles, acute triangle.

Name the quadrilateral.

Opposite sides are parallel. It is a parallelogram.

Remember that a quadrilateral can be a rectangle, square, trapezoid, parallelogram, or rhombus.

Classify each shape by its sides and angles.

1.

2.

3.

4.

Set F, pages 208–209

What is true about all of these shapes?

The number of sides in each is the same as the number of angles. Test your generalization.

4 sides, 4 angles

3 sides, 3 angles

4 sides, 4 angles

Remember to test your generalizations.

1. Look at each group of numbers below. Give a generalization for each group of numbers that does not apply to the other group of three numbers.

1   4   3
7   6   9

Understanding Fractions

1 The Maryland state flag is the only state flag that is made up of 2 family seals. Which family seals are on the flag? You will find out in Lesson 10-1.

2 How many gallons of milk does an average milk cow produce each day? You will find out in Lesson 10-6.

Review What You Know!

Vocabulary

Choose the best term from the box.

- fraction
- denominator
- thirds
- numerator

1. Three equal parts of a shape are called __?__.

2. A __?__ can name a part of a whole.

3. The number below the fraction bar in a fraction is the __?__ .

Division

Divide.

4. $454 \div 5$ **5.** $600 \div 3$ **6.** $336 \div 4$

7. $625 \div 5$ **8.** $387 \div 3$ **9.** $878 \div 7$

10. $240 \div 8$ **11.** $816 \div 2$ **12.** $284 \div 4$

13. $626 \div 6$ **14.** $312 \div 3$ **15.** $847 \div 9$

Fraction Concepts

Name the number of equal parts in each figure.

16.   **17.**   **18.**

19.   **20.**   **21.**

22. Writing to Explain Is $\frac{1}{4}$ of the figure below red? Why or why not?

③

Asia is the largest continent, covering about $\frac{3}{10}$ of Earth's total land area. About what fraction of the people on Earth live in Asia? You will find out in Lesson 10-3.

④

The world's largest pumpkin pie was made in 2005. How much did the pumpkin pie weigh? You will find out in Lesson 10-4.

Understand It!
Fractions name parts of a whole region or parts of a set of objects.

Regions and Sets

How can you name and show parts of a region and parts of a set?

A fraction is a symbol, such as $\frac{2}{3}$ or $\frac{5}{1}$, used to name a part of a whole, a part of a set, a location on a number line, or a division of whole numbers.

What fraction of the Nigerian flag is green?

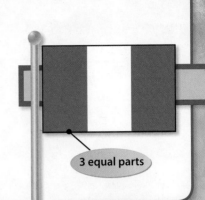

3 equal parts

Another Example How can you draw parts of a region and parts of a set?

Draw Parts of a Region

Draw a flag that is $\frac{3}{5}$ green.

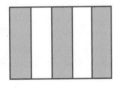

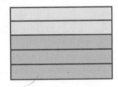

In both flags, there are 5 equal parts, and 3 of the parts are green. Both flags are $\frac{3}{5}$ green.

Draw Parts of a Set

Draw a set of shapes in which $\frac{4}{10}$ of the shapes are small triangles.

There are 4 small triangles out of 10 shapes. So, $\frac{4}{10}$, or four tenths, of the shapes are small triangles.

Explain It

1. Draw a flag that is $\frac{3}{6}$ green. How does this flag compare to a flag of the same size that is $\frac{3}{5}$ green?

2. What fraction of the set of shapes above is orange? What fraction of the shapes are squares? What is the same about these two fractions?

Parts of a region

The <mark>numerator</mark> <u>tells how many equal parts are described</u>. The <mark>denominator</mark> <u>tells how many equal parts there are in all</u>.

$$\frac{2}{3}$$ ← Numerator

← Denominator

In the Nigerian flag, $\frac{2}{3}$ of the flag is green.

Parts of a set

These flags show the first 4 letters in the International Code of Signals:

What fraction of these flags are rectangles? $\frac{2}{4}$ ← Number that are rectangles ← Total number in set

In this set of 4 flags, $\frac{2}{4}$ are rectangles.

Guided Practice*

Do you know HOW?

In **1** and **2**, write a fraction to describe the part of each region or set that is green.

1.

2.

In **3** and **4**, draw a model for each fraction.

3. $\frac{4}{5}$ of a region   4. $\frac{2}{9}$ of a set

Do you UNDERSTAND?

5. **Writing to Explain** What fraction of the signal flags at the top contain blue? What fraction of the flags contain yellow? Why do these fractions both have the same denominator?

6. What fraction of the squares below contain a red circle? What fraction of the circles are red?

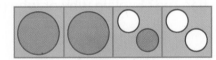

Independent Practice

In **7** and **8**, write a fraction to describe the part of each region or set that is green.

7.    8.

Animated Glossary
www.pearsonsuccessnet.com
DIGITAL

Independent Practice

In **9** and **10**, write a fraction to describe the part of each region or set that is blue.

9.

10.

In **11** through **18**, draw a model for each fraction.

11. $\frac{7}{10}$ of a region   **12.** $\frac{2}{8}$ of a region   **13.** $\frac{1}{6}$ of a region   **14.** $\frac{3}{9}$ of a region

15. $\frac{1}{8}$ of a set   **16.** $\frac{5}{6}$ of a set   **17.** $\frac{3}{7}$ of a set   **18.** $\frac{1}{10}$ of a set

Problem Solving

19. Maya tried a skateboard trick 12 times. She got it to work 3 times. What fraction describes the number of times the trick did **NOT** work?

20. Jane has a fish tank. Draw a model to show that $\frac{3}{10}$ of the fish are black and the rest of the fish are orange.

21. Students arranged 32 chairs in equal rows for a school concert. Describe two ways the students could have arranged the chairs.

22. When the numerator is the same as the denominator, what do you know about the fraction?

23. In the signal flag shown below, is $\frac{1}{3}$ of the flag red? Explain why or why not.

24. Alan's grandfather made 10 pancakes. Alan ate 3 pancakes. His sister ate 2 pancakes. What fraction of the pancakes did Alan eat?

  A $\frac{3}{10}$ **C** $\frac{5}{10}$

  B $\frac{2}{5}$ **D** $\frac{3}{5}$

Use the diagram at the right for **25**.

25. The Maryland state flag is made up of the Calvert and the Crossland family seals. Each family has their seal displayed twice. What fraction of the flag does one seal take up?

  A $\frac{1}{4}$ **B** $\frac{1}{3}$ **C** $\frac{1}{2}$ **D** $\frac{3}{4}$

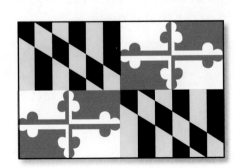

Find each sum. Estimate to check
if the answer is reasonable.

1.	4,572 + 2,391	**2.**	73,901 + 5,799	**3.**	3,468 + 947	**4.**	247 + 312

5. 5,474 + 723   **6.** 47,090 + 2,910   **7.** 6,685 + 37

Find each difference. Estimate to check
if the answer is reasonable.

8.	4,087 − 496	**9.**	8,354 − 2,568	**10.**	9,115 − 76	**11.**	6,000 − 1,473	**12.**	6,249 − 123

13. 5,302 − 88   **14.** 2,249 − 51   **15.** 8,001 − 4,832

Error Search Find each sum or difference that is not correct.
Write it correctly and explain the error.

16.	543 + 29 562	**17.**	6,043 + 972 7,025	**18.**	76,248 + 19,046 95,294	**19.**	354 − 74 320	**20.**	14,953 − 10,834 4;119

Number Sense

Estimating and Reasoning Write whether each
statement is true or false. Explain your answer.

21. The number 213,753 is ten thousand more than 223,753.

22. The sum of 6,823 and 1,339 is greater than 7,000
but less than 9,000.

23. The sum of 42,239 and 11,013 is less than 50,000.

24. The difference of 7,748 − 989 is greater than 7,000.

25. The sum of 596 + 325 is 4 less than 925.

26. The difference of 12,023 and 2,856 is closer
to 9,000 than 10,000.

Fractions and Division

How can you share items?

Tom, Joe, and Sam made clay pots using two rolls of clay. If they shared the clay equally, what fraction of the clay did each friend use?

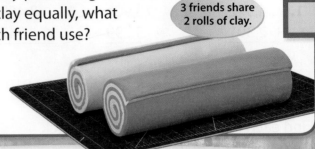

3 friends share
2 rolls of clay.

Choose an Operation
Divide to find a fraction
of the total.

Guided Practice*

Do you know HOW?

Tell what fraction each person gets.

1. Three people share 2 cans of paint.

2. Two students share 1 sheet of paper.

3. Four friends share 3 apples.

4. Five friends share 5 bagels.

Do you UNDERSTAND?

5. How do you write 3 ÷ 5 as a fraction?

6. In Exercises 1 through 4, did you use the number of items as the denominator or as the numerator?

7. If 6 people equally shared 3 rolls of clay to make pots, how much clay did each person use?

Independent Practice

In **8** through **13**, tell what fraction each person gets when they share equally.

 The number of items shared is the numerator and the number of people is the denominator.

8. Four students share 3 breakfast bars.

9. Ten friends share 7 dollars.

10. Five women each run an equal part of a 3-mile relay.

11. Ten students share 1 hour to give their reports.

12. Six soccer players share 5 oranges.

13. Five friends pay for a 4 dollar gift.

*For another example, see Set B on page 244.

Think about sharing 2 rolls of clay among 3 people. Divide each roll into 3 equal parts.

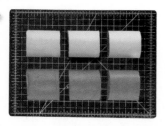

Each part is 1 ÷ 3 or $\frac{1}{3}$.

The parts were shared equally.

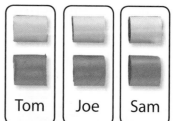

Tom | Joe | Sam

Each person used one part from each roll of clay for a total of 2 parts.

This is the same as $\frac{2}{3}$ of one roll of clay.

You can write division as a fraction. So, $2 \div 3 = \frac{2}{3}$.

Problem Solving

14. Eight friends divide 3 pizzas equally. How much pizza does each friend get?

15. Algebra Find the missing numbers in the following pattern.
1, 3, 9, ▢, 81, ▢

16. Reasoning A group of friends went to the movies. They shared 2 bags of popcorn equally. If each person got $\frac{2}{3}$ of a bag of popcorn, how many people were in the group?

17. When Sharon's reading group took turns reading aloud, every student had a chance to read. They finished a 12 page story. If each student read 3 pages, how many students are in the reading group?

18. There were 16 teams at a gymnastics meet. Each team had 12 members. How many gymnasts participated in the meet?

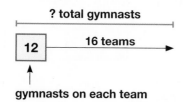

? total gymnasts

12 | 16 teams →

gymnasts on each team

19. Twenty-one soccer players were put into 3 equal teams. How many players were on each team?

21 players

? | ? | ?

players on each team

20. **Think About the Process** Four friends are baking bread. They equally share 3 sticks of butter. Which number sentence can be used to find the fraction of a stick of butter that each friend uses?

A 3 ÷ 12 = ▢   **C** 3 ÷ 4 = ▢

B 5 ÷ 12 = ▢   **D** 3 ÷ 5 = ▢

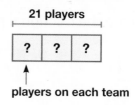

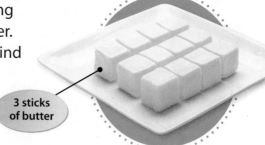

3 sticks of butter

Lesson
10-3

Understand It!
Use benchmark fractions to estimate fractional amounts.

Estimating Fractional Amounts

How can you estimate parts?

Emma helped her mom begin to paint a mural downtown. About what fraction of the wall has been painted?

Emma's mural

Guided Practice*

Do you know HOW?

For **1** through **3**, estimate the fractional part that is orange.

1.
2.
3.

Do you UNDERSTAND?

4. **Writing to Explain** How can you estimate whether a part of a region is about $\frac{1}{2}$ of the whole?

5. Which of the rectangles in Exercises 1 through 3 has the greatest fractional part that is orange?

6. About what fraction of the wall is **NOT** painted at all?

Independent Practice

In **7** through **9**, estimate the fractional part of each that is green.

7.   8.   9.

In **10** through **12**, estimate the fractional part of each that is flowers.

10.   11.   12.

Animated Glossary
www.pearsonsuccessnet.com

222   *For another example, see Set C on page 244.*

Step 1

Think about benchmark fractions. A **benchmark fraction** is a simple fraction that is easy to visualize, such as $\frac{1}{4}, \frac{1}{3}, \frac{1}{2}, \frac{2}{3}$, and $\frac{3}{4}$.

You can use benchmark fractions to estimate fractional parts.

Step 2

Compare the benchmark fractions to the part of the wall that has been painted.

The painted part is more than $\frac{1}{4}$, but less than $\frac{1}{2}$. About $\frac{1}{3}$ of the wall is painted.

Problem Solving

13. Asia has more people than any other continent. About what fraction of the people on Earth live in Asia?

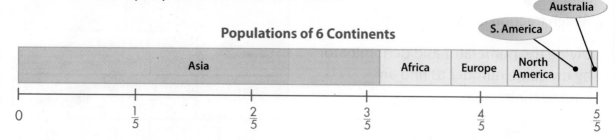

14. At the bowling alley, there are 32 bowling balls. Of these, 8 are blue, 5 are pink, 6 are red, and the rest are black. How many of the bowling balls are black?

15. Reasonableness If less than half of a garden is planted with corn, is it reasonable to estimate that $\frac{2}{3}$ of the garden is planted with corn? Explain.

16. Number Sense The numbers are missing from the graph below. Compare the bars to decide which farmer has about $\frac{1}{3}$ as many cows as Mr. Harris.

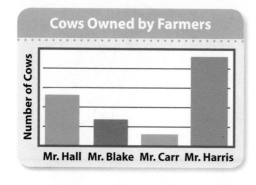

17. Geometry What is the perimeter of the figure shown below?

TIP *The perimeter of a rectangle equals the sum of the lengths of the 4 sides.*

A 6 units

B 8 units

C 12 units

D 16 units

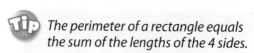

Equivalent Fractions

Hands-On
fraction strips

$\frac{1}{8}$

How can you find two fractions that name the same part of a whole?

Lee ate $\frac{1}{4}$ of a pizza. Write another fraction that is equivalent to $\frac{1}{4}$.

Equivalent fractions <u>name the same part of a whole</u>.

Lee ate 1/4 of a pizza.

Another Example How can you divide to find an equivalent fraction?

Sara ate $\frac{6}{8}$ of a small mushroom pizza. Which fraction is equivalent to $\frac{6}{8}$?

Divide the numerator and denominator by the same number to find an equivalent fraction.

$\div 2$

$\frac{6}{8} = \frac{3}{4}$ So, $\frac{3}{4}$ is equivalent to $\frac{6}{8}$.

$\div 2$

Check your answer using fractions strips.

Find $\frac{6}{8}$ by counting 6 of the $\frac{1}{8}$ strips.

Find $\frac{3}{4}$ by counting 3 of the $\frac{1}{4}$ strips.

Both $\frac{6}{8}$ and $\frac{3}{4}$ name the same part of a whole.

1											
$\frac{1}{2}$						$\frac{1}{2}$					
$\frac{1}{3}$				$\frac{1}{3}$				$\frac{1}{3}$			
$\frac{1}{4}$			$\frac{1}{4}$			$\frac{1}{4}$			$\frac{1}{4}$		
$\frac{1}{5}$		$\frac{1}{5}$		$\frac{1}{5}$		$\frac{1}{5}$		$\frac{1}{5}$			
$\frac{1}{6}$		$\frac{1}{6}$		$\frac{1}{6}$		$\frac{1}{6}$		$\frac{1}{6}$		$\frac{1}{6}$	
$\frac{1}{8}$	$\frac{1}{8}$	$\frac{1}{8}$	$\frac{1}{8}$	$\frac{1}{8}$	$\frac{1}{8}$	$\frac{1}{8}$	$\frac{1}{8}$				
$\frac{1}{10}$	$\frac{1}{10}$	$\frac{1}{10}$	$\frac{1}{10}$	$\frac{1}{10}$	$\frac{1}{10}$	$\frac{1}{10}$	$\frac{1}{10}$	$\frac{1}{10}$	$\frac{1}{10}$		
$\frac{1}{12}$	$\frac{1}{12}$	$\frac{1}{12}$	$\frac{1}{12}$	$\frac{1}{12}$	$\frac{1}{12}$	$\frac{1}{12}$	$\frac{1}{12}$	$\frac{1}{12}$	$\frac{1}{12}$	$\frac{1}{12}$	$\frac{1}{12}$

Explain It

1. Can you divide 6 and 8 by any number to find an equivalent fraction? Explain.

2. Using fraction strips, find two fractions that are equivalent to $\frac{9}{12}$.

You can multiply the numerator and the denominator by the same number to find an equivalent fraction.

$$\frac{1}{4} = \frac{2}{8}$$

Use fraction strips to find equivalent fractions.

Both $\frac{1}{4}$ and $\frac{2}{8}$ name the same part of a whole.

So, $\frac{1}{4}$ and $\frac{2}{8}$ are equivalent fractions.

Guided Practice*

Do you know HOW?

In **1** through **6**, multiply or divide to find an equivalent fraction.

1. 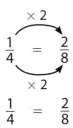 $\frac{2}{3} = \frac{}{}$

2. $\frac{10}{15} = \frac{}{}$ ÷ 5

3. $\frac{1}{4} = \frac{}{16}$

4. $\frac{10}{12} = \frac{5}{}$

5. $\frac{15}{20} = \frac{}{4}$

6. $\frac{3}{8} = \frac{9}{}$

Do you UNDERSTAND?

7. Suppose Lee's pizza had 12 equal slices instead of 4. How many slices are gone if he ate $\frac{1}{4}$ of the pizza? Explain.

8. Reasoning Josh, Lisa, and Vicki each ate $\frac{1}{2}$ of a pizza. The pizzas were the same size, but Josh ate 1 slice, Lisa ate 3 slices, and Vicki ate 4 slices. How is this possible?

Independent Practice

Leveled Practice For **9** through **16**, multiply or divide to find equivalent fractions.

 You can check your answers using fraction strips.

9. $\frac{4}{9} = \frac{}{}$

10. $\frac{9}{15} = \frac{}{}$

11. $\frac{5}{7} = \frac{}{}$

12. $\frac{2}{4} = \frac{}{}$

13. $\frac{10}{10} = \frac{1}{}$

14. $\frac{3}{4} = \frac{12}{}$

15. $\frac{10}{20} = \frac{}{4}$

16. $\frac{30}{40} = \frac{6}{}$

DIGITAL — Animated Glossary, eTools
www.pearsonsuccessnet.com

In **17** through **26**, find an equivalent fraction for each.

17. $\frac{8}{18}$ **18.** $\frac{2}{10}$ **19.** $\frac{1}{3}$ **20.** $\frac{3}{5}$ **21.** $\frac{24}{30}$

22. $\frac{60}{80}$ **23.** $\frac{2}{15}$ **24.** $\frac{21}{28}$ **25.** $\frac{12}{15}$ **26.** $\frac{12}{20}$

Problem Solving

For **27** and **28**, use the fraction strips at the right.

27. Name 10 pairs of equivalent fractions.

28. Reasoning How can you show that $\frac{6}{8}$ and $\frac{9}{12}$ are equivalent by multiplying and dividing?

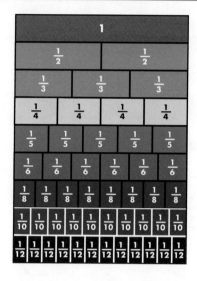

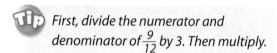 *First, divide the numerator and denominator of $\frac{9}{12}$ by 3. Then multiply.*

29. The world's largest pumpkin pie weighed 2,020 pounds. The pie was $12\frac{1}{3}$ feet across and $\frac{1}{3}$ foot thick. Write a fraction equivalent to $\frac{1}{3}$.

30. In a school poetry contest, 15 out of 45 students who entered will win a small prize. Half of the remaining students receive a certificate. How many students get a certificate?

31. Algebra James has 18 mystery books and 12 sports books. Rich has twice as many mystery books and three times as many sports books. How many books does Rich have?

32. Writing to Explain In the United States, $\frac{2}{5}$ of all states start with the letters M, A, or N. How can you use equivalent fractions to find out how many states this is?

33. Look at the model. Name three equivalent fractions for the area that is red.

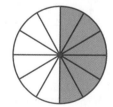

34. Where would the parentheses go for the following expression to be true?

$$7 + 5 - 8 - 3 = 7$$

A $(7 + 5) - 8 - 3$

B $7 + (5 - 8) - 3$

C $7 + 5 - (8 - 3)$

D $(7 + 5 - 8 - 3)$

Algebra Connections

Divisibility

A number is divisible by another number when the quotient is a whole number and the remainder is 0.

Find which numbers in each list are divisible by the number shown.

1. 5
(5, 8, 10, 12, 15)

2. 8
(8, 14, 16, 19, 24)

3. 12
(12, 18, 25, 36, 48)

4. 14
(14, 27, 42, 56, 96)

5. 15
(15, 35, 45, 70, 90)

6. 16
(16, 32, 63, 80, 98)

7. 17
(17, 28, 34, 51, 69)

8. 22
(22, 33, 44, 55, 66)

9. 31
(31, 62, 83, 91, 124)

10. 4
(4, 8, 9, 12, 17)

11. 6
(6, 18, 21, 24, 35)

12. 7
(12, 14, 20, 28, 35)

13. 9
(18, 26, 36, 55, 63)

14. 18
(18, 35, 54, 72, 91)

Example:

Which of these numbers are divisible by 3?

(11, 14, 23, 42)

Use divisibility rules for 3s:

Think *Is the sum of the digits of the number divisible by 3?*

Try 14.

1 + 4 = 5

5 is not divisible by 3, so 14 is not divisible by 3.

Now try 42.

4 + 2 = 6

6 is divisible by 3, so 3 is a factor of 42.

Check: **42 ÷ 3 = 14**

---

15. Bonnie has 64 packets of pepper. She wants to store the same amount of packets in bags so that each bag has the same number of packets. What are three different ways Bonnie can do this?

16. How many pieces of cloth 7 yards long could you cut from a piece of cloth that is 42 yards long? Explain.

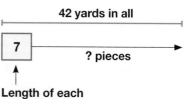

42 yards in all

7

? pieces

Length of each piece of cloth

Understand It!
Fractions can be written so that the numerator and denominator have no common factors other than 1.

Fractions in Simplest Form

How do you write a fraction in simplest form?

Jason ran $\frac{4}{12}$ of the way around the track. Write $\frac{4}{12}$ in simplest form.

Since 4 is a factor of 12, it is a common factor of 4 and 12.

A fraction is in simplest form when the numerator and denominator have no common factor other than 1.

$\frac{4}{12}$ of the way around the track

Guided Practice*

Do you know HOW?

For **1** through **6**, write each fraction in simplest form.

1. $\frac{6}{8}$

2. $\frac{15}{45}$

3. $\frac{10}{100}$

4. $\frac{16}{80}$

5. $\frac{21}{33}$

6. $\frac{12}{14}$

Do you UNDERSTAND?

7. **Writing to Explain** Explain how you can tell $\frac{4}{9}$ is in simplest form.

8. Jamal ran $\frac{8}{12}$ of the way around a track. Write this fraction in simplest form.

 If the numerator and denominator are even numbers, they have 2 as a common factor.

Independent Practice

In **9** through **33**, write each fraction in simplest form. If it is in simplest form, write simplest form.

9. $\frac{3}{12}$

10. $\frac{2}{10}$

11. $\frac{4}{8}$

12. $\frac{12}{16}$

13. $\frac{4}{6}$

14. $\frac{2}{5}$

15. $\frac{2}{6}$

16. $\frac{3}{16}$

17. $\frac{8}{10}$

18. $\frac{5}{12}$

19. $\frac{3}{7}$

20. $\frac{8}{20}$

21. $\frac{9}{10}$

22. $\frac{9}{15}$

23. $\frac{12}{20}$

24. $\frac{5}{6}$

25. $\frac{3}{9}$

26. $\frac{15}{18}$

27. $\frac{30}{40}$

28. $\frac{30}{35}$

29. $\frac{2}{3}$

30. $\frac{7}{14}$

31. $\frac{9}{16}$

32. $\frac{4}{12}$

33. $\frac{5}{15}$

 Animated Glossary
www.pearsonsuccessnet.com

Write $\frac{4}{12}$ in simplest form by dividing twice.

$\div 2$
$$\frac{4}{12} = \frac{2}{6}$$
$\div 2$

4 and 12 are both even. Two is a common factor.

$\div 2$
$$\frac{2}{6} = \frac{1}{3}$$
$\div 2$

2 and 6 are both even. Two is a common factor.

Write $\frac{4}{12}$ in simplest form by dividing by 4.

$\div 4$
$$\frac{4}{12} = \frac{1}{3}$$
$\div 4$

In simplest form, $\frac{4}{12} = \frac{1}{3}$.

Problem Solving

34. Reasoning If the numerator and the denominator of a fraction are both prime numbers and not equal to each other, can the fraction be simplified?

35. Estimation About what fraction of this model is red?

Use the table at the right for **36** and **37**.

36. What fraction of the band members practice for more than 2 hours a week? Write your answer in simplest form.

37. What fraction of the band members spend more time on lessons than on practice? Write your answer in simplest form.

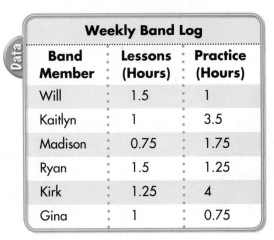

Weekly Band Log

Band Member	Lessons (Hours)	Practice (Hours)
Will	1.5	1
Kaitlyn	1	3.5
Madison	0.75	1.75
Ryan	1.5	1.25
Kirk	1.25	4
Gina	1	0.75

38. Think About the Process Which of the following helps you find the simplest form of $\frac{4}{8}$?

A Subtract 4 from 8.

B Divide 4 by 8.

C Compare fraction strips for fourths and eighths.

D Compare fraction strips for eighths and halves.

39. The year 2005 was a record year for panda births. In that year, 16 pandas were born in captivity. If a total of 180 pandas are living in captivity, what fraction of pandas were born in 2005? Write your answer in simplest form.

Understand It!
Fractions can have a value greater than 1.

Improper Fractions and Mixed Numbers

Hands-On
fraction strips

$\frac{1}{8}$

How can you name an amount in two different ways?

How many times will Matt need to fill his $\frac{1}{4}$-cup container to make $2\frac{1}{4}$ cups of punch?

$2\frac{1}{4}$ is a mixed number. A mixed number has a whole number part and a fraction part.

$2\frac{1}{4}$ cups

Another Example How can you write an improper fraction as a mixed number or whole number?

Jack used $\frac{10}{3}$ cups of water to make lemonade.
Write $\frac{10}{3}$ as a mixed number.

A $10\frac{1}{3}$ cups

B $3\frac{1}{3}$ cups

C $3\frac{1}{10}$ cups

D $\frac{3}{3}$ cups

Use a model. Show $\frac{10}{3}$ or 10 thirds.

There are 3 wholes shaded and $\frac{1}{3}$ of another whole shaded.

So, $\frac{10}{3} = 3\frac{1}{3}$.

Jack made $3\frac{1}{3}$ cups of lemonade.

The correct answer choice is **B**.

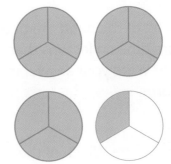

Explain It

1. Explain why $\frac{6}{3} = 2$. Draw a model to help you.

2. Jacquelyn made punch using $\frac{7}{2}$ cups of water. Write $\frac{7}{2}$ as a mixed number.

One Way

Use a model to write $2\frac{1}{4}$ as an improper fraction.

An **improper fraction** <u>has a numerator greater than or equal to its denominator.</u>

Count the shaded fourths.

There are 9 fourths or $\frac{9}{4}$ shaded. So, $2\frac{1}{4} = \frac{9}{4}$. $\frac{9}{4}$ is an improper fraction.

Matt needs to fill the $\frac{1}{4}$-cup container 9 times.

Another Way

Use fraction strips.

1			
$\frac{1}{4}$	$\frac{1}{4}$	$\frac{1}{4}$	$\frac{1}{4}$
$\frac{1}{4}$	$\frac{1}{4}$	$\frac{1}{4}$	$\frac{1}{4}$
$\frac{1}{4}$			

So, $2\frac{1}{4} = \frac{9}{4}$.

Guided Practice*

Do you know HOW?

Write each mixed number as an improper fraction. Write each improper fraction as a mixed number or whole number. Use models to help you.

1. $1\frac{3}{8}$

1							
$\frac{1}{8}$	$\frac{1}{8}$	$\frac{1}{8}$	$\frac{1}{8}$	$\frac{1}{8}$	$\frac{1}{8}$	$\frac{1}{8}$	$\frac{1}{8}$
$\frac{1}{8}$	$\frac{1}{8}$	$\frac{1}{8}$					

2. $\frac{4}{3}$

1		
$\frac{1}{3}$	$\frac{1}{3}$	$\frac{1}{3}$
$\frac{1}{3}$		

Do you UNDERSTAND?

3. How else could you model $2\frac{1}{4}$ using fraction strips?

4. If Matt filled a $2\frac{1}{5}$ cup container, how many $\frac{1}{5}$-cups would he need to use?

5. Nancy bought $7\frac{1}{2}$ gallons of milk for the school cafeteria. She bought only half-gallon containers. How many half-gallon containers did she buy?

Independent Practice

For **6** through **8**, write each number as a mixed number or improper fraction.

6. $1\frac{3}{4}$

1			
$\frac{1}{4}$	$\frac{1}{4}$	$\frac{1}{4}$	$\frac{1}{4}$
$\frac{1}{4}$	$\frac{1}{4}$	$\frac{1}{4}$	

7. $\frac{7}{3}$

1		
$\frac{1}{3}$	$\frac{1}{3}$	$\frac{1}{3}$
$\frac{1}{3}$	$\frac{1}{3}$	$\frac{1}{3}$
$\frac{1}{3}$		

8. $3\frac{1}{5}$

1				
$\frac{1}{5}$	$\frac{1}{5}$	$\frac{1}{5}$	$\frac{1}{5}$	$\frac{1}{5}$
$\frac{1}{5}$	$\frac{1}{5}$	$\frac{1}{5}$	$\frac{1}{5}$	$\frac{1}{5}$
$\frac{1}{5}$	$\frac{1}{5}$	$\frac{1}{5}$	$\frac{1}{5}$	$\frac{1}{5}$
$\frac{1}{5}$				

DIGITAL

Animated Glossary, eTools
www.pearsonsuccessnet.com

*For another example, see Set F on page 246.

For **9** through **11**, write each number as a mixed number or improper fraction.

9. $4\frac{2}{3}$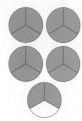

10. $\frac{10}{3}$

1		
$\frac{1}{3}$	$\frac{1}{3}$	$\frac{1}{3}$
$\frac{1}{3}$	$\frac{1}{3}$	$\frac{1}{3}$
$\frac{1}{3}$	$\frac{1}{3}$	$\frac{1}{3}$
$\frac{1}{3}$		

11. $1\frac{1}{2}$

1	
$\frac{1}{2}$	$\frac{1}{2}$
$\frac{1}{2}$	

Problem Solving

12. Jeremy used this recipe to make a smoothie. How many $\frac{1}{2}$-cups of ice does Jeremy need?

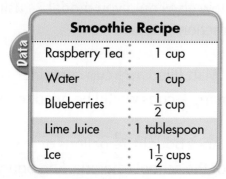

Smoothie Recipe

Raspberry Tea	1 cup
Water	1 cup
Blueberries	$\frac{1}{2}$ cup
Lime Juice	1 tablespoon
Ice	$1\frac{1}{2}$ cups

13. Chris finished eating his lunch in 11 minutes. His brother took 3 times as long. How many minutes did it take his brother to finish his lunch?

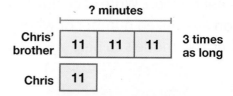

14. Sara bought a box of 6 granola bars. The total weight was $7\frac{1}{3}$ ounces. Write $7\frac{1}{3}$ as an improper fraction.

15. Kathy wrote the mixed number for $\frac{35}{5}$ as $\frac{7}{5}$. Is she correct? Why or why not?

16. Julia bought $3\frac{1}{4}$ yards of fabric. How many $\frac{1}{4}$-yards of fabric did Julia buy?

17. In one week, Nate drank $\frac{17}{3}$ cups of milk. Write $\frac{17}{3}$ as a mixed number.

18. What fraction or mixed number does this model show?

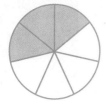

19. The average milk cow produces $4\frac{1}{2}$ gallons of milk a day. How much milk is this amount as an improper fraction?

A $\frac{11}{9}$ gallons   **C** $\frac{9}{2}$ gallons

B $\frac{19}{9}$ gallons   **D** $\frac{19}{2}$ gallon

Mixed Problem Solving

Artists frequently mix base colors together to create different hues of paint for use in paintings. They begin with three primary colors: blue, red, and yellow. The colors that are produced depend upon the fraction of paints that are combined.

Mr. McCrory is mixing paints together to create colors to use in some oil paintings.

Data			
Paint 1	$\frac{1}{4}$ blue	$\frac{1}{6}$ red	$\frac{5}{6}$ yellow
Paint 2	$\frac{3}{4}$ red	$\frac{1}{3}$ yellow	$\frac{5}{8}$ blue
Color	Light Purple	Orange	Deep Green

1. Use fraction strips to compare the fractions of color paint that were used to make the shade of deep green and the shade of light purple. Write the fractions from *greatest* to *least*.

2. Use fraction strips to order all the fractions of paint used from *least* to *greatest*.

3. Jared painted on a canvas using fractional amounts of colored paint. The chart at the right shows the fractional amount of each color that was used. Order each fraction from *least* to *greatest*.

Data				
Color of paint	Blue	Red	Yellow	White
Amount used	$\frac{2}{3}$	$\frac{6}{12}$	$\frac{8}{9}$	$\frac{4}{10}$

4. Elsie took a course on making stained glass at the community art center. She used $\frac{2}{6}$ of green-colored glass, $\frac{1}{2}$ of yellow-colored glass, and $\frac{1}{6}$ of red-colored glass to make a sun catcher. Was more of her sun catcher made up of green or yellow colored glass? Draw a model to show your answer.

5. A flag is made up of fractional colors. $\frac{1}{2}$ of the flag is blue, and $\frac{1}{4}$ is white. The rest of the flag is made up of $\frac{2}{12}$ red and $\frac{1}{12}$ green. Order the fractions of color from *least* to *greatest*.

Understand It!
There are different ways to compare fractions.

Comparing Fractions

How can you compare fractions?

Isabella's father is building a model dinosaur with spare pieces of wood that measure $\frac{1}{4}$ of an inch and $\frac{5}{8}$ of an inch.

Which are longer, the $\frac{1}{4}$ inch pieces or the $\frac{5}{8}$ inch pieces?

$\frac{1}{4}$ of an inch

Guided Practice*

Do you know HOW?

Compare. Write >, <, or = for each ◯. Use fraction strips or drawings to help.

1. $\frac{3}{4}$ ◯ $\frac{6}{8}$

2. $\frac{1}{4}$ ◯ $\frac{1}{10}$

3. $\frac{3}{5}$ ◯ $\frac{7}{15}$

4. $\frac{1}{2}$ ◯ $\frac{4}{5}$

Do you UNDERSTAND?

5. Mary says that $\frac{1}{8}$ is greater than $\frac{1}{4}$ because 8 is greater than 4. Is she right? Explain your answer.

6. Mr. Arnold used wood measuring $\frac{2}{5}$ foot, $\frac{1}{3}$ foot, and $\frac{3}{8}$ foot to build a birdhouse. Compare these lengths of wood.

Independent Practice

For **7** through **38**, compare. Then write >, <, or = for each ◯. Use fraction strips or benchmark fractions to help.

7. $\frac{5}{6}$ ◯ $\frac{10}{12}$

8. $\frac{3}{10}$ ◯ $\frac{7}{8}$

9. $\frac{5}{12}$ ◯ $\frac{1}{2}$

10. $\frac{7}{8}$ ◯ $\frac{3}{4}$

11. $\frac{1}{3}$ ◯ $\frac{2}{8}$

12. $\frac{1}{4}$ ◯ $\frac{2}{3}$

13. $\frac{7}{12}$ ◯ $\frac{3}{4}$

14. $\frac{2}{3}$ ◯ $\frac{2}{12}$

15. $\frac{3}{8}$ ◯ $\frac{2}{3}$

16. $\frac{3}{4}$ ◯ $\frac{1}{8}$

17. $\frac{2}{3}$ ◯ $\frac{5}{12}$

18. $\frac{1}{2}$ ◯ $\frac{3}{4}$

19. $\frac{7}{10}$ ◯ $\frac{11}{12}$

20. $\frac{7}{12}$ ◯ $\frac{4}{10}$

21. $\frac{5}{12}$ ◯ $\frac{4}{5}$

22. $\frac{2}{6}$ ◯ $\frac{3}{12}$

23. $\frac{8}{10}$ ◯ $\frac{3}{4}$

24. $\frac{3}{8}$ ◯ $\frac{11}{12}$

25. $\frac{2}{3}$ ◯ $\frac{10}{12}$

26. $\frac{7}{8}$ ◯ $\frac{1}{6}$

DIGITAL
eTools
www.pearsonsuccessnet.com

*For another example, see Set G on page 246.

Use benchmark fractions.

Compare $\frac{1}{4}$ and $\frac{5}{8}$.

You can use fraction strips to compare both fractions to $\frac{1}{2}$.

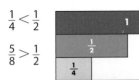

$\frac{1}{4} < \frac{1}{2}$

$\frac{5}{8} > \frac{1}{2}$

So, $\frac{1}{4} < \frac{5}{8}$.

The $\frac{5}{8}$ inch pieces are longer.

Compare $\frac{1}{4}$ and $\frac{3}{4}$.

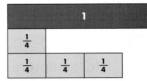

When the two fractions have the same denominators, you compare the numerators.

$$3 > 1$$

So, $\frac{3}{4} > \frac{1}{4}$.

27. $\frac{3}{8} \bigcirc \frac{7}{8}$ **28.** $\frac{2}{4} \bigcirc \frac{4}{8}$ **29.** $\frac{6}{8} \bigcirc \frac{8}{12}$ **30.** $\frac{1}{3} \bigcirc \frac{4}{9}$

31. $\frac{6}{8} \bigcirc \frac{8}{10}$ **32.** $\frac{3}{5} \bigcirc \frac{3}{6}$ **33.** $\frac{2}{10} \bigcirc \frac{2}{12}$ **34.** $\frac{5}{6} \bigcirc \frac{4}{5}$

35. $\frac{4}{4} \bigcirc \frac{1}{1}$ **36.** $\frac{2}{4} \bigcirc \frac{8}{10}$ **37.** $\frac{7}{8} \bigcirc \frac{3}{5}$ **38.** $\frac{3}{9} \bigcirc \frac{1}{3}$

Problem Solving

39. Number Sense Felicia drew the picture at the right to show that $\frac{3}{8}$ is greater than $\frac{3}{4}$. What was Felicia's mistake?

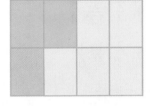

40. Writing to Explain Why can you compare two fractions with the same denominator by only comparing the numerators?

41. What can you conclude about $\frac{3}{5}$ and $\frac{12}{20}$ if you know that $\frac{3}{5} = \frac{6}{10}$ and that $\frac{6}{10} = \frac{12}{20}$?

42. Reasoning Which is longer, $\frac{1}{4}$ foot or $\frac{1}{4}$ yard? Explain.

43. If $34 \times 20 = 680$, then $34 \times 200 = \blacksquare$.

44. A melon was divided into 8 equal slices. Juan ate three slices. Tom and Stacy ate the remaining slices. What fraction of the melon did Tom and Stacy eat?

A $\frac{1}{4}$ **B** $\frac{2}{8}$ **C** $\frac{2}{3}$ **D** $\frac{5}{8}$

45. Neil is setting up for a dinner party. He has 6 tables each seating 5 guests and another table seating the left over 3 guests. How many people are coming to Neil's dinner party?

Understand It!
Equivalent fractions can be used to order fractions.

Ordering Fractions

How can you order fractions?

Hands-On
fraction strips $\frac{1}{8}$

Three students made sculptures for a school project. Jeff's sculpture is $\frac{9}{12}$ foot tall, Scott's sculpture is $\frac{1}{3}$ foot tall, and Kristen's sculpture is $\frac{3}{6}$ foot tall. List the heights of the sculptures in order from least to greatest.

$\frac{9}{12}$ foot tall

Guided Practice*

Do you know HOW?

For **1** through **6**, order the fractions from least to greatest. Use fraction strips or drawings to help.

1. $\frac{2}{3}, \frac{1}{2}, \frac{5}{12}$

2. $\frac{5}{6}, \frac{1}{3}, \frac{1}{6}$

3. $\frac{7}{8}, \frac{3}{8}, \frac{3}{4}$

4. $\frac{2}{3}, \frac{3}{12}, \frac{3}{4}$

5. $\frac{7}{9}, \frac{2}{3}, \frac{4}{9}$

6. $\frac{2}{3}, \frac{1}{4}, \frac{1}{6}$

Do you UNDERSTAND?

7. What denominator would you use to find equivalent fractions when comparing $\frac{2}{3}, \frac{2}{4}, \frac{2}{12}$?

8. Three other students made sculptures with these heights: $\frac{2}{3}$ foot, $\frac{5}{6}$ foot, and $\frac{2}{12}$ foot. Write these heights in order from least to greatest.

Independent Practice

For **9** through **20**, find equivalent fractions. Then order the fractions from least to greatest. Use drawings or fraction strips to help.

9. $\frac{1}{4}, \frac{1}{6}, \frac{1}{2}$

10. $\frac{2}{4}, \frac{2}{6}, \frac{2}{12}$

11. $\frac{2}{3}, \frac{5}{6}, \frac{7}{12}$

12. $\frac{5}{12}, \frac{2}{3}, \frac{1}{4}$

13. $\frac{3}{5}, \frac{4}{10}, \frac{1}{2}$

14. $\frac{1}{2}, \frac{3}{5}, \frac{2}{10}$

15. $\frac{5}{6}, \frac{3}{4}, \frac{8}{12}$

16. $\frac{8}{12}, \frac{1}{2}, \frac{3}{4}$

17. $\frac{6}{8}, \frac{1}{2}, \frac{3}{8}$

18. $\frac{2}{5}, \frac{3}{10}, \frac{3}{5}$

19. $\frac{10}{12}, \frac{1}{2}, \frac{3}{4}$

20. $\frac{2}{4}, \frac{3}{12}, \frac{2}{3}$

DIGITAL

eTools
www.pearsonsuccessnet.com

*For another example, see Set H on page 247.

Step 1

Find equivalent fractions with a common denominator.

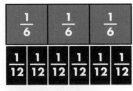

$$\frac{3}{6} = \frac{6}{12}$$

$$\frac{1}{3} = \frac{4}{12}$$

Step 2

Compare the numerators.

$$\frac{4}{12} < \frac{6}{12} < \frac{9}{12}$$

Order the fractions from least to greatest.

So, $\frac{1}{3} < \frac{3}{6} < \frac{9}{12}$.

The heights of the sculptures in order from least to greatest are $\frac{1}{3}$ foot, $\frac{3}{6}$ foot, $\frac{9}{12}$ foot.

Problem Solving

21. Writing to Explain Sandy's sculpture is taller than Jason's. Becca's sculpture is taller than Sandy's sculpture. If Sandy's sculpture is $\frac{2}{3}$ foot tall, how tall could Jason's and Becca's sculpture be?

22. Reasoning The fraction $\frac{2}{3}$ is $\frac{1}{3}$ less than 1 whole. Without finding equivalent fractions, order the fractions $\frac{7}{8}$, $\frac{2}{3}$, and $\frac{5}{6}$ from least to greatest.

23. The table at the right shows the number of pages four students read. Which lists the number of pages in order from least to greatest?

  A 25, 69, 96, 64   **C** 64, 25, 69, 96

  B 25, 64, 69, 96   **D** 25, 64, 96, 69

Students	Number of Pages
Francine	25
Ty	69
Greg	96
Vicki	64

Data

24. Algebra Find the missing numbers in the pattern below.

  ▨, 36, 54, ▨, ▨, 108, ▨

25. Katie asked Kerry to name 3 fractions between 0 and 1. Kerry said $\frac{5}{12}$, $\frac{1}{4}$, and $\frac{2}{6}$. Order Kerry's fractions from least to greatest.

26. Geena had 6 pairs of earrings. Kiera had 3 times as many. How many pairs of earrings did Kiera have?

27. Each student in fourth grade had the same book to read. Charles read $\frac{2}{3}$ of the book, and Drew read $\frac{3}{5}$ of the book. Who read more?

Understand It!
Using words, pictures, or symbols are ways to write a math explanation.

Writing to Explain

Jake found a piece of wood in the shape of an equilateral triangle. He cut off a section of the triangle as shown to the right.

Did Jake cut off $\frac{1}{3}$ of the triangle? Explain.

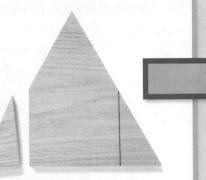

Section of wood cut off

Another Example

Erin says that $\frac{1}{2}$ is always the same amount as $\frac{2}{4}$. Matthew says that $\frac{1}{2}$ and $\frac{2}{4}$ are equivalent fractions, but they could be different amounts. Which student is correct? Explain.

The circles are the same size.

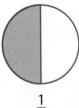

$\frac{1}{2}$

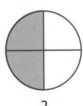

$\frac{2}{4}$

The amounts are the same.

The circles are not the same size.

$\frac{2}{4}$

$\frac{1}{2}$

The amounts are different.

Matthew is correct. $\frac{1}{2}$ and $\frac{2}{4}$ are equivalent fractions, but they could represent different amounts.

Explain It

1. When will amounts of $\frac{1}{2}$ and $\frac{2}{4}$ be equal?

2. When are the fractional amounts $\frac{3}{6}$ and $\frac{2}{4}$ not equal?

Read & Understand

What do I know?

The triangle is an equilateral triangle. One piece is cut off.

What am I asked to find?

Is the section that is cut off $\frac{1}{3}$ of the triangle?

Plan

Use words, pictures, numbers, or symbols to write a math explanation.

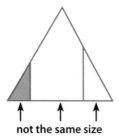

$\frac{1}{3}$ means that the whole has to be divided into 3 equal parts. The parts have to be the same size.

not the same size

The shaded section is not $\frac{1}{3}$ of the triangle.

Guided Practice*

Do you know HOW?

1. A board is cut into 12 equal pieces. How many pieces together represent $\frac{3}{4}$ of the board? Explain how you arrived at your answer.

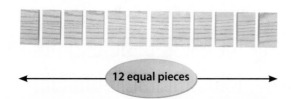

12 equal pieces

Do you UNDERSTAND?

2. Copy and draw the triangle above. Shade in $\frac{1}{3}$ of the triangle.

3. **Write a Problem** Write a problem that would use the figure below as part of its explanation.

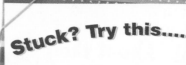

Independent Practice

Write to explain.

4. Devon and Amanda knit the same size scarf. Devon's scarf is $\frac{3}{5}$ yellow. Amanda's scarf is $\frac{3}{4}$ yellow. How can you use a picture to show whose scarf is more yellow?

5. The school newspaper has a total of 18 articles and ads. There are 6 more articles than ads. How many articles and ads are there? Explain how you found your answer.

Stuck? Try this....

- What do I know?
- What diagram can I use to help understand the problem?
- Can I use addition, subtraction, multiplication, or division?
- Is all of my work correct?
- Did I answer the right question?
- Is my answer reasonable?

*For another example, see Set J on page 247.

Lesson 10-9

6. Look at the cell pattern below. Explain how the number of cells changes as the number of divisions changes.

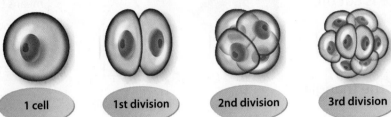

| 1 cell | 1st division | 2nd division | 3rd division |

7. Algebra Look at the number sentences below. What numbers replace ●, ▲, and ■? Explain your answer.

$$▲ + ■ = 18$$
$$● + ▲ = 20$$
$$■ + ■ = 14$$

8. Geometry Three streets intersect with one another. East Street runs horizontally, North Street runs vertically and Fourth Street runs diagonally and intersects both East Street and North Street. What geometric figure do the three streets form?

Use the data at the right for problems **9** and **10**.

9. How can you find the number of cards Linda has in her collection?

10. George has 100 rookie cards in his collection. How can you find the number of pictures in the pictograph that represent George's rookie cards?

Baseball Card Collections

George
Becky
Trent
Linda

Each 🂠 = 25 cards

Think About the Process

11. Janet gets $25 a week to buy lunch at school. She spends $4 each day and saves the rest. Which expression can be used to find how much money Janet will save at the end of the 5 days?

A $(4 \times 5) + 25$ **C** $(25 - 5) + 4$

B $25 + (5 - 4)$ **D** $25 - (5 \times 4)$

12. During recess, Rachel played on the bars and swings. She spent 10 minutes on the bars and twice as long on the swings. Which expression can be used to find how much time she spent on the equipment?

A $10 - (2 + 10)$ **C** $(10 + 2) - 10$

B $10 + (2 \times 10)$ **D** $(10 \div 2) + 10$

Equivalent Fractions

Use tools Fractions.

Find the numerator which makes the fractions equivalent. $\frac{3}{4} = \frac{\square}{8}$

Step 1 Go to the Fractions eTool. Select the equivalence workspace mode.

⊘ Select $\frac{1}{4}$ three times, to show $\frac{3}{4}$ in the first circle.

Step 2 Select the second circle by clicking on it. Select $\frac{1}{8}$ until the symbol changes from > to =. Read the fractions at the bottom of the workspace. $\frac{3}{4} = \frac{6}{8}$

Step 3 Use the Broom tool to clear the workspace before doing another problem.

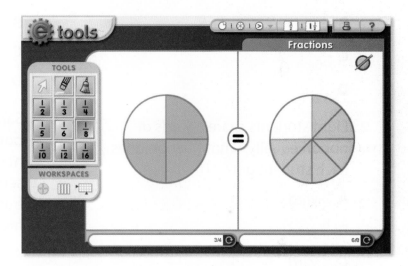

Practice

Use the Fractions eTool to find the numerator which makes the fractions equivalent.

1. $\frac{3}{4} = \frac{\square}{8}$

2. $\frac{2}{5} = \frac{\square}{10}$

3. $\frac{4}{6} = \frac{\square}{3}$

4. $\frac{6}{16} = \frac{\square}{8}$

5. $\frac{1}{2} = \frac{\square}{16}$

6. $\frac{1}{3} = \frac{\square}{12}$

7. $\frac{8}{10} = \frac{\square}{5}$

8. $\frac{3}{12} = \frac{\square}{4}$

9. $\frac{3}{4} = \frac{\square}{12}$

10. $\frac{5}{8} = \frac{\square}{16}$

11. $\frac{3}{4} = \frac{\square}{16}$

12. $\frac{4}{8} = \frac{\square}{2}$

13. $\frac{1}{2} = \frac{\square}{12}$

14. $\frac{1}{2} = \frac{\square}{10}$

15. $\frac{5}{6} = \frac{\square}{12}$

16. $\frac{4}{5} = \frac{\square}{15}$

1. Tonya bought the fruit shown below. What fraction of the fruit are apples? (10-1)

A $\frac{7}{10}$

B $\frac{3}{7}$

C $\frac{3}{10}$

D $\frac{3}{12}$

2. Eight students share 5 yards of ribbon equally. What fraction does each student get? (10-2)

A $\frac{8}{5}$ yard

B $\frac{8}{8}$ yard

C $\frac{5}{5}$ yard

D $\frac{5}{8}$ yard

3. Jase completed 8 out of the 10 laps required to pass his swimming test. What fraction, in simplest form, of the laps did he complete? (10-5)

A $\frac{8}{10}$

B $\frac{4}{5}$

C $\frac{3}{4}$

D $\frac{2}{3}$

4. Javier and Mark drew straws to see who went down the waterslide first. Javier's straw was $\frac{5}{12}$ inch long and Mark's was $\frac{7}{12}$ inch long. Which symbol makes the comparison true? (10-7)

$$\frac{5}{12} \bigcirc \frac{7}{12}$$

A $\times$

B $=$

C $<$

D $>$

5. Sandy had 3 bottles of juice. She poured the bottles into 7 glasses for her friends to drink. Which number sentence can be used to find the fraction of a bottle of juice that each friend gets? (10-2)

A $3 \times 7 = $ ▢

B $3 \div 4 = $ ▢

C $7 \div 3 = $ ▢

D $3 \div 7 = $ ▢

6. Yao drank $\frac{11}{4}$ bottles of water during a soccer game. What is this number written as a mixed number? (10-6)

A $3\frac{1}{4}$

B $2\frac{3}{4}$

C $2\frac{1}{2}$

D $2\frac{1}{4}$

7. Which statement would **NOT** be used in an explanation of how the drawing shows that $\frac{2}{3} = \frac{4}{6}$? (10-9)

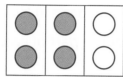

A 2 of the 3 rectangles are filled with shaded circles.

B 4 out of the 6 rectangles are shaded.

C Both $\frac{2}{3}$ and $\frac{4}{6}$ describe the part that is shaded.

D In the rectangles, 4 out of the 6 circles are shaded.

8. The student council ordered pizza for their meeting. Half of the members voted for cheese pizza, $\frac{1}{10}$ for hamburger, and $\frac{2}{5}$ for vegetable.

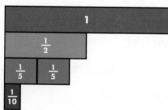

Which shows the fractions in order from least to greatest? (10-8)

A $\frac{1}{2}, \frac{1}{10}, \frac{2}{5}$

B $\frac{2}{5}, \frac{1}{10}, \frac{1}{2}$

C $\frac{1}{10}, \frac{1}{2}, \frac{2}{5}$

D $\frac{1}{10}, \frac{2}{5}, \frac{1}{2}$

9. What is the missing number which makes the fractions equivalent? (10-4)

$$\frac{3}{5} = \frac{9}{\square}$$

A 10

B 11

C 15

D 20

10. Elmer is painting one wall in his room. About what fraction of the wall has he painted blue? (10-3)

A $\frac{3}{4}$

B $\frac{1}{4}$

C $\frac{1}{2}$

D $\frac{2}{3}$

11. Mary weighed $7\frac{1}{2}$ pounds when she was born. What number makes the statement true? (10-6)

$$7\frac{1}{2} = \frac{\square}{2}$$

A 15

B 14

C 9

D 8

Set A, pages 216–218

You can write fractions to represent parts of a set. What part of the grapes are green?

$$\frac{\text{numerator}}{\text{denominator}} = \frac{\text{green grapes}}{\text{parts in all}}$$

$\frac{3}{5}$ of the grapes are green.

Remember the numerator tells how many equal parts are described, and the denominator tells how many equal parts in all.

Write a fraction for the part of each set that is red.

1.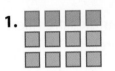
2.

3.
4. (circles)

Set B, pages 220–221

Four friends cut up 3 pieces of construction paper. If they shared the paper equally, what fraction of the paper did each friend use?

  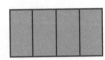

Each part is 1 ÷ 4, or $\frac{1}{4}$.

Each person used 3 parts. Each part is $\frac{1}{4}$, so each person used $\frac{3}{4}$ of a piece of construction paper.

Remember you can draw a model to show each fraction amount.

Tell what fraction each person gets.

1. Five students share 1 hour to give their reports.

2. Four people share two sandwiches.

3. Four friends share 3 cups of hot chocolate.

Set C, pages 222–223

Estimate the fractional part of the rectangle that is blue.

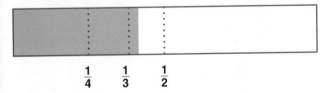

$\frac{1}{4}$ $\frac{1}{3}$ $\frac{1}{2}$

Compare the part that is blue. The blue part is more than $\frac{1}{3}$ but less than $\frac{1}{2}$ of the whole rectangle. About $\frac{1}{3}$ of the rectangle is blue.

Remember the benchmark fractions are basic fractions, such as $\frac{1}{4}, \frac{1}{3}, \frac{1}{2}, \frac{2}{3},$ and $\frac{3}{4}$.

Estimate the fractional part of each that is green.

1.
2. (rectangle)

244

Set D, pages 224–226

Find equivalent fractions for $\frac{2}{6}$ using multiplication and division.

Multiply the numerator and the denominator by the same number to find an equivalent fraction.

$$\overset{\times 2}{\underset{\times 2}{\frac{2}{6} = \frac{4}{12}}}$$ $\frac{2}{6}$ is equivalent to $\frac{4}{12}$.

Divide the numerator and denominator by 2.

$$\overset{\div 2}{\underset{\div 2}{\frac{2}{6} = \frac{1}{3}}}$$ $\frac{1}{3} = \frac{2}{6} = \frac{4}{12}$

Remember to find an equivalent fraction by dividing or multiplying the numerator and denominator by the same number.

Multiply or divide to find an equivalent fraction.

1. $\frac{8}{16} = \frac{\square}{8}$ **2.** $\frac{6}{36} = \frac{54}{\square}$

3. $\frac{8}{96} = \frac{\square}{12}$ **4.** $\frac{2}{11} = \frac{\square}{121}$

Find two equivalent forms for each fraction using multiplication and division.

5. $\frac{8}{12}$ **6.** $\frac{30}{40}$

7. $\frac{8}{72}$ **8.** $\frac{14}{22}$

Set E, pages 228–229

Write $\frac{4}{10}$ in simplest form.

The numerator, 4, and denominator, 10, have 2 as a common factor.

$$\overset{\div 2}{\underset{\div 2}{\frac{4}{10} = \frac{2}{5}}}$$

The only common factor for 2 and 5 is 1. In simplest form, $\frac{4}{10} = \frac{2}{5}$.

Write $\frac{12}{16}$ in simplest form.

$$\overset{\div 2}{\underset{\div 2}{\frac{12}{16} = \frac{6}{8}}}$$ then $$\overset{\div 2}{\underset{\div 2}{\frac{6}{8} = \frac{3}{4}}}$$

In simplest form, $\frac{12}{16} = \frac{3}{4}$.

Remember that a fraction is in simplest form if the numerator and the denominator have no common factor other than 1.

Write each fraction in simplest form.

1. $\frac{3}{6}$ **2.** $\frac{2}{10}$

3. $\frac{20}{30}$ **4.** $\frac{10}{12}$

5. $\frac{9}{12}$ **6.** $\frac{4}{6}$

7. $\frac{4}{10}$ **8.** $\frac{8}{12}$

9. $\frac{8}{16}$ **10.** $\frac{28}{32}$

Set F, pages 230–232

Write $\frac{7}{4}$ as a mixed number.

Use fraction strips.

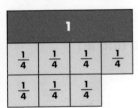

4 fourths in one whole

3 fourths

So, $\frac{7}{4} = 1\frac{3}{4}$.

Use a model.

There is 1 whole shaded and $\frac{3}{4}$ of another whole shaded.

So, $\frac{7}{4} = 1\frac{3}{4}$.

Remember you can use fraction strips to write a mixed number as an improper fraction.

Write each number as a mixed number or an improper fraction.

1. $2\frac{2}{5}$ **2.** $\frac{9}{4}$

Set G, pages 234–235

Compare $\frac{1}{6}$ and $\frac{3}{6}$.

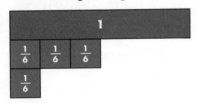

$1 < 3$

So, $\frac{1}{6} < \frac{3}{6}$.

Compare $\frac{4}{6}$ and $\frac{3}{4}$.

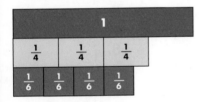

$\frac{4}{6}$ is less than $\frac{3}{4}$.

So, $\frac{4}{6} < \frac{3}{4}$.

Remember when comparing fractions with different denominators, you can use benchmark fractions such as $\frac{1}{4}, \frac{1}{3}, \frac{1}{2}, \frac{2}{3},$ and $\frac{3}{4}$.

Compare. Write $>$, $<$, or $=$ for each $\bigcirc$.

1. $\frac{5}{6} \bigcirc \frac{2}{3}$ **2.** $\frac{1}{3} \bigcirc \frac{3}{10}$

3. $\frac{5}{10} \bigcirc \frac{1}{2}$ **4.** $\frac{3}{4} \bigcirc \frac{5}{12}$

5. $\frac{3}{8} \bigcirc \frac{1}{3}$ **6.** $\frac{4}{10} \bigcirc \frac{3}{12}$

7. $\frac{7}{8} \bigcirc \frac{5}{8}$ **8.** $\frac{1}{5} \bigcirc \frac{2}{10}$

9. $\frac{2}{5} \bigcirc \frac{1}{4}$ **10.** $\frac{3}{6} \bigcirc \frac{3}{4}$

11. $\frac{2}{12} \bigcirc \frac{1}{6}$ **12.** $\frac{1}{7} \bigcirc \frac{7}{7}$

13. $\frac{9}{10} \bigcirc \frac{4}{5}$ **14.** $\frac{2}{6} \bigcirc \frac{2}{3}$

Set H, pages 236–237

Order $\frac{5}{6}$, $\frac{2}{3}$, and $\frac{1}{2}$ from least to greatest.

Find equivalent fractions with a common denominator.

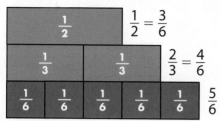

$\frac{1}{2} = \frac{3}{6}$

$\frac{2}{3} = \frac{4}{6}$

$\frac{5}{6}$

$\frac{3}{6} < \frac{4}{6} < \frac{5}{6}$ So, $\frac{1}{2}$, $\frac{2}{3}$, $\frac{5}{6}$.

Order $\frac{4}{6}$, $\frac{3}{4}$, and $\frac{1}{2}$ from least to greatest.

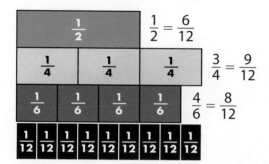

$\frac{1}{2} = \frac{6}{12}$

$\frac{3}{4} = \frac{9}{12}$

$\frac{4}{6} = \frac{8}{12}$

$\frac{6}{12} < \frac{8}{12} < \frac{9}{12}$.   So, $\frac{1}{2}$, $\frac{4}{6}$, $\frac{3}{4}$.

Remember you can use fraction strips to find equivalent fractions with common denominators.

Order from least to greatest.

1. $\frac{1}{2}$, $\frac{2}{3}$, $\frac{5}{12}$ 2. $\frac{7}{8}$, $\frac{3}{8}$, $\frac{3}{4}$

3. $\frac{1}{3}$, $\frac{1}{6}$, $\frac{3}{6}$ 4. $\frac{2}{5}$, $\frac{5}{6}$, $\frac{11}{12}$

5. $\frac{6}{8}$, $\frac{5}{8}$, $\frac{1}{2}$ 6. $\frac{2}{5}$, $\frac{3}{10}$, $\frac{6}{10}$

Order from greatest to least.

7. $\frac{1}{3}$, $\frac{2}{3}$, $\frac{5}{6}$ 8. $\frac{7}{8}$, $\frac{3}{4}$, $\frac{1}{1}$

9. $\frac{7}{10}$, $\frac{3}{12}$, $\frac{1}{3}$ 10. $\frac{1}{4}$, $\frac{3}{8}$, $\frac{2}{6}$

11. $\frac{2}{8}$, $\frac{1}{3}$, $\frac{2}{4}$ 12. $\frac{4}{5}$, $\frac{5}{6}$, $\frac{9}{12}$

Set J, pages 238–240

Suppose a square is cut as shown. Is each section $\frac{1}{4}$ of the square?

What do I know?   The square is cut into 4 pieces.

What am I asked to find?   Do all the cuts represent $\frac{1}{4}$ of the square?

If each part is $\frac{1}{4}$ then the whole is divided into 4 equal parts.
The parts are not the same size. Each is not $\frac{1}{4}$ of the square.

Remember to explain your answer.

1. Peter says that $\frac{3}{4}$ of a pizza is always the same as $\frac{6}{8}$ of a pizza. Nadia says that while they are equivalent fractions, $\frac{3}{4}$ and $\frac{6}{8}$ of a pizza could represent different amounts. Who is correct?

2. David says you can have an unlimited number of equivalent fractions to any given fraction. Is he right?

Adding and Subtracting Fractions

1 The Metrodome in Minnesota has an air-supported roof. What fraction of Major League baseball parks have a roof? You will find out in Lesson 11-3.

2

Mancala is one of the oldest games in the world. There are many names for this game which is played in different countries. How many stones are used in a game of Mancala? You will find out in Lesson 11-1.

Review What You Know!

Vocabulary

Choose the best term from the box.

- common factor
- numerator
- denominator
- simplest form

1. The factor that two or more numbers have in common is called a(n) ___?___.

2. A ___?___ represents the total number of equal parts in all.

3. The number above the fraction bar in a fraction is known as the ___?___.

Parts of a Region or Set

4. What fraction of the set below is red?

⬤⬤⬤⬤⬤
⬤⬤⬤⬤⬤

5. What fraction of the rectangle below is not green?

3

How many chemical elements are named for women scientists? You will find out in Lesson 11-2.

Fraction Concepts

Draw a model to show each fraction.

6. $\frac{5}{6}$ **7.** $\frac{1}{4}$ **8.** $\frac{2}{3}$

9. $\frac{1}{3}$ **10.** $\frac{6}{8}$ **11.** $\frac{3}{5}$

12. $\frac{6}{10}$ **13.** $\frac{11}{12}$ **14.** $\frac{5}{5}$

15. Writing to Explain Why are $\frac{3}{4}$ and $\frac{4}{8}$ not equivalent fractions?

11-1

Adding and Subtracting Fractions with Like Denominators

Hands-On
fraction strips

$\frac{1}{8}$

How can you add fractions with like denominators?

Jimmy painted $\frac{1}{8}$ of a fence in the morning and $\frac{4}{8}$ of a fence in the afternoon. How much did he paint in all?

$\frac{1}{8}$ of the fence

Another Example **How can you subtract fractions with like denominators?**

Mandy bought $\frac{1}{6}$ pound of popcorn and Jane bought $\frac{5}{6}$ pound of popcorn. How much more popcorn did Jane buy than Mandy?

One Way

Subtract $\frac{5}{6} - \frac{1}{6}$ using fraction strips.

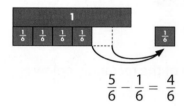

$$\frac{5}{6} - \frac{1}{6} = \frac{4}{6}$$

Simplify.

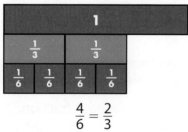

$$\frac{4}{6} = \frac{2}{3}$$

Jane bought $\frac{2}{3}$ of a pound more popcorn than Mandy.

Another Way

Subtract $\frac{5}{6} - \frac{1}{6}$.

$$\frac{5}{6} - \frac{1}{6} = \frac{5-1}{6} = \frac{4}{6}$$

Simplify.

$$\frac{4}{6} \overset{\div 2}{\underset{\div 2}{=}} \frac{2}{3}$$

Jane bought $\frac{2}{3}$ of a pound more popcorn than Mandy.

Explain It

1. How do you know that $\frac{4}{6}$ can be simplified to $\frac{2}{3}$?

One Way

Add $\frac{1}{8} + \frac{4}{8}$ using fraction strips.

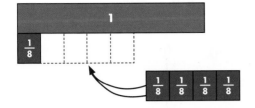

There are 5 eighths in all.
Jimmy painted $\frac{5}{8}$ of the fence.

Another Way

Add $\frac{1}{8} + \frac{4}{8}$.

The denominators are the same, so add the numerators.

$$\frac{1}{8} + \frac{4}{8} = \frac{1+4}{8} = \frac{5}{8}$$

Jimmy painted $\frac{5}{8}$ of the fence.

Guided Practice*

Do you know HOW?

Add or subtract the fractions. Write the answers in simplest form. You may use fraction strips to help.

1. $\frac{1}{5} + \frac{2}{5}$ **2.** $\frac{3}{12} + \frac{5}{12}$

3. $\frac{3}{6} - \frac{1}{6}$ **4.** $\frac{4}{10} - \frac{2}{10}$

Do you UNDERSTAND?

5. In the example above, how do you know that $\frac{5}{8}$ is in simplest form?

6. After painting $\frac{5}{8}$ of the fence, Jimmy painted another $\frac{2}{8}$ of the fence. How much had he painted in all?

Independent Practice

For **7** through **16**, add. Write the answer in simplest form. You may use fraction strips to help.

7. $\frac{1}{9}$
$+ \frac{3}{9}$

8. $\frac{2}{6}$
$+ \frac{1}{6}$

9. $\frac{4}{12}$
$+ \frac{4}{12}$

10. $\frac{1}{12}$
$+ \frac{9}{12}$

11. $\frac{3}{8}$
$+ \frac{3}{8}$

12. $\frac{1}{3}$
$+ \frac{1}{3}$

13. $\frac{2}{5}$
$+ \frac{1}{5}$

14. $\frac{1}{6}$
$+ \frac{3}{6}$

15. $\frac{1}{8}$
$+ \frac{3}{8}$

16. $\frac{1}{7}$
$+ \frac{4}{7}$

DIGITAL   eTools   www.pearsonsuccessnet.com

Independent Practice

For **17** through **26**, subtract. Write the answer in simplest form. You may use fraction strips to help.

17. $\frac{11}{12}$
$-\ \frac{2}{12}$

18. $\frac{5}{8}$
$-\ \frac{3}{8}$

19. $\frac{5}{9}$
$-\ \frac{2}{9}$

20. $\frac{10}{11}$
$-\ \frac{9}{11}$

21. $\frac{9}{12}$
$-\ \frac{3}{12}$

22. $\frac{3}{4}$
$-\ \frac{1}{4}$

23. $\frac{4}{5}$
$-\ \frac{2}{5}$

24. $\frac{5}{6}$
$-\ \frac{1}{6}$

25. $\frac{10}{12}$
$-\ \frac{6}{12}$

26. $\frac{6}{7}$
$-\ \frac{1}{7}$

For **27** through **36**, add or subtract. Write the answer in simplest form. You may use fraction strips to help.

27. $\frac{1}{8} + \frac{2}{8}$

28. $\frac{5}{7} - \frac{2}{7}$

29. $\frac{1}{12} + \frac{3}{12}$

30. $\frac{7}{10} - \frac{3}{10}$

31. $\frac{1}{5} + \frac{3}{5}$

32. $\frac{2}{6} - \frac{1}{6}$

33. $\frac{2}{4} + \frac{1}{4}$

34. $\frac{8}{10} - \frac{3}{10}$

35. $\frac{7}{10} + \frac{1}{10}$

36. $\frac{3}{4} - \frac{2}{4}$

Problem Solving

37. Algebra All 4 sides of a rectangle have the same length. If the perimeter is 16 inches, what is the length of each side?

38. Stan makes a smoothie with $\frac{2}{8}$ cup of water and $\frac{3}{8}$ cup of milk. How much water and milk does he use in all?

For **39** and **40**, use the diagram at the right.

39. Harriet took 7 horses from the barn to the pasture when she cleaned their stalls. If there was a horse in every stall, what fraction of the horses were in the pasture?

40. If Harriet took 3 more horses from the barn to the pasture, what fraction of the horses were then in the pasture? Write your answer in simplest form.

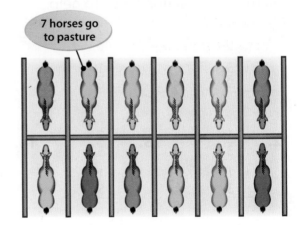

7 horses go to pasture

For **41** and **42**, use the picture to the right.

41. What fraction of the stained glass window is either green or purple?

42. What fraction of the stained glass window is either red or blue?

43. A new CD has 16 songs. Four of the songs are more than five minutes long, 7 of the songs are between three and five minutes long, and the remaining songs are less than three minutes long. What fraction of the songs on the CD are less than three minutes long?

44. Sandy, Josh, and Jeremy are all decorating a banner. Sandy decorates $\frac{4}{8}$ of the banner, Josh decorates $\frac{3}{8}$ of the banner, and Jeremy decorates $\frac{1}{8}$ of the banner. How much more of the banner do they have to decorate?

45. Terri says since 80 has 8 as one of its factors, it will also have 4 and 2 as factors because 4 and 2 are factors of 8. Is she correct?

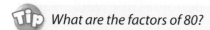 *What are the factors of 80?*

46. Austin walked $\frac{1}{6}$ mile to school. He then walked $\frac{2}{6}$ mile to the park. How far has Austin walked?

  A $\frac{1}{2}$ mile   **C** $\frac{3}{4}$ mile

  B $\frac{5}{8}$ mile   **D** $\frac{8}{6}$ miles

In the game, Mancala, there are 36 stones. When a stone is captured, it stays in one player's cala, or bin, for the rest of the game. The person who has the most captured stones at the end of the game wins.

47. Reasoning If Player 1 has captured $\frac{3}{36}$ of the stones and Player 2 has $\frac{7}{36}$ of the stones, what fraction of the stones have not been captured yet? Write your answer in simplest form.

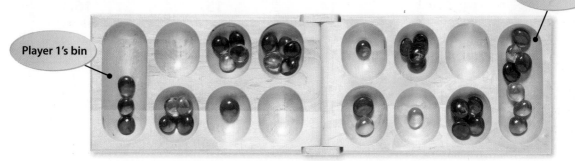

Player 2's bin

Player 1's bin

Understand It!
To add fractions with unlike denominators, it is necessary to change to like denominators.

Adding Fractions with Unlike Denominators

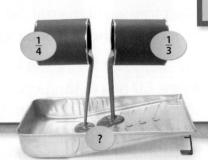

Hands-On
fraction strips

$\frac{1}{8}$

How can you add fractions with unlike denominators?

Terry mixed $\frac{1}{4}$ of a can of red paint and $\frac{1}{3}$ of a can of blue paint to make purple. What fraction of a can of purple paint does Terry have now?

Guided Practice*

Do you know HOW?

For **1** through **4**, add. Write the answer in simplest form. You may use fraction strips or drawings to help.

1. $\frac{1}{3} + \frac{1}{6}$

2. $\frac{3}{8} + \frac{1}{4}$

3. $\frac{1}{6} + \frac{2}{4}$

4. $\frac{1}{5} + \frac{4}{10}$

Do you UNDERSTAND?

5. If Terry mixed $\frac{1}{4}$ can of red paint and $\frac{2}{12}$ can of yellow paint, how much orange paint would he have?

6. What denominator would you use to add $\frac{1}{3}$ and $\frac{3}{5}$?

Independent Practice

For **7** through **21**, add. Write the answer in simplest form. You may use fraction strips or drawings to help.

7. $\frac{3}{4} + \frac{1}{8}$

8. $\frac{7}{10} + \frac{1}{5}$

9. $\frac{3}{6} + \frac{1}{3}$

10. $\frac{1}{5} + \frac{1}{10}$

11. $\frac{7}{12} + \frac{1}{3}$

12. $\frac{3}{10} + \frac{2}{5}$

13. $\frac{1}{6} + \frac{3}{4}$

14. $\frac{1}{5} + \frac{1}{2}$

15. $\frac{1}{6} + \frac{5}{12}$

16. $\frac{1}{4} + \frac{1}{6}$

17. $\frac{1}{8} + \frac{1}{4}$

18. $\frac{1}{12} + \frac{3}{4}$

19. $\frac{1}{10} + \frac{2}{5}$

20. $\frac{2}{4} + \frac{2}{8}$

21. $\frac{1}{5} + \frac{2}{10}$

eTools
www.pearsonsuccessnet.com

*For another example, see Set B on page 264.

One Way

Add $\frac{1}{4}$ and $\frac{1}{3}$ using fraction strips.

Both the $\frac{1}{4}$ and $\frac{1}{3}$ piece can be shown using twelfths.

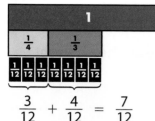

$$\frac{3}{12} + \frac{4}{12} = \frac{7}{12}$$

Terry has $\frac{7}{12}$ of a can of purple paint.

Another Way

Find $\frac{1}{4} + \frac{1}{3}$.

When you add fractions with unlike denominators, change the fractions to equivalent fractions that have a common denominator. Then add the numerators.

$$\frac{1}{4} \overset{\times 3}{=} \frac{3}{12} \underset{\times 3}{}$$

Think What number has 4 and 3 as factors?

$$+\ \frac{1}{3} \overset{\times 4}{=} \frac{4}{12} \underset{\times 4}{}$$

Add the new fractions. Write the sum in simplest form.

$$\frac{7}{12}$$

Terry has $\frac{7}{12}$ of a can of purple paint.

Problem Solving

22. Reasoning To trim a child's costume, Nora needs $\frac{1}{2}$ yard of lace at the neck and $\frac{1}{5}$ yard for each wrist. How much lace does Nora need?

23. Francis read $\frac{1}{3}$ of his book yesterday and $\frac{1}{2}$ of his book today. How much of the book has Francis read?

24. Add the two fractions represented by each circle. What is the sum in simplest form?

25. Number Sense Mary measures beads for a bracelet. Three clay beads are each $\frac{1}{8}$ inch long. Two glass beads are each $\frac{1}{4}$ inch long. What is the length of all five beads when strung together?

26. In all, 36 chemical elements were named after people or places. Of these, two were named for women scientists, and twenty-five were named for places. What fraction of these 36 elements were named for women and places? Write your answer in simplest form.

27. At the first stop, a trolley picks up $\frac{1}{6}$ of the number of passengers it can carry. At the second stop, it picks up $\frac{2}{3}$ of the number of passengers it can carry. Which sum is **NOT** the correct fraction of passengers that are on the trolley after 2 stops?

A $\frac{5}{6}$ **B** $\frac{9}{12}$ **C** $\frac{15}{18}$ **D** $\frac{20}{24}$

Understand It!
To subtract fractions with unlike denominators, it is necessary to change to like denominators.

Subtracting Fractions with Unlike Denominators

Hands-On fraction strips $\frac{1}{8}$

How can you subtract fractions with unlike denominators?

Zoe and Frank are making macaroni and cheese. They bought $\frac{2}{3}$ pound of cheese. How much cheese will they have left if they use $\frac{1}{2}$ pound of cheese?

$\frac{2}{3}$ of a pound

$\frac{1}{2}$ of a pound

Guided Practice*

Do you know HOW?

For **1** through **4**, subtract. Write the answer in simplest form. You may use fraction strips or drawings to help.

1. $\frac{2}{5} - \frac{2}{10}$
2. $\frac{4}{6} - \frac{4}{8}$
3. $\frac{5}{6} - \frac{2}{12}$
4. $\frac{7}{10} - \frac{2}{5}$

Do you UNDERSTAND?

5. How much cheese would Zoe and Frank have left if they used $\frac{1}{4}$ pound of cheese?

6. What denominator would you use to subtract $\frac{5}{6} - \frac{1}{5}$?

Independent Practice

For **7** through **21**, subtract. Write the answer in simplest form. You may use fraction strips or drawings to help.

7. $\frac{3}{4} - \frac{3}{8}$
8. $\frac{7}{10} - \frac{1}{5}$
9. $\frac{7}{9} - \frac{2}{3}$
10. $\frac{5}{6} - \frac{4}{12}$
11. $\frac{2}{3} - \frac{2}{6}$

12. $\frac{5}{10} - \frac{1}{5}$
13. $\frac{3}{4} - \frac{4}{8}$
14. $\frac{7}{12} - \frac{1}{3}$
15. $\frac{2}{5} - \frac{3}{10}$
16. $\frac{5}{6} - \frac{3}{4}$

17. $\frac{4}{5} - \frac{1}{10}$
18. $\frac{1}{4} - \frac{1}{6}$
19. $\frac{11}{12} - \frac{2}{3}$
20. $\frac{5}{8} - \frac{1}{4}$
21. $\frac{1}{4} - \frac{1}{8}$

eTools
www.pearsonsuccessnet.com

For another example, see Set C on page 265.

Use fraction strips to subtract $\frac{2}{3} - \frac{1}{2}$.

Both $\frac{2}{3}$ and $\frac{1}{2}$ can be shown using sixths.

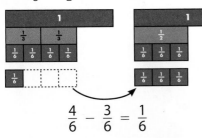

$$\frac{4}{6} - \frac{3}{6} = \frac{1}{6}$$

They have $\frac{1}{6}$ pound of cheese left.

Find $\frac{2}{3} - \frac{1}{2}$.

Rewrite the fractions using the same denominator.

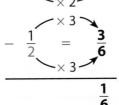

Think What number has 3 and 2 as factors?

Subtract the new fractions. Write the difference in simplest form.

$$\frac{1}{6}$$

They have $\frac{1}{6}$ pound of cheese left.

Problem Solving

22. Algebra Write an expression to represent the cost of a pizza for d dollars with a coupon for $2 off.

23. The sum of two fractions is $\frac{8}{9}$. The difference is $\frac{2}{9}$. What are the two fractions?

24. Geometry Tim used 28 straws to make squares and hexagons. If he made 4 squares, how many hexagons could he make?

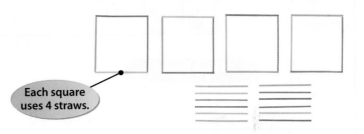

Each square uses 4 straws.

25. A banana bread recipe calls for $\frac{1}{4}$ cup of oil. A muffin recipe calls for $\frac{1}{2}$ cup of oil. How much more oil is needed to make the muffins?

26. Luke and Lydia ran for $\frac{3}{4}$ hour without stopping. This is $\frac{3}{16}$ hour more than Kevin and Sarah ran. How long did Kevin and Sarah run?

27. Of 30 Major League baseball teams, $\frac{7}{30}$ of the teams have a covered ballpark with a roof. If $\frac{1}{10}$ of the 30 ballparks are National League parks with a roof, what fraction of the ballparks are American League ballparks with a roof?

$\frac{7}{30}$ **covered ballparks**

$\frac{1}{10}$	?

28. Renee's pizza had 8 equal slices. She ate $\frac{3}{8}$ of her pizza. George's pizza had 12 equal slices. He ate $\frac{1}{4}$ of his pizza. If both pizzas were the same size, how much more pizza did Renee eat?

A $\frac{1}{8}$ more

C $\frac{1}{3}$ more

B $\frac{1}{4}$ more

D $\frac{5}{8}$ more

Understand It!
Learning how and when to draw a picture and write an equation can help you solve problems.

Draw a Picture and Write an Equation

Brad and his father hiked three trails. The Gadsen Trail is $\frac{9}{10}$ of a mile, the Rosebriar Trail is $\frac{1}{2}$ of a mile, and the Eureka Trail is $\frac{3}{5}$ of a mile. How far did they walk in all?

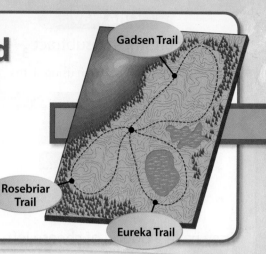

Gadsen Trail

Rosebriar Trail

Eureka Trail

Another Example Sandra and Ron are hiking a trail. They have already hiked $\frac{1}{10}$ of a mile. How much farther do they have to travel to reach the $\frac{3}{4}$ mile mark?

$\frac{3}{4}$ of a mile in all

$\frac{1}{10}$	?

One Way

$\frac{3}{4} - \frac{1}{10} = $ ▨

Find common denominators and subtract.

$\frac{3}{4} = \frac{15}{20}$ $\qquad$ $\frac{1}{10} = \frac{2}{20}$

$\frac{15}{20} - \frac{2}{20} = \frac{13}{20}$

Another Way

$\frac{1}{10} + $ ▨ $ = \frac{3}{4}$

Find common denominators and add.

$\frac{1}{10} = \frac{2}{20}$ $\qquad$ $\frac{3}{4} = \frac{15}{20}$

$\frac{2}{20} + \frac{13}{20} = \frac{15}{20}$

Sandra and Ron need to hike $\frac{13}{20}$ of a mile farther to reach the $\frac{3}{4}$ mile mark.

Explain It

1. How could you find how much farther Sandra and Ron will have to hike to reach one mile?

2. **Reasoning** If Sandra and Ron turn around and hike back $\frac{1}{10}$ of a mile, how can you find the difference between the length they traveled and $\frac{3}{4}$ of a mile?

What do I know?

Brad and his father hiked 3 trails.

Gadsen Trail = $\frac{9}{10}$ mi

Rosebriar Trail = $\frac{1}{2}$ mi

Eureka Trail = $\frac{3}{5}$ mi

What am I asked to find?

How far did Brad and his father walk in all?

Find a common denominator.

$$\frac{9}{10} = \frac{9}{10}$$
$$\frac{1}{2} = \frac{5}{10}$$
$$\frac{3}{5} = \frac{6}{10}$$

? miles in all

$\frac{9}{10}$	$\frac{5}{10}$	$\frac{6}{10}$

Then, add the fractions and simplify.

$$\frac{9}{10} + \frac{5}{10} + \frac{6}{10} = \frac{20}{10} \text{ or } \frac{10}{5} \text{ or 2 miles}$$

Brad and his father walked 2 miles in all.

Guided Practice*

Do you know HOW?

Draw a picture and write an equation to solve.

1. Hannah ran $\frac{1}{3}$ of a mile. David ran $\frac{1}{6}$ of a mile. How much farther did Hannah run than David?

Do you UNDERSTAND?

2. **Writing to Explain** If you were asked to find how far Brad and his father walked on the Rosebriar and Eureka Trails alone, would the common denominator be different?

3. **Write a Problem** Write a problem that you can solve by drawing a picture and writing an equation.

Independent Practice

Draw a picture and write an equation to solve.

4. Steve connected a wire extension that is $\frac{3}{8}$ foot long to another wire that is $\frac{1}{2}$ foot long. How long is the wire with the extension?

? foot

$\frac{3}{8}$	$\frac{1}{2}$

Stuck? Try this....

- What do I know?
- What diagram can I use to help understand the problem?
- Can I use addition, subtraction, multiplication, or division?
- Is all of my work correct?
- Did I answer the right question?
- Is my answer reasonable?

5. The smallest female spider measures about $\frac{1}{2}$ mm in length. The smallest male spider measures about $\frac{2}{5}$ mm in length. How much longer is the length of the female spider than the male spider?

$\frac{1}{2}$ mm long

$\frac{2}{5}$	?

*For another example, see Set D on page 265.

6. A recipe calls for 3 times as many carrots as peas. If Carmen used 2 cups of peas, how many cups of carrots will she use?

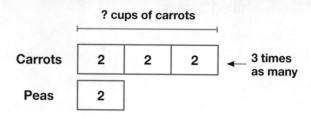

7. Felix bought $\frac{5}{6}$ pound of peanuts. He ate $\frac{3}{4}$ pound of the peanuts with his friends. How much did Felix have left?

$\frac{5}{6}$ pound of peanuts

$\frac{3}{4}$	?

8. Geometry Jack's dog has a rectangular pen. The length is two feet longer than the width. The width is 6 feet. What is the perimeter of the pen?

9. Writing to Explain Terrence has 8 comic books and 4 detective books. His sister says $\frac{2}{3}$ of his books are comic books. Terrence says that $\frac{8}{12}$ of his books are comic books. Who is correct?

10. Writing to Explain If the perimeter of the parallelogram below is 56 inches, and you know one side is 8 inches, will you be able to find the length of the other 3 sides? Why or why not?

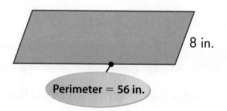

8 in.

Perimeter = 56 in.

Think About the Process

11. Four relay team members run an equal part of an 8-mile race. Which number sentence shows how far each member runs?

A $4 + 2 = 6$ **C** $2 + 2 + 2 = 6$

B $8 \div 4 = 2$ **D** $2 \times 4 = 8$

12. At an automobile dealership, there are 3 green cars, 4 blue cars, and 4 silver cars. Which number sentence tells how many cars are not silver?

A $7 + 4 = 11$ **C** $3 + 4 + 4 = 11$

B $11 - 4 = 7$ **D** $7 \times 4 = 28$

Adding and Subtracting Mixed Numbers

Adding and subtracting mixed numbers is similar to adding and subtracting fractions. You can use fraction strips to help.

Examples:

To add mixed numbers, add the fractions, add the whole numbers, and then simplify if necessary.

$$1\frac{3}{8}$$
$$+\ 1\frac{4}{8}$$
$$\overline{\ 2\frac{7}{8}}$$

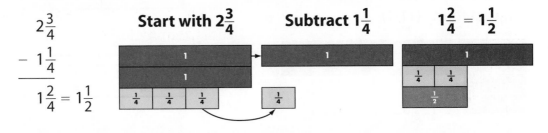

To subtract mixed numbers, subtract the fractions, subtract the whole numbers, and then simplify if necessary.

$$2\frac{3}{4}$$
$$-\ 1\frac{1}{4}$$
$$\overline{1\frac{2}{4}=1\frac{1}{2}}$$

Start with $2\frac{3}{4}$ **Subtract $1\frac{1}{4}$** $1\frac{2}{4}=1\frac{1}{2}$

Practice

Add or subtract. Write each answer in simplest form.

1. $3\frac{7}{8}-2\frac{3}{8}$ **2.** $2\frac{3}{5}+2\frac{1}{5}$ **3.** $7\frac{8}{9}-2\frac{4}{9}$ **4.** $6\frac{3}{8}+2\frac{1}{8}$

5. $6\frac{3}{4}-1\frac{3}{4}$ **6.** $7\frac{1}{3}+4\frac{2}{3}$ **7.** $5\frac{5}{6}-3\frac{1}{6}$ **8.** $4\frac{3}{12}+1\frac{2}{12}$

9. One day, a craft store sold $7\frac{2}{9}$ yards of green felt. The store sold $3\frac{1}{9}$ yards more purple felt than green felt. How many yards of purple felt did the store sell?

10. Josh ran $2\frac{2}{5}$ miles on Tuesday and $1\frac{1}{5}$ miles on Thursday. How many more miles did Josh run on Tuesday than on Thursday?

1. Mickie walked $\frac{1}{5}$ mile to her friend's house. Then they walked $\frac{3}{5}$ mile to the bus stop. How far did Mickie walk? (11-1)

A $\frac{5}{4}$ miles   C $\frac{2}{5}$ mile

B $\frac{4}{5}$ mile   D $\frac{4}{10}$ miles

2. Mrs. Garrison bought $\frac{7}{8}$ yard of fabric. She used $\frac{5}{8}$ yard to make a skirt. How much fabric does she have left? Write your answer in simplest form. (11-1)

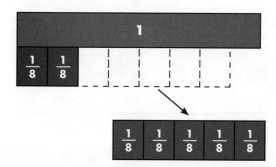

A $\frac{1}{4}$ yard

B $\frac{1}{3}$ yard

C $\frac{3}{4}$ yard

D $\frac{4}{3}$ yards

3. What is $\frac{3}{10} + \frac{1}{5}$ in simplest form? (11-2)

A $\frac{4}{15}$ C $\frac{4}{10}$

B $\frac{2}{5}$ D $\frac{1}{2}$

4. Darrell bought $\frac{1}{4}$ pound of American cheese and $\frac{1}{8}$ pound of Swiss cheese at the deli. Which picture models how much cheese Darrell bought? (11-4)

A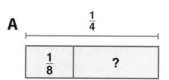

B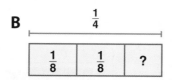

C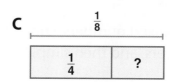

D

5. What is $\frac{5}{12} + \frac{1}{4}$ in simplest form? (11-2)

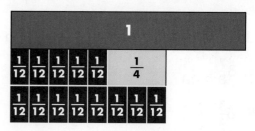

A $\frac{3}{4}$

B $\frac{9}{12}$

C $\frac{2}{3}$

D $\frac{3}{8}$

6. Joy bought $\frac{3}{4}$ of a quart of fruit salad and $\frac{1}{3}$ of a quart of three bean salad. How much more fruit salad did Joy buy? (11-3)

A $\frac{1}{3}$ of a quart

B $\frac{5}{12}$ of a quart

C $\frac{1}{2}$ of a quart

D $\frac{7}{12}$ of a quart

7. Bella used $\frac{1}{4}$ cup of white flour and $\frac{5}{8}$ cup of wheat flour in the bread recipe. How much more wheat flour did she use? (11-3)

A $\frac{1}{4}$

B $\frac{2}{4}$

C $\frac{3}{8}$

D $\frac{2}{8}$

8. Chen's mom bought $\frac{7}{8}$ pound of salmon. That night, the family ate $\frac{1}{4}$ pound. How much of the salmon was left? (11-3)

A $\frac{6}{4}$ pound

B $\frac{5}{8}$ pound

C $\frac{1}{3}$ pound

D $\frac{1}{4}$ pound

9. Walt ate $\frac{4}{10}$ of a pizza. Lakota also ate $\frac{3}{10}$ of the same pizza. How much of the pizza did they eat in all? (11-1)

A $\frac{1}{10}$

B $\frac{1}{2}$

C $\frac{3}{5}$

D $\frac{7}{10}$

10. Trent walked $\frac{3}{8}$ mile and jogged $\frac{1}{2}$ mile. How far did Trent go? (11-2)

A $\frac{7}{8}$ mile

B $\frac{3}{4}$ mile

C $\frac{2}{3}$ mile

D $\frac{2}{5}$ mile

11. A pitcher had $\frac{9}{10}$ gallon of juice. Manuella drank $\frac{2}{5}$ gallon of juice. Which number sentence can be used to find how much juice was left? (11-3)

A $\frac{9}{10} + \frac{2}{5} = \blacksquare$

B $\frac{9}{10} + \blacksquare = \frac{2}{5}$

C $\frac{9}{10} - \frac{2}{5} = \blacksquare$

D $\frac{2}{5} - \frac{9}{10} = \blacksquare$

12. What is $\frac{7}{12} - \frac{1}{3}$ in simplest form? (11-3)

A $\frac{1}{4}$ **C** $\frac{5}{12}$

B $\frac{1}{3}$ **D** $\frac{11}{12}$

Set A, pages 250–253

Find $\frac{1}{9} + \frac{5}{9}$.

Add the numerators. Write the sum over the like denominator.

$$\frac{1}{9} + \frac{5}{9} = \frac{1+5}{9} = \frac{6}{9}$$

Simplify if necessary.

$$\frac{6}{9} \xrightarrow[\div 3]{\div 3} = \frac{2}{3}$$

So, $\frac{1}{9} + \frac{5}{9} = \frac{2}{3}$.

Find $\frac{7}{9} - \frac{5}{9}$.

Subtract the numerators. Write the difference over the like denominator.

$$\frac{7}{9} - \frac{5}{9} = \frac{7-5}{9} = \frac{2}{9}$$

Remember you can use fraction strips to add or subtract fractions with like denominators.

Add or subtract. Write each answer in simplest form.

1. $\frac{1}{7} + \frac{2}{7}$ 2. $\frac{4}{15} + \frac{2}{15}$

3. $\frac{7}{8} - \frac{1}{8}$ 4. $\frac{8}{10} - \frac{5}{10}$

5. $\frac{1}{4} + \frac{1}{4}$ 6. $\frac{8}{9} - \frac{5}{9}$

7. $\frac{5}{12} + \frac{7}{12}$ 8. $\frac{4}{13} - \frac{2}{13}$

9. $\frac{8}{15} - \frac{3}{15}$ 10. $\frac{2}{6} + \frac{3}{6}$

Set B, pages 254–255

Add $\frac{1}{6} + \frac{1}{2}$ using fraction strips.

Find equivalent fractions with like denominators.

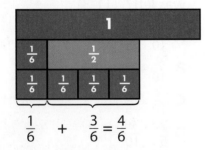

$$\frac{1}{6} \quad + \quad \frac{3}{6} = \frac{4}{6}$$

Simplify if necessary.

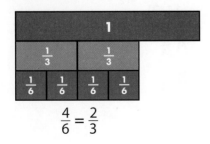

$$\frac{4}{6} = \frac{2}{3}$$

Remember to first find equivalent fractions to add fractions with unlike denominators.

Add the fractions. Write each answer in simplest form.

1. $\frac{2}{3} + \frac{1}{4}$ 2. $\frac{3}{5} + \frac{1}{3}$

3. $\frac{1}{3} + \frac{1}{9}$ 4. $\frac{1}{4} + \frac{1}{6}$

5. $\frac{3}{8} + \frac{1}{2}$ 6. $\frac{2}{3} + \frac{1}{9}$

7. $\frac{2}{6} + \frac{2}{3}$ 8. $\frac{1}{4} + \frac{4}{8}$

9. $\frac{1}{5} + \frac{3}{10}$ 10. $\frac{1}{3} + \frac{1}{4}$

11. $\frac{2}{6} + \frac{1}{4}$ 12. $\frac{3}{6} + \frac{1}{3}$

Set C, pages 256–257

Subtract $\frac{2}{3} - \frac{1}{4}$ using fraction strips.

Both $\frac{2}{3}$ and $\frac{1}{4}$ can be shown using twelfths.

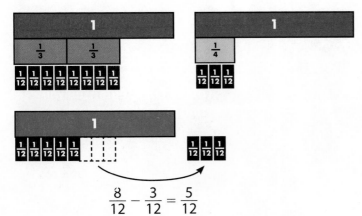

$$\frac{8}{12} - \frac{3}{12} = \frac{5}{12}$$

Remember to find equivalent fractions before subtracting fractions with unlike denominators.

Subtract the fractions. Write each answer in simplest form.

1. $\frac{3}{4} - \frac{3}{8}$ 2. $\frac{5}{12} - \frac{1}{6}$

3. $\frac{1}{2} - \frac{1}{3}$ 4. $\frac{7}{10} - \frac{1}{2}$

5. $\frac{4}{5} - \frac{1}{2}$ 6. $\frac{8}{9} - \frac{2}{9}$

7. $\frac{5}{6} - \frac{1}{12}$ 8. $\frac{7}{9} - \frac{1}{3}$

9. $\frac{4}{10} - \frac{1}{5}$ 10. $\frac{5}{6} - \frac{2}{3}$

Set D, pages 258–260

Tina and Andy are building a model airplane together. Tina built $\frac{1}{3}$ of the model, and Andy built $\frac{1}{5}$ of the model. How much more has Tina built than Andy?

$\frac{1}{3}$ of the model	
$\frac{1}{5}$	?

Find a common denominator and subtract.

$$\frac{1}{3} = \frac{5}{15}$$
$$-\ \frac{1}{5} = \frac{3}{15}$$
$$\overline{\frac{2}{15}}$$

Tina built $\frac{2}{15}$ more of the model than Andy.

Remember to use a picture to help you write a number equation.

Solve.

1. Bonnie ran $\frac{1}{4}$ of a mile. Olga ran $\frac{1}{8}$ of a mile. How much farther did Bonnie run than Olga?

2. Linda's plant was $\frac{9}{12}$ foot tall. Macy's plant was $\frac{2}{3}$ foot tall. How much taller is Linda's plant than Macy's?

Understanding Decimals

1 The Roman Colosseum is one of the best examples of Roman architecture. The arena is what fractional part of the Colosseum? You will find out in Lesson 12-3.

2 According to the Greek mathematician, Zeno, who lived in the fourth century B.C., this ball will never stop bouncing. You will find out why in Lesson 12-4.

3

The world's largest living tree, the General Sherman Giant Sequoia, is in Sequoia National Park in California. How tall is this tree? You will find out in Lesson 12-5.

GENERAL SHERMAN

Review What You Know!

Vocabulary

Choose the best term from the box.

> • greater   • tenth
> • hundredth   • decimal point

1. One of ten equal parts of a whole is one _?_.

2. A dot used to separate dollars from cents or ones from tenths in a number is a _?_.

3. One part of 100 equal parts of a whole is one _?_.

4. The number 3,704 is _?_ than the number 3,407.

Comparing Numbers

Compare. Write >, <, or = for each $\bigcirc$.

5. 1,909 $\bigcirc$ 1,990

6. 43,627 $\bigcirc$ 43,167

7. 629,348 $\bigcirc$ 629,348

8. 455,311 $\bigcirc$ 455,331

9. 101,101 $\bigcirc$ 101,011

10. 95,559 $\bigcirc$ 95,555

Ordering Numbers

Order the numbers from greatest to least.

11. 3,687   3,867   3,678   3,768

12. 41,101   41,011   41,110   41,001

13. 4,593   4,395   4,595   4,359

14. **Writing to Explain** How would you order the numbers below from least to greatest? Explain.

15,420   154,200   1,542

Topic 12   **267**

Lesson

12-1

Understand It!
There are many ways to represent decimal numbers.

Decimal Place Value

What are some ways to represent decimals?

A squirrel can weigh 1.64 pounds. There are different ways to represent 1.64.

1.64 pounds

Guided Practice*

Do you know HOW?

For **1** and **2**, write the expanded form for each number.

1. 3.91   **2.** 6.87

In **3** and **4**, draw and shade a grid for each number. Then, write the word form for each number.

3. 1.06   **4.** 2.36

Do you UNDERSTAND?

5. In Exercise 1, what digit is in the tenths place? in the hundredths place?

6. At the end of a basketball game, there are 3.29 seconds left on the clock. How would the referee say this number?

 When you read a number or write a number in word form, replace the decimal point with the word and.

Independent Practice

In **7** through **9**, write the decimal for each shaded part.

7.   **8.**   **9.**

In **10** through **12**, write the number in standard form.

10. four and thirty-six hundredths   **11.** $5 + 0.2 + 0.08$ **12.** $2 + 0.01$

For another example, see Set A on page 286.

One Way

Use a decimal model.

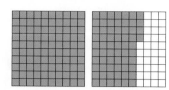

Expanded form: 1 + 0.6 + 0.04
Standard form: 1.64
Word form: one and sixty-four hundredths

Another Way

Use a place-value model.

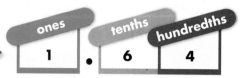

ones	tenths	hundredths
1	6	4

Expanded form: 1 + 0.6 + 0.04
Standard form: 1.64
Word form: one and sixty-four hundredths

In **13** through **17**, write the number in word form and give the value of the red digit for each number.

13. 2.47   **14.** 23.79   **15.** 1.85   **16.** 14.12   **17.** 9.05

In **18** through **22**, write each number in expanded form.

18. 3.19   **19.** 13.62   **20.** 0.78   **21.** 8.07   **22.** 17.2

Problem Solving

23. Reasoning Write a number that has a 4 in the tens place and a 6 in the hundredths place.

24. Mr. Cooper has 6 gallons of gas in his car. His car can hold 15 gallons in its gas tank. Will Mr. Cooper need more or less than 10 gallons to fill his tank?

25. Tisha wrote this amount: Five dollars and nine cents.

   a What is the decimal word form for this amount?

   b What is the decimal number?

26. Number Sense Write three numbers between 4.1 and 4.2.

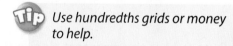

Use hundredths grids or money to help.

27. Writing to Explain Use the decimal model below to explain why 0.08 is less than 0.1.

28. What is the value of the 5 in 43.51?

   A five hundredths

   B five tenths

   C fifty-one hundredths

   D five

Lesson

12-2

Understand It!
Place value can be
used to compare and
order decimals.

Comparing and Ordering Decimals

How do you compare decimals?

A penny made in 1982 weighs
about 0.11 ounce. A penny made
in 2006 weighs about 0.09 ounce.
Which penny weighs more,
a 1982 penny or a 2006 penny?

1982 penny
0.11oz

2006 penny
0.09oz

Another Example How do you order decimals?

Patrick has a 1982 penny, a 2006 penny, and a dime
in his pocket. Order the weights of the coins from
least to greatest.

Dime
0.10 oz

First compare the tenths place.

0.1̲1

0.0̲9

0.1̲0

The least number is 0.09 because it has a 0 in the tenths place.

Compare the remaining numbers.
First compare the tenths. Both
decimals have a 1 in the tenths place.

0.1̲0

0.1̲1

Compare the hundredths place.

0.10̲

0.11̲

1 > 0, so 0.11 is the greatest decimal.

The order from least to greatest is 0.09, 0.10, 0.11.

Explain It

1. Order the numbers above from greatest to least.

2. Which place did you use to compare 0.10 and 0.11?

One Way

Use hundredths grids.

11 hundredths > 9 hundredths

0.11 > 0.09

Another Way

Use place value.

Start at the left. Look for the first place where the digits are different.

0.11   0.09

1 tenth > 0 tenths

0.11 > 0.09

A penny made in 1982 weighs more than a penny made in 2006.

Guided Practice*

Do you know HOW?

In **1** through **4**, write >, <, or = for each ◯. Use grids to help.

1. 0.7 ◯ 0.57   **2.** 0.23 ◯ 0.32

3. 1.01 ◯ 0.98   **4.** 0.2 ◯ 0.20

In **5** and **6**, order the numbers from least to greatest.

5. 0.65 0.6 0.71   **6.** 1.21 1.01 1.2

Do you UNDERSTAND?

7. Number Sense Which is greater, 2.02 or 0.22? Explain.

8. Maria told Patrick that her quarter weighs less than what a nickel weighs because 0.2 has fewer digits than 0.18. How can Patrick show Maria that 0.2 is greater than 0.18?

Quarter 0.2oz   Nickel 0.18oz

Independent Practice

For **9** through **16**, compare. Write >, <, or = for each ◯. Use grids to help.

9. 0.01 ◯ 0.1   **10.** 7.31 ◯ 7.29   **11.** 6.56 ◯ 5.98   **12.** 1.1 ◯ 1.10

13. 3.22 ◯ 4.44   **14.** 9.01 ◯ 9.1   **15.** 2.01 ◯ 1.7   **16.** 0.01 ◯ 1.02

For **17** through **22**, order the numbers from least to greatest.

17. 1.2, 1.23, 1.1   **18.** 0.56, 4.56, 0.65   **19.** 0.21, 0.12, 0.22

20. 3.8, 0.38, 3.08   **21.** 0.71, 0.07, 1.7   **22.** 0.5, 0.25, 1.05

*For another example, see Set B on page 286.

23. Number Sense A bag of 500 nickels weighs 5.5 pounds. A bag of 200 half dollars weighs 5 pounds. Which bag weighs more?

24. Writing to Explain Evan said the numbers 7.37, 7.36, 2.59, and 2.95 were in order from greatest to least. Is he correct?

25. Number Sense Tell which coin is worth more.

    a 1 quarter or 1 half dollar

    b 1 dime or 1 penny

    c 1 dollar or 1 penny

26. Which number is **NOT** greater than 0.64?

    A 6.4

    B 4.6

    C 0.46

    D 0.66

For **27** and **28**, use the clocks at the right.

27. Which clock shows the earliest time?

28. Order the clock times from latest to earliest.

29. Which numbers are **NOT** in order from least to greatest?

    A 0.3, 0.7, 0.9

    B 0.04, 0.09, 0.12

    C 0.15, 0.19, 0.23

    D 0.24, 0.09, 0.18

30. Ms. Alvarez has $0.83 in her change purse. She has 7 coins. She has the same number of pennies as quarters. What coins does she have?

31. Which number has a 3 in the ten-thousands place?

    A 23,604   **C** 593,100

    B 32,671   **D** 694,392

32. Which number is between 6.7 and 7.3?

    A 6.07   **C** 6.83

    B 6.26   **D** 7.4

33. Fishing lures are sold by weight. A yellow minnow lure weighs 0.63 ounce and a green minnow lure weighs 0.5 ounce. Which lure weighs more?

34. Tom has one $10 bill, one $5 bill, four $1 bills, 3 quarters, and 2 dimes. Janet has three $5 bills, three $1 bills, and 8 quarters. Who has more money?

Algebra Connections

Number Patterns

Number patterns can help you predict the next number or numbers that follow.

Example: 10, 20, 30, 40, ▨

Think *How is each number in the number pattern related?*

Compare 10 and 20.

10 + 10 = 20

Now, compare 20 and 30.

20 + 10 = 30

The pattern that best describes the list of numbers is: add 10.

The missing number in the number pattern is represented by a shaded box. Use the number pattern to find the missing number.

40 + 10 = 50

The missing number is 50.

Fill in each shaded box with the number that best completes the number pattern. Then, tell how you completed the pattern.

1. 2, 4, 6, 8, ▨

2. 5, 10, 15, 20, ▨

3. 5, 8, 11, 14, ▨

4. 1, 3, 5, ▨, 9

5. 5, 15, ▨, 35, 45

6. 30, 23, ▨, 9, 2

7. 28, ▨, 18, 13, 8

8. 32, 36, ▨, 44, 48, ▨

9. 47, 56, ▨, 74, ▨, 92

10. 98, 91, ▨, 77, ▨

11. 75, 59, 43, ▨, ▨

12. 3, 5, 4, 6, 5, 7, 6, ▨

· ·

13. What are the missing numbers in the number pattern? Describe the number pattern.

48, ▨, ▨, 33, 28, 23

15. Write a Problem Write a problem using one of the number patterns in Exercises 1 to 12.

14. Complete the table. Describe the pattern.

A	B	C
4	6	10
5	8	13
6		16
	11	19
15		30
20	14	

Understand It!
Fractions and decimals can be used to name the same amounts.

Fractions and Decimals

Hands-On
grid paper

How can you write a fraction as a decimal and a decimal as a fraction?

On Kelsey Street, six out of 10 homes have swing sets in their backyards.

Write $\frac{6}{10}$ as a decimal.

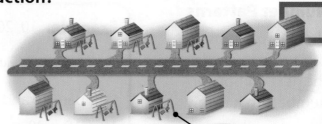

6 of 10 houses have swing sets.

Other Examples

Write 2.1 as a mixed number.

Since $0.1 = \frac{1}{10}$, $2.1 = 2\frac{1}{10}$.

Write $2\frac{14}{100}$ as a decimal.

Since $\frac{14}{100} = 0.14$, $2\frac{14}{100} = 2.14$.

Guided Practice*

Do you know HOW?

For **1** and **2**, write a decimal and a fraction in simplest form for the part of each grid that is shaded.

1.   **2.**

Do you UNDERSTAND?

3. Writing to Explain Why is the fraction $\frac{6}{10}$ not written 0.06?

4. On Kelsey Street, what fraction of homes do **NOT** have swings? Write your answer as a fraction and a decimal.

Independent Practice

For **5** through **9**, write a decimal and a fraction in simplest form for the part of each grid that is shaded.

5.   **6.**   **7.**   **8.**   **9.**

*For another example, see Set C on page 286.

Write $\frac{6}{10}$ as a decimal.

$\frac{6}{10}$ is six tenths, or 0.6.

$$\frac{6}{10} = 0.6$$

So, 0.6 of the houses have swing sets.

In Rolling Hills, 0.75 of the houses are two-story homes.

Write 0.75 as a fraction.

0.75 is seventy-five hundredths, or $\frac{75}{100}$.

$$0.75 = \frac{75}{100}$$

So, $\frac{75}{100}$, or $\frac{3}{4}$, of the houses are two-story homes.

For **10** through **19**, write an equivalent decimal, fraction, or mixed number in simplest form.

10. $9\frac{4}{10}$ **11.** $\frac{21}{100}$ **12.** 11.6 **13.** $1\frac{81}{100}$ **14.** 0.65

15. $\frac{50}{100}$ **16.** 0.48 **17.** $4\frac{7}{10}$ **18.** $\frac{20}{200}$ **19.** 1.45

Problem Solving

20. Estimation About what fraction of the rectangle to the right is shaded green?

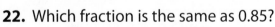

21. The arena of the Colosseum in Rome was about $\frac{3}{20}$ of the entire Colosseum. Write this amount as a decimal.

Tip $\frac{1}{20} = \frac{5}{100}$

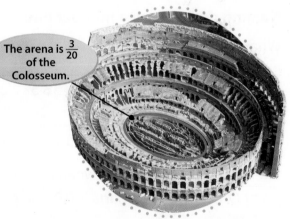

The arena is $\frac{3}{20}$ of the Colosseum.

22. Which fraction is the same as 0.85?

  A $\frac{85}{1,000}$ **C** $\frac{85}{1}$

  B $\frac{85}{100}$ **D** $\frac{85}{10}$

23. Reasoning James, Vicki, Jaime, and Jill are in line for tickets for the basketball game. Jaime is first. Vicki is behind Jill. Jill is not last. James is in front of Jill. How are they ordered?

24. Algebra Find the missing numbers in the pattern below.

  ▢, 18, 27, ▢, ▢, 54, ▢

DIGITAL
eTools
www.pearsonsuccessnet.com

Lesson

12-4

Understand It!
Fractions and decimals
can name a distance
on a number line.

Fractions and Decimals On the Number Line

How can you locate points on a number line?

In short-track speed skating, each lap is $\frac{1}{9}$ kilometer.
In long-track speed skating, each lap is 0.4 kilometer.
How can you use a number line to show these distances?

One lap = 0.4 km

One lap = $\frac{1}{9}$ km

Another Example **How can you name points on a number line?**

Naming fractions on a number line

What fraction is at point *P*?

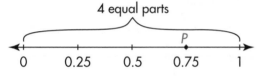

4 equal parts

			P	
0	0.25	0.5	0.75	1

There are 4 equal parts between 0 and 1. There are 3 equal
parts between 0 and point *P*. So, point *P* is at $\frac{3}{4}$.

Naming decimals on a number line

What number is at point *Q*?

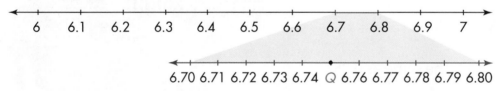

6   6.1   6.2   6.3   6.4   6.5   6.6   6.7   6.8   6.9   7

6.70 6.71 6.72 6.73 6.74 *Q* 6.76 6.77 6.78 6.79 6.80

There are 5 equal parts between 6.70 and
point *Q*. Each of these parts is 0.01, so point *Q* is at 6.75.

Explain It

1. Describe where you would place point *Q* on a number
   line that shows only tenths.

2. What number is at point *R*?

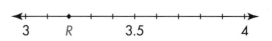

3   *R*   3.5   4

Locate $\frac{1}{9}$ on a number line.

Draw a number line, and label 0 and 1. Divide the distance from 0 to 1 into 9 equal parts.

Draw a point at $\frac{1}{9}$.

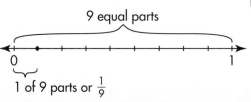

9 equal parts

1 of 9 parts or $\frac{1}{9}$

Locate 0.4 on a number line.

Draw a number line, and divide the distance from 0 to 1 into 10 equal parts to show tenths.

Draw a point at 0.4.

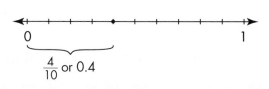

$\frac{4}{10}$ or 0.4

Guided Practice*

Do you know HOW?

For **1** and **2**, use the number line below to name the fraction.

1. *A*   **2.** *B*

For **3** and **4**, name the point on the number line for each decimal.

3. 1.33   **4.** 1.39

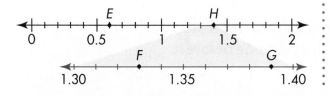

Do you UNDERSTAND?

5. Where would you locate 0.46 on the number line at the top?

6. Use the number line for Exercises 1 and 2. What fraction is located at point *C*?

7. A 1,500-meter speed-skating race is 13.5 laps around a short track. Show 13.5 on a number line.

8. Use the number line for Exercises 3 and 4. What point is at $\frac{6}{10}$?

Independent Practice

For **9** through **13**, use the number line below to name the decimal.

9. *J*   **10.** *K*   **11.** *L*   **12.** *M*   **13.** *N*

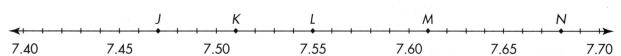

For **14** through **18**, name the fraction that should be written at each point.

14. *V* **15.** *Z* **16.** *X* **17.** *W* **18.** *Y*

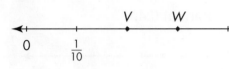

For **19** through **23**, name the point for each decimal or fraction.

19. 10.1 **20.** 10.28 **21.** 10.25 **22.** 9.6 **23.** 10.0

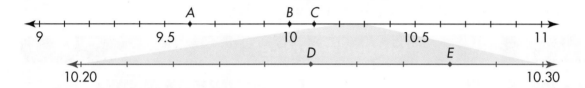

24. Writing to Explain Which two points on the number line to the right represent the same point?

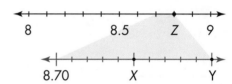

25. Jack walked $\frac{4}{5}$ mile to the library. What is this distance as a decimal?

26. Write an expression that tells how to find the perimeter of a triangle with each side 2 inches long.

Use the diagram below for **27** and **28**.

According to the Greek mathematician Zeno, a ball will never stop bouncing because each bounce is half as high as the one before it.

27. Name the fractions that should be written at points *D* and *E*.

28. Writing to Explain Do you think it would be possible for the ball to reach zero by moving halfway closer at every step? Why or why not?

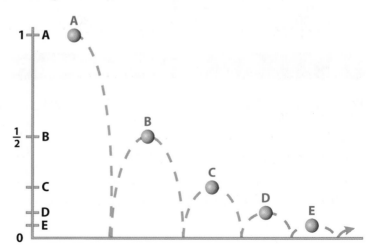

Find the quotient. Estimate to check
if the answer is reasonable.

1. 480 ÷ 8   **2.** 29 ÷ 3   **3.** 749 ÷ 8   **4.** 304 ÷ 3

5. 4)$\overline{608}$ **6.** 5)$\overline{528}$ **7.** 515 ÷ 3   **8.** 6)$\overline{87}$

9. 95 ÷ 5   **10.** 888 ÷ 9   **11.** 54 ÷ 4   **12.** 210 ÷ 3

13. 8)$\overline{807}$ **14.** 465 ÷ 2   **15.** 5)$\overline{64}$ **16.** 964 ÷ 4

Find the sum. Estimate to check if the answer is reasonable.

17.   46,037   **18.**   9,979   **19.**   73,678   **20.**   2,873   **21.**   21,165
 + 12,750   + 2,956   + 26,321   +   49   + 15,375

22. 54,893 + 3,746   **23.** 23,963 + 12 + 3,987   **24.** 48 + 40,287 + 834

Error Search Find each quotient that is not correct.
Write it correctly and explain the error.

25. 19 ÷ 2 = 9 R1   **26.** 808 ÷ 4 = 22   **27.** 354 ÷ 5 = 70 R4

28. 74 ÷ 6 = 12 R2   **29.** 377 ÷ 3 = 125   **30.** 940 ÷ 7 = 140

Number Sense

Estimating and Reasoning Write whether each
statement is true or false. Explain your answer.

31. The quotient of 398 ÷ 4 is closer to 100 than 90.

32. The product of 9 and 32 is greater than the product of 3 and 92.

33. The quotient of 154 ÷ 5 is less than 30.

34. The quotient of 1,500 ÷ 30 is 30.

35. The difference of 4,321 – 2,028 is less than 1,000.

36. The sum of 2,243 and 5,809 is greater than 7,000 but less than 9,000.

Lesson

12-5

Understand It!
Mixed numbers and decimals can name a distance on a number line.

Mixed Numbers and Decimals on the Number Line

How can you locate mixed numbers and decimals on a number line?

Laurie and Aaron went rollerblading. Laurie skated 1.6 miles, and Aaron skated $1\frac{3}{5}$ miles.

Who skated farther?

Aaron skated $1\frac{3}{5}$ miles.

Laurie skated 1.6 miles.

Other Examples

What fraction should be written at point *A*?

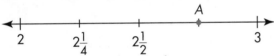

There are 4 equal parts between 2 and 3. Each part is $\frac{1}{4}$.
So, $2\frac{3}{4}$ should be written at point *A*.

What decimal should be written at point *B*?

There are 10 equal parts between 1.40 and 1.50. There are 8 equal parts between 1.40 and point *B*.
So, 1.48 should be written at point *B*.

Guided Practice*

Do you know HOW?

For **1** through **6**, what decimal and fraction or mixed number should be written at each point?

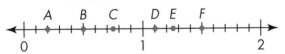

1. Point *A*
2. Point *B*
3. Point *C*
4. Point *D*
5. Point *E*
6. Point *F*

Do you UNDERSTAND?

7. The next day, Aaron skated 0.8 miles farther than the $1\frac{3}{5}$ miles he had skated the day before. Use a number line to show this distance as a decimal and as a mixed number.

   Tip *Convert 0.8 to a fraction.*

8. If Laurie skated between 3.5 and 4.0 miles, what distances could she have skated?

For another example, see Set D on page 287.

Show $1\frac{3}{5}$ and 1.6 on the same number line.

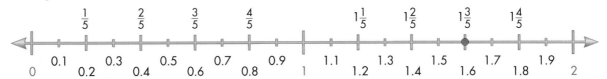

Draw a number line and label 0, 1, and 2.

| Divide the distance between each whole number into 5 equal lengths. Label the points $\frac{1}{5}, \frac{2}{5}$, and so on. | Then divide the distance between each whole number into 10 equal lengths. Label 0.1, 0.2, and so on. | Draw a point at $1\frac{3}{5}$ and 1.6. Laurie and Aaron skated the same distance. |

Independent Practice

For **9** through **13**, name the decimal for each point.

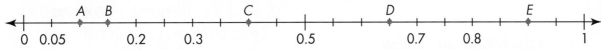

9. Point *A* **10.** Point *B* **11.** Point *C* **12.** Point *D* **13.** Point *E*

For **14** through **18**, name the mixed number that should be written at each point.

14. Point *F* **15.** Point *G* **16.** Point *H* **17.** Point *I* **18.** Point *J*

Problem Solving

19. The General Sherman Giant Sequoia in Sequoia National Park is the world's largest living tree. It is 83.8 meters high above its base. Write the height of the tree as a mixed number.

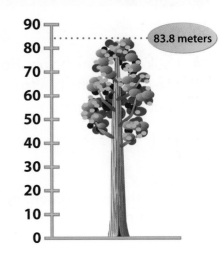

20. Jennifer lives $2\frac{1}{2}$ miles from school. Dorothy lives 2.4 miles from school. Does Dorothy or Jennifer live closer to the school? Use a number line to compare the two distances.

21. Renee and George are eating a pie they just baked. George cut himself a slice that was 0.2 of the pie. Renee cut herself a slice that was $\frac{2}{10}$ of the pie. How much of the pie did they eat together?

A $\frac{4}{15}$ **B** $\frac{1}{3}$ **C** $\frac{2}{5}$ **D** $\frac{1}{2}$

Lesson
12-6

Understand It!
Learning how and when to draw a picture can help solve problems.

Draw a Picture

A hiking path is being planned for the local park. The planner started marking the drawing of the path with distances, but stopped. Where should the 1-mile mark be placed?

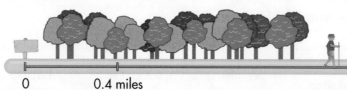

0   0.4 miles

Guided Practice*

Do you know HOW?

Solve.

1. Look at the hiking path below. Carla begins at the starting point and walks 0.8 miles. Where on the drawing would Carla end her walk?

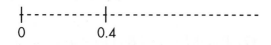

0   0.4

Do you UNDERSTAND?

2. How are the numbers 0.4 and 0.8 related? How can this help you to find where 0.8 is located on the drawing?

3. **Write a Problem** Write a problem that uses the drawing below to solve.

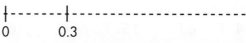

0   0.3

Independent Practice

Solve.

4. Look at the line below. How can you use the mark on the line to find where 1.0 should be located?

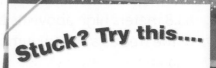

0   0.1

5. Copy the line segment from Problem 4. Find 1.0.

Stuck? Try this....

- What do I know?
- What diagram can I use to help understand the problem?
- Can I use addition, subtraction, multiplication, or division?
- Is all of my work correct?
- Did I answer the right question?
- Is my answer reasonable?

What do I know? The hiking path must be 1 mile long. The marker for 0.4 mile is located on the drawing.

What am I asked to find? Where the 1-mile mark should be located on the drawing

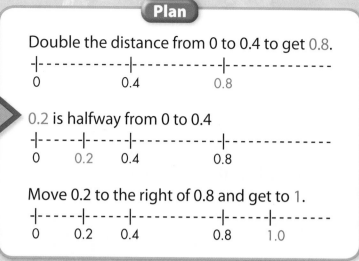

Double the distance from 0 to 0.4 to get 0.8.

0   0.4   0.8

0.2 is halfway from 0 to 0.4

0   0.2   0.4   0.8

Move 0.2 to the right of 0.8 and get to 1.

0   0.2   0.4   0.8   1.0

---

6. Allie needed to design a banner for field day. She wanted her banner to be 2 feet long. Allie marked 0.5 feet on her drawing. How can she use this distance to find 2 feet?

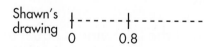

Allie's drawing   0   0.5

7. Dawn has 45 customers on her paper route. She delivers newspapers every day. How many newspapers does she deliver in five days?

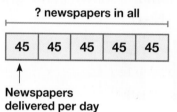

? newspapers in all

| 45 | 45 | 45 | 45 | 45 |

↑ Newspapers delivered per day

8. Writing to Explain Blake jogged 1.7 miles one morning. His sister jogged $1\frac{3}{4}$ miles that same day. Who jogged farther? Explain your answer.

9. What would a good estimate for point *G* be on the drawing below?

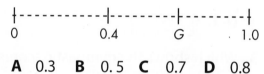

0   0.4   G   1.0

A 0.3 **B** 0.5 **C** 0.7 **D** 0.8

10. Shawn marked 0.8 feet on the chalkboard. How can Shawn use this distance to find 2 feet?

Shawn's drawing   0   0.8

11. Algebra John has twice as many brothers as Bob. If Bob has *b* brothers, how many brothers does John have?

12. Nick wrote a four-digit number. He used the digits 2, 4, 6, and 8. How many four-digit numbers could Nick have written?

13. Mary has 3 coin purses with 58 coins in each. How many coins does Mary have?

1. Quinton's frog leaped $2\frac{3}{4}$ feet on its first leap. Which point on the number line best represents the point where the frog landed? (12-5)

A L

B M

C N

D P

2. What decimal is shown in the grid below? (12-1)

A 6.12

B 2.61

C 1.62

D 1.26

3. Which shows the gymnastic scores in order from least to greatest? (12-2)

A 9.72, 9.8, 9.78, 9.87

B 9.78, 9.72, 9.87, 9.8

C 9.78, 9.8, 9.72, 9.87

D 9.72, 9.78, 9.8, 9.87

4. Which statement is true? (12-2)

0.14   0.09

A 0.14 > 0.09

B 0.14 < 0.09

C 0.09 = 0.14

D 0.09 > 0.14

5. What is 1.47 written as a fraction or mixed number? (12-3)

A $\frac{1}{147}$

B $\frac{47}{100}$

C $1\frac{47}{100}$

D $1\frac{47}{10}$

6. Which number is best represented by point R on the number line? (12-4)

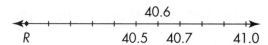

A 40.1

B 40.0

C 39.9

D 39.0

7. Which of the following is equal to $20 + 7 + 0.9 + 0.03$? (12-1)

A 20.79

B 20.93

C 27.39

D 27.93

8. Which fraction and decimal represent the part that is green? (12-3)

A $\frac{63}{100}$ and 0.63

B $\frac{63}{100}$ and 0.063

C $\frac{63}{100}$ and 6.3

D $\frac{63}{10}$ and 0.63

9. What fraction and decimal are best represented by point *B* on the number line? (12-5)

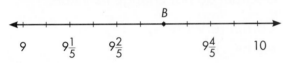

A $9\frac{3}{5}$ and 9.3

B $9\frac{3}{5}$ and 9.6

C $9\frac{3}{10}$ and 9.3

D $9\frac{3}{10}$ and 9.6

10. What fraction is best represented by point *D* on the number line? (12-4)

A $\frac{2}{5}$

B $\frac{3}{5}$

C $\frac{1}{2}$

D $\frac{3}{10}$

11. Louise is creating a 1-foot long comic strip. If she has marked 0.5 on her paper, what should she do to find 1 foot? (12-6)

A Subtract 0.5

B Add 0.2

C Multiply 0.5

D Add 0.5

12. Which of the following has the least value? (12-2)

A 5.45

B 8.02

C 4.99

D 13.2

13. Which of the following has a 9 in the hundredths place? (12-1)

A 28.79

B 65.91

C 79.88

D 926.7

14. Angie drew a number line and labeled 0 and 1. To show $\frac{5}{12}$, how many parts should she divide the distance from 0 to 1? (12-6)

A 5

B 10

C 11

D 12

Set A, pages 268–269

Write the decimal shown in expanded, standard, and word form.

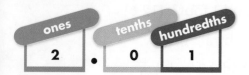

Expanded form: 2 + 0.01

Standard form: 2.01

Word form: Two and one hundredth

Remember to use the word *and* for the decimal point when you write a decimal in word form.

Write the following in word and expanded form.

1. 12.13

2. 1.09

3. 11.1

4. 88.08

Set B, pages 270–272

Compare 1.35 and 1.26 using place value.

Write the numbers, lining up the decimal points. Then compare digits by place value.

1.35

1.26

3 tenths > 2 tenths

So, 1.35 > 1.26.

Remember that zeros at the end of the decimal do not change its value.

Compare. Write >, <, or = for each ◯.

1. 1.82 ◯ 1.91

2. 1.1 ◯ 1.10

Order the numbers from greatest to least.

3. 22,981   14,762   21,046

Set C, pages 274-275

Write $\frac{37}{100}$ as a decimal.

$\frac{37}{100}$ is thirty-seven hundredths, or 0.37.

Write 1.7 as a mixed number.

Since 0.7 = $\frac{7}{10}$,

1.7 = $1\frac{7}{10}$.

Remember you can write a decimal and a fraction for the shaded part of each grid.

1.   2.

3.   4.

Set D, pages 276–278, 280-281

Show $6\frac{1}{4}$ on a number line.

Divide the distance from 6 to 7 into 4 equal lengths. Label the tick marks and draw a point at $6\frac{1}{4}$.

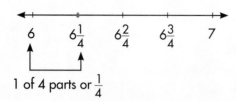

1 of 4 parts or $\frac{1}{4}$

Show 7.7 on a number line.
Divide the distance from 7 to 8 into 10 equal lengths.

Label the tick marks, and draw a point at 7.7.

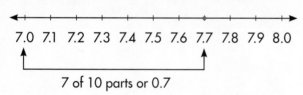

7 of 10 parts or 0.7

Remember each tick mark is set evenly apart.

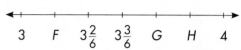

3   F $3\frac{2}{6}$ $3\frac{3}{6}$ G   H   4

Name the fraction at each point.

1. G   **2.** F   **3.** H

J   K L   M   N   O

5.40 5.45 5.50 5.55 5.60 5.65 5.70

Name the decimal at each point.

4. K   **5.** M   **6.** O

Identify the point on the number line for each number.

7. $5\frac{3}{5}$ **8.** $5\frac{1}{2}$ **9.** 5.42

Set E, pages 282–283

A biking trail is being planned for a town. Where should the 2-mile marker be placed?

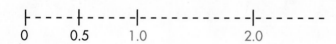

0   0.5   1.0   2.0

What do I know?   The biking trail must be at least 2 miles long. The 0.5 mile mark is located on the drawing.

What am I asked to find?   Where would the 2-mile mark be located on the drawing?

Think 1.0 is double 0.5, and 1.0 is half of 2.0.

Measure the distance from 0 to 0.5. Double this distance. Mark 1.0. Now double this distance and mark 2.0.

Remember you can use a ruler to measure the distance between each mark.

1. Look at the walking path below. Will begins at the starting point and walks 0.6 miles. Where on the path would Will end his walk?

0   0.3

Operations with Decimals

1 What is a sidereal day? You will find out in Lesson 13-5.

2 One of the smallest dinosaurs was Compsognathus. How long was this dinosaur? You will find out in Lesson 13-4.

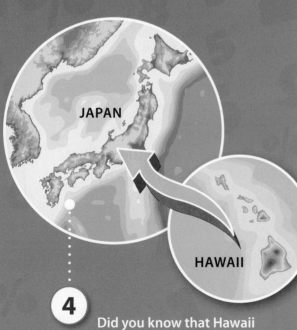

Review What You Know!

Choose the best term from the box.

- fraction
- decimal
- mixed number
- whole number

1. A ? names part of a whole.

2. A number that has a whole number and a fraction is a ?.

3. The ? equivalent of $\frac{1}{4}$ is 0.25.

Ordering Decimals

Order the numbers from least to greatest.

4. 0.4, 0.32, 0.25   5. 18.75, 18.7, 19.5

6. 2.4, 4.1, 1.5, 0.9   7. 3.5, 2.9, 4.6

Decimals and Fractions

Write each fraction as a decimal. Write each decimal as a fraction.

8. $\frac{2}{10}$ 9. 0.4   10. $\frac{41}{100}$

11. $\frac{6}{100}$ 12. 0.7   13. 0.75

Equivalent Fractions

Write each fraction in simplest form.

14. $\frac{2}{4}$ 15. $\frac{4}{10}$

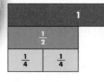

16. **Writing to Explain** How do you know that $\frac{3}{8}$ is in simplest form?

3 How many Earth days does it take Mercury to revolve around the sun? You will find out in Lesson 13-6.

JAPAN

HAWAII

4 Did you know that Hawaii is moving closer to Japan every year? Find out how much closer in Lesson 13-2.

Understand It!
Place value can be used to round decimals.

Rounding Decimals

How can you round decimals?

A passenger train travels from Emeryville to Sparks. Sacramento is one of the stops along the route.

Rounded to the nearest whole number, what is the distance from Emeryville to Sparks?

Emeryville to Sacramento: 77.86 miles   Sacramento to Sparks: 134.12 miles

211.98 miles

Another Example **How do you round to the nearest tenth?**

You have learned how to round whole numbers. Now you will learn how to round decimals.

What is 211.98 rounded to the nearest tenth?

A 211.0

B 211.9

C 211.99

D 212.0

Step 1

Look at the tenths place

211.9̲8

Step 2

Look at the digit to the right.

211.9̲8

If the digit to the right is less than 5, round to 211.9. If the digit is 5 or greater than 5, round to 212.

Step 3

211.9̲8 rounds to **212.0**.

Since this digit is 8, the digit in the tenths place increases by 1.

So, 211.98 rounded to the nearest tenth is 212.0. The correct choice is **D**.

Explain It

1. **Reasonableness** Why does the ones place change when you round 211.98 to the nearest tenth?

Look at the ones place.

211.98

Look at the digit to the right.

211.98

Since 9 > 5, round to the next whole number.

The distance from Emeryville to Sparks is about 212 miles.

A number line shows that the rounded answer is reasonable.

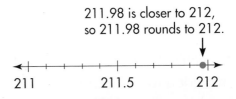

211.98 is closer to 212, so 211.98 rounds to 212.

211   211.5   212

Guided Practice*

Do you know HOW?

For **1** through **6**, round each decimal to the nearest whole number and to the nearest tenth.

1. 17.23   **2.** 19.80

3. 49.56   **4.** 67.59

5. 5.74   **6.** 82.19

Do you UNDERSTAND?

7. Writing to Explain In the example above, explain why the number line shows that 212 is a reasonable answer.

8. Round 77.86 to the nearest whole number.

9. Round 134.12 to the nearest tenth.

Independent Practice

For **10** through **24**, round each decimal to the nearest whole number.

10. 60.82   **11.** 88.3   **12.** 2.28   **13.** 0.69   **14.** 72.56

15. 41.48   **16.** 0.81   **17.** 7.61   **18.** 57.95   **19.** 63.66

20. 78.61   **21.** 4.10   **22.** 12.12   **23.** 91.95   **24.** 7.45

For **25** through **34**, round each decimal to the nearest tenth.

25. 3.78   **26.** 9.04   **27.** 23.97   **28.** 73.23   **29.** 99.94

30. 6.44   **31.** 0.32   **32.** 2.48   **33.** 44.54   **34.** 50.05

*For another example, see Set A on page 312.

35. Number Sense Name 3 decimals which, when rounded to the nearest tenth, round to 7.8.

36. Aaron filled his car with 8.53 gallons of gasoline. To the nearest tenth of a gallon, how much gasoline did Aaron purchase?

37. Which of these decimals, when rounded to the nearest whole number, does **NOT** round to 6?

A 5.71   **C** 6.2

B 5.91   **D** 6.82

38. What is 17.63 rounded to the nearest tenth?

A 17   **C** 17.63

B 17.6   **D** 18

39. Use a number line to explain why 0.28 rounded to the nearest whole number is 0.

40. Barbara's dog weighs 35.5 pounds. To the nearest whole number, how much does Barbara's dog weigh?

41. Reasonableness Danny had weighed two pieces of volcanic rock. The first piece had a weight of 4.99 grams and the second had a weight of 2.85 grams. Danny needs to record the combined weight of the two pieces of volcanic rock to the nearest gram. Is 4.0 + 2.9 a reasonable estimate of the weights to the nearest gram?

42. Dawn jogs 12 miles a week. How many miles does Dawn jog in 1 year?

 1 year = 52 weeks

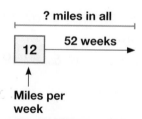

43. Reasoning Round 4.97 to the nearest tenth. Did the ones place change? Explain.

44. Writing to Explain What do the decimal numbers below have in common?

3.6, 4.2, 4.1

45. Number Sense Marissa was asked to round 89.36 to the nearest tenth. She answered 89.3. Is she correct? Explain.

46. Geometry If a circle has a diameter of 86 centimeters, what is the radius of the circle?

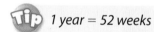 *The diameter is twice as long as the radius.*

47. According to Mica's rain gauge, it had rained 2.28 inches in 24 hours. What is 2.28 rounded to the nearest tenth? whole number?

48. The distance between Happy Valley and Rolling Meadow is 53.19 miles. What is this distance rounded to the nearest mile?

Mixed Problem Solving

The density of a material tells you how many grams are in a cubic centimeter of that material. For example, the density of water is 1.0 gram per cubic centimeter. So, 1.0 cubic centimeter of water has a mass of 1.0 gram.

Use the table at the right for **1** through **4**.

Data

Material	Density ($\frac{g}{cm^3}$)
Water	1.0
Ice	0.9
Aluminum	2.7
Iron	7.9
Balsa wood	0.13
Oak wood	0.79

1. Order the densities in the table from least to greatest.

2. Materials with greater density than water sink in water. Which materials in the table will sink in water?

3. Which material in the table has the greatest density?

4. Write an inequality to show which has a greater density, water or ice.

When you look closely at a rock, you may see different minerals. A mineral has properties you can measure, such as hardness or density.

Use the table at the right for **5** and **6**.

Mineral Sample	Mass (grams)	Volume (cubic centimeters)	Density (grams per cubic centimeter)
#1	6	2	
#2	26	13	
#3	16	4	

5. The density of a material equals its mass divided by its volume. What is the density of each mineral shown in the table?

6. Granite has a density of about 2.75 grams per cubic centimeter. If rounded to the nearest whole number, which of the samples could be granite?

7. Iron has a density of about 7.86 grams per cubic centimeter. What is this number rounded to the nearest tenth?

8. If a mineral has a mass of 33 grams and its density is 3 grams per cubic centimeter, what is its volume?

Lesson
13-2

Understand It!
To estimate, round decimals to whole numbers to add and subtract.

Estimating Sums and Differences of Decimals

How do you estimate when you add and subtract decimals?

In Beijing, China, it rained 5.82 inches in the first half of the year. In the second half of the year, it rained 18.63 inches. Estimate the rainfall for the whole year.

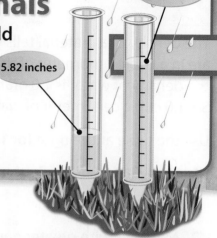

18.63 inches

5.82 inches

Guided Practice*

Do you know HOW?

In **1** through **4**, estimate each sum or difference.

1. 0.72 + 0.56

2. 18.54 − 1.99

3.   13.94
     +   4.72

4.   47.31
     − 11.25

Do you UNDERSTAND?

5. Explain why 1.4 and 0.75 both round to 1.

6. Reasonableness In the example above, explain why 2.5 inches is not a reasonable estimate of the rainfall for the whole year.

Independent Practice

In **7** through **22**, round to the nearest whole number to estimate each sum or difference.

 You can write rounded numbers in vertical format before adding or subtracting.

7. 9.6 + 3.27

8. 9.51 + 8.61

9. 7.11 + 0.15

10. 1.45 + 6.85

11. 18.85 − 6.8

12. 4.31 − 1.28

13. 31.12 − 4.86

14. 0.66 − 0.34

15.   82.43
     −   3.90

16.   5.78
     − 3.86

17.   63.93
     +   3.31

18.   3.73
     + 0.81

19.   2.1
     + 7.5

20.   3.45
     − 2.44

21.   19.06
     +   1.99

22.   4.84
     + 0.73

For another example, see Set B on page 312.

Estimate 5.82 + 18.63.

Round each decimal to the nearest whole number. Then add.

$$5.82 \longrightarrow 6$$
$$+ \ 18.63 \longrightarrow + \ 19$$
$$\overline{ \quad 25}$$

About 25 inches of rain fell in Beijing.

In August, 6.7 inches of rain fell in Beijing. In September, it rained 2.3 inches. About how much more did it rain in August than in September?

$$6.7 \longrightarrow 7$$
$$- \ 2.3 \longrightarrow - \ 2$$
$$\overline{ \quad 5}$$

Round each decimal to the nearest whole number. Then subtract the rounded numbers.

It rained about 5 inches more in August.

Problem Solving

In **23** and **24**, use the table at the right.

23. The table shows the weight of each type of vegetable Vanessa bought to make a large salad for her family picnic. About how much more did the cucumbers weigh than the lettuce?

24. About how much did all of the vegetables weigh altogether?

Vegetable	Weight (pounds)
	2.0
	2.6
	1.2
	3.5

25. Hawaii is moving toward Japan at a rate of approximately 2.8 inches per year. About how much closer will Hawaii be to Japan in 3 years?

26. Sunny has $50 to buy painting supplies. She wants to buy brushes for $7.33, paper for $14.97, and an easel for $38.19. Do you need to find the exact total or an estimate?

27. Neil is installing 38 square yards of carpet in his home. He uses 12.2 square yards in one room and 10.5 square yards in another room. About how much carpet does he have left?

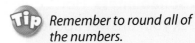

Remember to round all of the numbers.

A about 13 square yards

C about 17 square yards

B about 15 square yards

D about 20 square yards

Understand It!
Adding and subtracting decimals is similar to adding and subtracting whole numbers.

Modeling Addition and Subtraction of Decimals

Hands-On
grid paper

How do you add decimals using grids?

Use the table at the right to find the total monthly cost of using the dishwasher and the DVD player.

Data

Device	Cost/month
DVD player	$0.40
Microwave oven	$3.57
Ceiling light	$0.89
Dishwasher	$0.85

Another Example **How do you subtract decimals with grids?**

Find the difference between the cost per month to run the microwave oven and the ceiling light.

Use hundredths grids to subtract 3.57 − 0.89.

Shade three grids and 57 squares to show 3.57.

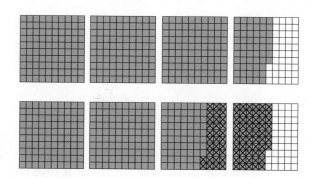

Cross out 8 columns and 9 squares of the shaded grid to show 0.89 being subtracted from 3.57.

Count the squares that are shaded but not crossed out to find the difference.
3.57 − 0.89 = 2.68

Explain It

1. **Reasonableness** How could you use the grids to check your answer above?

2. How would the grid above be different if the cost per month to run the microwave is $2.57?

Step 1

Use hundredths grids to add $0.85 + $0.40.

It costs $0.85 to use the dishwasher per month.

Shade 85 squares to show $0.85.

Step 2

It costs $0.40 to use the DVD player per month.

Use a different color and shade 40 more squares to show $0.40. Count all of the shaded squares to find the sum.

$0.85 + $0.40 = $1.25

The monthly cost of using the dishwasher and DVD player is $1.25.

Guided Practice*

Do you know HOW?

In **1** through **6**, use hundredths grids to add or subtract.

1. 1.22 + 0.34   **2.** 0.63 + 0.41

3. 2.73 − 0.94   **4.** 1.38 − 0.73

5. 0.47 − 0.21   **6.** 2.02 + 0.8

Do you UNDERSTAND?

7. If you were to shade 40 squares first, and then shade 85 more, would the answer be the same as shading 85 squares and then 40 more?

8. Show the difference between the monthly cost of using the DVD player and the dishwasher.

Independent Practice

In **9** through **18**, add or subtract. Use hundredths grids to help.

9. 0.1 + 0.73

10. 0.37 + 0.47

11. 1.2 + 0.56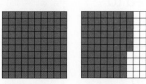

12. 1.33 − 0.35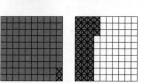

13. 3.0 − 1.47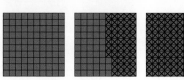

14. 1.11 + 0.89

DIGITAL eTools www.pearsonsuccessnet.com

15. 2.23 − 1.8

16. 0.4 − 0.21

17. 0.58 + 2.4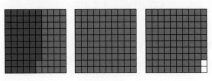

18. 1.31 − 0.55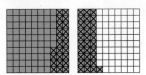

Problem Solving

19. Writing to Explain How is adding 4.56 + 2.31 similar to adding $2.31 + $4.56?

20. Number Sense Do you think the difference of 1.4 − 0.95 is less than one or greater than one? Explain.

21. Number Sense Is the sum of 0.46 + 0.25 less than or greater than one? Explain.

22. Estimation Estimate to decide if the sum of 314 + 175 is more or less than 600.

23. Which choice represents the problem below?

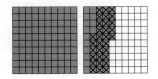

A 2.00 + 0.31 **C** 1.76 − 1.45
B 1.76 − 0.31 **D** 1.45 − 0.31

24. Geometry What kind of angle is made when two lines are perpendicular?

A acute angle **C** obtuse angle
B right angle **D** vertex

25. Think About the Process Which expression can be used to find the perimeter of the pool shown to the right?

A 50 + 25 **C** 50 + 50 + 25 + 25
B 25 + 25 + 25 + 25 **D** 50 + 50 + 50 + 50

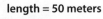
length = 50 meters

width = 25 meters

26. Write the number sentence that is shown by the hundredths grids to the right.

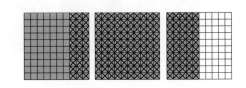

Reasonableness of Sums

Estimate 2,968 + 983 + 5,442. Use a calculator to find the sum. Then, explain whether or not the sum you found is reasonable.

Step 1 Estimate 2,968 + 983 + 5,442.

3,000 + 1,000 + 5,000 = 9,000

Step 2 Use a calculator to add.

Press: 2,968 ⊞ + ⊞ 983 ⊞ + ⊞ 5,442

Display:

9393

Step 3 Explain whether or not the sum is reasonable.

Since 9,393 is close to the estimate of 9,000, the sum is reasonable.

Practice

Estimate each sum. Find the sum on a calculator.
Remember to check whether or not the sum is reasonable.

1. 956 + 1,495

2. 1,872 + 3,216

3. 4,857 + 5,679 + 3,298

4. 8,542 + 875 + 6,425

5. 1,978 + 7,435 + 2,986

6. 9,650 + 2,348 + 5,822

7. 2,726 + 1,247 + 3,476

8. 3,214 + 7,981 + 2,148 + 6,542

9. 872 + 2,729 + 221

10. 6,742 + 7,231

11. 8,792 + 3,864 + 298

12. 8,898 + 6,281

13. 1,372 + 6,261 + 204

14. 7,671 + 3,341

15. 3,634 + 8,916 + 192

16. 3,456 + 7,654 + 211

17. 101 + 3,561 + 41

18. 99 + 3,795 + 4,319

Understand It!
Adding and subtracting
decimals is like adding
and subtracting whole
numbers.

Adding and Subtracting Decimals

How can you add or subtract decimals?

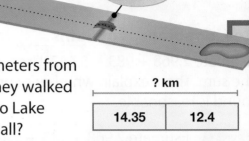

Crystal River

The Patel family walked 14.35 kilometers from their cabin to Crystal River. Later, they walked 12.4 kilometers from Crystal River to Lake Dorrance. How far did they walk in all?

? km

| 14.35 | 12.4 |

Another Example **How can you subtract decimals?**

You know how to subtract whole numbers. In this lesson, you will learn how to subtract decimals.

23.23 kilograms

| 11.6 | ? |

Roger's backpack has a mass of 23.23 kilograms. Marta's backpack has a mass of 11.6 kilograms. What is the difference in the masses of their backpacks?

Estimate 23.23 rounds to 23 and 11.6 rounds to 12.
23 − 12 = 11.

Step 1

Line up the decimal points. Write zeros as placeholders, if necessary.

$$23.23$$
$$-\ 11.60$$

Step 2

Regroup, if necessary. Subtract hundredths.

$$23.23$$
$$-\ 11.60$$
$$\overline{3}$$

Step 3

Regroup, if necessary. Subtract tenths.

$$\overset{2\ 12}{2\cancel{3}.\cancel{2}3}$$
$$-\ 11.60$$
$$\overline{63}$$

Step 4

Subtract ones and tens, regrouping as necessary. Place the decimal point.

$$\overset{2\ 12}{2\cancel{3}.\cancel{2}3}$$
$$-\ 11.60$$
$$\overline{11.63}$$

Roger's backpack has a mass that is of 11.63 kilograms more than Marta's backpack. The answer is reasonable because 11.63 is close to 11.

Explain It

1. In Step 4, how do you know where to place the decimal point?

2. **Reasonableness** Is it reasonable to say that the mass of Roger's backpack is twice as much as Marta's backpack?

Step 1	Step 2	Step 3	Step 4
Line up the decimal points. Write zeros as place holders, if necessary.	Add the hundredths. Regroup if necessary.	Add the tenths. Regroup if necessary.	Add the ones, then the tens. Place the decimal point.

Step 1:
```
  14.35
+ 12.40
```

Step 2:
```
  14.35
+ 12.40
      5
```

Step 3:
```
  14.35
+ 12.40
     75
```

Step 4:
```
  14.35
+ 12.40
  26.75
```
The Patel family walked 26.75 km in all.

Guided Practice*

Do you know HOW?

For **1** through **6**, add or subtract.

1.
```
   8.24
+ 19.16
```

2.
```
  37.68
- 14.53
```

3.
```
   5.93
+ 87.82
```

4.
```
  62.53
- 43.75
```

5. 7.7 + 0.85

6. 0.6 − 0.42

Do you UNDERSTAND?

7. How many miles farther is the distance from the cabin to Crystal River than the distance from Crystal River to Lake Dorrance?

8. Is the answer in the example above reasonable?

Independent Practice

For **9** through **24**, add or subtract. Estimate to check the reasonableness of your answer.

9.
```
  2.73
+ 0.44
```

10.
```
  46.81
- 12.43
```

11.
```
  35.78
+ 70.71
```

12.
```
  17.15
-  2.38
```

13.
```
  4.83
- 0.56
```

14.
```
  12.55
+ 53.59
```

15.
```
  88.25
-  7.52
```

16.
```
  59.32
+  4.31
```

17. 70.1 − 65.81

18. 55.7 + 0.52

19. 89.82 − 46.3

20. 92.78 − 37.97

21. 9.12 + 82.4

22. 69.63 + 0.99

23. 39.65 − 17.69

24. 91.5 − 66.13

25. Number Sense Is 8.7 − 0.26 greater or less than 8? Explain.

26. Geometry Heather says an obtuse triangle always has no equal sides. Is she correct?

27. On Oak Street, 66.32 kilograms of trash was collected, and 31.21 kilograms of recyclables were collected in one week. How many kilograms were collected in all?

? kilograms	
66.32	31.21

28. Reasoning When Matt left his home in Red Grove, his odometer read 47,283.5 kilometers. By the time he had arrived in Grand City, his odometer read 48,163.7 kilometers. How many kilometers did Matt travel?

48,163.7 kilometers	
47,283.5	?

29. One of the largest dinosaurs ever found, the *Puertasaurus,* measured 39.92 meters long. One of the smallest dinosaurs, the *Compsognathus,* measured 1.43 meters long. What was the difference in length of these dinosaurs?

30. Think About the Process Throughout the world, about 270 babies are born each minute. Which expression would you use to find about how many babies are born in one hour?

A $270 + 60$ **C** 270×6

B 270×60 **D** 270×30

31. Think About the Process The distance from Don's house to his school is twice the length of the distance from Don's house to the post office. The post office is 2.4 kilometers from the school. How could you find the distance from Don's house to the school?

A $2.4 + 2.4$ **C** $2.4 + 1.2$

B $2.4 - 1.2$ **D** $2.4 - 0.2$

32. In one week, Jessica spent 2.35 hours walking from her house to work. Together, Jessica and her friend, Constance, will spend 4.21 hours of their week walking from their homes to work. How many hours does Constance spend each week walking from home to work?

4.21 hours	
2.35	?

33. In a butterfly garden, there are 36 butterflies. Nine of them are yellow swallowtails. What fraction of the butterflies are yellow swallowtails?

Algebra Connections

Solving Equations

Remember that an equation is a number sentence which uses an equal sign to show that two expressions have the same value. You can use basic facts and mental math to help you find missing values in an equation.

Example:

$18 \div \boxed{} = 3$

Think *What number times 3 is 18?*

Since $6 \times 3 = 18$, the value of $\boxed{}$ must be 6.

Copy and complete. Check your answers.

1. $20 + \boxed{} = 34$ **2.** $64 \div \boxed{} = 8$ **3.** $5 \times \boxed{} = 45$ **4.** $54 - \boxed{} = 14$

5. $\boxed{} \times 6 = 42$ **6.** $36 \div \boxed{} = 4$ **7.** $\boxed{} + 15 = 31$ **8.** $\boxed{} - 8 = 6$

9. $26 - \boxed{} = 18$ **10.** $9 + \boxed{} = 20$ **11.** $12 \div \boxed{} = 6$ **12.** $4 \times \boxed{} = 28$

13. $72 \div \boxed{} = 8$ **14.** $\boxed{} \times 9 = 54$ **15.** $\boxed{} - 5 = 7$ **16.** $\boxed{} + 7 = 29$

17. $\boxed{} + 32 = 46$ **18.** $28 - \boxed{} = 9$ **19.** $\boxed{} \div 4 = 12$ **20.** $\boxed{} \times 3 = 30$

. . . .

For **21** through **24**, copy and complete the equation using information from the problem. Then find the answer.

21. Jaina has $4. She needs $12 to buy a book. How much more money does Jaina need?

$4 + \boxed{} = 12$

22. Harrison's allowance is $5 a week. How much money will he have if he saves his whole allowance for 4 weeks?

$\boxed{} \times 5 = \boxed{}$

23. There are 49 fourth graders. The gym teacher needs to divide them into groups of 7. How many groups can be made?

$49 \div \boxed{} = \boxed{}$

24. **Write a Problem** Write a problem in which 4 is subtracted from 28 to find a difference. Write the number sentence and then solve.

Lesson
13-5

Understand It!
Multiplying a whole number by a decimal is like multiplying whole numbers.

Multiplying a Whole Number by a Decimal

How do you multiply whole numbers and decimals?

The sailfish can swim at a speed that is about 3.09 times faster than that of a Pacific leatherback turtle. How fast can the sailfish swim?

A sailfish swims ? mph.

A sea turtle swims 22 mph.

Guided Practice*

Do you know HOW?

For **1** through **6**, find each product.

1.
$$\begin{array}{r} 7.2 \\ \times\ 3 \\ \hline \end{array}$$

2.
$$\begin{array}{r} 6.18 \\ \times\ 5 \\ \hline \end{array}$$

3.
$$\begin{array}{r} 6.21 \\ \times\ 8 \\ \hline \end{array}$$

4.
$$\begin{array}{r} 9.47 \\ \times\ 76 \\ \hline \end{array}$$

5.
$$\begin{array}{r} 43.2 \\ \times\ 23 \\ \hline \end{array}$$

6.
$$\begin{array}{r} 3.74 \\ \times\ 9 \\ \hline \end{array}$$

Do you UNDERSTAND?

7. Suppose you wrote 6,798 instead of 67.98 as the product in the example above. How does estimation help you know your answer is incorrect?

8. Writing to Explain If you multiplied 22 by 6.8, how many decimal places would be in the product?

Independent Practice

For **9** through **20**, find each product.

9.
$$\begin{array}{r} 3.63 \\ \times\ 4 \\ \hline \end{array}$$

10.
$$\begin{array}{r} 27.4 \\ \times\ 7 \\ \hline \end{array}$$

11.
$$\begin{array}{r} 58.8 \\ \times\ 65 \\ \hline \end{array}$$

12.
$$\begin{array}{r} 8.19 \\ \times\ 18 \\ \hline \end{array}$$

13.
$$\begin{array}{r} 9.4 \\ \times\ 34 \\ \hline \end{array}$$

14.
$$\begin{array}{r} 7.62 \\ \times\ 44 \\ \hline \end{array}$$

15.
$$\begin{array}{r} 5.39 \\ \times\ 93 \\ \hline \end{array}$$

16.
$$\begin{array}{r} 17.46 \\ \times\ 35 \\ \hline \end{array}$$

17. 61×2.2

18. 72×4.8

19. 8.31×55

20. 49×7.3

For another example, see Set E on page 313.

Find 22 × 3.09.

Estimate: 22 × 3 = 66

Multiply as you would with whole numbers.

$$\begin{array}{r} \overset{1}{\underset{1}{}} \\ 3.09 \\ \times \quad 22 \\ \hline 618 \\ + \; 6180 \\ \hline 6798 \end{array}$$

Write the decimal point in the product.

$$\begin{array}{r} 3.09 \\ \times \quad 22 \\ \hline 618 \\ + \; 6180 \\ \hline 67.98 \end{array}$$

3.09   **2** decimal places

× 22   **0** decimal places

67.98   2 decimal places

Count the decimal places in both factors. The total is the number of decimal places in the product.

Look at your estimate to see if your answer is reasonable. 67.98 is close to 66.

A sailfish can swim 67.98 miles per hour.

Problem Solving

21. Karen is setting up chairs in two rooms for a banquet. The first room has 5 rows of chairs with 12 chairs in each row. The second room has 8 rows of chairs with 9 chairs in each row. Which room has more chairs? How many more?

22. Dana is 3 times as old as Liz. Their combined age is 32. How old are they?

  A Dana: 27   **C** Dana: 18
       Liz: 9   Liz: 6

  B Dana: 24   **D** Dana: 9
       Liz: 8   Liz: 3

23. **Number Sense** Write two fractions that name the shaded part in the figure at the right. Explain why the fractions are equivalent.

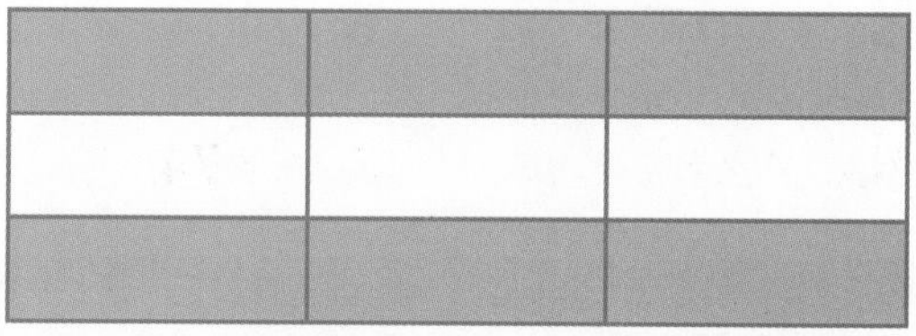

24. The amount of time it takes the Earth to make a full rotation is known as a "sidereal day." A sidereal day is about 23.9 hours long. How long are seven sidereal days?

25. If you use 40 × 5 to estimate 36 × 5, is 800 greater or less than the exact answer? Is 800 an overestimate or an underestimate? Explain.

26. A recipe for cinnamon bread calls for 1.5 cups of flour. How many cups of flour are needed if the recipe is tripled?

27. **Algebra** Use the number sentences below. What numbers replace $\bigcirc$ and $\triangle$?

$$\bigcirc + \triangle = 14$$
$$\bigcirc + \bigcirc = 16$$

Understand It!
Dividing a decimal by a whole number is like dividing whole numbers.

Dividing a Decimal by a Whole Number

How do you divide decimals by whole numbers?

The average length of an adult giraffe's neck is 1.8 meters long. This is about three times the length of its heart. How long is the heart of an average adult giraffe?

1.8 meters

Guided Practice*

Do you know HOW?

For **1** through **6**, find each quotient. Check your answer by multiplying.

1. $9\overline{)7.2}$

2. $4\overline{)24.4}$

3. $8\overline{)8.24}$

4. $4\overline{)42.8}$

5. $3\overline{)20.7}$

6. $2\overline{)0.6}$

Do you UNDERSTAND?

7. The legs of an adult giraffe are about as long as its neck. About how long are the legs of an adult giraffe?

8. **Writing to Explain** How is dividing a decimal by a whole number different from dividing a whole number by a whole number?

Independent Practice

For **9** through **28**, find each quotient. Check your answer by multiplying.

9. $4.64 \div 4$

10. $42.7 \div 7$

11. $57.6 \div 6$

12. $8.95 \div 5$

13. $9.89 \div 1$

14. $7.32 \div 4$

15. $51.9 \div 3$

16. $14.4 \div 4$

17. $36.4 \div 4$

18. $31.2 \div 8$

19. $5.13 \div 9$

20. $91.8 \div 6$

21. $2.4 \div 8$

22. $93.8 \div 7$

23. $5.32 \div 2$

24. $4.32 \div 3$

25. $24.65 \div 5$

26. $43.68 \div 7$

27. $24.9 \div 3$

28. $16.8 \div 4$

For another example, see Set E on page 313.

Find 1.8 ÷ 3.

You can use the same process here as you used to divide whole numbers.

1.8 meters

| Neck | | | | 3 times as long |
| Heart | ? | | | |

An average adult giraffe's heart is 0.6 meters long.

Place the decimal point in the quotient and divide.

$$
\begin{array}{r}
0.6 \\
3\overline{)1.8} \\
-1.8 \\
\hline
0
\end{array}
$$

Check your answer by multiplying.

$0.6 \times 3 = 1.8$

Problem Solving

29. A cyclist travels 25.5 miles in 3 hours. What is the average speed of the cyclist in miles per hour?

30. Isabella made 7 calls last week that lasted a total of 68.6 minutes. If each call lasted the same amount of time, how many minutes did each phone call last?

31. Paul drew three lines. The first line was 7.6 centimeters long. The second line was half the length of the first line. The third line was half the length of the second line. How long is the third line?

32. One day, the high temperature in Kansas City, Missouri, was 77.4°F. This was 3 times as high as the temperature in Nome, Alaska, on the same day. What was the high temperature in Nome?

33. Reasonableness Is 91 a reasonable answer to 27.3 ÷ 3? Why or why not?

34. Writing to Explain Is 7,777,777 a prime number? Why or why not?

35. **Think** **About the Process** One day on Mercury is equal to 59 days on Earth. How would you find how many Earth days are equal to three Mercury days?

A 59 ÷ 3
C 59 × 3
B 59 ÷ 1
D 365 × 3

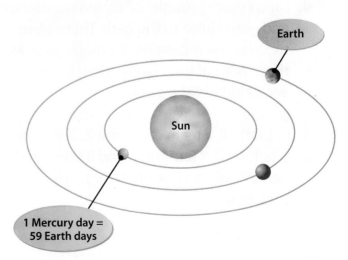

1 Mercury day = 59 Earth days

Lesson
13-7

Understand It!
Using the Try, Check, and Revise strategy can help solve problems.

Problem Solving

Try, Check, and Revise

Wilma bought supplies for her dog at the pet store. She spent a total of $26.18 not including tax. She bought two of one item in the chart and one other item. What did she buy?

Dog Toy:
$7.98

Dog Supplies	
Leash	$11.50
Collar	$5.59
Bowls	$7.48
Medium Beds	$15.00
Toys	$7.98

Guided Practice*

Do you know HOW?

Use the Try, Check, and Revise strategy to solve this problem. Write the answer in a complete sentence.

1. Annie and Matt spent a total of $29 on a gift. Annie spent $7 more than Matt. How much did each spend?

Do you UNDERSTAND?

2. How do you know that two beds are too much?

3. **Write a Problem** Write a problem using the Try, Check, and Revise strategy.

Independent Practice

Use the Try, Check, and Revise strategy to solve the problems. Write the answer in a complete sentence.

4. Lana's mom brought 27 cartons of orange and grape juice to the park. There were twice as many cartons of orange juice as there were of grape juice. How many of each kind did she bring?

5. In football, a team can score 2, 3, 6, 7, or 8 points. The Terriers scored 3 times and had 19 points. How did they score their points?

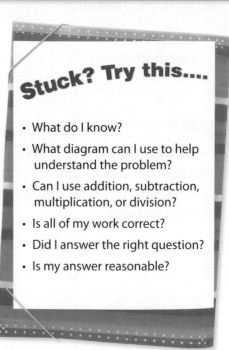

Stuck? Try this....

- What do I know?
- What diagram can I use to help understand the problem?
- Can I use addition, subtraction, multiplication, or division?
- Is all of my work correct?
- Did I answer the right question?
- Is my answer reasonable?

Make a reasonable first try.

Two beds are too much.

Try one bed. Then try two of the smaller priced items, like the toy.

Check using the information given in the problem.

$7.98 + $7.98 + $15 = $30.96

That's too high but is close.

Revise. Use your first try to make a reasonable second try.

The first try was $4.78 too high. If you keep the bed, you need to come down $4.78 total or $2.39 for each item.

Try two collars.

$5.59 + $5.59 + $15 = $26.18

Wilma bought two collars and one medium bed.

For **6** through **8**, use the data at the right.

6. Trent spent $16.34, before tax, at Fun Town. He bought 3 different items. What did he buy?

7. Alicia spent $14.10, before tax, on 3 items at Fun Town. Two of her three items were the same. What did she buy?

8. Rich spent $30.80, before tax, at Fun Town. He bought two of one item and two of another item. What did Rich buy?

Fun Town	
Jump Rope	$2.35
Skateboard	$26.95
Basketball	$8.75
Football	$6.00
Baseball	$5.24
Bat	$9.40

9. Mr. Mill took all of the tires off of the old bicycles and tricycles in his garage. He got 12 tires off of 5 cycles. How many of each type of cycle did he have?

10. Linda earned $8 per hour and Susan earned $10 per hour. Linda and Susan worked the same number of hours. Linda earned $72. How much did Susan earn?

11. If Chuck's Sports sold 12 fishing poles each week, how many fishing poles would be sold in one month?

? fishing poles

12	12	12	12

Fishing poles sold each week

12. Lizzy bought six notebooks at the beginning of the school year. They were $2.19 each. How much did the six notebooks cost?

A $4.38   **C** $10.95

B $6.57   **D** $13.14

1. The distance across the widest part of a quarter is 24.26 millimeters. What is 24.26 rounded to the nearest tenth? (13-1)

   A 24

   B 24.2

   C 24.3

   D 25

2. Lee's turtle has a shell that is 14.42 centimeters long. Ty's turtle has a shell that is 12.14 centimeters long. Which is the best estimate of the difference? (13-2)

   A 1 centimeter

   B 2 centimeters

   C 4 centimeters

   D 6 centimeters

3. Larry spent $1.89 on a bottle of paint and $0.45 on a sponge brush. What was the total amount he spent? (13-3)

   A $2.34

   B $1.34

   C $1.32

   D $1.24

4. Tatum weighs 47.39 kilograms. What is her mass rounded to the nearest whole number? (13-1)

   A 50 kilograms

   B 48 kilograms

   C 47.4 kilograms

   D 47 kilograms

5. A penny has a mass of 2.5 grams. A quarter has a mass of 5.67 grams. What is the difference in their masses? (13-4)

   A 2.17 grams

   B 3.17 grams

   C 5.42 grams

   D 8.17 grams

6. What is 39.2 ÷ 8? (13-6)

   A 0.49

   B 3.9

   C 4.9

   D 5.8

7. Mr. Treveses bought 2.72 kilograms of hamburger meat and 1.48 kilograms of turkey meat. How many kilograms of meat did he buy? (13-4)

   A 1.24 kilograms

   B 3.10 kilograms

   C 4.10 kilograms

   D 4.20 kilograms

8. What is 6×19.37? (13-5)

A 116.22

B 114.22

C 64.82

D 56.22

9. Which symbol makes the comparison true? (13-4)

$12.63 - 5.94 \bigcirc 3.8 + 2.88$

A <

B =

C +

D >

10. Jason spent $8.76, not including tax, on breakfast food. He bought 4 items. Two of the items were the same thing. What did he buy? (13-7)

Breakfast Food	
Bagel	$0.89
Box of Cereal	$2.79
Loaf of Bread	$1.59
Gallon of Juice	$3.19
Gallon of Milk	$3.79

A 2 bagels, a gallon of juice, and a gallon of milk

B 2 bagels, a box of cereal, and a gallon of milk

C 2 loaves of bread, a box of cereal, and a gallon of juice

D 2 boxes of cereal, a bagel, and a gallon of milk

11. Samantha rode her bicycle 6.79 miles on Saturday and 8.21 miles on Sunday. Which is the best estimate of the total miles she rode during the weekend? (13-2)

A 20 miles

B 15 miles

C 12 miles

D 1 mile

12. Mrs. Smith bought 6.25 yards of material to make 5 costumes. If each costume uses the same amount of material, how many yards does one costume use? (13-6)

A 31.25 yards

B 12.5 yards

C 1.25 yards

D 0.125 yards

13. Mr. Kwan loaded 8 boxes into his truck. If each box weighed 26.4 pounds, how many pounds did he load into his truck? (13-5)

A 3.3 pounds

B 210.4 pounds

C 211.2 pounds

D 2,112 pounds

14. What is 15.52 rounded to the nearest whole number? (13-1)

A 16

B 15.6

C 15.5

D 15

Set A, pages 290–292

Round 306.87 to the nearest whole number.

Look at the ones place: 30**6**.87

Now look at the digit to the right: 306.**8**7

If the digit to the right is less than 5, round to 306. If the digit is 5 or greater, round to 307.

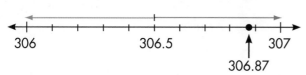

8 > 5
So, 306.87 rounds to 307.

Remember you must look at the digit to the right of the digit you are rounding.

Round each decimal to the nearest whole number and then to the nearest tenth.

1. 18.34   **2.** 17.60

3. 68.58   **4.** 2.78

5. 6.83   **6.** 80.12

Set B, pages 294–295

Estimate 23.64 + 7.36.

Round each decimal to the nearest whole number. Then add.

23.64 rounds to 24.
7.36 rounds to 7.

24 + 7 = 31

Remember to compare the digit in the tenths place to 5 when you round to the nearest whole number.

1. 19.35 + 8.74   **2.** 12.3 − 9.7

3.   14.04   **4.**   7.48
       + 9.33   − 3.92

Set C, pages 296–298

Use hundredths grids to subtract 1.86 − 0.95.

Shade one whole grid and 86 squares to show 1.86.

To subtract 0.95, cross out 95 shaded squares on the grids.

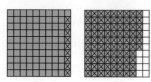

Count the squares that are shaded but not crossed out.

1.86 − 0.95 = 0.91

Remember when adding decimals, shade the first number in one color and then continue on shading the second number with another color.

1. 0.02 + 0.89   **2.** 0.67 − 0.31

 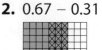

3. 0.34 + 0.34   **4.** 0.81 − 0.78

Set D, pages 300–302

Add 15.85 23.3.

Line up the decimal points.

Add the hundredths.	Add the tenths.	Add the ones. Place the decimal in the answer.
15.85 + 23.30 ——— 5	¹ 15.85 + 23.30 ——— 1 5	¹ 15.85 + 23.30 ——— 39.15

Remember to place the decimal in the answer.

Add or subtract.

1.   6.32
     + 15.12

2.   43.42
     − 15.28

3.   8.34
     + 97.25

4.   71.35
     − 67.82

5. 5.2 + 0.74   **6.** 0.8 + 0.56

Set E, pages 304–307

Find 2.78 × 5.

Estimate.
2.78 rounds to 3.

$3 \times 5 = 15$

³ ⁴
2.78   Multiply the same way as with whole numbers.
×   5   Count two decimal places in the factors.
———   Place the decimal in the answer.
13.90

Remember to divide with a decimal the same way as with whole numbers.

Multiply or divide.

1.   2.37
     ×   3

2.   65.88
     ×   6

3. 4)5.12   **4.** 9)4.68

Set F, pages 308–309

Dan spent $72.82 on 4 items at the store. Two of his items were the same. What did he buy?

Kids Mart	
Video games	$15.86
Shoes	$32.96
Sports hat	$12

Try two video games, one pair of shoes, and one hat.
$31.72 + $32.96 + $12.00 = $76.68

That's too high but close.

Revise. Try two sports hats, one video game, and one pair of shoes.
$24.00 + $15.86 + $32.96 = $72.82

Dan bought 1 video game, 1 pair of shoes, and 2 sports hats.

Remember to write the answer in a complete sentence.

Use Try, Check, and Revise to solve the problem.

1. Terry, Corey, and Chris together made 20 baskets in a basketball game. Terry made 5 more baskets than Corey. Chris made 3 times as many baskets as Corey. How many baskets did they each have?

Topic 14

Area and Perimeter

1 You can use different polygons to estimate the perimeter of the United States. You will find out how in Lesson 14-6.

2 Central Park is one of the most visited city parks in the world. How many square kilometers does it cover? You will find out in Lesson 14-2.

Vocabulary

Choose the best term from the box.

> • addition • multiplication
> • area • perimeter

1. The ? is the distance around a figure.

2. The number of square units needed to cover a region is the ? .

3. ? is the operation you use to find the area of a region.

Multiplication Facts

Find each product.

4. 6×5	**5.** 7×9	**6.** 8×8
7. 7×4	**8.** 3×6	**9.** 5×4
10. 4×9	**11.** 8×5	**12.** 9×6
13. 8×4	**14.** 3×9	**15.** 8×7

Shapes

Identify each shape.

16. 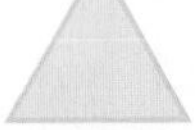 **17.** 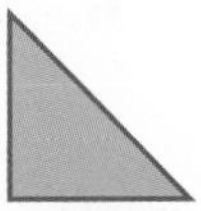 **18.**

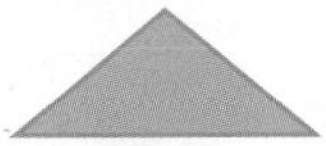

19.  **20.** 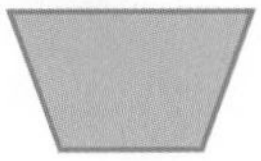 **21.**

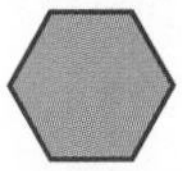

22.  **23.**  **24.**

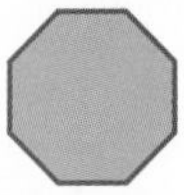

25. **Writing to Explain** Explain how the figures in Exercises 16–18 are alike and how they are different.

③ A Sierpinski Triangle is a famous fractal, or geometric shape, in which the shape itself is recurring. How can you find the area of the triangle in the middle? You will find out in Lesson 14-5.

Lesson
14-1

Understand It!
Find the area of figures by counting the number of square units that cover a region.

Understanding Area

How do you measure area?

Emily made a collage in art class. She cut shapes to make her design.

What is the area of one of the shapes?

Area is the number of square units needed to cover a region.

Guided Practice*

Do you know HOW?

For **1** and **2**, count to find the area. Tell if the area is exact or an estimate.

1.

2.

Do you UNDERSTAND?

3. If the first shape above had two more rows of 4 squares, what would the new area be?

4. Make two different figures that each have an area of 16 square units.

Independent Practice

For **5** through **12**, count to find the area. Tell if the area is exact or an estimate.

5.

6.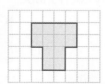

7.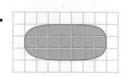

8.

9.

10.

11.

12.

For another example, see Set A on page 342.

Count the square units inside the shape. The exact count is the area of the shape.

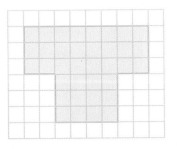

There are 36 squares inside the shape.

The area of the shape is 36 square units.

Sometimes you can estimate the area.

Count the squares inside the shape.

There are about 27 squares inside the shape.

The area of the shape is about 27 square units.

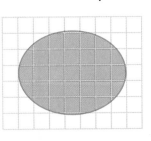

Problem Solving

For **13** through **15**, use the picture to the right.

Mr. Sanchez's Farm

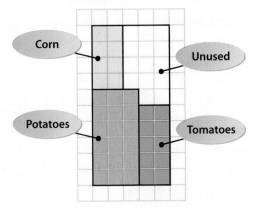

13. Mr. Sanchez grows three types of vegetables on his farm. What is the area of the section he uses to grow potatoes?

14. Mr. Sanchez leaves one section unused each growing season. What is the area of the farm that is being left unused this season?

15. What is the area of the farm that is being used to grow crops?

16. Maggie bought 4 sketch pads and 2 boxes of art pencils. If each sketch pad costs $3.59 and each box of art pencils costs $4.12, how much money did Maggie spend on her supplies?

17. What would be a good estimate (in units) of the green shaded area shown below?

   A About 13

   B About 10

   C About 4

   D About 2

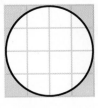

18. A bookstore is having a sale. When customers buy 2 books, they get another book free. If Pat buys 8 books, how many books will he get for free?

Understand It! There are different ways to find the square units needed to cover a figure.

Area of Squares and Rectangles

How can you find the area of a figure?

A small can of chalkboard paint covers 40 square feet. Does Mike need more than one small can to paint one wall of his room?

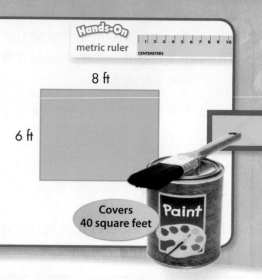

8 ft

6 ft

Covers 40 square feet

Paint

Hands-On
metric ruler

Guided Practice*

Do you know HOW?

For **1** through **4**, find the area of each figure.

1.
7 in
3 in

2.
5 m
4 m

3.
14 ft
8 ft

4.
9 cm

Do you UNDERSTAND?

5. What is the formula for the area of a square? Explain how you know.

6. Mike plans to paint another wall in his room blue. That wall measures 12 feet by 8 feet. How much area does Mike need to paint?

Independent Practice

Leveled Practice In **7** and **8**, measure the sides, and find the area of each figure.

7.
cm
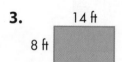
cm

8.
cm

cm

In **9** through **12**, find the area of each figure.

9.
4 ft
9 ft

10.
13 mm
9 mm

11.
5 in.
7 in.

12.
4 yd

For another example, see Set B on page 342.

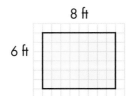

One Way

You can count the square units to find area.

8 ft

6 ft

There are 48 square units.

The area of Mike's wall is 48 square feet.

Another Way

You can measure to find the length of each side and use a formula to find area.

Area = length × width

$A = \ell \times w$
$A = 8 \times 6$
$A = 48$

length

width

The area of Mike's wall is 48 square feet. He will need more than one small can of paint.

Problem Solving

13. Reasoning Jen's garden is 4 feet wide and has an area of 28 square feet. What is the length of the garden?

14. Diane drew a polygon with 4 sides and 1 set of parallel sides. What type of polygon did Diane draw?

15. Mr. Chen is putting tile down in his kitchen. The kitchen is 16 feet long and 8 feet wide. The tile costs $5 per square foot. How much will it cost Mr. Chen to tile his kitchen?

For **16** and **17**, use the map at the right.

16. Central Park is in New York City. What is its area?

    A 1.2 square kilometers

    B 3.2 square kilometers

    C 4.8 square kilometers

    D 32 square kilometers

17. Which polygon best describes the shape of Central Park?

    A Triangle   **C** Quadrilateral

    B Pentagon   **D** Hexagon

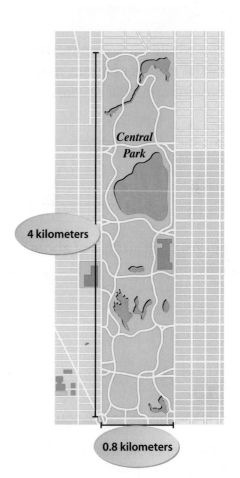

Central Park

4 kilometers

0.8 kilometers

DIGITAL Animated Glossary, eTools
www.pearsonsuccessnet.com

14-3

Understand It!
A formula can be used to find the square units needed to cover an irregular shape.

Area of Irregular Shapes

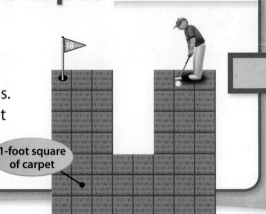

Hands-On
metric ruler

How can you find the area of an irregular figure?

Mr. Fox is covering a miniature golf course hole with artificial grass. How many 1-foot squares of carpet will Mr. Fox need to cover the miniature golf course hole?

1-foot square of carpet

Another Example How can you estimate area?

Some shapes contain partial square units.

Estimate the area of the trapezoid to the right.

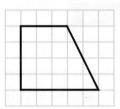

One Way

Count the whole square units. Then estimate the number of units made from combining partial squares.

There are 14 whole square units. The partial square units make about 2 more square units.

14 + 2 = 16

The trapezoid has an area of about 16 square units.

Another Way

Draw a rectangle around the trapezoid and find the rectangle's area.
$A = 4 \times 5 = 20$

Find the area outside the trapezoid but inside the rectangle.

There are about 4 square units not in the trapezoid.

Subtract to find the difference between the two areas.

20 − 4 = 16

The trapezoid has an area of about 16 square units.

Explain It

1. Why is the answer of 16 square units considered an estimate?

2. Can the trapezoid be divided into rectangles to find the area?

eTools
www.pearsonsuccessnet.com

DIGITAL

cut here

One Way

Count the square units to find the area.

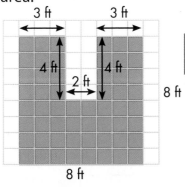

The area of the golf course hole is 56 square feet.

Another Way

Divide the hole into rectangles. Find the area of each rectangle and add.

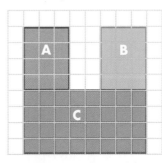

Rectangle A
$A = 4 \times 3 = 12$

Rectangle B
$A = 4 \times 3 = 12$

Rectangle C
$A = 4 \times 8 = 32$

Add the areas: $12 + 12 + 32 = 56$
The area of the golf course hole is 56 square feet.

Guided Practice*

Do you know HOW?

For **1** and **2**, find the area of each figure.

1.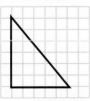

2.
4 cm
3 cm
9 cm
6 cm

For **3** and **4**, estimate the area of each figure.

3.

4.

Do you UNDERSTAND?

5. Writing to Explain Could the golf course hole be divided into any other set of rectangles?

6. Suppose Mr. Fox bought 75 square feet of artificial grass. How much artificial grass will be left over?

7. Mr. Fox decided the area of the hole was too large. What would the new area of the hole be if he only uses rectangles A and C in the example above?

Independent Practice

For **8** and **9**, measure and find the area of each figure.

8.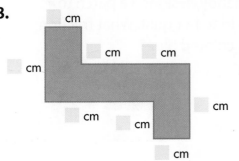
cm
cm
cm
cm
cm
cm
cm
cm

9.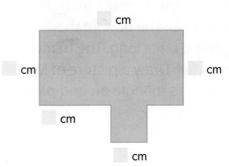
cm
cm
cm
cm
cm

result

result

For another example, see Set B on page 342.

Lesson 14-3

321

For **10** through **13**, estimate the area of each figure.

10.   **11.** 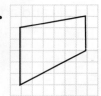 **12.**   **13.**

14. Think About the Process Jared drew the figure to the right on grid paper. Which is **NOT** a way in which the figure could be divided to find the total area?

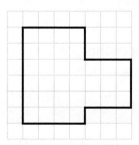

A $(4 \times 6) + (3 \times 3)$

B $(3 \times 7) + (4 \times 2) + (4 \times 1)$

C $(4 \times 6) + (3 \times 7)$

D $(2 \times 4) + (3 \times 3) + (4 \times 1) + (4 \times 3)$

15. Writing to Explain Laurie's family is building a new house. The design for the house is shown to the right. What is the area of the new house? How big will their yard be?

Tip *90′ means 90 feet.*

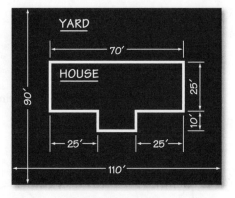

16. Algebra Write an algebraic expression to represent the phrase "six times a number is 24." Solve the expression.

17. Writing to Explain Each student on a field trip got a sandwich, a salad, and a juice. If you know that there were 10 students on the field trip, would you be able to tell how much they paid for lunch in all? Why or why not?

18. Mrs. Washington drew a triangle on grid paper. The base of the triangle is 6 units long. The triangle is 8 units tall. Draw a picture of Mrs. Washington's triangle on grid paper. Estimate the area.

19. Mandy designed a patch to add to her quilt. What fraction is colored blue?

A $\frac{2}{8}$

B $\frac{4}{8}$

C $\frac{8}{8}$

D $\frac{8}{4}$

Find each product. Estimate to check
if the answer is reasonable.

1. 21
× 4

2. 843
× 6

3. 6,318
× 5

4. 5,008
× 9

5. 40
× 3

6. 17
× 8

7. 92,075
× 2

8. 796
× 7

9. 24,927
× 6

10. 1,234
× 9

11. 700
× 5

12. 99
× 9

13. 50,000
× 4

Find each difference. Estimate to check
if the answer is reasonable.

14. 3,427 − 648　　**15.** 7,005 − 6,496　　**16.** 502 − 89

Error Search Find each product that is not correct.
Write it correctly and explain the error.

17. 56,829
× 5
──────
284,145

18. 408
× 9
──────
3,602

19. 2,365
× 3
──────
7,098

20. 45
× 4
──────
49

21. 777
× 7
──────
5,439

Number Sense

Estimating and Reasoning Write whether each
statement is true or false. Explain your answer.

22. The product of 6 and 39 is less than 240.

23. The sum of 3,721 and 1,273 is greater than 4,000 but less than 6,000.

24. The product of 5 and 286 is greater than 1,500.

25. The product of 4 and 3,103 is closer to 12,000 than 16,000.

26. The difference of 4,637 − 2,878 is greater than 2,000.

27. The quotient of 4 divided by 1 is 1.

Understand It!
Use the formula for the area of a rectangle to find a formula for the area of a parallelogram.

Area of Parallelograms

How can you find the area of a parallelogram?

One shape in a quilt is shaped like a parallelogram. It has a base of 9 inches and a height of 4 inches. What is the area of the parallelogram?

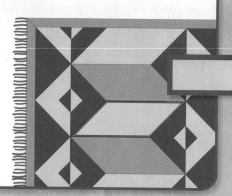

Guided Practice*

Do you know HOW?

For **1** through **4**, find the area of each parallelogram.

1.

6 in
2 in

2.
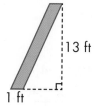
13 ft
1 ft

3.
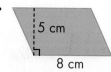
5 cm
8 cm

4.
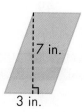
7 in.
3 in.

Do you UNDERSTAND?

5. In the example above, which parts of the parallelogram and the rectangle are congruent?

6. Why would the formula to find the area of a parallelogram be similar to the formula to find the area of a rectangle?

7. Writing to Explain A parallelogram has an area of 16 square feet and a height of 8 feet. What is the length of the parallelogram? Explain.

Independent Practice

For **8** through **15**, find the area of each parallelogram.

8.
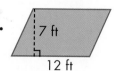
2 ft
5 ft

9.
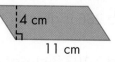
1 m
11 m

10.
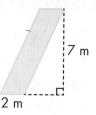
4 cm
11 cm

11.
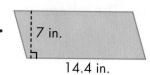
7 m
2 m

12.

7 ft
12 ft

13.
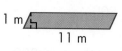
4 in.
5.1 in.

14.
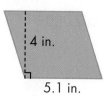
16 cm
22 cm

15.
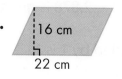
7 in.
14.4 in.

For another example, see Set C on page 342.

If you slide the triangle to the other side, you have a rectangle.

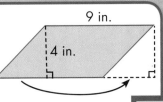

9 in.

4 in.

Multiply the length and width of the rectangle to find the area.

$A = \ell \times w$

$A = 9 \times 4$

$A = 36$ square inches

The area of the parallelogram is 36 square inches.

The base (b) and the height (h) correspond to the dimensions of the rectangle.

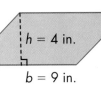

$h = 4$ in.

$b = 9$ in.

$A = b \times h$

$A = 9 \times 4$

$A = 36$ square inches

The area of the parallelogram is 36 square inches.

Problem Solving

16. Writing to Explain Quinn says the parallelogram to the right has an area of 50 square centimeters. Is Quinn correct? Explain.

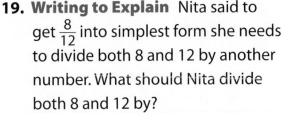

4 cm

5 cm

10 cm

17. A parallelogram has an area of 32 square inches. If the parallelogram is 16 inches long, what is its height?

18. Geometry What is the name of a quadrilateral that has one set of parallel sides?

19. Writing to Explain Nita said to get $\frac{8}{12}$ into simplest form she needs to divide both 8 and 12 by another number. What should Nita divide both 8 and 12 by?

20. Geometry Line *AB* is parallel to line *CD*. Line *AC* is perpendicular to line *CD*. Line *AC* is parallel to line *BD*. What figure do points *ABCD* create?

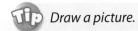 *Draw a picture.*

21. Which parallelogram would have the greatest area?

   A Base: 11 in.   **C** Base: 7 in.
      Height: 2 in.   Height: 3 in.

   B Base: 5 in.   **D** Base: 6 in.
      Height: 5 in.   Height: 4 in.

22. Which unit below could be used to measure the area of a figure?

   A Miles

   B Meters

   C Square feet

   D Kilometers

Lesson
14-5

Understand It!
Use the relationship between triangles and parallelograms to find the area of a triangle.

Area of Triangles

How can you find the area of a triangle?

Kendra's model sailboat has a triangular sail with a base measuring 6 inches in length and a height of 7 inches.

What is the area of the sail?

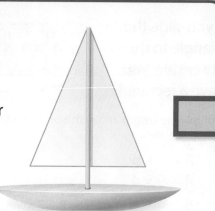

Guided Practice*

Do you know HOW?

For **1** through **4**, find the area of each triangle.

1.
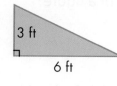
2 m
9 m

2.
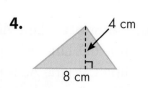
3 yd
12 yd

3.
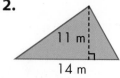
8 ft
6 ft

4.
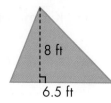
4 cm
8 cm

Do you UNDERSTAND?

5. In the example above, how do you know that the area of the triangle is exactly half the area of the parallelogram?

6. In the example above, why must the second triangle be congruent to the first?

7. **Number Sense** Will the area of a triangle be different if you divide by two rather than multiply by $\frac{1}{2}$?

Independent Practice

For **8** through **15**, find the area of each triangle.

8.
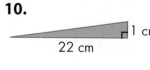
3 ft
6 ft

9.
5 yd
4 yd

10.
1 cm
22 cm

11.
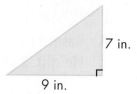
7 in.
9 in.

12.
11 m
14 m

13.
8 ft
6.5 ft

14.
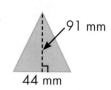
91 mm
44 mm

15.
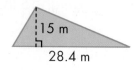
15 m
28.4 m

For another example, see Set C on page 342.

You can use what you have learned about finding the area of a parallelogram to find the area of the sail.

If you position a congruent triangle as shown, you have a parallelogram.

$h = 7$ in.

$A = b \times h$

$A = 6 \times 7$

$A = 42$ square inches

$b = 6$ in.

The area of the parallelogram is 42 square inches.

The area of each triangle is half the area of a parallelogram.

$A = \frac{1}{2} \times \text{base} \times \text{height}$

$A = \frac{1}{2} \times b \times h$

$h = 7$ in.

$A = \frac{1}{2} \times 6 \times 7$

$A = 21$ square inches

$b = 6$ in.

The area of the sail is 21 square inches.

Problem Solving

16. Writing to Explain Patricia says the triangle to the right has an area of 300 square inches. Is she correct? Explain.

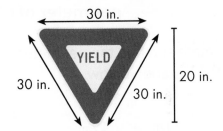

30 in.

YIELD

30 in.

20 in.

30 in.

17. What is the area of the triangle below?

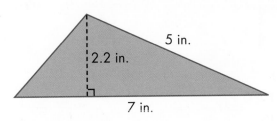

5 in.

2.2 in.

7 in.

18. Algebra A triangle has an area of 32 square inches. If the triangle has a base of 16 inches, what is its height?

19. The Sierpinski triangle is a geometric pattern formed by connecting the midpoints of the sides of a triangle, creating 4 smaller equal-sized triangles. Use the drawing at the right to find the area of the triangle in the middle.

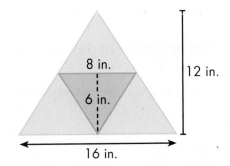

8 in.

12 in.

6 in.

16 in.

20. Writing to Explain Tim is making apple pies. The recipe for each pie calls for six apples. Tim has 20 apples and can make three pies. Tim divides 20 by 6 and gets 3 R2. What does the remainder mean?

21. Which measurements for a triangle have the greatest area?

A Base: 9 in.
Height: 6 in.

B Base: 10 in.
Height: 5 in.

C Base: 18 in.
Height: 2 in.

D Base: 52 in.
Height: 1 in.

Understand It! There
are different ways to
find the distance around
a figure.

Perimeter

Hands-On
metric ruler

36 in.

How do you find the distance around an object?

Fred wants to put a border around the bulletin board in his room. How much border will he need?

22 in.

Perimeter is the distance around a figure.

Another Example How do you estimate and find the perimeter of different figures?

Estimate and find the perimeter of the hexagon below.

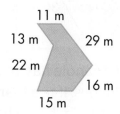

11 m
13 m   29 m
22 m
16 m
15 m

Use rounding to estimate:
$30 + 20 + 20 + 20 + 10 + 10 = 110$

Add the actual numbers:
$29 + 16 + 15 + 22 + 13 + 11 = 106$

The perimeter of the hexagon is 106 m.

Find the perimeter of the square below. All 4 sides of a square are the same length. So, the formula is:
$P = s + s + s + s$
or, $P = 4 \times s$

9 cm

$s = 9$
$P = 4 \times 9$
$P = 36$

The perimeter of the square is 36 cm.

Explain It

1. How can you use addition to find the perimeter of a square? How can you use multiplication?

2. Why couldn't you use a formula to find the perimeter of the hexagon? Could you ever use a formula to find the perimeter of a hexagon? Explain.

One Way

Measure to find the length of each side. Then add to find the perimeter.

$$36 + 22 + 36 + 22 = 116$$

The perimeter of the bulletin board is 116 inches.

Another Way

Use a formula.

Perimeter = $(2 \times \text{length}) + (2 \times \text{width})$

$P = (2 \times \ell) + (2 \times w)$

$P = (2 \times 36) + (2 \times 22)$

$P = 72 + 44$

$P = 116$

The perimeter of the bulletin board is 116 inches.

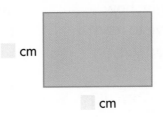

length

width

Guided Practice*

Do you know HOW?

For **1** through **4**, estimate. Then find the perimeter of each figure.

1.
11 in.   16 in.
13 in.

2.
9 ft
17 ft

3.
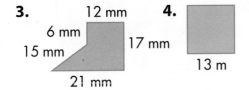
12 mm
6 mm
15 mm
17 mm
21 mm

4.
13 m

Do you UNDERSTAND?

5. How can you use a formula to find the perimeter of a polygon that has sides of equal length?

6. How can you estimate to see if the value you found for the perimeter of Fred's bulletin board is reasonable?

7. Fred is making a frame for an autographed photo. If the picture is 8 inches by 10 inches, how much wood will Fred need for the frame?

Independent Practice

For **8** through **10**, measure the sides and find the perimeter of each figure.

8.
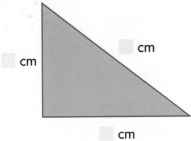
cm
cm
cm

9.
cm
cm

10.
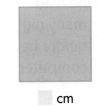
cm

DIGITAL
Animated Glossary, eTools
www.pearsonsuccessnet.com

For another example, see Set D on page 343.

For **11** through **18**, estimate, and then find the perimeter of each figure.

11. 39 in.

12. 12 ft
16 ft

13. 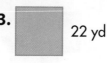 22 yd

14. 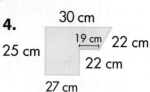 30 cm
25 cm 19 cm 22 cm
22 cm
27 cm

15. 14 m

16. 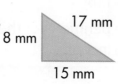 17 mm
8 mm
15 mm

17. 8 ft
20 ft 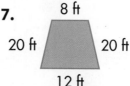 20 ft
12 ft

18. 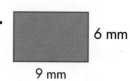 6 mm
9 mm

Problem Solving

19. Tom drew the 2 rectangles at the right. What is the difference between the perimeter of Rectangle A and the perimeter of Rectangle B?

A 3 cm   **B** 6 cm   **C** 12 cm   **D** 54 cm

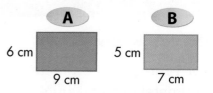
A   B
6 cm   5 cm
9 cm   7 cm

20. Reasoning Which has a greater perimeter, a 28-inch square or a 21-inch by 31-inch rectangle? Explain.

21. Charles wanted to estimate the perimeter of the United States, so he drew several polygons and placed them over a map of the United States. Estimate the perimeter of the United States to the nearest thousand.

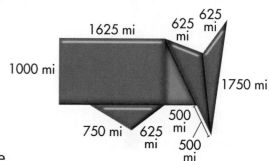
1625 mi   625 mi   625 mi
1000 mi   1750 mi
750 mi   625 mi   500 mi
500 mi

22. Paula built a play area for her dog in the shape of a regular pentagon. If the perimeter is 35 feet, what is the length of each side of the play area?

23. Myles gets to play on the computer every time he reads 120 pages. If he reads 10 pages a night, how many nights will he have to read before he gets to play on the computer?

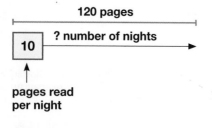
120 pages
? number of nights
10
pages read
per night

24. Think About the Process James wants to draw a rectangle with a perimeter of 42 units and a length of 13 units. How can he determine the width?

A Subtract 13 from 42, then divide by 2.

B Multiply 13 by 2.

C Add 13 to 42. Then divide by 2.

D Multiply 13 by 2. Subtract the product from 42. Divide the difference by 2.

Enrichment

Circumference

Circumference is the distance around a circle. For any circle, the circumference divided by the diameter equals pi (π).

The **center** is a point within a circle that is the same distance from all points on a circle.

A **chord** is a line segment that connects any two points on a circle.

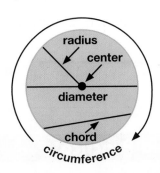

A **radius** is any line segment that connects the center to a point on the circle.

A **diameter** is any line segment that connects two points on the circle and passes through the center. The length of the diameter is twice the radius.

Examples: Since the relationship between the circumference and diameter of all circles is always the same, you can use a formula to describe it.

Formula for Circumference

Circumference = π × diameter
$C = \pi \times d$

Find the circumference.

$C = \pi \times d$
$C = 3.14 \times 6$
$C = 18.84$ cm

6 cm

Formula for Circumference

Circumference = π × 2 × radius
$C = \pi \times 2 \times r$ or
$C = 2 \times \pi \times r$

Find the circumference.

$C = 2 \times \pi \times r$
$C = 2 \times \pi \times 4$
$C = 3.14 \times 8$
$C = 25.12$ m

4 m

Practice

For **1** through **6**, find the circumference. Use 3.14 for π.

1.

9 cm

2.

1 in.

3.

2 m

4. $d = 7$ cm

5. $r = 5$ m

6. $r = 2.5$ mm

Lesson

14-7

Understand It!
Rectangles with the
same perimeter can have
different areas.

Same Perimeter, Different Area

Can rectangles have the same perimeter but different areas?

Beth has 12 feet of fence to build a rectangular pen for her rabbits. She wants the pen to have as much space as possible. Which rectangular pen has the greatest area?

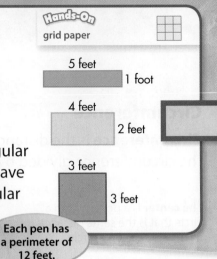

Hands-On
grid paper

5 feet
1 foot

4 feet
2 feet

3 feet
3 feet

Each pen has a perimeter of 12 feet.

Guided Practice*

Do you know HOW?

For **1** through **4**, use grid paper to draw two different rectangles with the given perimeter. Tell the dimensions and area of each rectangle. Circle the one that has the greater area.

1. 16 feet

2. 20 centimeters

3. 24 inches

4. 40 meters

Do you UNDERSTAND?

5. In the example at the top, what do you notice about the area of the rectangles as the shape becomes more like a square?

6. Alex is building a rabbit pen with 25 feet of fence. What rectangle can he build that has the greatest possible area?

Independent Practice

For **7** through **10**, use grid paper to draw two different rectangles with the given perimeter. Tell the dimensions and area of each rectangle. Circle the one that has the greater area.

7. 10 inches

8. 22 centimeters

9. 26 yards

10. 32 feet

For **11** through **14**, describe a different rectangle with the same perimeter as the one shown. Then tell which rectangle has the greater area.

11.

4 in.

5 in.

12.

4 ft

3 ft

13.

9 cm

5 cm

14.

5 m

3 m

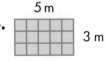

eTools
www.pearsonsuccessnet.com

*For another example, see Set E on page 343.

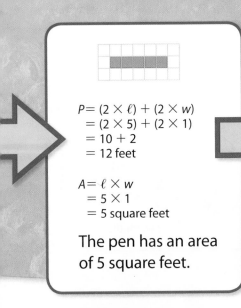

$P = (2 \times \ell) + (2 \times w)$
$\quad = (2 \times 5) + (2 \times 1)$
$\quad = 10 + 2$
$\quad = 12$ feet

$A = \ell \times w$
$\quad = 5 \times 1$
$\quad = 5$ square feet

The pen has an area
of 5 square feet.

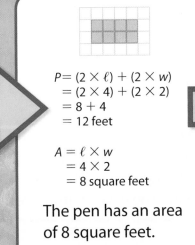

$P = (2 \times \ell) + (2 \times w)$
$\quad = (2 \times 4) + (2 \times 2)$
$\quad = 8 + 4$
$\quad = 12$ feet

$A = \ell \times w$
$\quad = 4 \times 2$
$\quad = 8$ square feet

The pen has an area
of 8 square feet.

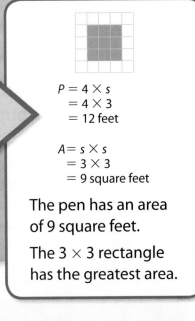

$P = 4 \times s$
$\quad = 4 \times 3$
$\quad = 12$ feet

$A = s \times s$
$\quad = 3 \times 3$
$\quad = 9$ square feet

The pen has an area
of 9 square feet.

The 3×3 rectangle
has the greatest area.

Problem Solving

15. **Reasoning** The rectangles at the right
have the same perimeter. Without
measuring or multiplying, how can
you tell which has the greater area,
Rectangle X or Rectangle Y?

16. Suppose you arrange 48 counters
into groups. The first group has
3 counters. Each group after that has
2 more counters than the group
before. How many groups do you
need to make to use all 48 counters?

17. **Writing to Explain** Karen drew
a rectangle with a perimeter of
20 inches. The smaller side measured
3 inches and the longer side of the
rectangle was 7 inches. Is she correct?

18. Mr. Gardner is building a fence
around his garden. He has a total
of 42 feet of fencing to make the
perimeter. How much fencing should
he use along the width and length
to create the pen with the largest
possible area?

19. **Estimation** Three towns are sharing
the cost of library repairs for a
regional high school. The total cost
will be $7,200. If the cost is shared
equally, will each town pay more or
less than $3,000?

For **20**, use the diagram at the right.

20. Which statement about the rectangles is true?

   A They both have the same width.

   B They both have the same length.

   C They both have the same perimeter.

   D They both have the same area.

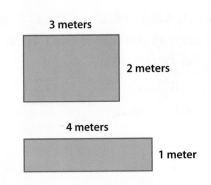

3 meters

2 meters

4 meters

1 meter

Understand It!
Rectangles with the same area can have different perimeters.

Same Area, Different Perimeter

Hands-On
grid paper

Can rectangles have the same area but different perimeters?

In a video puzzle game, you have 16 castle tiles to make a rectangular castle and 16 water tiles for a moat. How can you completely surround the castle with water?

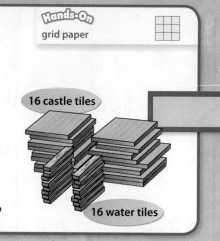
16 castle tiles

16 water tiles

Guided Practice*

Do you know HOW?

For **1** through **4**, find two different rectangles that have the given area. Give the dimensions and perimeter of each rectangle, and tell which one has the smaller perimeter.

1. 6 square feet   **2.** 36 square yards

3. 64 square meters   **4.** 80 square inches

Do you UNDERSTAND?

5. In the example above, what do you notice about the perimeter of the rectangles as the shape becomes more like a square?

6. In Round 2 of the video puzzle game, you have 24 castle tiles. What is the fewest number of water tiles you will need to surround your castle?

Independent Practice

For **7** through **10**, use grid paper to draw two different rectangles with the given area. Tell the dimensions and perimeter of each rectangle. Circle the one that has the smaller perimeter.

7. 9 square inches   **8.** 18 square feet   **9.** 30 square meters   **10.** 32 square centimeters

For **11** through **14**, describe a different rectangle with the same area as the one shown. Then tell which rectangle has a smaller perimeter.

11.
6 m
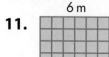
4 m

12.
3 yd
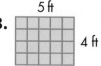
4 yd

13.
5 ft
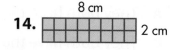
4 ft

14.
8 cm

2 cm

DIGITAL
eTools
www.pearsonsuccessnet.com

*For another example, see Set E on page 343.

Make rectangles that have an area of 16 square units. Find the perimeter of each rectangle.

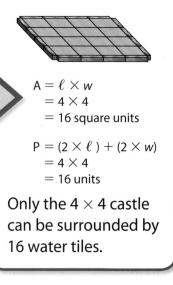

$A = \ell \times w$
$= 16 \times 1$
$= 16$ square units

$P = (2 \times \ell) + (2 \times w)$
$= (2 \times 16) + (2 \times 1)$
$= 32 + 2$
$= 34$ units

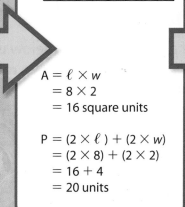

$A = \ell \times w$
$= 8 \times 2$
$= 16$ square units

$P = (2 \times \ell) + (2 \times w)$
$= (2 \times 8) + (2 \times 2)$
$= 16 + 4$
$= 20$ units

$A = \ell \times w$
$= 4 \times 4$
$= 16$ square units

$P = (2 \times \ell) + (2 \times w)$
$= 4 \times 4$
$= 16$ units

Only the 4 × 4 castle can be surrounded by 16 water tiles.

Problem Solving

15. Writing to Explain Park School and North School cover the same area. In physical education classes, each student runs one lap around the school. At which school do the students have to run farther?

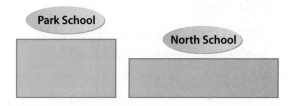

Park School

North School

16. Estimation Sue bought 2 sweaters for $18.75 each and mittens for $11.45. About how much money will she get in change if she pays with 3 twenty-dollar bills?

17. Geometry Which of the following shapes cannot be congruent to a rectangle: a square, a rhombus, a quadrilateral, or a circle?

18. Number Sense The perimeter of rectangle P is 12 feet. The perimeter of rectangle Q is 18 feet. Both rectangles have the same area. Find the area and the dimensions of each rectangle.

19. Ms. Fisher is using 64 carpet tiles to make a reading area in her classroom. Each tile is a square that measures 1 foot by 1 foot. What is the length and width of the rectangular area she can make with the smallest possible perimeter?

20. Which statement about the rectangles to the right is true?

   A They both have the same width.

   B They both have the same length.

   C They both have the same perimeter.

   D They both have the same area.

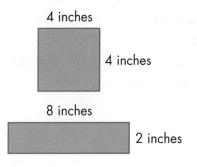

4 inches

4 inches

8 inches

2 inches

Understand It!
Learning how and when to solve a simpler problem can help when solving problems.

Solve a Simpler Problem and Make a Table

Each side of a triangle cracker below is one inch long. If there are 12 triangle crackers in a row, what is the perimeter of the figure?

1 inch

Guided Practice*

Do you know HOW?

1. Cora is cutting a piece of paper to get equal sized pieces. After the first cut, she stacks the two pieces and makes another cut. After she makes the second cut, she stacks the pieces again. If this pattern continues, how many pieces will she have after the fourth cut?

Do you UNDERSTAND?

2. How was the problem above broken into simpler problems?

3. **Write a Problem** Write a problem that you can solve by making a table.

Independent Practice

Solve.

4. Troy is helping his father build a fence. Each section of the fence has a post at each end. Make a table showing how many posts will be needed if there are 1, 3, 5, 10, 15, or 20 sections of the fence. Look for a pattern.

5. How many posts will be needed if the fence has 47 sections?

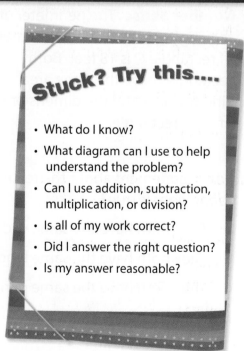

Stuck? Try this....

- What do I know?
- What diagram can I use to help understand the problem?
- Can I use addition, subtraction, multiplication, or division?
- Is all of my work correct?
- Did I answer the right question?
- Is my answer reasonable?

For another example, see Set F on page 343.

Plan

Change the problem into problems that are simpler to solve.

Look at 1 triangle, then 2 triangles, then 3 triangles.

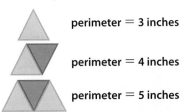

perimeter = 3 inches

perimeter = 4 inches

perimeter = 5 inches

Solve

The perimeter is 2 more than the number of triangles.

Number of triangles	1	2	3
Perimeter (inches)	3	4	5

So, for 12 triangles the perimeter is 14 inches.

Problem Solving

6. Helen is part of a 32-player one-on-one basketball tournament. As soon as a player loses, she is out of the tournament. The winners will continue to play until there is one champion. How many games are there in all in this tournament?

7. The figure below is a square. If sides A and B are doubled, will this figure still be a square?

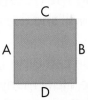

For **8** through **10**, use the table at the right.

8. The missing classes in the schedule to the right are Math, Science, Reading, Spelling, and Social Studies. Math is after morning break. Spelling is at 9:40. Reading and Science are the two afternoon classes. At what time is Math class?

9. What class is at 8:45?

10. Science class is before Reading. What time is Science class?

Class Schedule	
Morning	**Afternoon**
8:30: Opening	12:15:
8:45:	1:00: Break
9:30: Break	1:30:
9:40:	1:55: Recess
10:25: Recess	2:05: Art, Music or P.E.
10:55:	2:40: Pack Up
11:30: Lunch	2:45: School's Out

11. Six friends are playing checkers. If each friend plays against every other friend once, how many games of checkers will they play all together?

12. Mr. McNulty's classroom library has 286 books. If he buys 12 books each month for five months, how many books will he have in all?

13. Jolene, Timmy, Nicholas, Paul, and Kathryn are all planting in a community garden. If each of their plots holds 7 rows and 13 columns, how many plants will they be able to grow all together?

14. Thomas is training for a marathon. He runs for 2 miles and then he walks for a half a mile. If he trains by running 22 miles every day, how many miles will he walk?

15. Every day, James spends $\frac{5}{10}$ of an hour on the phone, $\frac{6}{12}$ of an hour reading, and $\frac{3}{6}$ of an hour on the computer. Use the fraction strips to the right to tell which activity James spends the most time doing.

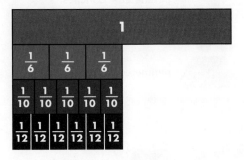

16. Maya is putting 3 ice cubes in each red cup and 4 ice cubes in each blue cup. The cups alternate colors starting with red. How many ice cubes will she use if she has 15 cups?

17. Shaina has a necklace she wants to have cut to give to her friends. The jeweler chargers $3 for each cut. How much does Shaina need to pay for 5 cuts?

18. Danielle can type 15 words per minute. How many words can she type in 7 minutes?

Minutes	1	2	3
Words Typed	15	30	45

Think About the Process

19. It takes a plumber 4 minutes to cut a pipe. Which expression would you use to find how long it would take the plumber to cut 7 pipes?

A $4 + 7$

B 4×4

C 7×4

D 7×7

20. On every train car there are two connectors, one at the front and one at the back. These connectors are there so each car can be linked with another car. If a train has 30 cars, how would you find out the number of connections made?

A The number of cars minus 1

B The number of connectors on all the cars minus 1

C Same as the number of cars

D The number of cars plus 1

Finding Area with a Calculator

One Way Find the area of the figure shown at the right:

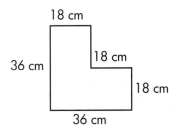

Divide the figure into two rectangles.
Rectangle A is 18 cm by 18 cm.
Rectangle B is 18 cm by 36 cm.

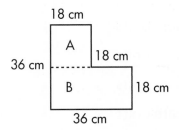

Find the area of each rectangle and add.

Press: 18 × 18 ENTER =   18 × 36 ENTER =   324 + 648 ENTER =

Display: *324*   *648*   *972*

Another Way Find the area of the figure in one step.

Press: 18 × 18 + 18 × 36 ENTER =

Display: *972*

The area of the figure is 972 square centimeters.

Practice

Use a calculator to find the area of each figure.

1.

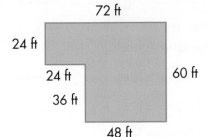

2.

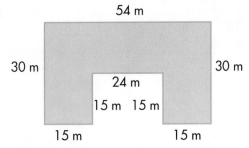

1. A drawing of the floor in Curt's fort is shown. What is the area of the fort's floor? (14-1)

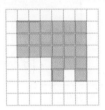

   A 23 square units

   B 22 square units

   C 21 square units

   D 20 square units

2. Each cube has 6 faces. If Tandra stacks 2 cubes on top of each other, she can see 10 faces. If Tandra stacks 7 cubes one on top of the other, how many faces of the cubes will she be able to see? (14-9)

Cubes	2	3	4	5	6	7
Faces	10	14	18			

   A 42

   B 32

   C 30

   D 28

3. Mrs. Gee has 24 carpet squares. How should she arrange them so that she has the smallest perimeter? (14-8)

   A 12 by 2 rectangle

   B 1 by 24 rectangle

   C 8 by 3 rectangle

   D 4 by 6 rectangle

4. What is the perimeter of the flag? (14-6)

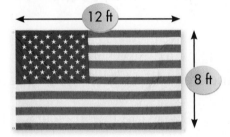

   A 96 feet

   B 40 feet

   C 28 feet

   D 20 feet

5. A diagram of Izzi's bedroom is shown below. What is the area of her room? (14-3)

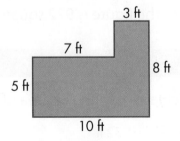

   A 44 square feet

   B 59 square feet

   C 74 square feet

   D 80 square feet

6. Which is the best estimate of the area of the shape shown below? (14-1)

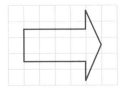

A 19 square units

B 17 square units

C 11 square units

D 5 square units

7. What is the area of the parallelogram? (14-4)

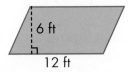

A 72 square feet

B 68 square feet

C 62 square feet

D 36 square feet

8. What is the area of the triangle? (14-5)

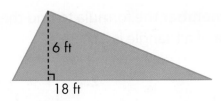

A 54 square feet

B 68 square feet

C 108 square feet

D 216 square feet

9. Howie used 20 feet of edging to design four different gardens. He wants the garden with the greatest area. Which should Howie use? (14-7)

A
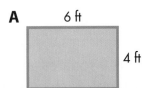
6 ft
4 ft

B
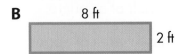
8 ft
2 ft

C

7 ft
3 ft

D
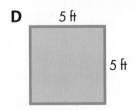
5 ft
5 ft

10. A picnic table is 9 feet long and 3 feet wide. What is the area of the rectangular surface of the table? (14-2)

A 27 square feet

B 36 square feet

C 45 square feet

D 54 square feet

11. Pepper's dog pen measures 4 meters wide and 5 meters long. What is the perimeter of the pen? (14-6)

A 20 meters

B 18 meters

C 14 meters

D 11 meters

Set A, pages 316–317

You can count square units to find area.

The shape fully covers 9 squares and partially covers 7 squares. Each partial cover is about a half of a square.

So, the shape has an area of about 13 square units.

Remember you can count partial squares to get an estimate of an area.

Find each area. Tell if each area is exact or an estimate.

1.   2.

Set B, pages 318–322

You can divide a figure into rectangles to find the area.

Find the area of each rectangle.

Rectangle A   Rectangle B
$A = 9 \times 6$ $A = 2 \times 4$
  $= 54$ $= 8$

Add the partial areas:
54 ft + 8 ft = 62 square feet

Remember you can count the units to find the area.

Find the area of each figure.

1. 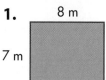   2.

Set C, pages 324–327

Find the area of the parallelogram. Use a formula to calculate the area.

Parallelogram
$A = b \times h$
$A = 10 \times 4$
$A = 40$ square inches

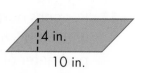

The area of the parallelogram is 40 square inches.

Remember the formula to find the area of a triangle is $\frac{1}{2} b \times h$.

1.   2.

3. 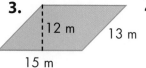   4.

Set D, pages 328–330

Use a formula to find the perimeter.

$P = (2 \times \ell) + (2 \times w)$
$P = (2 \times 14) + (2 \times 6)$
$P = 28 + 12$
$P = 40$

6 m
14 m

The perimeter of the rectangle is 40 meters.

Remember you can add the lengths of each side to find the perimeter.

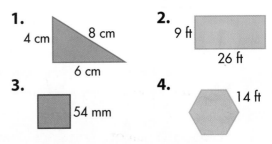

1.
4 cm   8 cm
6 cm

2.
9 ft
26 ft

3.
54 mm

4.
14 ft

Set E, pages 332–335

Draw a different rectangle with the same perimeter as the one shown, and find its area.

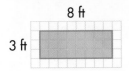

8 ft
3 ft

$P = (2 \times \ell) + (2 \times w)$ $A = \ell \times w$
$\quad = (2 \times 8) + (2 \times 3)$ $\quad = 8 \times 3$
$\quad = 16 + 6$ $\quad = 24$ square feet
$\quad = 22$ ft

A 4 ft by 7 ft rectangle has the same perimeter.

$P = (2 \times 7) + (2 \times 4) = 22$ ft
$A = 7 \times 4$
$A = 28$ square feet

7 ft
4 ft

Remember that two rectangles can have the same area but different perimeters.

Draw two different rectangles with the perimeter listed. Find the area of each rectangle.

1. $P = 24$ feet

2. $P = 40$ centimeters

Draw two different rectangles with the area listed. Find the perimeter of each rectangle.

3. $A = 64$ square feet

4. $A = 80$ square yards

Set F, pages 336–338

Each side of each triangle is two inches. What is the perimeter of the figure with 5 triangles?

2 in
2 in

The perimeter increases by 2.

Number of Triangles	1	2	3	4	5
Perimeter	6 in.	8 in.	10 in.	12 in.	14 in.

The perimeter of 5 triangles is 14 inches.

Remember you can break the problem apart and solve.

1. Each side of a square in the figure is one inch. If there are 14 squares in a row, what is the perimeter of the figure?

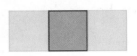

1 Eartha is the world's largest rotating scale model of Earth. Where is this model located? You will find out in Lesson 15-1.

2 The Pyramids at Giza were built by the Egyptians. What is the length of one of the sides of the Great Pyramid of Khufu? You will find out in Lesson 15-3.

3 In December 2005, a movie theater broke a world record by filling the largest box of popcorn with over 2,200 pounds of popcorn. How many cubic feet was the box? You will find out in Lesson 15-4.

Vocabulary

Choose the best term from the box.

- line
- ray
- quadrilateral
- line segment
- rhombus
- triangle

1. A polygon with three sides is known as a ? .

2. A part of a line that has one endpoint is a ? .

3. A four-sided polygon in which opposite sides are parallel, and all sides are the same length is a ? .

4. A ? is a straight path of points that goes on forever in two directions.

Solid Figures

Name the solid figure for each object.

5.   **6.**   **7.**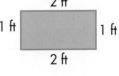

Perimeter

Find the perimeter of each polygon.

8.
2 in   2 in
2 in

9.
2 ft
1 ft   1 ft
2 ft

10.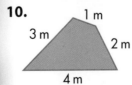
1 m
3 m   2 m
4 m

11.
1 cm   1 cm
1 cm   1 cm
1 cm

12. Writing to Explain Describe when you might need to know the perimeter of something at home.

15-1

Understand It!
A solid figure can be described by its curved surfaces or flat surfaces.

Solids

How can you describe and classify solids?

A solid figure has three dimensions: length, width, and height.

Solids can have curved surfaces.

Sphere   Cylinder   Cone

Another Example How can you build a solid figure?

A net is a pattern that can be used to make a solid.

This is a net for a cube. Each of the faces is connected to at least one other face.

This is a net for a triangular prism.

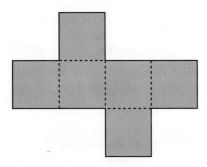

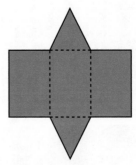

Explain It

1. Explain why the net for a cube has six squares.

2. Why does the net for a triangular prism have two triangles and three rectangles?

Some solids have all flat surfaces. They are named by referring to their faces.

face-flat surface of a solid

vertex-point where 3 or more edges meet (plural: vertices)

edge-line segment where 2 faces meet

rectangular prism
6 rectangular faces

cube
6 square faces

triangular prism
2 triangular faces
3 rectangular faces

rectangular pyramid
1 rectangular face
4 triangular faces

square pyramid
1 square face
4 triangular faces

Guided Practice*

Do you know HOW?

For **1** through **4**, identify each solid.

1.

2.

3.

4.

Do you UNDERSTAND?

5. Which solid figure has four triangular faces and one square face?

6. Why is a cube a special kind of rectangular prism?

7. Does a sphere have any edges or vertices? Explain.

Independent Practice

Leveled Practice For **8** through **10**, copy and complete the table.

	Solid Figure	Faces	Edges	Vertices	Shape(s) of Faces
8.	Rectangular prism	▢	▢	▢	6 rectangles
9.	Cube	6	▢	▢	▢
10.	Rectangular pyramid	▢	8	▢	▢

DIGITAL
Animated Glossary
www.pearsonsuccessnet.com

In **11** through **14**, trace each net and cut it out. Fold and tape it together to make a solid. The dotted lines shown are the fold lines.

11.

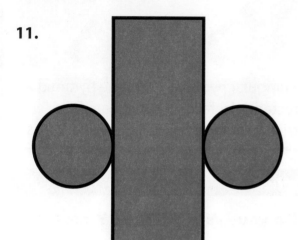

12.

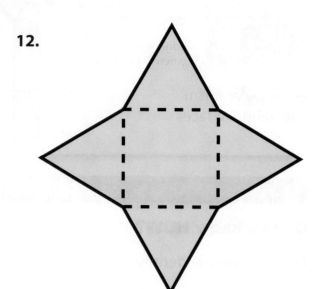

13.

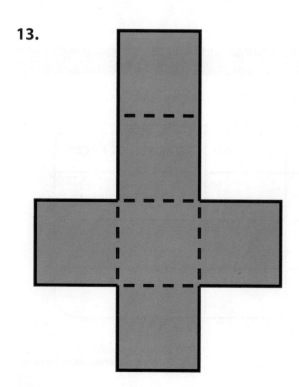

14.

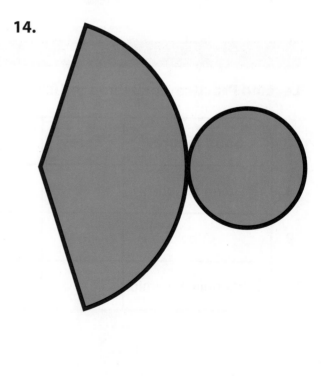

For **15** through **18**, tell what solid figure best represents each object.

15.

16.

17.

18.

19. Todd's father offered to drive some members of the soccer team to a game. His car can fit 4 players. He drives 10 players from his home to the game. How many one-way trips must he make if he stays to watch the game?

 Draw a picture to show each one-way trip.

20. How many edges does this cube have?

A 6 edges   **C** 10 edges

B 8 edges   **D** 12 edges

For **21** and **22**, use the rectangular pyramid shown at the right.

21. How many edges does the rectangular pyramid have?

22. How many vertices does the rectangular pyramid have?

23. A square pyramid is a special kind of rectangular pyramid. It has 1 square face and 5 vertices. How many triangular faces does a square pyramid have?

24. Which number is **NOT** between 0.5 and $\frac{3}{4}$ on a number line?

A $\frac{5}{8}$ **C** $\frac{13}{16}$

B 0.6   **D** 0.7

25. Eartha is located in Yarmouth, Maine. Identify the solid that best describes Eartha.

26. In one soccer season, the Cougars scored six times as many goals as Jason made all season. Jason scored 12 goals. How many goals did the Cougars score throughout the season?

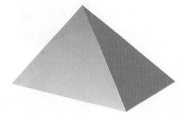

Lesson

15-2

Undertand It!
There is a unique
connection between solid
figures and flat shapes.

Views of Solids: Nets

How can you use a two-dimensional shape to represent a three-dimensional solid?

You can open up a three-dimensional
solid to show a pattern. This pattern is
called a net. The faces or flat surfaces
of a solid figure are shown by a net.

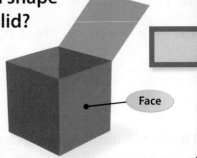

Face

Guided Practice*

Do you know HOW?

For **1** through **4**, identify how many
faces each solid has.

1.

2.

3.

4.

Do you UNDERSTAND?

5. How is a cube like a rectangular
prism?

6. Name a solid that has exactly
3 rectangular faces.

7. Draw a different net for the cube
in the example above.

Independent Practice

For **8** through **11**, name the solid figure that can be made.

8.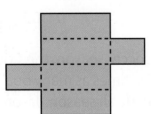

9.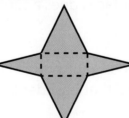

10.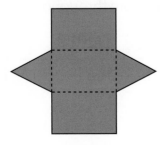

11.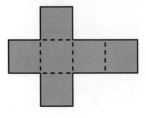

*For another example, see Set B on page 360.

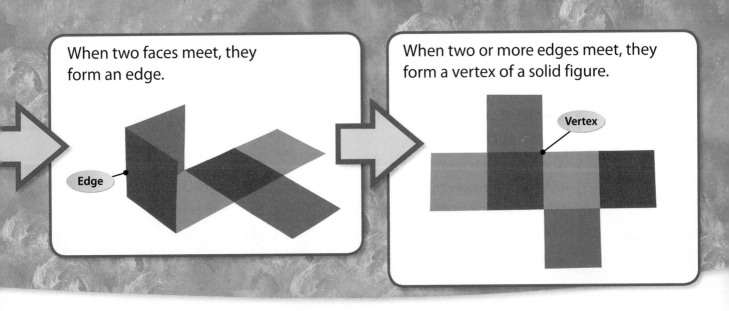

When two faces meet, they form an edge.

Edge

When two or more edges meet, they form a vertex of a solid figure.

Vertex

For **12** through **14**, name the solid figure that can be made.

12.

13.

14.

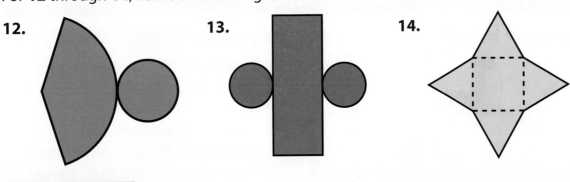

15. Helga has baseball pennants hanging on all 4 walls of her bedroom. There are 7 pennants on each wall. How many pennants are there?

16. The net of what figure is shown below?

17. Draw a net for the figure below.

18. A jet plane travels at 450 miles per hour. It takes about 4 hours to fly from San Francisco to Wichita. What is the approximate distance between the two cities?

19. What is the name of the quadrilateral shown to the right?

  A Parallelogram **C** Rhombus

  B Rectangle **D** All of the above

Understand It!
Polygons can be used to describe different perspectives of solids.

Views of Solids: Perspective

How can you get information about a solid from different perspectives?

You can think about solids from different perspectives. What would this solid look like from the front? From the side? From the top?

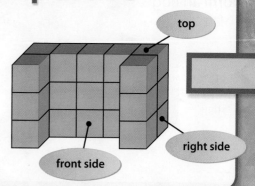

top

right side

front side

Guided Practice*

Do you know HOW?

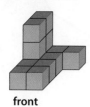

front

1. Draw the top view of the solid figure.

2. Draw a side view of the solid figure.

3. Draw a front view of the solid figure.

Do you UNDERSTAND?

4. How many blocks make up the three-dimensional figure above?

5. How many blocks are not visible from the top view of the three-dimensional figure above?

6. In Exercise 1, how many blocks are not visible in the front view of the three-dimensional figure?

Independent Practice

For **7** through **12**, draw front, right, and top views of each stack of unit blocks.

7.

front

8.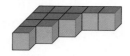

front

9.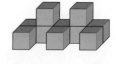

front

10.

front

11.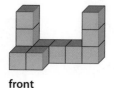

front

12.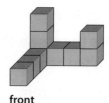

front

*For another example, see Set C on page 361.

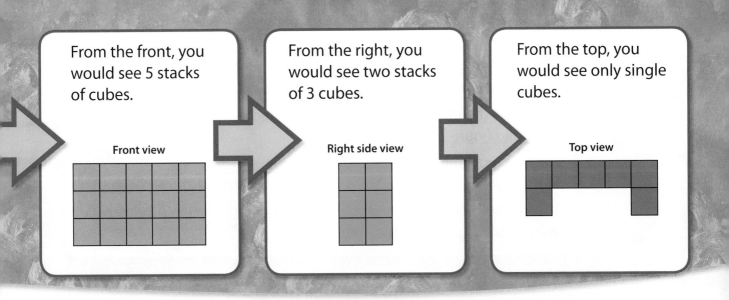

From the front, you would see 5 stacks of cubes.

Front view

From the right, you would see two stacks of 3 cubes.

Right side view

From the top, you would see only single cubes.

Top view

Problem Solving

13. How many edges does this rectangular prism have?

A 4 edges   **C** 8 edges

B 6 edges   **D** 12 edges

14. The net of what figure is shown below?

15. Explain why the net of a cube has six squares.

16. What would the top view of a cylinder look like?

17. Which choice below gives the number of faces, edges, and vertices of a cube?

A 6, 12, 8   **C** 4, 5, 6

B 6, 8, 12   **D** None of the above

18. Number Sense Without dividing, tell whether $320 \div 4$ has a two-digit or a three-digit quotient. Explain how you know.

19. Writing to Explain The length of the base of each side of the Great Pyramid of Khufu is about 756 feet long. If the Great Pyramid of Khufu is a square pyramid, what is the distance around the base of the pyramid?

15-4

Understand It!
Count cubic units or use a formula to measure the volume of a solid figure.

Volume

How can you measure volume?

Volume is <u>the number of cubic units needed to fill a solid figure</u>.

How can you find the volume of the figure at the right?

You can count cubes or multiply to find the volume of a figure in cubic units.

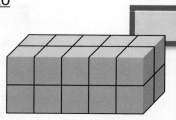

Guided Practice*

Do you know HOW?

For **1** through **4**, find the volume of each figure.

1.

2.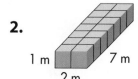
   1 m   2 m   7 m

3.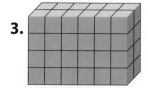

4.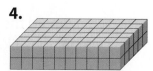

Do you UNDERSTAND?

5. Two more layers of 10 blocks each were added to the solid figure above. Find the volume using the formula.

6. **Writing to Explain** A box has a length of 4 yards and a width of 3 yards. Its volume is 96 cubic yards. What is its height? Explain.

Independent Practice

For **7** through **12**, find the volume for each figure.

7.

8.

9.

10.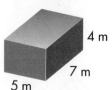
    4 m   7 m   5 m

11.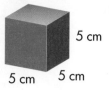
    5 cm   5 cm   5 cm

12.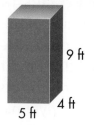
    9 ft   4 ft   5 ft

For another example, see Set D on page 361.

Count the cubes.

Each cube is 1 cubic unit.
There are 20 cubes in all.

The volume is 20 cubic units.

Use a formula.

Volume = length × width × height

$V = \ell \times w \times h$

$V = 5 \times 2 \times 2$

$V = 20$

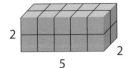

The volume is 20 cubic units.

Problem Solving

13. Writing to Explain Jack measured the box to the right and said the volume was 18 cubic units. Is he correct? Why or why not?

2 feet

9 inches

1 yard

14. Writing to Explain A box has a volume of 40 cubic inches. Will any object that has a volume less than 40 cubic inches fit into the box?

15. Algebra A box measures 4 inches long and 2 inches wide. If the box has a volume of 96 cubic inches, what is the height of the box?

16. The world's largest box of popcorn is 18 feet tall. The box has a square base. One side is 10 feet. What is the volume of the box?

10 ft

17. What is the volume of the rectangular prism below?

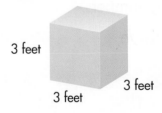

3 feet

3 feet

3 feet

A 3 cubic feet   **C** 18 cubic feet

B 9 cubic feet   **D** 27 cubic feet

18. A triangle has a base 12 inches long and a height of 6 inches. What is the area of the triangle?

19. What is the volume of a jewelry box that measures 12 centimeters by 5 centimeters by 20 centimeters?

Lesson
15-5

Understand It!
Learning how and when
to look for a pattern can
help you solve problems.

Problem Solving

Look for a Pattern

Ella is learning how to play a waltz on the piano. Her teacher gives her a beginner's exercise for her left hand.

The music shows 4 measures. If this pattern continues, how many notes will she play in 8 measures?

3, 6, 9, 12, ▦, ▦, ▦, ▦

measure

Guided Practice*

Do you know HOW?

Solve. Find a pattern.

1. Julia is printing files. The first file is 2 pages, the second file is 4 pages, the third file is 6 pages, and the fourth file is 8 pages. If this pattern continues, how many pages will be in the eighth file?

Do you UNDERSTAND?

2. What multiplication facts can you use to help find the answer to Problem 1? Why?

3. **Write a Problem** Write a problem that uses a pattern for multiples of 5. Then answer your question.

Independent Practice

Look for a pattern. Use the pattern to find the missing numbers.

4. 5, 10, 15, 20, ▦, ▦, ▦, ▦

5. 9, 18, 27, ▦, ▦, ▦, ▦

Look for a pattern, Draw the next two shapes.

6.

7.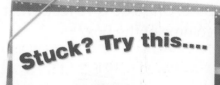

Stuck? Try this....

- What do I know?
- What diagram can I use to help understand the problem?
- Can I use addition, subtraction, multiplication, or division?
- Is all of my work correct?
- Did I answer the right question?
- Is my answer reasonable?

What do I know? The pattern for the first 4 measures is: 3, 6, 9, and 12.

What am I asked to find? The number of notes she will play in 8 measures.

Find a pattern. Skip count by 3s.

3, 6, 9, 12,...

What are the next four numbers?

3, 6, 9, 12, 15, 18, 21, 24

Ella plays 24 notes in 8 measures.

Is the answer reasonable?

There are 12 notes in 4 measures.

The number of notes in 8 measures is double the number in 4 measures.

The answer is reasonable.

Look for a pattern. Copy and complete each number sentence.

8. $30 + 5 = 35$
$300 + 5 = 305$
$3,000 + 5 = $ ▨
$30,000 + 5 = $ ▨

9. $50 + 5 = 55$
$505 + 50 = 555$
$5,005 + 550 = $ ▨
$50,505 + 5,050 = $ ▨

10. $60 + 8 = 68$
$608 + 60 = 668$
$6,008 + 660 = $ ▨
$60,008 + 6,660 = $ ▨

11. Kaylee delivers invitations to everyone on her floor of her apartment building. There are 10 apartments on her floor. The numbers of the first four apartments are 2, 4, 6, and 8. If the pattern continues, what are the rest of the apartment numbers?

12. Look for a pattern in the table below to find the missing numbers.

300	320	340	▨	380
400	▨	440	460	▨
500	520	▨	560	580

13. Kerry has a newspaper route. The first four houses she delivers to are numbered 322, 326, 330, and 334. If this pattern continues, what will be the next four numbers?

14. Marvin is looking for a radio station on the AM dial. He tries these three stations: 1040, 1080, and 1120. If this pattern continues, what will be the next three numbers?

15. Jonas saves coins in his piggy bank. He drops in these two groups of coins: 1 penny, 2 nickels, 3 dimes, 4 quarters and 5 pennies, 6 nickels, 7 dimes, 8 quarters. If this pattern continues, what is the next group of coins?

16. **Writing to Explain** Suppose there are 18 bowls arranged in this pattern: big bowl, little bowl, big bowl, little bowl, and so on. Is the last bowl a big bowl or a little bowl? Explain.

1. Which view is shown of this solid?
(15-3)

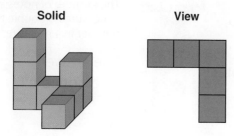

Solid   View

A Front view

B Top view

C Side view

D The view is not from this solid.

2. A model of the box that Ben's dune buggy was delivered in is shown. What is the volume of the box? (15-4)

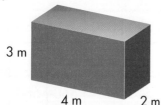

3 m

4 m   2 m

A 6 cubic meters

B 8 cubic meters

C 12 cubic meters

D 24 cubic meters

3. Which solid's net would be made with 6 squares? (15-2)

A Rectangular pyramid

B Triangular prism

C Square pyramid

D Cube

4. Which best describes the tissue box? (15-1)

A 5 faces and 12 edges

B 6 faces and 8 edges

C 6 faces and 12 edges

D 12 faces and 6 edges

5. Tad applies numbers on the back of football jerseys. Below are the first five numbers he applied. If the pattern continues, what are the next three numbers he will apply? (15-5)

9, 18, 27, 36, 45, ▢, ▢, ▢

A 54, 63, 72

B 54, 63, 71

C 63, 64, 72

D 63, 72, 81

6. Fionna used cubes to build a model of the figure below. What is the volume of the figure? (15-4)

A 10 cubic units

B 15 cubic units

C 20 cubic units

D 24 cubic units

7. What solid figure can be made from the net shown below? (15-2)

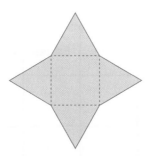

A Triangular pyramid

B Square pyramid

C Rectangular pyramid

D Rectangular prism

8. What is the volume of this figure? (15-4)

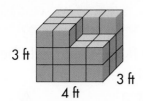

A 24 cubic units

B 28 cubic units

C 32 cubic units

D 36 cubic units

9. Which solid best describes the roll of paper towels? (15-1)

A Cylinder

B Sphere

C Cube

D Cone

10. The box Mrs. Lawry's porcelain doll was shipped in is shown below. What is the volume of the box? (15-4)

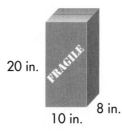

20 in.   8 in.   10 in.

A 200 cubic inches

B 800 cubic inches

C 1,200 cubic inches

D 1,600 cubic inches

11. Which view is shown of this solid? (15-3)

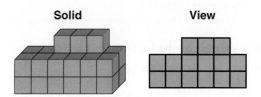

Solid   View

A Front view

B Top view

C Side view

D The view is not from this solid.

12. How many edges does this triangular prism have? (15-1)

A 5

B 6

C 8

D 9

Set A, pages 346–349

Name the solid figure.

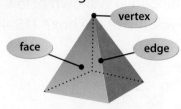

The solid figure has four faces that are triangles and one face that is a square.

How many faces, edges, and vertices does this figure have?

The figure has 5 faces, 8 edges, and 5 vertices.

Remember that the flat surface of a solid is the face.

		Faces	Edges	Vertices
1.	Triangular prism	5		
2.	Square pyramid			5
3.	Cube		12	
4.	Rectangular prism	6		
5.	Triangular pyramid			4

Set B, pages 350–351

Tell which solid figure can be made from the nets below.

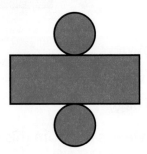

When folded and taped together, the net would form a cylinder.

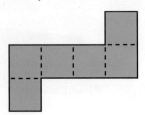

When folded and taped together, the net would form a cube.

Name the solid figure that could be made from each net.

1. 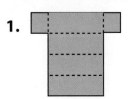   2.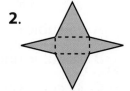

3. 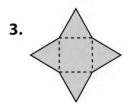   4.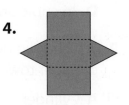

Draw nets for each solid figure.

5. Draw two different nets for a triangluar prism.

6. Draw two different nets for a cone.

Set C, pages 352–353

Draw the front, right side, and top views of this solid.

Here is the front view of the solid.

Here is the right side view of the solid.

Here is the top view of the solid.

Remember to consider blocks that might be hidden from your view in the drawings.

Draw the top, right side, and front views of each solid figure.

1.

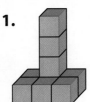

Front

2.

Front

Set D, pages 354–355

Find the volume.

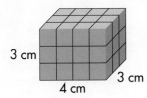

3 cm

3 cm

4 cm

$V = \ell \times w \times h$

$V = 4 \times 3 \times 3$

$V = 36$

The rectangular prism has a volume of 36 cubic centimeters.

Remember that volume is measured in cubic units.

Find the volume.

1.

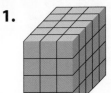

2.

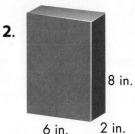

8 in.

6 in.   2 in.

Set E, pages 356–357

Look for a pattern. Tell the missing numbers.

1, 5, 9, 13, ▢ **,** ▢

Find the pattern.

1 + 4 = 5

5 + 4 = 9

9 + 4 = 13

Finish the pattern.

13 + 4 = 17

17 + 4 = 21

The missing numbers are 17 and 21.

Remember that in some patterns, you do not add the same number each time.

1. 2, 10, 18, 26, ▢ , ▢ , ▢

2. 1, 2, 4, 7, 11, 16, 22, ▢ , ▢ , ▢

3. 3, 6, 9, 12, ▢ , ▢ , ▢

4. 5, 11, 17, 23, ▢ , ▢ , ▢

5. 14, 21, 28, 35, ▢ , ▢ ,

Topic 16

Measurement, Time, and Temperature

1 The ENIAC was built in 1946 and is known as the first computer ever built. It weighed 30 tons. What units of weight are used to weigh most computers today? You will find out in Lesson 16-3.

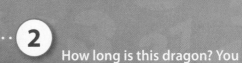

2 How long is this dragon? You will find out in Lesson 16-5.

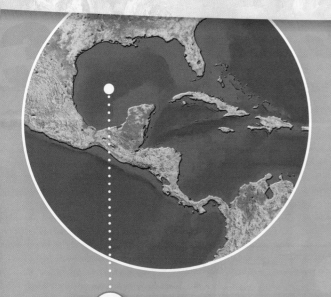

Review What You Know!

Vocabulary

Choose the best term from the box.

> • capacity   • length
> • foot   • volume

1. A _?_ is a unit of length equal to 12 inches.

2. _?_ represents the amount a container can hold in liquid units.

3. The _?_ of a solid figure is the number of cubic units needed to fill it.

Capacity

Choose the best unit to measure the capacity of each. Write cups or gallons.

4. bathtub   5. fish tank

6. soup bowl   7. mug

8. gasoline tank   9. sugar in a recipe

Weight

Choose the best unit to measure the weight of each. Write ounces or pounds.

10. bicycle   11. slice of bread

12. pencil   13. bag of wood chips

14. bowling ball   15. banana

Area and Volume

16. What is the width of a rectangle if its area is 16 square feet, and its length is 8 feet?

17. **Writing to Explain** The length of the edge of a cube is 4 feet. Find the volume.

3 The Gulf of Mexico is a massive body of water. How much water is deposited into the Gulf of Mexico every second? You will find out in Lesson 16-2.

4 How could an ancient Mayan pyramid be a type of calendar? You will find out in Lesson 16-9.

Lesson

16-1

Understand It!
Customary units are used to estimate and measure length.

Using Customary Units of Length

inch ruler

How do you estimate and measure length?

The United States uses customary units of measure. About how long is Greg's toy car?

About 1 inch (in.)

Other Examples

A notebook is about **1 foot (ft)**.

Almost 1 foot

1 ft = 12 in.

A baseball bat is about **1 yard (yd)**.

1 yd = 36 in.   1 yd = 3 ft

1 mile (mi) is about twice around the track.

1 mi = 5,280 ft   1 mi = 1,760 yd

Guided Practice*

Do you know HOW?

For **1** through **4**, choose the most appropriate unit to measure the length of each. Write in., ft, yd, or mi.

1. highway
2. CD case
3. football field
4. room

Do you UNDERSTAND?

5. How long is your textbook to the nearest inch? Explain how you measured.

6. Greg wants to measure how tall his 2-year-old sister is. What two units could he use? Explain your answer.

Independent Practice

For **7** through **10**, choose the most appropriate unit to measure the length of each. Write in., ft, yd, or mi.

7. pencil
8. building
9. mountain
10. spool of ribbon

Animated Glossary, eTools
www.pearsonsuccessnet.com

*For another example, see Set A on page 396.

Step 1

The toy car is shorter than a foot. So, the best unit to use would be inches.

The car is about 3 inches long.

Step 2

Measure to the nearest inch.

Line one end of the toy car up with the zero mark on the ruler. Then, find the inch mark closest to the other end of the toy car.

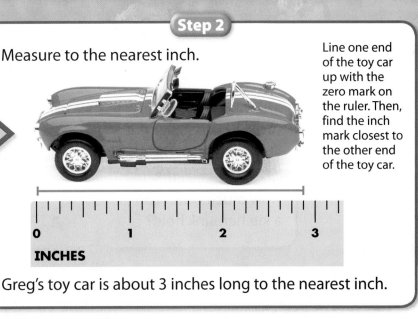

INCHES

Greg's toy car is about 3 inches long to the nearest inch.

For **11** through **13**, estimate and then measure each length to the nearest inch.

11.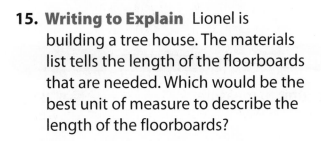

12.

13.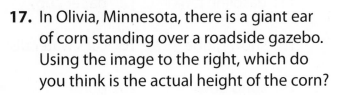

Problem Solving

14. Geometry If the perimeter of the triangle at the right is 14 yards, what is the length of the third side?

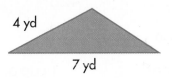
4 yd
7 yd

15. Writing to Explain Lionel is building a tree house. The materials list tells the length of the floorboards that are needed. Which would be the best unit of measure to describe the length of the floorboards?

16. Reasoning Trini took some photos. The number of photos she took is a two-digit number. The sum of the digits is 11. The tens digit is 3 more than the ones digit. How many photos did Trini take?

17. In Olivia, Minnesota, there is a giant ear of corn standing over a roadside gazebo. Using the image to the right, which do you think is the actual height of the corn?

  A 25 miles   **C** 25 inches

  B 25 feet   **D** 25 centimeters

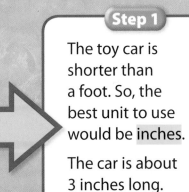

Understand It!
Customary units are
used to estimate and
measure capacity.

Customary Units of Capacity

How do you measure capacity in customary units?

Capacity is the volume of a container measured in liquid units. Here are some customary units for measuring capacity.

How much water can a kitchen sink hold?

| 1 cup (c) | 1 pint (pt) | 1 quart (qt) | 1 gallon (gal) |

Guided Practice*

Do you know HOW?

Which is the best estimate for the capacity of each item?

1.

3 gallons or
30 gallons?

2.

2 cups or
2 quarts?

3.

1 pint or
4 gallons?

4.

1 cup or
1 quart?

Do you UNDERSTAND?

5. Look at the quart and gallon containers above. Estimate how many quarts are in 1 gallon.

6. Estimate how many quarts it would take to fill the kitchen sink.

7. Which is greater, one cup or one quart?

8. Which is greater, one cup or one pint?

Independent Practice

In **9** through **20**, choose the most appropriate unit to measure the capacity of each item. Write c, pt, qt, or gal.

9. juice carton

10. bucket

11. gasoline tank

12. paper cup

13. fish bowl

14. bathtub

15. snow globe

16. cat's water dish

17. spray bottle

18. aquarium

19. soup bowl

20. pond

DIGITAL

Animated Glossary
www.pearsonsuccessnet.com

*For another example, see Set B on page 396.

Step 1	Step 2	Step 3

Step 1

Choose the most appropriate unit to measure:

It would take too long to fill the sink with the cup, pint, or quart.

The best unit would be the gallon.

Step 2

Estimate:

Visualize how many gallons of water it would take to fill the sink.

The sink has a capacity of about 4 gallons.

Step 3

Measure:

Fill the gallon jug with water and pour it into the sink. Do this until the sink is full, and count how many gallon jugs were used to fill the sink.

The sink has a capacity of about 5 gallons.

In **21** through **24**, choose the best estimate for the capacity of each item.

21.

1 gallon or 10 gallons?

22.

1 gallon or 1 quart?

23.

20 quarts or 200 quarts?

24.

2 quarts or 2 pints?

Problem Solving

25. In one second, 3,300,000 gallons of water from the Mississippi River enters the Gulf of Mexico. In one day, Houston's water system can carry 900,000 gallons. Which is greater, 3,300,000 gallons or 900,000 gallons?

26. Number Sense A lemonade recipe calls for 1 cup of sugar and 1 quart of water. This recipe makes 4 servings. If you want to make 12 servings, how many cups of sugar will you need?

27. You need 1 teaspoon of bubble bath for every 25 gallons of water. How much bubble bath is needed for a 50-gallon bathtub?

28. The lines on the measuring cup below show fluid ounces (oz) and cups (c). Which is greater, one fluid ounce or one cup?

29. Reasoning Which would be the better unit to measure the water in a swimming pool, the number of juice glasses or the number of bathtubs?

Understand It!
Customary units are used to estimate and measure weight.

Units of Weight
How do you measure weight?

Weight <u>is how heavy an object is</u>. Below are some customary units for measuring weight.

How much does a peach weigh?

1 ounce (oz)

1 pound (lb)

1 ton (T)

A key weighs about 1 ounce.

A kitten weighs about 1 pound.

A giraffe weighs about 1 ton.

Guided Practice*

Do you know HOW?

For **1** through **4**, give the best unit to measure the weight of each item.

1.

a slice of bread

2.

a sheep

3.

a helicopter

4.

a bicycle

Do you UNDERSTAND?

5. **Writing to Explain** How can you tell that the weight of the peach is **NOT** 8 ounces?

6. If you placed 3 keys on the same pan with the peach, how many ounces would be needed to balance the keys and the peach?

Independent Practice

For **7** through **18**, choose the most appropriate unit to measure the weight of each item.

Tip *Think of a familiar object that weighs one pound, one ounce, or one ton. Use that object to estimate the weight of other objects measured with the same unit.*

7. sea lion	**8.** orange	**9.** nail polish	**10.** greeting card
11. paper clip	**12.** canoe	**13.** ocean liner	**14.** football player
15. telephone	**16.** car	**17.** fork	**18.** bag of potatoes

Animated Glossary
www.pearsonsuccessnet.com

For another example, see Set C on page 396.

Choose the appropriate unit to measure:

A peach weighs less than a pound.

So, the best unit would be the ounce.

Estimate:

Think A key weighs about one ounce. How many keys would weigh the same as a peach?

About 8 keys would weigh the same.

A peach weighs about 8 ounces.

Measure:

Place the peach on one pan of the balance. Place an ounce weight on the other pan. Add ounce weights until the balance is level, and count the ounce weights.

The peach weighs 7 ounces.

Problem Solving

19. One of the first computers built weighed 30 tons. What would be an appropriate unit of weight to measure the weight of most desktop computers today?

21. Which is a greater number, the number of pounds a rooster weighs or the number of ounces the same rooster weighs?

For **22** through **25**, use the chart at the right.

22. About how many ounces do two dozen medium apples weigh?

23. Estimate the weight of one apple.

24. Do five dozen large watermelons weigh more or less than 1,000 pounds?

25. About how many pounds do three dozen bananas weigh?

26 . What is a good estimate for the weight of a bicycle?

    A 30 ounces   **C** 30 pounds

    B 3 pounds   **D** 3,000 ounces

20. Reasoning Name 3 things about the box below that you can measure. Give a reasonable estimate for each measure.

Fruit	Weight of one dozen
(apple)	72 ounces
(banana)	3 pounds
(watermelon)	264 pounds

16-4

Changing Customary Units

How do you change customary units?

The table at the right can be used to change one customary unit of measure to another.

Customary Units

Length	Capacity	Weight
1 ft = 12 in.	1 tbsp = 3 tsp	1 lb = 16 oz
1 yd = 36 in.	1 fl oz = 2 tbsp	1 T = 2,000 lb
1 yd = 3 ft	1 c = 8 fl oz	
1 mi = 5,280 ft	1 pt = 2 c	
1 mi = 1,760 yd	1 qt = 2 pt	
	1 gal = 4 qt	

Another Example How do you compare customary measures?

Kylie brought 2 gallons of punch to the school picnic. Each person gets 1 cup of punch.

Did Kylie bring enough punch for 24 people?

2 gal $\bigcirc$ 24 c

Step 1

Change gallons into cups.

Think 1 gal = 4 qt
So, 2 gal × 4 qt = 8 quarts.

Think 1 qt = 2 pt
So, 8 qt × 2 pt = 16 pints.

Think 1 pt = 2 c
So, 16 pt × 2 c = 32 cups.

Kylie brought enough punch for 24 people.

Step 2

Compare.

32 c > 24 c
So, 2 gal > 24 c.

Explain It

1. How do you change quarts to gallons?

2. How do you change pounds to ounces?

3. **Reasonableness** What are two ways to find how many inches are in a mile?

How many pints are in five quarts?

To change larger units to smaller units, multiply.

$$5 \text{ qt} = \quad \text{pt}$$

Think 1 qt = 2 pt

$$5 \times 2 = 10$$

$$5 \text{ qt} = 10 \text{ pt}$$

There are 10 pints in five quarts.

How many feet are equal to 84 inches?

To change smaller units to larger units, divide

$$84 \text{ in.} = \quad \text{ft}$$

Think 12 in. = 1 ft

$$84 \div 12 = 7$$

$$84 \text{ in.} = 7 \text{ ft}$$

There are 7 feet in 84 inches.

Guided Practice*

Do you know HOW?

In **1** through **4**, find each missing number.

1. 6 T = ▨ lb

2. 12 qt = ▨ gal

3. 7 lb = ▨ oz

4. 3 yd = ▨ in.

In **5** through **8**, compare. Write > or < for each ◯.

5. 5 ft ◯ 57 in.

6. 16 fl oz ◯ 3 c

7. 2 tbsp ◯ 4 tsp

8. 3 gal ◯ 8 qt

Do you UNDERSTAND?

9. In the first example, why do you multiply 5×2?

10. Do you multiply or divide to change inches to yards?

11. Writing to Explain A 4-foot stick is longer than one yard. A 32-inch stick is shorter than one yard. Is a 4-foot stick longer or shorter than a 32-inch stick.

Independent Practice

Leveled Practice For **12** through **19**, find each missing number.

12. 4 pt = ▨ qt
$$4 \div 2 = \quad \text{qt}$$

13. 18 tsp = ▨ tbsp
$$18 \div 3 = \quad \text{tbsp}$$

14. 2 c = ▨ fl oz
$$2 \times 8 = \quad \text{fl oz}$$

15. 4 tbsp = ▨ tsp
$$4 \times 3 = \quad \text{tsp}$$

16. 8 yd = ▨ ft

17. 60 in. = ▨ ft

18. 3 lb = ▨ oz

19. 7 ft = ▨ in.

For **20** through **27**, compare. Write > or < for each ◯.

20. 1 pt ◯ 1 qt

21. 16 tbsp ◯ 2 c

22. 14 in. ◯ 1 yd

23. 5 c ◯ 2 pt

24. 9 ft ◯ 2 yd

25. 2 T ◯ 2,500 lb

26. 2 mi ◯ 2,000 yd

27. 24 oz ◯ 2 lb

Problem Solving

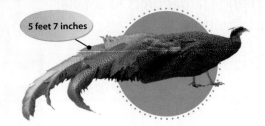

5 feet 7 inches

28. The longest tail feathers of any bird are those of the Argus Pheasant. The feathers measure 5 feet 7 inches in length. How many inches long are these feathers?

29. A super-stretch limousine is 240 inches long. A pickup truck is 19 feet long. Which is longer?

30. Geometry If one side of a square measures 5 inches, what is the area of the square?

Use the table at the right for **31** through **33**.

The weight of objects on other planets and the Moon is different than it is on Earth.

31. What is the approximate weight in ounces of a fourth grader on Venus?

32. What is the approximate weight in ounces of a fourth grader on the Moon?

Approximate Weight of a 4th-Grader			
Earth	Jupiter	Venus	Moon
85 lb	215 lb	77 lb	14 lb

33. Writing to Explain Would an adult weigh more on Earth or on Venus? Explain your reasoning.

34. Reasonableness A magazine reports that a giraffe's height is 180 inches, or 15 yards. What mistake was made?

35. Writing to Explain Which unit of measure would you use to measure the length of your shoe?

36. Mr. Kunkle uses a bowling ball that weighs 13 pounds. How many ounces does the bowling ball weigh?

   A 116 oz   **C** 180 oz

   B 140 oz   **D** 208 oz

37. Jeremiah bought 2 pounds of lettuce and 3 pounds of tomatoes for a salad. How many ounces of each did he purchase?

38. Every day, more than 17,000,000 gallons of water flow through the Trevi Fountain. How many quarts of water is this?

   A 68 qt   **C** 68,000 qt

   B 6,800 qt   **D** 68,000,000 qt

17 million gallons per day

Find the difference. Estimate to check
if the answer is reasonable.

1. 54.3 − 0.28   **2.** 14.8 − 3.76   **3.** 15.23 − 3.17

4. 25.78 − 9.8   **5.** 18.1 − 3.45   **6.** 12.7 − 3.81

Find the product. Estimate to check if the answer is reasonable.

7.   23,418   **8.**   6,223   **9.**   33,478   **10.**   406   **11.**   4,000
     ×   5   ×   2   ×   5   ×   36   ×   12

Find the sum. Estimate to check if the answer is reasonable.

12.   12,345   **13.**   4,402   **14.**   403   **15.**   5,474   **16.**   13,985
   + 87,654   + 3,912   + 737   + 723   + 7,539

Error Search Find each answer that is not correct.
Write it correctly and explain the error.

17.   33.90   **18.**   34,890   **19.** $1.05   **20.** $\frac{5}{6}$ **21.**   5,007
   + 25.76   ×   8   2)$2.10   − $\frac{1}{4}$ ×   35
    58.66   279,120 $\frac{4}{2}$ 175,215

Number Sense

Estimating and Reasoning Write whether each statement is true or false.
Explain your answer.

22. The product of 3 and $5.87 is greater than $18.

23. The sum of 59,703 and 24,032 is greater than 70,000,
but less than 90,000.

24. The difference of 466 − 103 is 3 less than 366.

25. The product of 21 and 4,076 is greater than 80,000.

26. The quotient of 534 ÷ 6 is greater than 90.

27. The sum of 11.35 and 5.2 is less than 16.

Lesson

16-5

Understand It!
Metric Units are
used to estimate
and measure length.

Using Metric Units of Length

Hands-On
metric ruler

How do you estimate and measure length?

The meter is the basic metric unit of length.

How long is the beetle at the right?

About 1 cm

Metric Units of Length

1 centimeter (cm) =
10 millimeters (mm)

1 decimeter (dm) =
10 centimeters (cm)

1 meter (m) =
100 centimeters (cm)

1 kilometer (km) =
1,000 meters (m)

Other Examples

1 millimeter (mm) is about the thickness of a dime.

1 meter (m) is about the length of a snake.

1 kilometer (km) is about the length of 4 city blocks.

Guided Practice*

Do you know HOW?

For **1** through **4**, choose the most appropriate unit to measure each. Write mm, cm, dm, m, or km.

1. height of a house

2. length of a cat

3. width of a sunflower seed

4. distance traveled by plane

Do you UNDERSTAND?

5. How wide is your textbook to the nearest centimeter? Explain how you measured.

6. Joni wants to measure the width of a narrow ribbon she is using to tie around the pinecone. Which metric unit should she use? Explain.

Independent Practice

For **7** through **9**, choose the most appropriate unit to measure each item. Write mm, cm, dm, m, or km.

7. length of a shoe

8. height of a tree

9. width of a strand of yarn

DIGITAL
Animated Glossary, eTools
www.pearsonsuccessnet.com

*For another example, see Set E on page 397.

Step 1

The beetle is shorter than a decimeter, but longer than a millimeter. So the best unit would be centimeters.

The beetle's length is about 4 centimeters long.

Step 2

Measure to the nearest centimeter.

Line one end of the beetle up with the zero mark on the ruler. Then find the centimeter mark closest to the other end of the beetle.

| | 1 | 2 | 3 | 4 | 5 | 6 | 7 | 8 |

CENTIMETERS

The beetle is 4 centimeters long to the nearest centimeter.

For **10** through **12**, estimate. Then measure each length to the nearest centimeter.

10.

11.

12.

Problem Solving

13. The fourth-grade teachers are planning a pizza party. Each pizza has 8 slices. The teachers want enough pizza so that each student can have 2 slices. If there are 22 students in each of the 3 fourth-grade classes, how many pizzas must be ordered?

14. Writing to Explain June measured the height from the top of her window to the floor and wrote 3. She forgot to write the unit. Which metric unit of measure did June most likely use?

15. In the year 2000, the world's largest Chinese dancing dragon was part of a celebration at the Great Wall of China. It took 3,200 people working inside the dragon to move it. Which is the best estimate of the length of the dragon?

    A 3,048 mm   **C** 3,048 cm

    B 3,048 dm   **D** 3,048 m

16. Measure to find the length of the bead below. What is the length of 32 of these beads on a necklace?

    A 30 cm   **C** 64 cm

    B 32 cm   **D** 100 cm

Lesson
16-6

Understand It!
Metric units are
used to estimate
and measure capacity.

Metric Units of Capacity

How do you measure capacity with metric units?

Below are two metric units for measuring capacity. How much liquid can the bottle to the right hold?

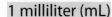
1 milliliter (mL)

1 liter (L)

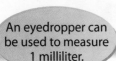

An eyedropper can be used to measure 1 milliliter.

Some water bottles hold 1 liter.

Guided Practice*

Do you know HOW?

Which is the best estimate for the capacity of each item?

1.

5 liters or 500 liters?

2.

10 liters or 100 liters?

3.

100 milliliters or 10 liters?

4.

10 milliliters or 1 liter?

Do you UNDERSTAND?

5. Which unit of measure is greater, a liter or a milliliter?

6. Which would be the best unit of measure to use to measure the amount of gasoline in a car's gas tank, a milliliter or a liter?

7. Which would be the best unit of measure to use to fill a large milk container?

Independent Practice

In **8** through **15**, choose the most appropriate unit to measure the capacity of each item. Write L or mL.

8. bucket

9. ink pen

10. juice glass

11. washing machine

12. soup pot

13. coffee mug

14. medicine cup

15. pitcher

Animated Glossary
www.pearsonsuccessnet.com

*For another example, see Set F on page 397.

Step 1	Step 2	Step 3

Step 1

Choose the most appropriate unit to measure:

The milliliter is a very small amount. A larger unit would be more appropriate to measure with.

The best unit would be the liter.

Step 2

Estimate:

Visualize how many liter bottles it would take to fill the bottle.

The bottle has a capacity of about 2 liters.

Step 3

Measure:

Fill the liter bottle with water and pour it into the bottle. Do this until the bottle is full, and count how many liter bottles were used.

The bottle has a capacity of about 2 liters.

In **16** through **19**, choose the best estimate for the capacity of each.

16.

200 milliliters or 200 liters?

17.

4 liters or 14 liters?

18.

20 milliliters or 200 milliliters?

19.

3 liters or 300 liters?

Problem Solving

20. Number Sense Which number would be greater, the number of liters of juice in a pitcher or the number of milliliters of juice in the same pitcher?

21. Reasonableness Zack said he poured lemonade from a 300-liter pitcher into a 20-milliliter glass. Are these numbers reasonable? Why or why not?

22. Which capacities are written in order from greatest to least?

  A   5 milliliters, 2 liters, 1 liter

  B   2 liters, 5 milliliters, 1 liter

  C   1 liter, 2 liters, 5 milliliters

  D   2 liters, 1 liter, 5 milliliters

23. Marcus filled a bottle with 1,000 milliliters of water to take with him on his jog. After his jog, he had about 450 milliliters left in his bottle. How much water did he drink while he jogged?

1,000 mL of water	
450	?

24. Geometry What is the perimeter of the triangle?

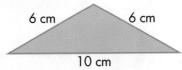

25. How much more water does a 0.75-liter sports bottle hold than a 0.6-liter bottle?

Understand It! Metric units are used to estimate and measure mass.

Units of Mass

What are metric units of mass?

Mass is the amount of matter that something contains.

What is the mass of a red brick?

1 gram (g)

A dollar bill has a mass of about 1 gram (g).

1 kilogram (kg)

A cantaloupe has a mass of about 1 kilogram (kg).

The mass of a red brick is?

Other Examples

Weight and Mass are different.

The **weight** of an object changes depending on its location.

The weight of the red brick on the moon is not the same as its weight on Earth.

The **mass** of an object always stays the same.

The mass of the red brick on the moon is the same as its mass on Earth.

Guided Practice*

Do you know HOW?

For **1** and **2**, choose the most appropriate unit to measure the mass of each item.

1.

   hamster

2.

   gorilla

Do you UNDERSTAND?

3. Which number would be less, the mass of a grapefruit in grams or the mass of the same grapefruit in kilograms?

4. How many cantaloupes would be needed to have the same mass as two red bricks?

Independent Practice

For **5** through **12**, choose the most appropriate unit to measure the mass of each item.

5. pencil

6. baseball player

7. baseball

8. honeydew melon

Animated Glossary
www.pearsonsuccessnet.com

*For another example, see Set G on page 398.

Step 1

Choose the appropriate unit to measure:

A brick has a greater mass than a cantaloupe.

So, the best unit would be the kilogram.

Step 2

Estimate:

Think A cantaloupe has a mass of about one kilogram. How many cantaloupes would have the same mass as a red brick?

About 3 cantaloupes would have the same mass.

The brick has a mass of about 3 kilograms.

Step 3

Measure:

Place the brick on one pan of the balance. Add kilograms to the other pan until the balance is level. Count the kilograms.

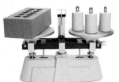

The brick has a mass of 3 kilograms.

9. strawberry

10. penguin

11. sailboat

12. dragonfly

Problem Solving

For **13** through **15**, use the table at the right.

13. Order the coins from least mass to greatest mass.

14. A dollar bill has a mass of about 1 gram. About how many dollar bills have the same mass as a nickel?

15. There are 40 nickels in a roll of nickels. What is the total mass of the nickels in one roll?

Tip *Find the mass of 4 nickels and multiply by 10.*

Coin	Mass
	2.500 grams
	5.000 grams
	2.268 grams
	5.670 grams

16. Writing to Explain Mandy says that she has a mass of 32 kg on the Earth. What is her mass on the moon?

17. Which number is greater, the mass of a carrot in grams or the mass of the same carrot in kilograms?

18. Use the bar diagram below. José needs $78 for a present. He has already saved $33. How much more does he need to save?

$78 in all

?	$33

19. What is a good estimate for the mass of an American saddlebred horse?

A 5 kg

B 50 kg

C 500 kg

D 5,000 kg

Lesson
16-8

Understand It!
Compare measures by
changing metric units.

Changing Metric Units

How do you change metric units?

The table at the right can be used to change one metric unit of measure to another.

Metric Units		
Length	**Capacity**	**Weight**
1 m = 1,000 mm	1 L = 1,000 mL	1 g = 1,000 mg
1 cm = 10 mm		1 kg = 1,000 g
1 dm = 10 cm		
1 m = 100 cm		
1 km = 1,000 m		

Data

Another Example **How do you compare metric measures?**

Sela went to the market to buy some fruit. She bought a bag of oranges that had a mass of 1 kg 125 g and a bag of apples that had a mass of 1,380 g.

Which bag had a greater mass?

1 kg 125 g ◯ 1,380 g

Step 1

Change kilograms into grams.

Think 1 kg = 1,000 g

1,000 + 125 = 1,125

1 kg 125 g = 1,125 g

The bag of apples has a greater mass.

Step 2

Compare.

1,125 kg < 1,380 kg

So, 1 kg 125 g < 1,380 g.

Explain It

1. How do you change centimeters to meters?

2. How do you change liters to milliliters?

3. **Reasonableness** Why do you have to change kilograms to grams when comparing these two units of mass?

A large monarch butterfly's wingspan is about 10 centimeters long. How long is this in millimeters?

To change larger units to smaller units, multiply.

10 cm = ▢ mm

(Think) 1 cm = 10 mm

10 × 10 = 100

10 cm = 100 mm

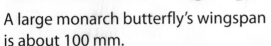

10 cm

A large monarch butterfly's wingspan is about 100 mm.

A small monarch butterfly's wingspan is about 60 millimeters long. How long is this in centimeters?

To change smaller units to larger units, divide.

60 mm = ▢ cm

(Think) 10 mm = 1 cm

60 ÷ 10 = 6

60 mm = 6 cm

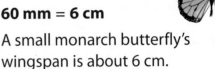

60 mm

A small monarch butterfly's wingspan is about 6 cm.

Guided Practice*

Do you know HOW?

In **1** through **4**, find each missing number.

1. 1 kg = ▢ g　　**2.** 3 cm = ▢ mm

3. 600 cm = ▢ m　　**4.** 4 dm = ▢ cm

In **5** through **8**, compare. Write > or < for each ◯.

5. 3 m ◯ 200 cm　**6.** 4 L ◯ 7,000 mL

7. 1 kg ◯ 100 g　**8.** 1 km ◯ 3,000 m

Do you UNDERSTAND?

9. In the second example, why do you divide 60 by 10?

10. Do you multiply or divide to change meters to centimeters?

11. Writing to Explain Explain how to change 600 mm to centimeters.

Independent Practice

Leveled Practice In **12** through **23**, find each missing number.

12. 8 km = ▢ m
8 × 1,000 = ▢ m

13. 6 L = ▢ mL
6 × 1,000 = ▢ mL

14. 32 kg = ▢ g
32 × 1,000 = ▢ g

15. 5 m = ▢ cm

16. 11 kg = ▢ g

17. 57 dm = ▢ cm

18. 8,632 m = ▢ cm

19. 552 km = ▢ m

20. 13,000 g = ▢ kg

21. 680 cm = ▢ dm

22. 61 km = ▢ m

23. 16 L = ▢ mL

Independent Practice

For **24** through **29**, compare. Write > or < for each $\bigcirc$.

24. 100 mL $\bigcirc$ 1 L

25. 10 cm $\bigcirc$ 100 dm

26. 2 kg $\bigcirc$ 200 g

27. 30 cm $\bigcirc$ 30 mm

28. 2 km $\bigcirc$ 200 m

29. 600 kg $\bigcirc$ 6 g

Problem Solving

Use the data to the right for **30** through **32**.

30. How many meters does a lion travel in 1 minute?

31. List the animals in order from fastest to slowest.

32. **Writing to Explain** Edgar says a giant tortoise is faster than a spider because 450 is greater than 31. Is he correct?

Distances Animals Can Travel in One Minute	
Elephant	670 m
Giant Tortoise	450 cm
Spider	31 m
Lion	1 km 340 m

33. **Algebra** Find the value of $n \div 6$ when n is 4,200.

34. **Estimation** The mass of 5 tomatoes is about 1 kilogram. Estimate the mass of 1 tomato in grams.

35. Use the diagram below to write a subtraction sentence.

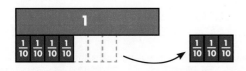

36. Which measure is **NOT** equal to 6 meters?

    A 60 kilometers

    B 60 decimeters

    C 600 centimeters

    D 6,000 millimeters

37. **Geometry** Two sides of an equilateral triangle both measure 3 inches. How long is the third side? Explain.

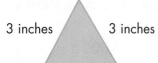

3 inches   3 inches

38. **Reasoning** There are about 5 milliliters in one teaspoon. There are 3 teaspoons in one tablespoon. How many milliliters are there in 10 tablespoons?

Enrichment

Comparing Metric and Customary Measures

The symbol ≈ is read as "is approximately equal to."
The table to the right lists the comparable measures.

Customary and Metric Unit Equivalents

Length:
1 in. = 2.54 cm
1 ft = 30.48 cm
1 m ≈ 3.28 ft
1 m ≈ 1.09 yd
1 km ≈ 0.62 mi
1 mi ≈ 1.61 km

Capacity:
1 L ≈ 1.06 qt
1 gal ≈ 3.79 L

Weight and Mass:
1 oz ≈ 28.35 g
1 kg ≈ 2.2 lb

Examples:

About how many pounds are equal to 5 kilograms?

Think 1 kilogram is approximately equal to 2.2 pounds.

Multiply to convert.

$5 \times 2.2 = 11$

5 kilograms is approximately 11 pounds.

About how many miles are equal to 5 kilometers?

Think 1 kilometer is approximately equal to 0.62 miles.

Multiply to convert.

$5 \times 0.62 = 3.1$

5 kilometers is approximately 3.1 miles.

Practice

For **1** through **8**, copy and complete by writing < or > for each ◯.

1. 1 m ◯ 1 yd

2. 1 mi ◯ 1 km

3. 1 cm ◯ 1 in.

4. 1 gal ◯ 1 L

5. 1 cm ◯ 1 ft

6. 1 L ◯ 1 qt

7. 1 lb ◯ 1 kg

8. 1m ◯ 1 ft

For **9** through **16**, copy and complete.

9. 2 oz ≈ ▢ g

10. 12 in = ▢ cm

11. 5 m ≈ ▢ ft

12. 7 mi ≈ ▢ km

13. 4 gal ≈ ▢ L

14. 3 kg ≈ ▢ lb

15. 10 L ≈ ▢ qt

16. 9 ft = ▢ cm

Lesson
16-9

Understand It!
Time can be measured
in different units.

Units of Time

How do you compare units of time?

On her birthday, Kara calculated that she was 108 months old. Her friend Jordan has the same birthday. If Jordan turned 8 years old, who is older, Kara or Jordan?

You can convert different units of time in order to compare them.

Units of Time	
1 minute	= 60 seconds
1 hour	= 60 minutes
1 day	= 24 hours
1 week	= 7 days
1 month	= about 4 weeks
1 year	= 52 weeks
1 year	= 12 months
1 year	= 365 days
1 leap year	= 366 days
1 decade	= 10 years
1 century	= 100 years
1 millennium	= 1,000 years

Guided Practice*

Do you know HOW?

For **1** through **4**, write >, <, or = for each ◯. Use the chart above to help.

1. 9 months ◯ 27 weeks

2. 17 years ◯ 2 decades

3. 5 minutes ◯ 300 seconds

4. 44 months ◯ 3 years

Do you UNDERSTAND?

5. Writing to Explain How can you tell which is longer, 63 hours or 3 days?

6. Do you multiply or divide if you want to change months to years?

7. How many years old is Kara?

Independent Practice

For **8** through **13**, write >, <, or = for each ◯.

8. 35 weeks ◯ 340 days   **9.** 7 days ◯ 120 hours   **10.** 2 years ◯ 730 days

11. 40 hours ◯ 2 days   **12.** 8 weeks ◯ 56 days   **13.** 12 months ◯ 40 weeks

For **14** through **22**, complete each number sentence.

14. 6 days = ▢ hours   **15.** 2 years = ▢ months   **16.** 6 minutes = ▢ seconds

17. 3 decades = ▢ years   **18.** 4 hours = ▢ minutes   **19.** 4 centuries = ▢ years

20. 36 months = ▢ years   **21.** 104 weeks = ▢ years   **22.** 5,000 years = ▢ millennia

Change 8 years to months.

1 year = 12 months

To find the number of months in 8 years, multiply.

$8 \times 12 = 96$

So, 8 years = 96 months.

Compare the amounts.

Kara's age   Jordan's age

108 months ◯ **8 years**

108 months ⧁ **96 months**

So, Kara is older than Jordan.

Problem Solving

23. Estimation About how many minutes does it take you to do your homework? How many seconds is this?

24. Trish is going to camp for 2 months. Which is greater than 2 months?

   A 35 days   **C** 6 weeks

   B 40 days   **D** 10 weeks

25. Reasoning Gina has 3 yards of fabric. She needs to cut 8 pieces, each 1 foot long. Does she have enough fabric? Explain.

26. A girl from England set a world record by sneezing 978 days in a row. About how many weeks did she sneeze in a row?

27. Estimation If you brush your teeth 10 minutes a day, about how many hours do you brush in a year?

28. A theater has 358 seats on the main level and 122 seats in the balcony. How many people can see 6 shows in one day?

29. It is believed that the Mayan pyramid of Kukulkan in Mexico was used as a calendar. It has 4 stairways leading to the top platform. Including the one extra step at the top, it has a total of 365 steps. How many steps are in each stairway?

Tip *Subtract 1 from the total number of steps before you divide.*

Each stairway has the same number of steps.

Lesson
16-10

Understand It!
Time can be used to tell
how long an event takes.

Elapsed Time

Hands-On
clock

How can you find and use elapsed time?

The dress rehearsal for the school
play started at 8:15 A.M. It ended at
10:25 A.M. How long was the rehearsal?

Elapsed time is the amount of time
that passes between the beginning
and the end of an event.

Another Example **How can you use elapsed time to
find when an event began or ended?**

At 11:50 A.M., Kerry's father dropped Kerry off at
a Saturday rehearsal for the school play. He was told
the rehearsal would last 1 hour and 30 minutes.
At what time should he pick her up?

Rehearsal starts
at 11:50 A.M.

One Way

The rehearsal started at 11:50 A.M.

Count 1 hour to 12:50 P.M.

Count 10 minutes to 1:00 P.M.

Count another 20 minutes to 1:20 P.M.

Kerry's father should pick her
up at 1:20 P.M.

Another Way

From 11:50 A.M. to 12:00 P.M. is
10 minutes.

From 12:00 P.M. to 12:20 P.M. is
20 minutes.

From 12:20 P.M. to 1:20 P.M. is 1 hour.

Kerry's father should pick her
up at 1:20 P.M.

Explain It

1. On Sunday, rehearsal starts at 10:30 A.M.
   When will rehearsal end if it lasts 1 hour
   and 30 minutes?

2. **Reasonableness** Is the elapsed time from 5:35 P.M.
   to 8:52 P.M. more or less than three hours?

One Way

From 8:15 A.M.
to 10:15 A.M. is
2 hours.

From 10:15 A.M.
to 10:25 A.M. is
10 minutes.

So, the dress rehearsal lasted
2 hours and 10 minutes.

Another Way

From 8:15 A.M. to 9:00 A.M. is 45 minutes.

From 9:00 A.M. to 10:00 A.M. is 1 hour.

From 10:00 A.M. to 10:25 A.M. is 25 minutes.

45 minutes + 1 hour + 25 minutes
is 1 hour and 70 minutes,
or 2 hours and 10 minutes.

The dress rehearsal lasted 2 hours and
10 minutes.

Guided Practice*

Do you know HOW?

Find the elapsed time.

1. Start: 9:00 P.M.
   Finish: 11:10 P.M.

2. Start: 6:10 A.M.
   Finish: 10:25 A.M.

3. Start: 1:11 A.M.
   Finish: 3:26 A.M.

4. Start: 2:37 P.M.
   Finish: 4:05 P.M.

Do you UNDERSTAND?

5. Is the elapsed time between
   4:40 P.M. and 6:20 P.M. more or
   less than 2 hours? Explain.

6. Based on the rehearsal time,
   if the play begins at 7:15 P.M.,
   at what time will it end?

Independent Practice

For **7** through **12**, find the elapsed time. Use a clock or stopwatch to help.

7. Start: 5:00 A.M.
   Finish: 9:20 A.M.

8. Start: 7:15 P.M.
   Finish: 11:00 P.M.

9. Start: 4:55 A.M.
   Finish: 5:37 A.M.

10. Start: 4:25 P.M.
    Finish: 6:41 P.M.

11. Start: 3:07 P.M.
    Finish: 10:12 P.M.

12. Start: 11:44 A.M.
    Finish: 1:05 P.M.

In **13** through **16**, write the time each clock will show in 2 hours and 15 minutes.

13.

14.

15.

16.

DIGITAL Animated Glossary, eTools
www.pearsonsuccessnet.com

For **17** through **22**, find each start or finish time.
Use a clock or stopwatch to help.

17. Start: 9:00 A.M.
Elapsed time: 2 hours
and 35 minutes
Finish:

18. Start: 5:25 P.M.
Elapsed time: 3 hours
and 23 minutes
Finish:

19. Start:
Elapsed time: 2 hours
and 20 minutes
Finish: 3:40 A.M.

20. Start:
Elapsed time: 6 hours
and 13 minutes
Finish: 8:27 P.M.

21. Start: 3:16 P.M.
Elapsed time: 2 hours
and 51 minutes
Finish:

22. Start:
Elapsed time: 5 hours
and 9 minutes
Finish: 11:21 A.M.

Problem Solving

For **23** and **24**, use the table at the right.

23. Which activities are scheduled to last more than 1 hour and 30 minutes?

24. Paulo's family arrived at the reunion at 8:30 A.M. How long do they have before the trip to Scenic Lake Park?

Suarez Family Reunion Schedule	
Trip to Scenic Lake Park	10:15 A.M. to 2:30 P.M.
Slide show	4:15 P.M. to 5:10 P.M.
Dinner	5:30 P.M. to 7:00 P.M.
Campfire	7:55 P.M. to 9:30 P.M.

25. **Algebra** Thomas saved $256. He used the money to buy 4 model trains. Each train cost the same amount. Write and solve a equation to find the cost of each train.

26. The "Trek Across Maine" bike ride is about 180 miles long. If the average cyclist bikes 50 miles per day, how many days will it take to complete the trek?

27. Which is greater, 13,400 seconds or 2,000 minutes?

28. Which is greater, 104 weeks or 3 years?

29. In 1999, a chain of 2,751,518 dominoes was toppled in Beijing, China. It took a total of 32 minutes and 22 seconds for the dominoes to fall. If the first domino fell at 11:22 P.M., at what time did the last domino fall? Round your answer to the nearest minute.

30. In April, Julie's puppy weighed 14 ounces. In July, the puppy weighed 4 times this much. How much did the puppy weigh in July?

A 2 pounds 10 ounces

B 3 pounds 8 ounces

C 4 pounds 8 ounces

D 7 pounds

Title

Use 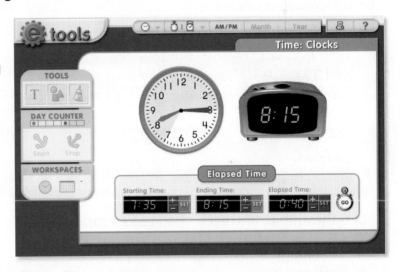 tools Time.

Jessica gets to play video games from 7:35 P.M. until 8:15 P.M. each evening. She sleeps from 9:40 P.M. until 6:25 A.M. How long does she play video games? How long does she sleep?

Step 1 Go to the Time eTool. Select Elapsed Time from the pull-down menu at the top of the page. Move the minute hand on the clock until it shows 7:35. The digital clock should change to match. Click the ➕ button under the starting time to change the time to 7:35. Hold down the button to change the time faster.

Step 2 Change the ending time to 8:15. Push Go to start the elapsed time animation.

Jessica gets to play video games for 40 minutes.

Step 3 Move the hands of the analog clock to show 9:40. Change the starting time to 9:40 by holding down the ➕ button. Change the ending time to 6:25 by holding down the ➖ button. Push Go to see the animation.

Jessica sleeps 8 hours and 45 minutes.

Practice

Use the Time eTool to find each elapsed time.

1. 1:25 P.M. to 3:15 P.M.

2. 5:45 A.M. to 8:05 A.M.

3. 12:45 P.M. to 7:20 P.M.

4. 11:52 A.M. to 2:19 P.M.

5. 3:31 P.M. to 6:46 P.M.

6. 11:43 A.M. to 4:39 P.M.

7. 2:12 P.M. to 3:09 P.M.

8. 7:28 A.M. to 5:30 P.M.

9. 7:30 A.M. TO 11:45 A.M.

Understand It!
Temperature can be read in degrees Fahrenheit or degrees Celsius.

Temperature

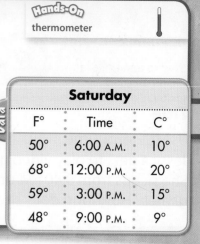

Hands-On
thermometer

How can you solve problems involving changes in temperature?

On Saturday, how many degrees Fahrenheit did the temperature increase between 6:00 A.M. and 12:00 P.M.? How many degrees Celsius did the temperature decrease between 3:00 P.M. and 9:00 P.M.?

	Saturday	
F°	Time	C°
50°	6:00 A.M.	10°
68°	12:00 P.M.	20°
59°	3:00 P.M.	15°
48°	9:00 P.M.	9°

Guided Practice*

Do you know HOW?

For **1** and **2**, find each temperature change. Then tell whether each change is an increase or decrease.

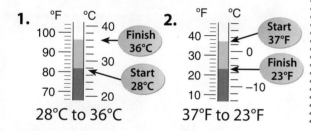

1. Finish 36°C / Start 28°C
   28°C to 36°C

2. Start 37°F / Finish 23°F
   37°F to 23°F

Do you UNDERSTAND?

3. On the Celsius side of the thermometer above, there are 4 tick marks between 10°C and 20°C. What does each tick mark represent?

4. **Writing to Explain** If a temperature increases in degrees Fahrenheit, will it increase or decrease in degrees Celsius?

Independent Practice

For **5** through **8**, find each change in temperature. Tell whether each change is an increase or decrease.

5. 24°C to 58°C   **6.** 40°F to 15°F   **7.** 44°F to 61°F   **8.** 42°C to 14°C

For **9** through **12**, read each temperature. Then tell what the temperature would be after each change described.

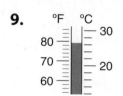

9. Decrease of 14°C

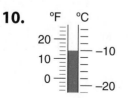

10. Increase of 17°F

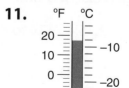

11. Increase of 35°F

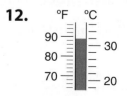

12. Decrease of 27°C

Degrees Fahrenheit (°F) are <u>customary units of temperature</u>.

Add to find the change in temperature between 6:00 A.M. and 12:00 P.M.

$50 + 10 = 60$

$60 + 8 = 68$

$\mathbf{50 + 18 = 68}$

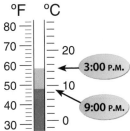

Between 6:00 A.M. and 12:00 P.M., the temperature increased by 18°F.

Degrees Celsius (°C) are <u>metric units of temperature</u>.

Subtract to find the change in temperature between 3:00 P.M. and 9:00 P.M.

$\mathbf{15 - 9 = 6}$

Between 3:00 P.M. and 9:00 P.M., the temperature decreased by 6°C.

Problem Solving

13. Crocodiles are cold-blooded animals with body temperatures from 86°F to 89°F. Crocodiles control their body temperature by moving to warmer or cooler environments. What is the difference between the highest normal body temperature and the lowest normal body temperature?

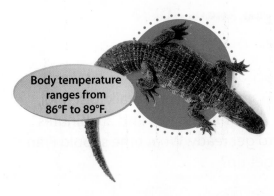

Body temperature ranges from 86°F to 89°F.

14. Reasoning Annie, Bart, and Consuela live in three different cities. One day, the high temperature in Bart's city was 9°C less than in Annie's city. The high temperature in Consuela's city was 14°C more than in Bart's city. Which city was warmer, Consuela's city or Annie's city?

15. The high temperature for a day in June was 68°F. The low temperature that day was 29°F less. What was the low temperature?

  A 39°F   **C** 39°C

  B 97°F   **D** 97°C

16. As a general rule, the air temperature drops about 7°C for every 1,000 meters of elevation. If the temperature at sea level is 33°C, what is the temperature at 4,000 meters?

17. Heather and Irene are reading the same 439-page book. Heather read 393 pages. Irene read 121 fewer pages than Heather. How many pages does Irene have left to read?

18. On the Celsius scale, water boils at 100°C and freezes at 0°C. What is the temperature difference between boiling and freezing?

19. On the Fahrenheit scale, water boils at 212°F and freezes at 32°F. What is the temperature difference between boiling and freezing?

Understand It!
Learning how and when to work backward can help when problem solving.

Work Backward

Between 6:00 A.M. and 7:00 A.M., the temperature rose 2 degrees. Every hour after that, the temperature rose 4 degrees. At 1:00 P.M., the temperature was 62°F. What was the temperature at 6:00 A.M.?

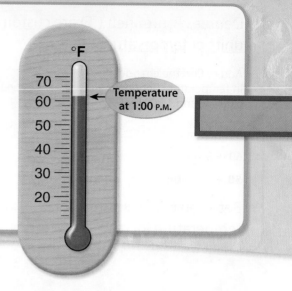

Temperature at 1:00 P.M.

Guided Practice*

Do you know HOW?

Solve.

1. School starts at 7:45 A.M. It takes Fran 30 minutes to walk to school, 15 minutes to eat, and 20 minutes to get ready. What time should Fran get up?

Do you UNDERSTAND?

2. **Reasonableness** Is the answer to the problem above reasonable? Explain.

3. **Write a Problem** Write a problem that uses working backward. Then answer your question.

Independent Practice

Solve. Write the answer in a complete sentence.

4. Wanda walked for 25 minutes from the mall to the train station. She waited 20 minutes for the train, and then had a 20 minute ride. Her train arrived at 12:20 P.M. What time did she leave the mall?

5. Art rode his bike from his house to Jay's house. The boys rode their bikes 3 miles to the park and then 4 miles to the mall. Art rode 9 miles in all. How many miles is Art's house from Jay's house?

Stuck? Try this....

- What do I know?
- What diagram can I use to help understand the problem?
- Can I use addition, subtraction, multiplication, or division?
- Is all of my work correct?
- Did I answer the right question?
- Is my answer reasonable?

For another example, see Set M on page 399.

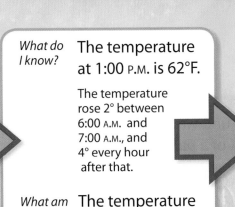

What do I know?	The temperature at 1:00 P.M. is 62°F.
	The temperature rose 2° between 6:00 A.M. and 7:00 A.M., and 4° every hour after that.
What am I asked to find?	The temperature at 6:00 A.M.

Work backward:

Draw a picture to show each change.
Work backward starting at 1:00 P.M.

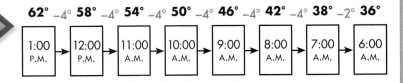

62° –4° **58°** –4° **54°** –4° **50°** –4° **46°** –4° **42°** –4° **38°** –2° **36°**

| 1:00 P.M. | 12:00 P.M. | 11:00 A.M. | 10:00 A.M. | 9:00 A.M. | 8:00 A.M. | 7:00 A.M. | 6:00 A.M. |

The temperature at 6:00 A.M. was 36°F.

6. Nina walked 1 mile on Monday. She walked twice as far on Tuesday. On Wednesday, she walked three more miles than she did on Monday. On Thursday, she walked a mile less than she had walked on Wednesday. How many miles did Nina walk on Thursday? Explain.

7. Georgette bought some craft items. The silk flowers cost three times as much as the ribbon. The ribbon cost double what the foam cost. The vase cost $12, which was three times as much as the foam. How much did the silk flowers cost?

8. Sylvia had $43 after she went shopping. She spent $9 on pet food, $6 on salad items, $12 on soup, and $24 on vegetables. How much money did Sylvia start with?

? money Sylvia started with

| $6 | $9 | $12 | $24 | $43 |

9. Mrs. Harris is planning to drive the twins to a soccer game at 6:00 P.M. They need to arrive 20 minutes early to warm up for the game. It takes 25 minutes to get to the soccer field. What time does Mrs. Harris and the twins need to leave the house?

10. Leslie has 3 boxes of tea in her cupboard. Each box contains 11 tea bags. Each tea bag uses 3 cups of hot water to make a mug of hot tea. How many cups of water will Leslie use if she makes all the tea?

11. The Declaration of Independence was signed in 1776. Three years earlier, the Boston Tea Party took place. Boston was settled 143 years before the Boston Tea Party. What year was Boston settled?

12. Number Sense Use the digits 7, 1, 5, 9, and 3 to write the largest number possible. Use each digit exactly once.

13. Number Sense Use the digits 6, 2, 5, and 4 to write 2 numbers less than 6,000 but greater than 5,500. Use each digit exactly once.

1. Which is the best estimate for the length of an earthworm? (16-1)

A About 3 feet

B About 3 yards

C About 3 miles

D About 3 inches

2. Which is the best estimate of the capacity of a bathroom sink? (16-2)

A 3 gallons

B 3 cups

C 300 cups

D 300 pints

3. Which is the best estimate of the mass of a football? (16-7)

A 400 grams

B 400 kilograms

C 4,000 grams

D 4,000 kilograms

4. A flight departs at 9:56 A.M. It arrives 2 hours and 15 minutes later. What time does the flight arrive? (16-10)

A 12:11 P.M.

B 12:11 A.M.

C 11:11 P.M.

D 11:11 A.M.

5. Which unit would best measure the weight of a pair of scissors? (16-3)

A Pounds

B Ounces

C Tons

D Kilograms

6. It takes a guinea pig about 68 days to develop completely before it is born. Which of these is greater than 68 days? (16-9)

A 1 month

B 1,200 hours

C 9 weeks

D 10 weeks

7. The Hutson family arrived at the Balloon Festival at 7:15 P.M. They left the festival at 9:30 P.M. How long did the family stay at the Balloon Festival? (16-10)

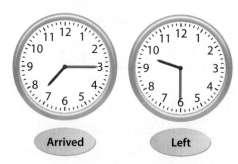

Arrived   Left

A 2 hours and 30 minutes

B 2 hours and 15 minutes

C 1 hour and 30 minutes

D 1 hour and 15 minutes

8. Which is the appropriate unit to measure the length of a school hallway? (16-5)

  A Meters

  B Millimeters

  C Centimeters

  D Kilometers

9. Which of the following holds about 2 liters of water? (16-6)

  A Bathtub

  B Drinking glass

  C Pitcher

  D Eye dropper

10. Which symbol makes the comparison true? (16-4)

  4 yd ◯ 124 in.

  A ×

  B =

  C <

  D >

11. The next total solar eclipse that will be able to be seen in the United States will be on August 21, 2017. It will last 160 seconds. Which symbol makes the comparison true? (16-9)

  160 seconds ◯ 3 minutes

  A ×

  B =

  C <

  D >

12. What would the temperature be if the temperature decreased by 8°F? (16-11)

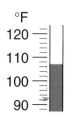

  A 97°F

  B 99°F

  C 101°F

  D 113°F

13. Which symbol makes the comparison true? (16-8)

  200 mL ◯ 2 L

  A ×

  B =

  C <

  D >

14. At 4:30 P.M., the thermometer outside of Yasmine's window read 40°C. It had risen 8° between noon and 4:30 P.M. and 5° between 7:00 A.M. and noon. What was the temperature at 7:00 A.M.? (16-12)

  A 27°C

  B 32°C

  C 35°C

  D 53°C

Set A, pages 364–365

Estimate and measure the length of the piece of ribbon.

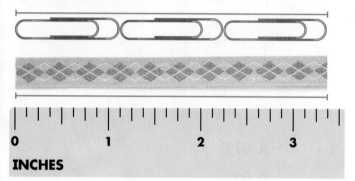

0   1   2   3
INCHES

The ribbon's length is about 3 small paper clips. It is 3 inches long to the nearest inch.

Remember to add when combining measurements.

Choose the most appropriate unit to measure the length of each.

1. airport runway   **2.** bridge

Estimate and measure the length of the eraser below to the nearest inch.

3.

Set B, pages 366–367

Which is the best estimate for the capactiy of the bucket?

2 pints or 2 gallons?

The pint is too small of a unit. The best unit to use is the gallon.

The best estimate is 2 gallons.

Remember that a cup is a smaller measure than a pint.

Which is the best estimate for the capacity of each item?

1.   **2.**

2 cups or 20 cups?   1 gallon or 8 gallons?

Set C, pages 368–369

Which is the best unit to measure the weight of a pear?

Most pears weigh less than a pound.

So, the best unit to use would be the ounce.

Remember to use benchmark weights to compare.

Give the best unit to measure the weight of each item. Write oz, lb, or T.

1. a whale   **2.** an apple

3. a puppy   **4.** a baseball

5. a box of books   **6.** a horse

396

Set D, pages 370–372

Convert 3 gallons to cups.

There are 4 quarts in 1 gallon.
3 gallons × 4 quarts = 12 quarts

There are 2 pints in 1 quart.
12 quarts × 2 pints = 24 pints

There are 2 cups in 1 pint.
24 pints × 2 cups = 48 cups

There are 48 cups in 3 gallons.

Remember when changing from a larger to a smaller unit, you multiply.

1. 5 T = ☐ lb

2. 10 mi = ☐ ft

3. 36 c = ☐ qt

4. 8 fl oz = ☐ tbsp

5. 4 yd = ☐ in.

6. 16 pt = ☐ gal

Set E, pages 374–375

Estimate and measure the length of the crayon.

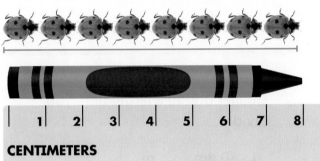

CENTIMETERS

The crayon's length is about 8 ladybugs. It is 8 centimeters long to the nearest centimeter.

Remember you can use objects to help you estimate length.

Give the best unit to measure the length of each. Write cm or m.

1. baseball bat   2. penny

Estimate and measure the length of the magnet below to the nearest centimeter.

3.

Set F, pages 376–377

How much liquid will the bucket hold?

8 mL or 8L?

The milliliter is too small of a unit. The best unit to use is the liter.

The best estimate is 8 liters.

Remember that a liter is a greater measure than a milliliter.

Which is the best estimate for the capacity of each item?

1.   2.

3 mL or 30 mL?   10 liters or 100 milliliters?

Set G, pages 378–379

What is the mass of a cell phone?

1 kilogram is too large for a cell phone. So, a gram would be a better unit to use.

A dollar bill has a mass of about 1 gram.

Estimate how many one-dollar bills have the same mass as a cell phone. About 20 one-dollar bills would have the same mass. So, the mass of a cell phone is about 20 grams.

Measure the mass of a cell phone on a balance.

Place the cell phone on one pan of the balance. Add 1 gram masses to the other side, and count the number of grams.

The cell phone has a mass of 17 grams.

Remember that weight depends on location. Mass always stays the same.

Choose the most appropriate unit, a gram or kilogram, to measure the mass of each item.

1. crayon
2. watermelon
3. carrot
4. wallet
5. bicycle
6. table
7. penny
8. paper clip
9. If you had a mass of 25 kg on Earth, what would your mass be on the planet Mars? Explain.

Set H, pages 380–382

Convert 3 kilograms to grams.

1 kg = 1,000 g
3 kg = 3 × 1,000 g
3 kg = 3,000 g

There are 3,000 grams in 3 kilograms.

Remember when going from a smaller unit to a larger unit, you divide.

1. 50 dm = ▢ m
2. 200 mm = ▢ cm
3. 8,000 g = ▢ kg
4. 90 L = ▢ mL

Set J, pages 384–385

Which is longer, 12 years or 120 months?

Change 12 years to months.

Since 1 year = 12 months, multiply the number of years by 12.

12 years × 12 = 144 months

144 months > 120 months

So, 12 years > 120 months.

Remember to first convert the measurements to the same unit. Then compare the measurements.

1. 36 months ◯ 104 weeks
2. 33 years ◯ 3 decades
3. 90 minutes ◯ 540 seconds
4. 96 months ◯ 8 years
5. 5 centuries ◯ 5,000 years

Set K, pages 386–388

Find the time that has elapsed between 8:45 A.M. and 1:25 P.M.

From 8:45 A.M. to 9:00 A.M. is 15 minutes.
From 9:00 A.M. to 1:00 P.M. is 4 hours.
From 1:00 P.M. to 1:25 P.M. is 25 minutes.
15 minutes + 4 hours + 25 minutes =
4 hours and 40 minutes

Remember to double check your answers for reasonableness.

Find each elapsed time.

1. Start: 8:00 A.M.
Finish: 10:50 A.M.

2. Start: 3:20 P.M.
Finish: 9:35 P.M.

3. Start: 2:39 P.M.
Finish: 4:06 P.M.

4. Start: 3:45 P.M.
Finish: 5:15 P.M.

Set L, pages 390–391

Find the change in temperature.

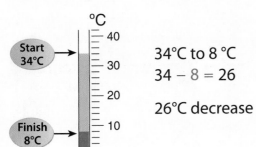

34°C to 8 °C
34 − 8 = 26

26°C decrease

Remember to check whether you are asked to find an answer in Fahrenheit or Celsius degrees.

Find the change in temperature. Tell whether the change is an increase or decrease.

1. 85°F to 29°F **2.** 28°C to15°C

3. 38°F to 62°F **4.** 3°C to 22°C

Set M, pages 392–393

Solve by working backward.

Jerrold checks the thermometer every hour between 12:00 P.M. and 7:00 P.M. He noticed that the temperature decreased 3° each hour from 12:00 P.M. to 4:00 P.M. Then from 4:00 P.M. to 7:00 P.M., the temperature decreased 4° each hour. At 7:00 P.M., the temperature was 57°F. What was the temperature at 12:00 P.M.?

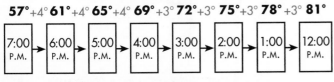

The temperature at 12:00 P.M. was 81°F.

Remember a picture can help you work backward.

1. Brad has trumpet practice at 10:45 A.M. It takes him 15 minutes to get from home to practice and 10 minutes to warm up. What time should he leave home to get to practice on time?

Data and Graphs

1 How many species of endangered mammals were there in the year 2000? You will find out in Lesson 17-5.

2 This long-horned beetle can grow to 7 inches long. How many kinds of beetles are there? You will find out in Lesson 17-2.

3 Emperor penguins cannot fly, but they are great swimmers. How deep can an Emperor penguin dive? You will find out in Lesson 17-6.

④

Japan's Akashi Kaikyo Bridge, shown above, is the longest suspension bridge in the world. How does its length compare to Florida's Sunshine Skyway Bridge, shown below? You will find out in Lesson 17-2.

Review What You Know!

Vocabulary

Choose the best term from the box.

- minute
- seconds
- negative
- thermometer

1. A ? is used to measure temperature.

2. Temperatures below 0 are ? temperatures.

3. There are 60 ? in one minute.

Telling Time

Find the time.

4.

5.

6.

7.

Reading a Thermometer

Find the temperature in Fahrenheit and Celsius.

8. °F   °C
    90
    80   30

9. °F   °C
    80
    70   20
    60

10. **Writing to Explain** Yolanda practices piano 2 hours a week. Pete practices piano 120 minutes a week. They both think that they spend more time practicing. Who is correct?

Understand It!
Taking a survery can
provide information to
solve a problem or answer
a question.

Data from Surveys

How do you take a survey and record the results?

Pizza Plus took a survey to decide which high school team they should sponsor.

In a survey, information is collected by asking different people the same question and recording their answers.

Please Take One

Which of these high school sports teams do you think Pizza Plus should sponsor?

❑ Football

❑ Baseball

❑ Basketball

Guided Practice*

Do you know HOW?

For **1** through **3**, use the tally chart below.

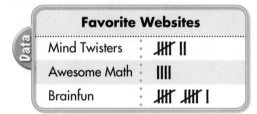

Favorite Websites

Data		
Mind Twisters	卌 II
Awesome Math	IIII
Brainfun	卌 卌 I

1. How many people were surveyed?

2. How many people in the survey liked the Awesome Math website best?

3. Which website was the favorite of more people than any other?

Do you UNDERSTAND?

4. In the survey at the top, do you know whether people thought Pizza Plus should sponsor the soccer team? Why or why not?

5. What question do you think was asked for the survey below?

High School Games Attended Last Year

Data	
Football	卌 卌 II
Basketball	卌
Soccer	卌 卌 IIII
Baseball	卌 III

Independent Practice

For **6** through **8**, use the tally chart at the right.

 Before answering the questions, add up all of the tallies.

6. How many people liked using a pencil the best?

7. How many people were surveyed?

8. Which type of project was the favorite of more people than any other?

Favorite Type of Drawing Project

Data	
Pencil	卌 II
Ink	卌 II
Paint	卌 IIII
Charcoal	IIII

*For another example, see Set A on page 426.

Step 1	Step 2	Step 3
Write a survey question. "Which of these high school sports teams do you think Pizza Plus should sponsor: football, baseball, or basketball?"	Make a tally chart and record the data. Count the tallies and record the results.	Explain the results of the survey. Football was chosen by the most people. So, Pizza Plus should sponsor the football team.

Team to Sponsor

Data			
Football	~~IIII~~ ~~IIII~~ III	13
Basketball	~~IIII~~ III	8
Baseball	~~IIII~~ ~~IIII~~ I	11

Problem Solving

For **9** through **12**, use the tally chart at the right.

9. How many of the people surveyed have pet fish?

10. Which type of pet was owned by the most people?

11. Reasoning Can you tell how many people were surveyed? Why or why not?

12. Reasoning Can you tell how many of the people surveyed have no pets? Why or why not?

Pets Owned

Data	
Dog	~~IIII~~ ~~IIII~~
Cat	~~IIII~~ IIII
Fish	~~IIII~~ III
Hamster	III
Snake	III

13. Elisa bought a camera for $29.50 and 2 rolls of film for $3.50 each. How much did Elisa spend in all?

For **14** and **15**, use the tally chart at the right.

14. What was the total count for each type of show?

15. How many people were surveyed?

Favorite Type of TV Show

Data	
Action	IIII
Animated	III
Comedy	~~IIII~~ III
Sports	~~IIII~~

16. **Think About the Process** At a barbeque, 8 out of 10 people ate hot dogs, and 4 out of 5 people ate hamburgers. Which number sentence shows that the same fraction of people ate hot dogs and hamburgers?

A $10 - 8 = (5 - 4) + 1$

B $10 + 8 = 2 \times (5 + 4)$

C $\frac{10}{8} = \frac{5}{4}$

D $\frac{8}{10} = \frac{4}{5}$

DIGITAL Animated Glossary www.pearsonsuccessnet.com

Interpreting Graphs

Understand It!
Data can be organized and interpreted in a bar graph.

How can you read a bar graph?

A **bar graph** uses bars to show data.

About how many more species of animals are in the Minnesota Zoo than the Phoenix Zoo?

The **interval** is the amount between tick marks on the scale.

The **scale** consists of numbers that show the units used on a graph.

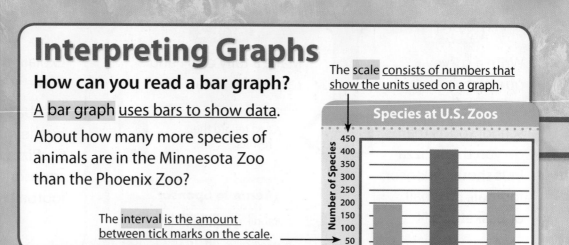

Guided Practice*

Do you know HOW?

For **1** and **2**, use the bar graph below.

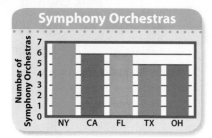

1. Which state shown on the graph has the most symphony orchestras?

2. Which state has the same number of symphony orchestras as Texas?

Do you UNDERSTAND?

3. What is the interval of the scale for the bar graph above?

4. The Miami Metro Zoo has 300 species of animals. Which zoos have a fewer number of species than the Miami Metro Zoo?

5. **Writing to Explain** Explain how you find the difference between the number of species at the San Francisco Zoo and the Phoenix Zoo.

Independent Practice

For **6** through **8**, use the bar graph at the right.

6. About how much longer does a lion live than a giraffe?

7. Which animals have the same average lifespan?

8. The average lifespan of a gorilla is 20 years. How would you change the graph to add a bar for gorillas?

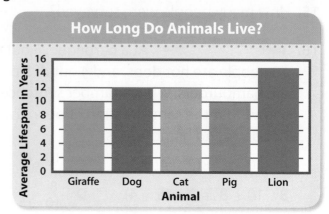

For another example, see Set B on page 426.

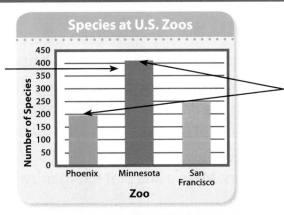

Species at U.S. Zoos

The purple bar is just above the number 400. The Minnesota Zoo has about 400 species of animals.

Skip count by 50s from the top of the green bar (Phoenix Zoo) until you are even with the top of the purple bar (Minnesota Zoo). Count: 50, 100, 150, 200.

The Minnesota Zoo has about 200 more species than the Phoenix Zoo.

Problem Solving

For **9** through **11**, use the graph at the right.

9. Describe the scale of the graph.

10. The Akashi Kaikyo Bridge is about 12,828 feet long. The Sunshine Skyway Bridge is about 29,040 feet long. How many fewer feet is the Akashi Kaikyo Bridge than the Sunshine Skyway Bridge?

11. **Estimation** About how many feet longer is the Sunshine Skyway Bridge than the Tappan Zee Bridge?

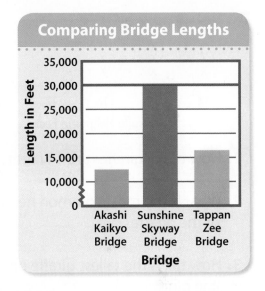

For **12** and **13**, use the graph at the right.

12. There are over 350,000 species of beetles. How does this compare to the number of species shown for moths and butterflies?

13. Which two insects have about the same number of species?

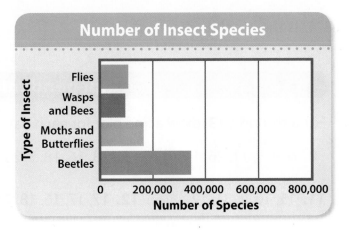

DIGITAL
Animated Glossary
www.pearsonsuccessnet.com

Lesson
17-3

Understand It!
Data can be organized
and displayed in a
line plot.

Line Plots

How can you organize data using a line plot?

A line plot <u>shows data along a number line</u>. Each X represents one number in the data set. An outlier <u>is any number that is very different from the rest of the numbers</u>.

The table below shows the average lifespans of certain animals in years. Make a line plot to organize the data.

Average Animal Lifespan (years)						
Kangaroo	Chicken	Fox	Cow	Wolf	Deer	Black Bear
7	8	9	10	10	10	18

Average
Lifespan:
18 years

Guided Practice*

Do you know HOW?

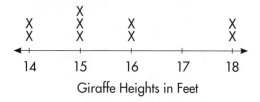

Giraffe Heights in Feet

1. How many giraffes are 14 feet tall?

2. What is the most common height of the giraffes?

3. How tall is the tallest giraffe on the line plot?

4. Is the number 18 an outlier?

Do you UNDERSTAND?

5. Which animals listed above have a lifespan of 10 years?

6. **Writing to Explain** How do you know that the lifespan of the bear is an outlier by looking at the line plot?

7. A mouse has an average lifespan of 2 years. If you included this information on the line plot above, how would it affect the line plot?

Independent Practice

For **8** through **13**, draw a line plot for each data set and identify any outliers.

8. 6, 9, 3, 11, 26

9. 13, 16, 18, 3, 25

10. 18, 17, 11, 15, 29, 14, 16

11. 15, 16, 2, 31, 12

12. 17, 17, 16, 18, 21

13. 25, 28, 22, 24, 27, 28, 21

DIGITAL
Animated Glossary
www.pearsonsuccessnet.com

*For another example, see Set C on page 426.

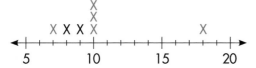

Read the line plot.

```
              X
              X
    X  X  X  X              X
  <-+--+--+--+--+--+--+--+--+--+->
    5     10    15    20
```

The most Xs are above 10 so the most common lifespan of the animals in the table is 10 years.

The greatest lifespan shown is 18 years and the shortest lifespan shown is 7 years.

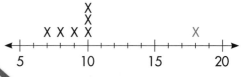

Identify any outliers.

```
              X
              X
    X  X  X  X              X
  <-+--+--+--+--+--+--+--+--+--+->
    5     10    15    20
```

The number 18 is far away from the rest of the numbers on the line plot.

The lifespan of the black bear, 18 years, is an outlier.

Problem Solving

For **14** through **16**, use the data to the right.

14. Trisha's swimming coach recorded the times it took her to swim one lap each day last week. Make a line plot of Trisha's lap times.

15. Which day is an outlier in the data?

16. If you made a line plot of Trisha's time using 0 and 5 minutes as the boundaries, would the outlier be more or less obvious than if the boundaries of your line plot were 50 and 75 seconds? Explain.

Day	Time
Monday	55 seconds
Tuesday	57 seconds
Wednesday	51 seconds
Thursday	72 seconds
Friday	51 seconds

17. Algebra A sheet of coupons is in an array with 12 rows. Each row has six coupons. How many coupons are there on 100 sheets?

18. Writing to Explain Bob listed the weights of his friends (in pounds). They were 87, 93, 89, 61, and 93. Bob said there were no outliers. Is Bob correct?

19. Six friends shared some CDs. Each friend received 3 CDs. How many CDs were there in all?

? CD's shared in all

3	3	3	3	3	3

↑ CDs for each friend

20. Henry and some friends went to play miniature golf. Their scores are shown below. Make a line plot of their scores.

51, 70, 52, 51, 48, 54, 55, 52, 52

Understand It!
A coordinate grid is used to identify the location of points or ordered pairs.

Ordered Pairs
How do you name a point located on a coordinate grid?

A coordinate grid is used to show ordered pairs. An ordered pair is a pair of numbers that name a point on a coordinate grid. Where is point *D* located on the grid?

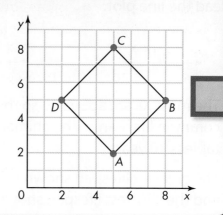

Guided Practice*

Do you know HOW?

For **1** through **6**, write the ordered pair, or name the point.

1. *C* **2.** *E*

3. *D* **4.** (4, 1)

5. (3, 4) **6.** (0, 3)

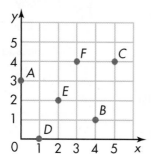

Do you UNDERSTAND?

7. Writing to Explain Without plotting the points, how can you tell that a point at (12, 6) is to the right of a point at (10, 6)?

8. In the example above, which point is at (5, 8)?

9. The coordinates for point *M* are (8, 3). Does point *M* lie inside or outside of the diamond above?

Independent Practice

For **10** through **18**, write the ordered pair for each point.

10. *I* **11.** *J* **12.** *K*

13. *L* **14.** *M* **15.** *N*

16. *O* **17.** *P* **18.** *Q*

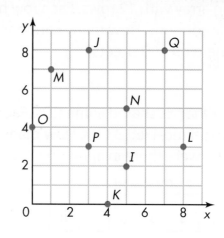

Animated Glossary
www.pearsonsuccessnet.com

For another example, see Set D on page 427.

A location on a coordinate grid is named by an ordered pair (x, y) of numbers.

The x-coordinate, or the first number, tells how many units to move to the right.

The y-coordinate, or second number, tells how many units to move up.

Point D is located at (2, 5).

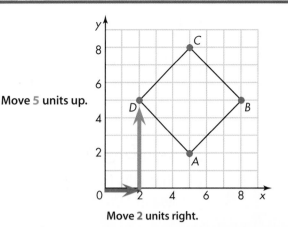

Move 5 units up.

Move 2 units right.

For **19** through **26**, name the point for each ordered pair.

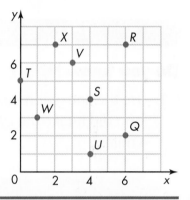

19. (4, 4)   **20.** (1, 3)   **21.** (4, 1)   **22.** (3, 6)

23. (2, 7)   **24.** (6, 2)   **25.** (6, 7)   **26.** (0, 5)

Problem Solving

27. Joanne, Terry, and Shira drank 2 liters of lemonade in all. How many liters did Terry drink if all three drank equal amounts of lemonade?

28. Place these ordered points on a graph: (2, 4), (2, 6), and (2, 8). What do you notice about these points?

29. Bernice ran a 26-mile marathon in 4 hours. In the first two hours, she ran 7 miles each hour. If she also ran equal distances in the third and fourth hours, how many miles did she run in the fourth hour?

30. Geometry A square measures 8 inches by 8 inches. A rectangle measures 4 inches by 16 inches. Both figures have the same area, 64 square inches. Which figure has a greater perimeter?

31. Writing to Explain In the coordinate grid at the right, why is the point (2, 5) different from the point (5, 2)?

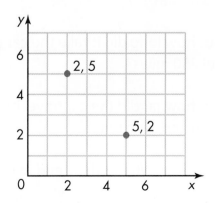

2, 5

5, 2

Lesson
17-5

Understand It!
~~Use line graphs to see~~
changes in data over time.

Line Graphs

How do you read and interpret line graphs?

A line graph <u>connects points to show how data changes over time</u>.

What was the population of Iowa in 1965?

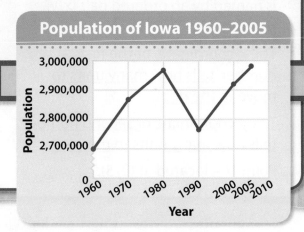

Population of Iowa 1960–2005

Guided Practice*

Do you know HOW?

1. Use the line graph below. About how long did it take the cyclist to travel 4 miles?

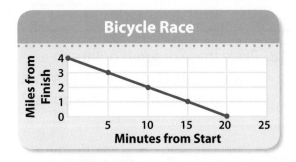

Bicycle Race

Do you UNDERSTAND?

2. Did Iowa's population increase more between 1970 and 1980 or between 1990 and 2000?

3. Would you expect the population of Iowa in 2010 to be more or less than 3 million? Explain your answer.

4. How can you tell when there is an increase from the data on a graph?

Independent Practice

For **5** through **8**, use the graph at the right.

5. About how far did the car travel in the first 8 hours?

6. About how long did it take the car to travel 250 miles?

7. About how far did the car travel between the 6th and 10th hours?

8. **Reasoning** What is the trend in the data?

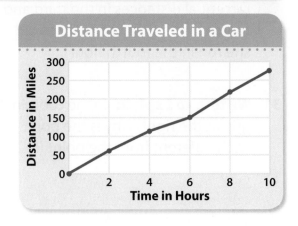

Distance Traveled in a Car

Animated Glossary
www.pearsonsuccessnet.com

The grid line for 2,800,000 crosses the graph between 1960 and 1970.

The population was about 2,800,000 in 1965.

What was the general trend in the population?
<u>The pattern in the data showing an increase or decrease</u> is the trend.

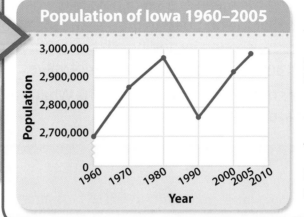
Population of Iowa 1960–2005

The line goes up from 1960 to 1980, decreases from 1980 to 1990, and then increases from 1990 to 2005.

The trend in the population was an increase.

Problem Solving

For **9** through **11**, use the graph to the right.

9. Between which times did Mary ride the fastest?

10. What do you think happened between 9:00 and 9:30?

11. How far did Mary ride in two hours and thirty minutes?

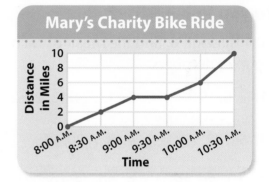
Mary's Charity Bike Ride

For **12** through **16**, use the graph to the right.

12. About how many species of mammals were endangered in 1996?

13. During which four years did the number of endangered mammals increase the least?

14. Estimation About how many more species of endangered mammals were there in 2004 than in 1992?

15. Between which four years did the number of endangered mammals stay the same?

    A 1988–1992   **C** 1996–2000

    B 1992–1996   **D** 2000–2004

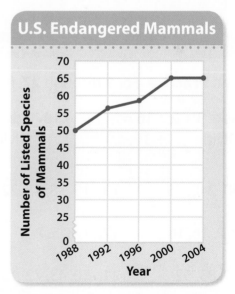
U.S. Endangered Mammals

16. Reasoning What does this graph tell you about the number of endangered species of reptiles?

Lesson
17-6

Understand It!
The mean describes the average of the numbers in a set of data.

Mean

How can you find the mean?

Finding the mean of a set of data tells what is typical of the numbers in the set. The mean, <u>or average, is found by adding all the numbers in a set and dividing by the number of values.</u>

Kara's quiz scores were 7, 7, and 10. What was her average quiz score?

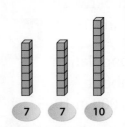

7 7 10

Guided Practice*

Do you know HOW?

For **1** through **6**, find the mean of each group of numbers.

1. 2, 6, 19   **2.** 13, 24, 15, 28, 25

3. 64, 72, 56   **4.** 8, 7, 20, 145

5. 3, 5, 30, 38   **6.** 20, 58, 190, 84

Do you UNDERSTAND?

7. Writing to Explain Why do you need to divide by 4 to find Kara's average test score?

8. Juan's bowling scores were 88, 96, and 113. What is his mean score?

Independent Practice

Leveled Practice For **9** through **27**, find the mean.

9. Add: 3 + 2 + 16 = ▢
Divide: ▢ ÷ 3 = ▢

10. Add: 1 + 5 + 2 + 4 = ▢
Divide: ▢ ÷ 4 = ▢

11. Add: 56 + 32 + 62 = ▢
Divide: ▢ ÷ 3 = ▢

12. 80, 248, 68   **13.** 15, 38, 25, 22   **14.** 35, 45, 75, 85   **15.** 16, 25, 86, 45

16. 2, 2, 16, 16   **17.** 1, 3, 5, 2, 4   **18.** 56, 72, 84, 68   **19.** 18, 19, 20

20. 51, 83, 52   **21.** 30, 43, 72, 15   **22.** 87, 33, 123   **23.** 52, 19, 71, 26

24. 12, 112, 221   **25.** 8, 21, 28   **26.** 1, 1, 106   **27.** 102, 123, 9, 358

DIGITAL

Animated Glossary
www.pearsonsuccessnet.com

To find the average, the items are combined and then divided equally.

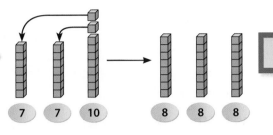

| 7 | 7 | 10 | | 8 | 8 | 8 |

Kara's average quiz score is 8.

Kara's test scores were 82, 76, 94, and 88.

Add the scores.

```
  2
  82
  76
  94
+ 88
 340
```

Divide the sum by the number of addends.

```
     85
  4)340
   - 32
     20
   - 20
      0
```

Kara's average test score is 85.

Problem Solving

28. Number Sense The mean of 16, 16, and 16 is 16. The mean of 15, 16, and 17 is also 16. Find 3 other sets of numbers that have the mean of 16.

29. Algebra What number goes in the box to make this number sentence true?
$(8 - 2) \times 4 = 6 \times$ ☐

30. Geometry Use geometric terms to describe one common characteristic of the shapes in each group.

Group A	△ △ ◁
Group B	▢ ⬠ ⬡

31. Reasoning Jacob worked 5 hours on Thursday, 4 hours on Friday, and 6 hours on Saturday. The number of hours he worked on Sunday did not change the mean. How many hours did Jacob work on Sunday?

Use the chart at the right for **32** through **34**.

32. Estimate how deep an Emperor Penguin dives in yards.

Tip *Remember 1 yard = 3 feet.*

33. How many fewer feet does a Peruvian Petrel dive than a Thick-billed Murre?

34. Find the mean of the dives as listed in the table.

Deepest Dives of Birds in Feet	
Emperor Penguin	1,772 ft
Thick-billed Murre	689 ft
Peruvian Petrel	272 ft

35. Which of these is the number six million, sixteen thousand, one hundred six?

  A 6,160,106   **B** 6,106,106   **C** 6,016,106   **D** 6,016,160

Lesson

17-7

Understand It!
Numbers in a set of
data can be described
by finding the median,
mode, and range.

Median, Mode, and Range

How do you find and use median, mode, and range?

The median is the middle number when the numbers in a data set are listed in order. The mode is the number or numbers that occur most often in the data. The range is the difference between the greatest and the least number in the data set.

What is the median, mode, and range for the heights in inches of a group of fourth graders listed below?

Height (in inches)
57, 55, 50, 52, 51, 56, 55

Data

Guided Practice*

Do you know HOW?

In **1** through **4**, find the median, mode, and range of each set of data.

1. 41, 15, 51, 51, 41

2. 36, 54, 43, 43, 67, 43, 39, 66

3. 11, 67, 34, 14, 42, 12, 34, 62, 33, 57

4. 42, 62, 54, 50, 62, 60, 48

Do you UNDERSTAND?

5. In the example above, how many numbers are less than the median? How many numbers are greater than the median?

6. Writing to Explain Can a group of numbers have more than 1 mode?

7. Does every set of data have a mode? Explain.

Independent Practice

In **8** through **16**, find the median, mode, and range of each set of data.

8. 58, 54, 62, 58, 60

9. 8, 9, 8, 10, 13, 3, 15, 15, 8, 13, 14

10. 23, 46, 52, 41, 41, 52, 66

11. 42, 13, 41, 41, 57, 52, 36

12. 6, 4, 12, 12, 5, 7, 8

13. 31, 63, 24, 15, 15, 26, 53

14. 56, 76, 66, 86, 59

15. 43, 64, 24, 14, 32, 47, 63, 63, 79

16. 49, 19, 45, 45, 48, 21, 19

DIGITAL

Animated Glossary
www.pearsonsuccessnet.com

For another example, see Set G on page 428.

Find the median.

List the data in order from least to greatest, and find the middle number.

50, 51, 52, 55, 55, 56, 57

The median is 55.

Find the mode.

Find the number or numbers that occur most often.

50, 51, 52, 55, 55, 56, 57

The mode is 55.

Find the range.

Subtract the greatest value minus the least value.

50, 51, 52, 55, 55, 56, 57

57 − 50 = 7
The range is 7.

Problem Solving

17. Geometry The perimeter of a triangle is $\frac{5}{6}$ inch. Two sides are $\frac{1}{8}$ inch each. What is the length of the third side?

18. Reasoning Liz said that the mode of the set of data below is 6. Is Liz correct? Explain.

2, 4, 6, 4, 4, 6, 6

19. Geometry If side A of a rectangle is 12.87 cm and side B is 4.89 cm, what is the perimeter of the rectangle?

20. Writing to Explain Could 23 be the median of 6, 8, 23, 4, and 5? Explain.

For **21** through **23**, use the chart to the right. Each X represents how much a person bought at the bake sale.

21. How many people bought 2 items?

22. What is the mode of the data?

23. How many people bought 3 or more items?

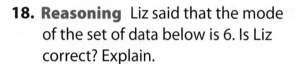

Number of Items Bought

24. What division sentence do the beads to the right model?

  A 24 ÷ 6 = 4

  B 24 ÷ 8 = 3

  C 29 ÷ 5 = 5 R4

  D 28 ÷ 4 = 4 R5

Stem-and-Leaf Plots

How do you read stem-and-leaf plots?

Understand It!
Stem-and-leaf plots organize data using place value.

Shelby's scores in a game of horseshoe are listed to the right.

What are the median, mode, and range of Shelby's scores?

A display that shows data in order of place value is a stem-and-leaf plot.

Data

Shelby's Horseshoe Toss Scores
4, 6, 12, 16, 20, 18, 14, 12, 10, 4, 8, 12, 20

Guided Practice*

Do you know HOW?

For **1** and **2**, use the stem-and-leaf plot below.

1. How many numbers are there in the stem-and-leaf plot?

Stem	Leaf
2	0 1
3	0 0 2 8
4	0 1 4 7

2. Find the mode of the data.

Do you UNDERSTAND?

3. For the number 18, what digit is the stem? What digit is the leaf?

4. Writing to Explain What is Shelby's lowest score? How does the stem-and-leaf plot help you find the least number?

Independent Practice

For **5** through **10**, use the stem-and-leaf plot to the right.

5. How many scores are greater than 48 points?

6. Which stem is **NOT** needed for the stem-and-leaf plot? Why?

7. Find the least score.

8. Find the median.

9. Find the mode.

10. Find the range.

Park County School Basketball Scores

Stem	Leaf
3	2 3 9
4	7 8 8 8
5	2 2
6	1
7	

Animated Glossary
www.pearsonsuccessnet.com

*For another example, see Set H on page 428.

The numbers can be organized using a stem-and-leaf plot.

The tens digit in each number is a **stem**.

The ones digit in each number is a **leaf**.

Stem	Leaf
0	4 4 6 8
1	0 2 2 2 4 6 8
2	0 0

The stems and leaves are arranged in order from least to greatest.

Use the stem-and-leaf plot to find the median, mode, and range.

median The seventh number in the stem-and-leaf plot is the median. The median is 12.

mode The number that appears most often has a stem of 1 and a leaf of 2. The mode is 12.

range The least number is 4. The greatest number is 20. $20 - 4 = 16$. The range is 16.

Problem Solving

For **11** through **13**, use the stem-and-leaf plot to the right.

11. What number is represented by the 8 in the second row?

12. How many of Gary's test scores were more than 85?

13. Find the median, mode, and range of Gary's test scores.

Gary's Math Test Scores

Stem	Leaf
7	2 7 7
8	5 8
9	2 2 2 9

14. Writing to Explain How does looking at the data in a stem-and-leaf plot help you find the median and mode of the data?

15. Writing to Explain The information in stem-and-leaf plots can be used to make bar graphs. Explain how you could turn a stem-and-leaf plot into a bar graph.

For **16** and **17**, use the net to the right.

16. What solid does the net create?

17. Algebra If the volume of the solid is 250 cubic units, what is the length of x?

Net of a Solid

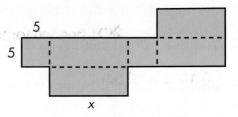

18. Reasoning Which leaf in a stem-and-leaf plot belongs to the greatest number?

19. What is the mode of data below?

A 3

B 4

C 13

D 24

Stem	Leaf
0	4 6
1	3 3 3 4 7
2	1 4 4

Reading Circle Graphs

How do you read and interpret circle graphs?

Kelli surveyed her classmates about their favorite music types. Her results are shown in the circle graph to the right.

<u>A graph in the shape of a circle that shows how a whole is broken into parts</u> is a circle graph.

What fraction of students liked country music?

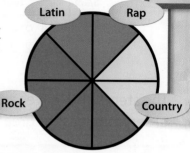

Guided Practice*

Do you know HOW?

For **1** and **2**, use the circle graph at the right.

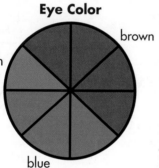

Eye Color

1. What fraction of the people surveyed have blue eyes?

2. Which eye color do half of the people surveyed have?

Do you UNDERSTAND?

3. One-half of the students surveyed in the example above liked which type of music?

4. What fraction of the students surveyed preferred Latin music to rock music?

5. **Writing to Explain** What information can you tell from a circle graph more easily than from a table? Explain.

Independent Practice

For **6** through **10**, use the circle graph to the right.

6. What fraction of planets have more than 2 moons?

7. What fraction of the planets have 20 or more moons?

8. What fraction of planets have between 3 and 19 moons?

9. What fraction of planets have less than 20 moons?

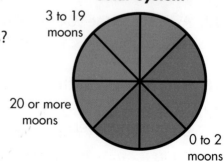

The Number of Moons for Each Planet in Our Solar System

Animated Glossary
www.pearsonsuccessnet.com

The circle graph is divided into eight equal sections. Two of the eight sections are yellow.

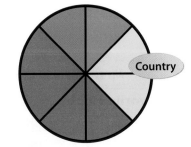

Country

$\frac{2}{8} = \frac{1}{4}$

One-fourth of the students surveyed liked country music.

What fraction of the students liked Latin and rap music combined?

Look at the graph. Think about benchmark fractions.

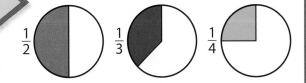

$\frac{1}{2}$ $\frac{1}{3}$ $\frac{1}{4}$

One-fourth of the people liked Latin and rap music combined.

Problem Solving

For **10** through **12**, use the circle graph at the right.

10. What fraction of the people drank between 6 to 8 glasses of water per day?

11. What fraction of the people drank 4 to 5 glasses of water?

12. Writing to Explain Could you use the circle graph to find out how many people drank exactly 7 glasses each day?

Glasses of Water Per Day

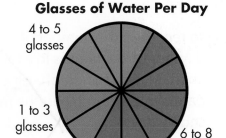

4 to 5 glasses

1 to 3 glasses

6 to 8 glasses

13. Geometry A box measures 4.7 feet long, 3 feet wide, and 4 feet tall. What is the volume of the box?

14. Tom's five practice run times in minutes were 12, 14, 15, 12, and 12. What was his mean time?

15. Don is taking a survey to see how many hours the 4th graders sleep each night. If he wants to show all of his data, would it be better for him to use a circle graph or a stem-and-leaf plot? Explain.

16. Gabriella mixed $\frac{2}{3}$ of a can of red paint with $\frac{1}{4}$ of a can of yellow paint to make a dark orange. How much of a can of orange paint does she have?

Nick's Budget

Entertainment   Clothes

Food

Apartment

17. The circle graph to the right shows Nick's budget for the month. What fraction of his budget does he spend on food?

  A $\frac{1}{20}$ **B** $\frac{1}{4}$ **C** $\frac{1}{2}$ **D** $\frac{3}{4}$

Understand It!
Learning how and when to make a graph can help you solve problems.

Problem Solving

Make a Graph

Students in two fourth-grade classes completed a survey about their favorite hobbies. How were the two classes similar? How were they different?

Mr. Foster's Class	
Favorite Hobby	**Tally**
Swimming	~~||||~~ ~~||||~~ ~~||||~~
Cycling	~~||||~~ ~~||||~~
Art	~~||||~~

Mrs. Lopez's Class	
Favorite Hobby	**Tally**
Swimming	~~||||~~ ~~||||~~	
Cycling	~~||||~~ ~~||||~~ |||
Art	~~||||~~

Guided Practice*

Do you know HOW?

Solve. Make a graph.

1. Jo recorded the number of snowy days for three months in a tally chart. Make a bar graph using this data. Which month had the most snowy days?

Month	Tally Snowy Days	Number
December	~~||||~~	5
January	~~||||~~ ~~||||~~		11
February	~~||||~~ |||	8

Do you UNDERSTAND?

2. How could you make different bar graphs to display the same data from the tally charts above?

3. Suppose you added the numbers from both classes to make one data table. Which hobby was the most popular overall?

4. **Write a Problem** Write a problem that uses the data charts above. Then answer your question.

Independent Practice

For **5** and **6**, use the table below.

	Morning	Afternoon	Evening
Cars	142	263	120
Trucks	42	181	64

5. Make two graphs of this data, one for cars and one for trucks.

6. Why is it useful to use the same scale for both graphs?

Stuck? Try this....
- What do I know?
- What diagram can I use to help understand the problem?
- Can I use addition, subtraction, multiplication, or division?
- Is all of my work correct?
- Did I answer the right question?
- Is my answer reasonable?

For another example, see Set K on page 429.

Make a bar graph for each data chart.

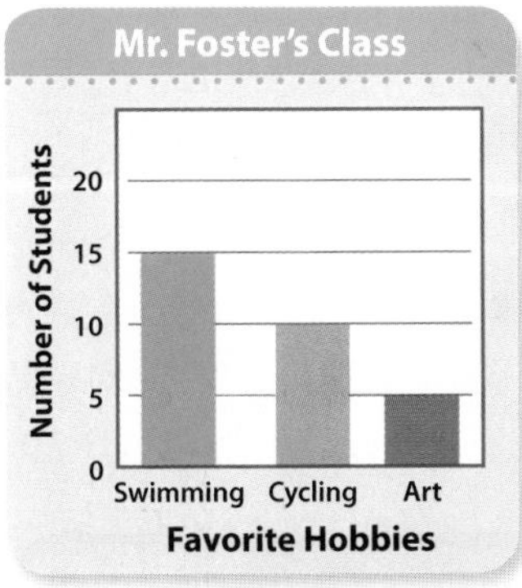

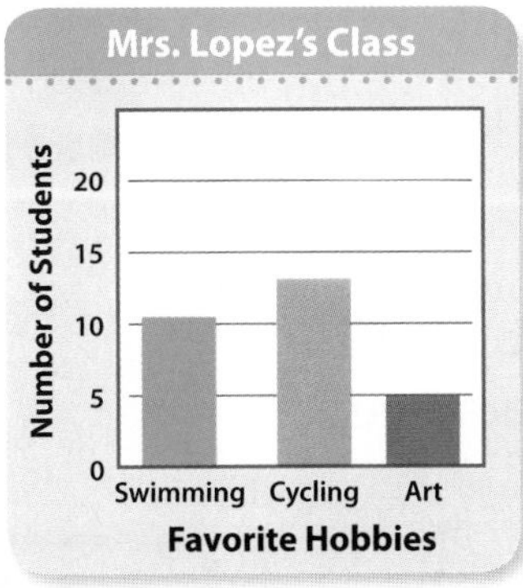

Mr. Foster's Class

Number of Students

20
15
10
5
0

Swimming Cycling Art

Favorite Hobbies

Mrs. Lopez's Class

Number of Students

20
15
10
5
0

Swimming Cycling Art

Favorite Hobbies

Read the graphs.
Make comparisons.

How they are similar:

Art was the least popular hobby in both classes, and the same number of students in each class liked art.

How they are different:

Swimming was the favorite hobby in Mr. Foster's class, and cycling was the favorite hobby in Mrs. Lopez's class.

For **7** through **10**, use the tally chart below.

Data

Activity	2008	2009
Newspaper	𝍷𝍷𝍷𝍷𝍷 𝍷𝍷𝍷𝍷𝍷	𝍷𝍷𝍷𝍷𝍷 𝍷𝍷𝍷𝍷𝍷
Dance Troupe	𝍷𝍷𝍷𝍷𝍷	𝍷𝍷𝍷𝍷𝍷 𝍷
Book Club	𝍷𝍷𝍷𝍷𝍷	𝍷𝍷𝍷𝍷𝍷
Marching Band	𝍷𝍷𝍷𝍷	𝍷𝍷𝍷𝍷𝍷 𝍷

7. The fourth grade students chose which of four activities they wanted to join. Make a bar graph for 2008 and another bar graph for 2009.

8. If 3 people in 2009 left the book club to join the dance troupe, which club would have the most students?

9. Identify two clubs in 2009 that together were chosen by more than half of the fourth grade students.

10. How many more students joined a club in 2009 than in 2008?

For **11** through **13**, use the table to the right.

11. Who biked 15 miles less than Sherry in Week 1?

12. Which person biked fewer miles in Week 2 than in Week 1?

13. **Reasoning** Use the table to compare the total miles biked in Week 1 to the total miles biked in Week 2. Which was greater?

Data

Distances Biked		
Name	Week 1	Week 2
Peter	17 miles	26 miles
Sherry	25 miles	29 miles
Jorgé	22 miles	20 miles
Carla	10 miles	20 miles

For **14** and **15**, use the diagram to the right.

14. Stella picks one marble from Bag 1. How many possible outcomes are there?

15. **Writing to Explain** How many marbles will Stella have to take from Bag 3 to guarantee she will draw a blue marble?

For **16** and **17**, use the table at the right.

16. Marcia recorded the number of sit-ups and push-ups she did last week. Make two graphs using the data in the table.

17. Compare the number of sit-ups each day to the number of push-ups. What pattern do you notice? What can you conclude?

Bag 1	Bag 2

Bag 3

Marcia's Sit-ups and Push-ups

Day	Sit-ups	Push-ups
Monday	25	12
Tuesday	21	16
Thursday	55	24
Friday	32	12
Sunday	68	28

For **18** and **19**, use the diagram at the right.

18. Ms. Michael planted the flowers in her garden in an array. After she fills in the fifth row, how many flowers will her garden have?

19. If Ms. Michael continues to plant using the same pattern of colors, what will be the colors of the next three flowers that she plants?

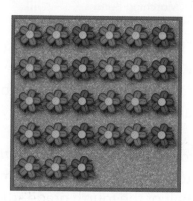

Think About the Process

20. There are 14 park benches in the park. Each bench holds 4 people. Which number sentence shows the greatest number of people who can sit on park benches at one time?

   A $14 \times 4 =$ ▇

   B $14 + 4 =$ ▇

   C $14 \times 14 =$ ▇

   D $4 \times 4 =$ ▇

21. Hanna walked to and from school on Monday, Wednesday, and Friday. What information is needed to find how far she walked?

   A The distance from home to school

   B Who she walked with

   C The number of streets she crossed

   D The time school starts

Misleading Graphs

Use 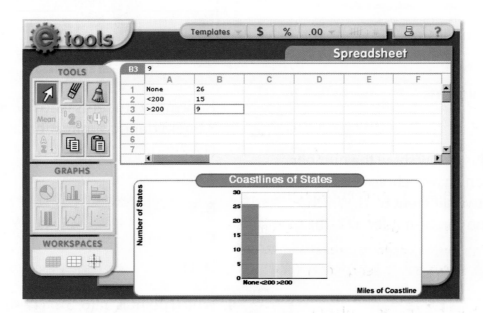e tools Spreadsheet/Data/Grapher.

In the United States, 26 states have no coastline along an ocean, 15 states have less than 200 miles of coastline, and 9 states have more than 200 miles.

Step 1 Go to the Spreadsheet/Data/Grapher eTool. Enter the data as shown below.

Step 2 Use the arrow tool to select the 2 columns and 3 rows with information. Click on the bar graph icon. Enter the graph title and label the x- and y- axes. Make the interval 5, the minimum 0, and the maximum 30. Click OK.

Step 3 Click in the graph area. Change the minimum to 5 and click OK. Compare the graphs. The second graph is misleading.

Practice

1. Alaska has 19 mountain peaks that are more than 14,000 feet high and Colorado has 54 mountain peaks. Graph the data. First, use a scale from 0 to 60, and make the interval 10. Then change the minimum to 10. Describe the different impressions each graph gives.

1. Which subject was the favorite of more students than any other? (17-1)

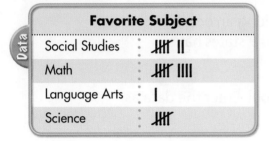

Favorite Subject	
Social Studies	JHT II
Math	JHT IIII
Language Arts	I
Science	JHT

A Social Studies

B Math

C Language Arts

D Science

2. The graphs below show the number of times an answer choice was used on two different tests. Which conclusion can be made? (17-10)

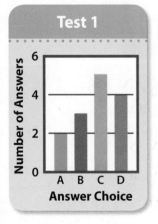

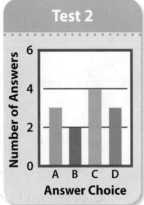

A Answer C was used most often in both tests.

B Answer B was used least often in both tests.

C Answer D was used the same number of times in both tests.

D No conclusions can be made.

3. Mrs. Chi made a bar graph of the number of books students read over summer break.

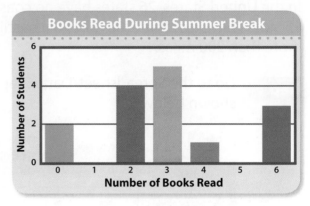

How many students read fewer than 3 books during summer break? (17-2)

A 4

B 5

C 6

D 11

4. Which point is at (6, 3)? (17-4)

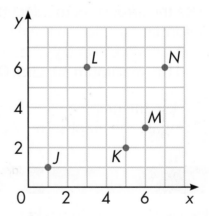

A Point J

B Point K

C Point L

D Point M

5. As part of a class fundraiser, students received money for each lap they ran around the school's parking lot.

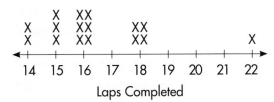

Laps Completed

What is the outlier in this set of data? (17-3)

A 8

B 16

C 22

D There is no outlier in this data set.

6. Jared's scores on his last four math assignments are listed below. What was his mean score? (17-6)

82, 76, 82, and 100

A 24

B 79

C 82

D 85

7. What fraction of the people surveyed like Mexican food best? (17-9)

A $\frac{1}{3}$

B $\frac{1}{4}$

C $\frac{1}{8}$

D $\frac{2}{3}$

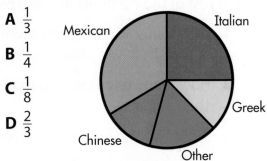

8. What is the median of the data? (17-8)

Stem	Leaf
2	2 4
3	5 5 8 8 9
4	1 1 1 4

A 22

B 38

C 39

D 41

9. Between which times did the temperature increase 10°F? (17-5)

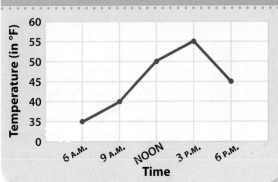

A Between 6 A.M. and 9 A.M.

B Between 9 A.M. and noon

C Between noon and 3 P.M.

D Between 3 P.M. and 6 P.M.

10. What is the range for this set of data? (17-7)

12, 10, 48, 64, 36, 48, 12, 32, 48

A 10

B 36

C 48

D 54

Set A, pages 402–403

How many people in the survey liked to watch the rings event?

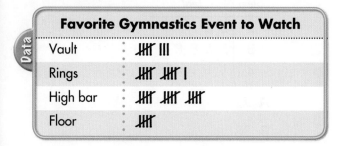

Favorite Gymnastics Event to Watch	
Vault	𝍷𝍷𝍷𝍷𝍷 III
Rings	𝍷𝍷𝍷𝍷𝍷 𝍷𝍷𝍷𝍷𝍷 I
High bar	𝍷𝍷𝍷𝍷𝍷 𝍷𝍷𝍷𝍷𝍷 𝍷𝍷𝍷𝍷𝍷
Floor	𝍷𝍷𝍷𝍷𝍷

Eleven people liked to watch the rings event best.

Remember that you can answer a question by taking a survey.

1. How many people in the survey liked to watch the vault best?

2. Which event was the favorite of more people than any other event?

3. Can you tell from the survey whether people liked to watch the uneven bars? Explain.

Set B, pages 404–405

Which animal has about 34 teeth?

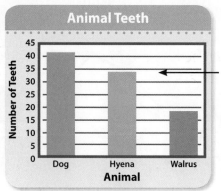

The top of the bar for hyenas is below the line for 35.

Hyenas have about 34 teeth.

Remember that looking at the scale can help you interpret the data.

1. What is the graph about?

2. What is the scale of the graph? What is the interval?

3. Which animal has 18 teeth?

4. About how many more teeth does a dog have than a hyena?

Set C, pages 406–407

The data set below shows the number of goals scored by 20 teams in a soccer tournament. What is the mode?

4, 8, 7, 0, 3, 3, 7, 4, 6, 1, 2, 7, 6, 4, 2, 7, 2, 6, 7, 4

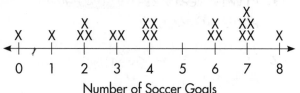

The mode is 7.

Remember that an outlier is a number that is very different from the rest of the numbers in a line plot.

1. How many soccer teams scored 3 goals?

2. How many teams scored more than 5 goals?

3. What was the greatest number of goals scored by a team?

4. How many teams scored only 2 goals?

Set D, pages 408–409

Write the ordered pair for point *M*.

Move **4** units to the right. The *x*-value is 4.

Move **8** units up. The *y*-value is 8.

The ordered pair for *M* is (4, 8).

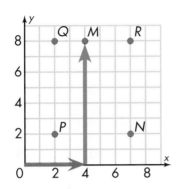

Remember that the first coordinate is the *x*-value, and the second coordinate is the *y*-value.

Write the ordered pair or name the point.

1. A   **2.** C   **3.** D   **4.** F

5. (7, 4) **6.** (6, 2) **7.** (5, 2) **8.** (6, 9)

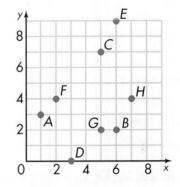

Set E, pages 410–411

Look at the graph below.

How much money was made in charity donations in the year 2000?

When the year is 2000, the amount of donations is $4,000.

Between what years did the amount in donations decrease?

When the y-value decreases, the graph will appear to go downhill.

The amount in donations decreased between 2001 and 2002.

Remember the line graph shows the trend of the data points.

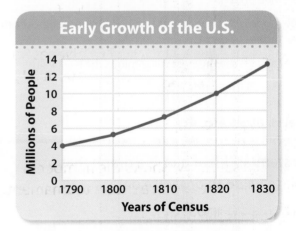

1. In what year was the population about 10 million?

2. What is the change in population from 1790 to 1820?

3. What is the overall trend?

Set F, pages 412–413

What is the mean of 77, 95, 78, and 86?

Add the numbers in the set.

```
  2
 77
 95
 78
+ 86
───
336
```

Divide the sum by the number of addends.

```
      84
  4)336
   - 32
   ───
     16
   - 16
   ───
      0
```

The mean of the set is 84.

Remember that the mean is found by adding all the numbers in a set first.

Find the mean of each group of numbers.

1. 5, 8, 17   **2.** 18, 19, 14, 29, 35

3. 68, 73, 51   **4.** 6, 2, 22, 146

5. 10, 10, 30, 34   **6.** 28, 52, 195, 89

Set G, pages 414–415

What is the median, mode, and range of this set of numbers?

12, 4, 8, 3, 26, 8, 17, 6, 12, 7, 5, 23

The median is the middle number when the data is ordered.

3, 4, 5, 6, 7, 8, 8, 12, 12, 17, 23, 26

The median is 8.

The mode is the number or numbers that occur most often. The mode is 8 and 12.

The range is the greatest value minus the least value.

26 − 3 = 23. The range is 23.

Remember there can be more than one mode.

Find the median, mode, and range of each set of data.

1. 1, 3, 10, 8, 7, 3, 11

2. 48, 50, 62, 50, 54

3. 92, 99, 100, 99, 106, 99, 97

4. 80, 85, 87, 80, 89

Set H, pages 416–417

A stem-and-leaf plot is a graph that uses place value to organize data.

The stem is the digit in the tens place, and the leaves are the digits in the ones place.

Stem	Leaf
1	2 8
2	
3	9
4	
5	1 1 2 2 2 9

What number is represented by the 9 in the third row?

Remember that the stems and leaves are in order from least to greatest.

Use the stem-and-leaf plot on the left.

1. Find the median.

2. Find the mode.

3. Find the range.

The stem is 3, and the leaf is 9.
The number is 39.

Set J, pages 418–419

What fraction of the people surveyed liked game shows?

Favorite Types of Shows

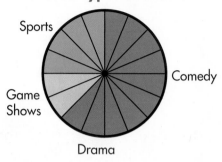

Two of the 16 sections are yellow.

$$\frac{2}{16} = \frac{1}{8}$$

$\frac{1}{8}$ of the people liked game shows.

What fraction of the people liked sports shows?

$\frac{1}{4}$ of the circle graph is shaded green for sport shows.

Remember the part of the circle filled in for a value is the fraction of the data represented by that value.

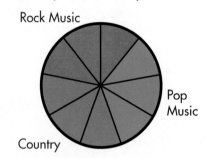

1. What fraction of people liked rock music?

2. What fraction of people liked country music?

3. Do more or less than half of the people like country music or pop music?

Set K, pages 420–422

How can you use a bar graph to find which team is in second place in the standings?

Volleyball Wins	
Hawks	10
Lions	14
Falcons	12
Bears	7

Choose a scale. Choose an interval. Make a bar for each team. Label the axis and give the graph a title.

The Falcons are in second place.

Remember to use a scale that starts at 0 and goes beyond the highest number in the data when you draw a bar graph.

1. How can you check whether the bars on the graph are correctly drawn?

2. What is the interval of the graph?

3. Which team came in third place?

Topic 18

Equations

1 The United States produces about 17.2 million bales of cotton each year. In the fields, cotton is compressed into modules that can weigh more than 6 tons. How many bales are in a module? You will find out in Lesson 18-2.

2 How hot does it get in Death Valley? You will find out in Lesson 18-4.

Review What You Know!

Vocabulary

Choose the best term from the box.

- data
- survey
- scale
- mean

1. A _?_ is a series of numbers along the axis of a graph.

2. Collected information is called _?_ .

3. The _?_ is found by adding all numbers in a set and dividing by the number of values.

Comparing Units of Time

Copy and complete. Write >, <, or = in the ◯.

4. 3 years ◯ 365 days

5. 4 weeks ◯ 40 days

6. 48 hours ◯ 2 days

Subtract Whole Numbers

Use the bar graph. How much higher is

7. Peak 1 than Peak 3?

8. Peak 3 than Peak 4?

9. **Writing to Explain** Why is this statement incorrect? The heights of Peak 2 and Peak 4 have the greatest difference.

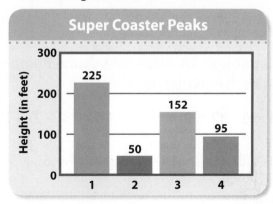

3

In 1969, Apollo 11 became the first space mission to land people on the moon. How long did the trip to the moon take? You will find out in Lesson 18-3.

Lesson
18-1

Understand It!
Expressions on each
side of an equation
are equal.

Equal or Not Equal

How can you change both sides of an equation so that it stays true?

An equation is <u>a number sentence stating that two expressions are equal.</u>

Decide if these equations are true. Use the balance scale to the right.

Does $5 + 3 - 3 = 8 - 3$?

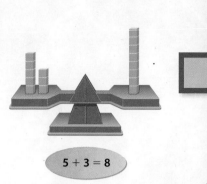

$5 + 3 = 8$

Guided Practice*

Do you know HOW?

For **1** through **4**, tell if the equation is true or false.

1. $8 + 6 + 2 = 14 + 2$

2. $50 \div 5 \div 2 = 8 \div 2$

3. $12 \times 2 = 24 \times 2$

4. $15 - 5 = 10 - 5$

Do you UNDERSTAND?

5. In the first example above, how can you tell that the equation is true using a pan balance?

6. Writing to Explain If 5 is being subtracted from different numbers on both sides of an equation, is the equation true?

Independent Practice

For **7** through **12**, tell if the equation is true or false.

7. $5 \times 3 - 8 = 12 - 8$

8. $8 \div 2 + 4 = 4 + 4$

9. $4 + 7 - 2 = 11 - 9$

10. $6 \times 3 + 10 = 18 + 10$

11. $2 \times 3 + 6 = 6 + 6$

12. $18 \div 3 - 2 = 6 - 2$

For **13** through **18**, write the missing number that makes each equation true.

13. $4 \times 6 = (2 \times 2) \times \boxed{}$

14. $(14 - 2) \div 2 = \boxed{} \div 2$

15. $6 + \boxed{} = (3 \times 2) + 9$

16. $(6 + 8) \div \boxed{} = 14 \div 2$

17. $(4 + 5) \div 3 = \boxed{} \div 3$

18. $\boxed{} + (9 - 5) = 8 + (9 - 5)$

Animated Glossary
www.pearsonsuccessnet.com

DIGITAL

For another example, see Set A on page 444.

Is this true?

$5 + 3 - 3 = 8 - 3$

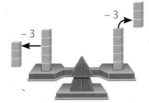

−3

−3

You can add or subtract the same number from both sides of an equation and the sides remain equal.

Check by finding the value of each side.

$5 + 3 - 3 = 8 - 3$
$8 - 3 = 5$
$5 = 5$

The equation is true.

Is this true?

$10 \div 2 = 5 \times 2 \div 5$

You can multiply both sides of an equation by the same number or divide both sides of an equation by the same number except 0 and the sides remain equal.

Check by finding the value of each side.

$10 \div 2 = 5 \times 2 \div 5$
$5 = 10 \div 5$
$5 \neq 2$

The equation is false.

Problem Solving

19. The equation $8 + 4 = 7 + 5$ shows that Hope and Cole have the same number of bookmarks. What equation would show how many bookmarks each has after giving away 3 bookmarks?

20. Rich delivers newspapers in his neighborhood. He started with 27 customers. Then 9 customers canceled their orders, and he gained 9 new customers. How many customers does Rich have now?

21. Harry has 8 autographed baseballs. He gave 2 to his sister and half of what he had left to his brother. How many autographed baseballs does he have now?

22. Becky says $16 - 2 \times 7$ is equal to 14×7. Is Becky correct? Why or why not?

For **23** and **24**, use the table at the right.

A class was asked how many siblings each student had. The results are listed in the table.

23. What fraction of the students has more than 1 sibling?

24. What fraction of the class has fewer than 2 siblings?

Students' Siblings	
Number of Siblings	Fraction of Class
Zero	$\frac{2}{3}$
One	$\frac{1}{30}$
Two	$\frac{1}{5}$
Three or more	$\frac{1}{10}$

Data

25. If ☆ $+ 25 = $ △ $+ 25$ which statement is true?

A ☆ $=$ △

B ☆ $=$ △ $- 25$

C ☆ $>$ △

D ☆ $>$ △ $+ 25$

26. Writing to Explain Explain why $4 \times 3 + 6$ has a different value than $4 \times (3 + 6)$.

Understand It!
Use an inverse operation to solve addition and subtraction equations.

Solving Addition and Subtraction Equations

How can you use addition and subtraction to solve equations?

Two operations that undo each other are called inverse operations. How many blocks should be removed from each side to get b by itself? Solve for b.

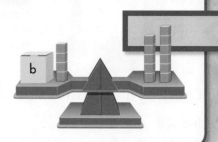

Guided Practice*

Do you know HOW?

1. $r + 3 = 12$

$r + 3 -$ ▢ $= 12 -$ ▢

$r =$ ▢

2. $s - 5 = 9$

$s - 5 +$ ▢ $= 9 +$ ▢

$s =$ ▢

3. $t + 23 = 61$

$t + 23 -$ ▢ $= 61 -$ ▢

$t =$ ▢

Do you UNDERSTAND?

4. In the second example above, why do you add 10 to both sides?

5. Henry balanced box n and 12 blocks on one side of a pan balance and 16 blocks on the other side. How many blocks should he remove from both sides to find the weight of n?

Independent Practice

Leveled Practice For **6** through **11**, solve for each ▢.

6. $c - 4 = 16$

$c - 4 +$ ▢ $= 16 +$ ▢

$c =$ ▢

7. $e + 7 = 19$

$e + 7 -$ ▢ $= 19 -$ ▢

$e =$ ▢

8. $z - 6 = 21$

$z - 6 +$ ▢ $= 21 +$ ▢

$z =$ ▢

9. $p + 8 = 18$

$p + 8 -$ ▢ $= 18 -$ ▢

$p =$ ▢

10. $q - 5 = 17$

$q - 5 +$ ▢ $= 17 +$ ▢

$q =$ ▢

11. $m + 1 = 8$

$m + 1 -$ ▢ $= 8 -$ ▢

$m =$ ▢

For another example, see Set B on page 444.

A **solution** is <u>the value of the variable that makes the equation true</u>.

Solve $b + 4 = 11$.

Undo adding 4 by subtracting 4 from each side.

$b + 4 - 4 = 11 - 4$

Simplify each side.

$b = 7$

The solution to $b + 4 = 11$ is 7.

Solve $n - 10 = 30$.

Undo subtracting 10 by adding 10 to each side.

$n - 10 + 10 = 30 + 10$

Simplify each side.

$n = 40$

The solution to $n - 10 = 30$ is 40.

For **12** through **19**, solve each equation.

12. $c - 4 = 23$ **13.** $e + 7 = 53$ **14.** $d - 6 = 3$ **15.** $4 + s = 17$

16. $x + 200 = 400$ **17.** $z - 8 = 3$ **18.** $y + 37 = 42$ **19.** $m - 51 = 29$

Problem Solving

20. There are 3 bones in each finger and 2 bones in each thumb. How many bones are in two hands?

21. Reasonableness Debra solved the equation $f - 17 = 40$ and got 50. Is this solution reasonable? Explain.

22. Estimation Grace is exactly 9 years old. Is she more or less than 500 weeks old today?

23. A factory can produce 30,000 pairs of sneakers each day. About how many days will it take to produce 600,000 pairs?

24. Think About the Process A school is selling magazine subscriptions to raise money. The first week they sold 435 subscriptions. If their goal is to sell 640 subscriptions in two weeks, which equation would you use to find how many subscriptions need to be sold in the second week?

A $s - 435 = 640$

B $s - 640 = 435$

C $s + 435 = 640$

D $640 + 435 = s$

25. Reasoning At harvest time, most of the cotton in the fields is compressed into modules. A large module weighs 7 tons. How many bales of cotton are in a large module?

Tons of Cotton	1	3	5	7
Bales of Cotton	4	12	20	

Lesson
18-3

Understand It!
Use an inverse
operation to solve
multiplication and
division equations.

Solving Multiplication and Division Equations

n books in
7 groups

How can you use multiplication and division to solve equations?

Jolene organized *n* books into 7 groups. Each group had 6 books. How many books did Jolene have? She wrote the equation $n \div 7 = 6$ to show the result. What is the value of *n*?

Guided Practice*

Do you know HOW?

1. $m \div 6 = 6$
$m \div 6 \times \boxed{} = 6 \times \boxed{}$
$m = \boxed{}$

2. $t \times 9 = 63$
$t \times 9 \div \boxed{} = 63 \div \boxed{}$
$t = \boxed{}$

3. $n \div 7 = 4$
$n \div 7 \times \boxed{} = 4 \times \boxed{}$
$n = \boxed{}$

Do you UNDERSTAND?

4. In the first example above, what is another way to describe the problem?

5. In the second example above, why must the solution to $w \times 4 = 32$ be less than 32?

6. Write an equation to show the following: Jolene put 16 books into *g* groups. Each group had 4 books. Find the value of *g*.

Independent Practice

Leveled Practice For **7** through **12**, solve for each ▨ .

7. $p \div 3 = 6$
$p \div 3 \times \boxed{} = 6 \times \boxed{}$
$p = \boxed{}$

8. $r \times 7 = 49$
$r \times 7 \div \boxed{} = 49 \div \boxed{}$
$r = \boxed{}$

9. $t \div 6 = 1$
$t \div 6 \times \boxed{} = 1 \times \boxed{}$
$t = \boxed{}$

10. $n \times 9 = 45$
$n \times 9 \div \boxed{} = 45 \div \boxed{}$
$n = \boxed{}$

11. $q \div 5 = 4$
$q \div 5 \times \boxed{} = 4 \times \boxed{}$
$q = \boxed{}$

12. $s \times 3 = 15$
$s \times 3 \div \boxed{} = 15 \div \boxed{}$
$s = \boxed{}$

For another example, see Set C on page 445.

Solve $n \div 7 = 6$ to find the number of books, n.

$n \div 7 = 6$

The inverse of dividing by 7 is multiplying by 7.

$n \div 7 \times 7 = 6 \times 7$

Simplify each side.

$n = 42$

The solution to $n \div 7 = 6$ is 42.

Jolene has 42 books.

Solve $w \times 4 = 32$.

The inverse of multiplying by 4 is dividing by 4.

$w \times 4 \div 4 = 32 \div 4$

Simplify each side.

$w = 8$

The solution to $w \times 4 = 32$ is 8.

For **13** through **22**, solve each equation.

13. $t \div 5 = 7$ **14.** $3 \times e = 18$ **15.** $j \div 4 = 8$ **16.** $d \div 3 = 3$ **17.** $c \div 5 = 5$

18. $2 \times r = 32$ **19.** $s \div 7 = 3$ **20.** $m \times 7 = 63$ **21.** $p \div 3 = 2$ **22.** $7 \times a = 56$

Problem Solving

23. Howard did homework from 5:05 P.M. until 6:23 P.M. Half of that time was spent studying for a science exam. How long did Howard study for the science exam?

24. Thomas spent 140 minutes every week practicing guitar. Write and solve an equation using multiplication to find out how many minutes Thomas practiced every day.

25. Algebra If the pattern below continues, what will the next three numbers be?

22, 23, 25, 28, 32, ▢ **,** ▢ **,** ▢

26. Writing to Explain Why must the solution to $6 \times k = 12$ be less than 12?

27. *Apollo 11* was the first mission to land people on the moon. Launched in 1969, the flight to the moon took about 75 hours. The average speed of the spacecraft was 5,200 kilometers per hour. Use the formula $d = r \times t$, distance = rate × time, to find the distance from Earth to the moon.

Tip *The rate is 5,200 kilometers per hour.*

28. A little league team is selling T-shirts. If their goal is to sell 90 T-shirts total and they average 15 T-shirts a week, which equation would you **NOT** use to find out how many weeks they will be selling T-shirts?

A $15 \times w = 90$ **C** $90 \div w = 15$

B $w \times 15 = 90$ **D** $w \div 90 = 15$

Understand It!
To solve an inequality, find values of the variables that make the inequality true.

Understanding Inequalities

How can you solve an inequality?

An inequality uses > and < to show that two expressions do not have the same value.

One solution to the inequality $x > 5$ is $x = 7$ because $7 > 5$. Inequalities have more than one solution. Graph all of the solutions of $x > 5$.

0 1 2 3 4 5 6 7

Guided Practice*

Do you know HOW?

For **1** and **2**, write the inequality that each graph represents.

1. $z \bigcirc \blacksquare$

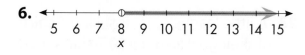

10 11 12 13 14 15 16 17 18 19 20
z

2. $c \bigcirc \blacksquare$

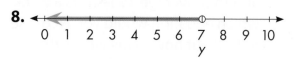

0 1 2 3 4 5 6 7 8 9 10
c

Do you UNDERSTAND?

3. Explain why 7 is a solution to $x > 5$.

4. Explain why 2 is **NOT** a solution to $x > 5$.

5. How does the number line above imply that 5.1 and 50 are solutions to $x > 5$?

Independent Practice

For **6** through **11**, write the inequality that each graph represents.

6.
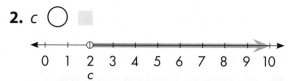
5 6 7 8 9 10 11 12 13 14 15
x

7.
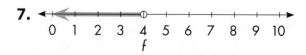
0 1 2 3 4 5 6 7 8 9 10
f

8.
0 1 2 3 4 5 6 7 8 9 10
y

9.
0 1 2 3 4 5 6 7 8 9 10
b

10.
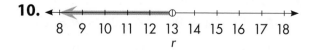
8 9 10 11 12 13 14 15 16 17 18
r

11.
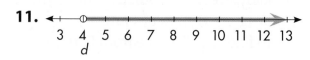
3 4 5 6 7 8 9 10 11 12 13
d

DIGITAL

Animated Glossary
www.pearsonsuccessnet.com

For another example, see Set D on page 445.

Step 1

To graph x > 5, draw an open circle at 5 on a number line.

0 1 2 3 4 5 6 7 8 9 10

The open circle shows that 5 is not a solution.

Step 2

Find several solutions and color those on a number line.

0 1 2 3 4 5 6 7 8 9 10

7 and 9 are solutions because 7 > 5 and 9 > 5.

Step 3

Start at the open circle and color over the solutions you found. Draw an arrow to show that the solutions go on forever.

0 1 2 3 4 5 6 7 8 9 10

For **12** through **16**, name three solutions to each inequality, and graph all the solutions on a number line.

12. $y < 3$ **13.** $c > 5$ **14.** $m > 22$ **15.** $z < 11$ **16.** $h > 8$

Problem Solving

17. Writing to Explain For the inequality $g > 6$, Patty said 6 is a solution. Is she correct? Why or why not?

18. An airline allows passengers to take one piece of carry-on luggage. The carry-on has to be less than 20 pounds. Use the inequality $c < 20$ to find three possible weights of carry-on luggage.

19. A square has 4 right angles and 4 congruent sides. If one side is 9 inches, what is its perimeter and area?

20. In 5 basketball games, Janelle scored 10, 7, 8, 12, and 8 points. What is the mean, median, and mode of her scores?

21. Number Sense The number line to the right shows the inequality $x > 7$. Is 7.1 a solution? Is 7.01 a solution? Explain how you can tell.

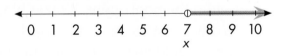

22. Death Valley is the hottest place in the United States. The highest temperature recorded there was 134°F. The lowest temperature recorded was 15°F. Name three possible temperatures recorded in Death Valley.

23. What number below would NOT be a solution to the inequality $v > 12$?

A 12   **C** 12.1

B 15   **D** 13.11

Understand It!
Learning how and when to work backward can help you solve problems.

Work Backward

We can use operation trains to build numbers.
Here is one example:

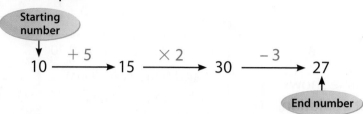

Starting number

$$10 \xrightarrow{+5} 15 \xrightarrow{\times 2} 30 \xrightarrow{-3} 27$$

End number

Guided Practice*

Do you know HOW?

Solve by working backward. Use an operation train to find your answer.

1. Charlie picked some peppers from his garden. He gave 14 peppers to his brother and 7 peppers to his neighbor. He has 24 peppers left. How many peppers did Charlie pick from his garden?

Do you UNDERSTAND?

2. In the example above, how can you check the answer?

3. **Write a Problem** Write a problem that uses an operation train. Then work backward to answer your question.

Independent Practice

Work backward to solve each problem. Write the answer in a complete sentence.

4. Kenny wants to get to the pool 25 minutes before the pool opens. It takes him 20 minutes to drive, and 15 minutes to pack up. At what time should he start packing up if the pool opens at 5:30 P.M.?

5. Drew drove to Karen's house. He drove 2 miles west, then 4 miles south, and 1 mile east. How can Drew drive home from Karen's house using the same path?

Stuck? Try this....

- What do I know?
- What diagram can I use to help understand the problem?
- Can I use addition, subtraction, multiplication, or division?
- Is all of my work correct?
- Did I answer the right question?
- Is my answer reasonable?

Use the operation train below. Find the starting number, *x*.

If you know the end number and how the number was built, you can work backward to find the beginning number.

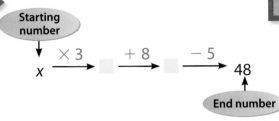

Starting number

x $\xrightarrow{\times 3}$ ▪ $\xrightarrow{+ 8}$ ▪ $\xrightarrow{- 5}$ 48

End number

Do the inverse of the given operations and work backward.

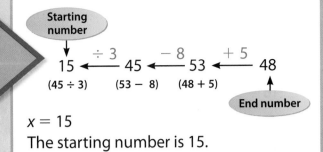

Starting number

15 $\xleftarrow{\div 3}$ 45 $\xleftarrow{- 8}$ 53 $\xleftarrow{+ 5}$ 48

(45 ÷ 3) (53 − 8) (48 + 5)

End number

$x = 15$
The starting number is 15.

6. Alice shredded cheese to top 6 pizzas. She spread 4 ounces of cheese on 5 of the pizzas. On the sixth pizza, she added twice as many ounces. She had 2 ounces of shredded cheese left. How many ounces of cheese did Alice shred?

7. Andy bought a 78-piece puzzle. He put some of the pieces together by himself. He and his brother put 24 more pieces together. Andy's sister then put 33 more pieces together to finish the puzzle. How many pieces did Andy put together himself?

8. Tara is 6 years older than Karen. Karen is 5 years younger than Dave. Dave is 3 years older than Luz. If Luz is 10 years old, how old is Tara?

9. Jason is thinking of a number. He adds 8, multiplies by 2, subtracts 4, and then divides by 2. The result is 24. What number is Jason thinking of?

10. Wendy took the bus to get to the mall. At the first stop, 8 people got off and 5 came on. At the next stop, 4 people got off and 3 more came on. There were 26 people left on the bus. How many people were on the bus when Wendy got on?

   A 5 people   C 22 people

   B 20 people   D 30 people

11. Kristy has band practice at 10:40 A.M. It takes her 15 minutes to get from home to practice. She spends 5 minutes before practice warming up. What time should she leave home to get to practice on time?

   A 10:15 A.M.   C 10:45 A.M.

   B 10:20 A.M.   D 11:00 A.M.

12. Joel took home a list of words to practice for a spelling bee competition. He already knew 12 of the words on the list. His mom tested him on 23 words. His dad asked him to spell 18 words. Joel had 22 words left to practice on his own. How many words were on Joel's list?

? Spelling words in all			
12	23	18	22

1. Find the missing number that makes the equation true. (18-1)

   $(6 + 9) \div 3 = \boxed{} \div 3$

   A 54

   B 15

   C 5

   D 3

2. How many counters equal the weight of box s? (18-2)

   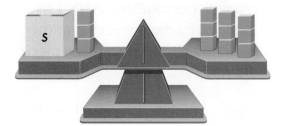

   A 3

   B 6

   C 9

   D 12

3. Mrs. Iverson bought 8 identical packages of pencils. She bought a total of 48 pencils. How many pencils did each package have? Let p equal the number of pencils in each package. Use the equation $8 \times p = 48$ to solve the problem. (18-3)

   A 384 pencils

   B 40 pencils

   C 6 pencils

   D 4 pencils

4. Solve the equation below. (18-2)

   $w - 28 = 59$

   A 89

   B 87

   C 32

   D 31

5. Which number makes the equation true? (18-1)

   $12 \div \boxed{} = 6 + 6 \div 2$

   A 2

   B 3

   C 4

   D 6

6. Which equation is true? (18-1)

   A $45 \div 9 \times 9 = 5 + 9$

   B $45 \div 9 - 9 = 5 + 9$

   C $45 \div 9 + 9 = 5 + 9$

   D $45 \div 9 \div 5 = 5 \div 5$

7. Which graph represents the inequality $x < 14$? (18-4)

   A
   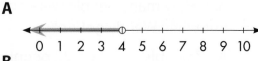

   B
   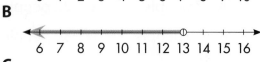

   C
   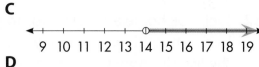

   D

8. Gentry has won a number of trophies. He put the trophies on 4 different shelves. Each shelf had 5 trophies. Gentry used the equation $t \div 4 = 5$ to find the number of trophies he had. What should Gentry do to find the value of t? (18-3)

A Divide each side by 4.

B Divide each side by 5.

C Multiply each side by 4.

D Multiply each side by 5.

9. The equation below shows that Joseph and Dillon both had some money, spent some of the money, and then earned more money.

Joseph   Dillon

$(17 - 8) + 5 = (12 - \boxed{}) + 5$

How much money did Dillon spend? (18-1)

A 8

B 5

C 4

D 3

10. What is the value of n? (18-2)

$n - 15 = 8$

A 38

B 33

C 23

D 7

11. Veronica bought a bouquet of 14 flowers for her mother. The bouquet had 8 daisies and some roses. Which equation would Veronica use to find how many roses, r, were in the bouquet? (18-2)

A $8 + r = 14$

B $8 \times r = 14$

C $r - 8 = 14$

D $8 + 14 = r$

12. Which inequality is graphed on the number line below? (18-4)

0 1 2 3 4 5 6 7 8 9 10

A $m > 0$

B $m < 7$

C $m > 7$

D $m < 10$

13. What is the value of x in the diagram below? (18-5)

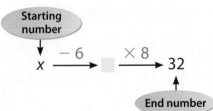

A 4

B 6

C 8

D 10

Set A, pages 432–433

Is this equation true?

$6 + 4 - 4 = 10 - 4$

When you perform the same operation on both sides of an equation, the equation is true.

$6 + 4 - 4 = 10 - 4$ Subtract 4 from both sides.

$10 - 4 = 6$ Find the value of each side.

$6 = 6$

The equation is true.

Is this equation true?

$12 \div 2 = 6 \times 2 \div 4$

The equation is false because both sides were not divided by the same number.

Remember that both sides of an equation must have the same value for the equation to be true.

Tell whether each equation is true or false.

1. $7 + 7 - 4 = 14 - 4$

2. $3 + 5 \times 8 = 8 \times 4$

3. $3 + 9 - 2 = 12 - 2$

4. $6 \times 8 + 12 = 48 + 12$

Write the number that makes each equation true.

5. $11 + 4 = 5 + \boxed{} + 4$

6. $18 - 9 - 2 = 9 - \boxed{}$

7. $2 \times 2 \times 2 = \boxed{} \times 2$

Set B, pages 434–435

Solve $x + 7 = 41$.

Use subtraction to undo addition.

$x + 7 - 7 = 41 - 7$ Subtract 7 from each side.

$x = 34$ Simplify each side.

The solution to $x + 7 = 41$ is 34.

Solve $y - 14 = 50$.

Use addition to undo subtraction.

$y - 14 + 14 = 50 + 14$ Add 14 to each side.

$y = 64$ Simplify each side.

The solution to $y - 14 = 50$ is 64.

Remember to add or subtract the same amount from both sides of the equation.

Solve each equation.

1. $y + 20 = 31$ **2.** $n - 10 = 36$

3. $r + 16 = 40$ **4.** $v - 25 = 25$

5. $l + 5 = 20$ **6.** $n - 8 = 17$

7. $x + 32 = 42$ **8.** $y - 18 = 13$

9. $p + 15 = 30$ **10.** $q - 11 = 19$

11. $s + 16 = 95$ **12.** $m - 15 = 0$

Set C, pages 436–437

Solve $n \div 6 = 5$.

Use multiplication to undo division.

$n \div 6 \times 6 = 5 \times 6$ Multiply each side by 6.

$n = 30$ Simplify each side.

The solution to $n \div 6 = 5$ is 30.

Remember to use division to undo multiplication.

1. $n \times 2 = 18$ **2.** $y \div 10 = 36$

3. $m \times 12 = 36$ **4.** $y \div 6 = 5$

5. $z \times 5 = 125$ **6.** $t \div 7 = 4$

Set D, pages 438–439

Name three solutions for $r < 15$, and graph the inequality on a number line.

Draw a number line with an open circle at 15.

10 11 12 13 14 15 16 17 18 19 20

On the number line, r can be any number less than 15. Find three solutions and mark those on a number line.

Start at the open circle and color over the solutions you found. Draw an arrow to show that all numbers less than 15 are solutions.

10 11 12 13 14 15 16 17 18 19 20

Remember you use an open circle to show that the number the circle is on is not a solution.

Write the inequality that each graph represents.

1.

5 6 7 8 9 10 11 12 13 14 15
s

2.

0 1 2 3 4 5 6 7 8 9 10
m

3.

20 21 22 23 24 25 26 27 28 29 30
j

Set E, pages 440–441

What is the value of x?

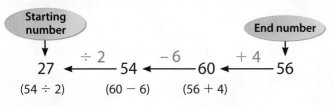

Start with the end number. Use inverse operations to work backward to find x.

Starting number

$27 \xleftarrow{\div 2} 54 \xleftarrow{-6} 60 \xleftarrow{+4} 56$ End number

$(54 \div 2)$ $(60 - 6)$ $(56 + 4)$

The value of x is 27.

Remember to identify all the steps in the process before working backward.

Work backward to solve.

1. For a school play, Juan sold 18 tickets, Teri sold 14 tickets, and Al sold 22 tickets. If they ended up with 45 unsold tickets, how many tickets did they start with?

Transformations, Congruence, and Symmetry

1 The Hall of Mirrors in Versailles, France, contains 357 mirrors. How long is the room? You will find out in Lesson 19-2.

2 How many lines of symmetry does the Thomas Jefferson Memorial in Washington, D.C. have? You will find out in Lesson 19-5.

In this M.C. Escher drawing, what are some of the ways these horses have been moved? You will find out in Lesson 19-1.

Review What You Know!

Vocabulary

Choose the best term from the box.

- inequality
- congruent
- symmetric
- equation

1. A figure is ? if it can be folded on a line to form two congruent halves.

2. A number sentence that uses the equal sign to show that two expressions have the same value is an ?.

3. Figures that are the same size and shape are ?.

Inequalities

Write the inequality for each number line.

4. 0 1 2 3 4 5 6 7 8 9 10

5. 5 6 7 8 9 10 11 12 13 14 15

6. 10 11 12 13 14 15 16 17 18 19 20

7. 35 36 37 38 39 40 41 42 43 44 45

Multiplying Three Factors

8. $3 \times 5 \times 5$ 9. $6 \times 2 \times 4$ 10. $1 \times 15 \times 2$

11. $8 \times 8 \times 6$ 12. $4 \times 10 \times 9$ 13. $20 \times 7 \times 3$

14. $2 \times 5 \times 4$ 15. $3 \times 3 \times 3$ 16. $4 \times 10 \times 2$

17. **Writing to Explain** Leo can make 3 dozen bagels an hour. If he makes bagels for 8 hours, how many bagels will be made?

Understand It!
The size and shape of a figure do not change when it is translated.

Translations

What is one way to move a figure?

A translation moves a figure up, down, left, or right.

In this honeycomb, the hexagon is translated to the right.

Hands-On
set of polygons
grid paper

Guided Practice*

Do you know HOW?

For **1** through **4**, tell if the figures are related by a translation.

1.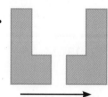

2.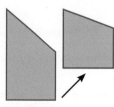

3.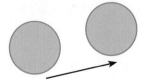

4.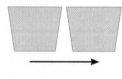

Do you UNDERSTAND?

5. Does a translation change a figure's shape or size?

6. Is moving a figure horizontally a translation?

7. Does moving a ruler across your desk affect its shape?

8. **Writing to Explain** Can a translation of a figure be done in many different directions?

Independent Practice

For **9** through **17**, tell if the figures are related by a translation. You may use grid paper or pattern blocks to decide.

Tip *Another name for translation is slide.*

9.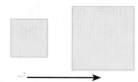

10.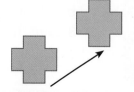

11.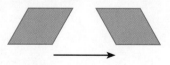

12.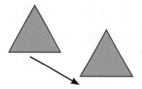

13.

14.

DIGITAL

Animated Glossary, eTools
www.pearsonsuccessnet.com

For another example, see Set A on page 464.

When a figure is translated, the size and shape of the figure do not change.

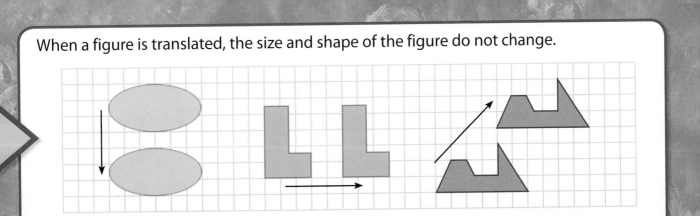

15.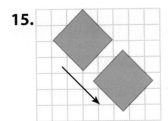

16.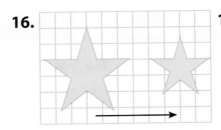

17.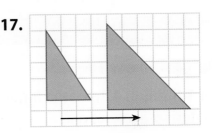

For **18** and **19**, use the table at the right.

18. How many sticks would you need to make 10 kites?

19. How many kites could you make with 60 sticks?

Number of Kites	Number of Sticks
1	2
2	4
3	6

Data

20. A triangle has two congruent sides and a 140° angle. What type of triangle is it?

21. Which of the following best represents a translation?

    A A bouncing ball   **C** A snake slithering

    B A leaf falling   **D** A hockey puck sliding

22. In the M.C. Escher drawing at the right, which horse(s) are a translation of the horse labeled X?

    A Horse A   **C** Horses A and C

    B Horse B   **D** Horses A, B, and C

Symmetry Drawing 78 By M.C. Escher

23. On grid paper, draw a rectangle that moves to the right 3 units and then down 5 units. Is this a translation (slide)? Explain.

Lesson
19-2

Understand It!
The size and shape of a figure do not change when it is reflected.

Reflections

Hands-On
set of polygons

grid paper

What is one way to move a figure?

A reflection of a figure <u>gives its mirror image</u>.

The guitar below has been reflected across the line.

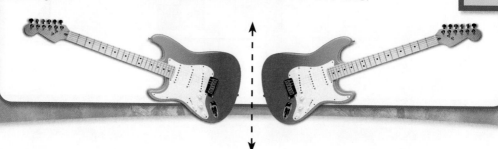

Guided Practice*

Do you know HOW?

For **1** through **4**, tell if the figures are related by a reflection.

1.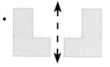

2.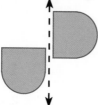

3.

4.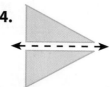

Do you UNDERSTAND?

5. Does a reflection change a figure's size or shape?

6. **Writing to Explain** Is the second triangle a reflection of the first triangle?

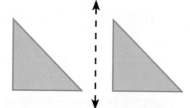

Independent Practice

For **7** through **12**, tell if the figures are related by a reflection. You may use grid paper or pattern blocks to decide.

Tip *Another name for reflection is flip.*

7.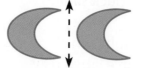

8.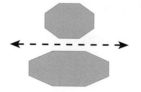

9.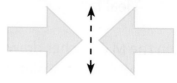

10.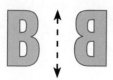

11.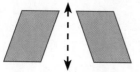

12.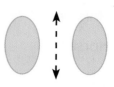

DIGITAL Animated Glossary, eTools
www.pearsonsuccessnet.com

For another example, see Set A on page 464.

When a figure is reflected, the size and shape of the figure do not change.

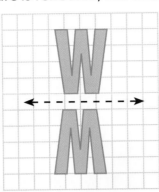

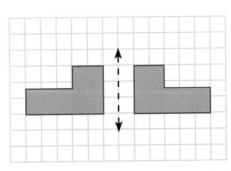

For **13** through **15**, draw the reflection (flip) of the given figure.

13.
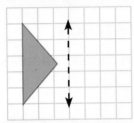

14.
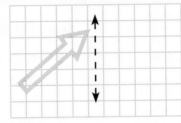

15.
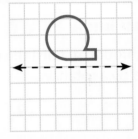

Problem Solving

16. In the drawing below, explain why the figure on the right is not a reflection of the figure on the left.

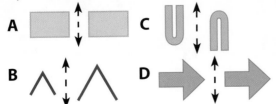

17. Draw an example of two figures that look the same when they are translated and when they are reflected.

18. Vanessa can run five miles in fifty minutes. If she keeps this pace, how many miles can she run in sixty minutes?

19. Number Sense How can you tell that you have made a mistake if you find that $540 \div 5 = 18$?

20. Which shows a pair of figures related by reflection (flip)?

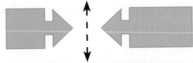

21. The Hall of Mirrors in the Palace of Versailles in France is 73 meters long. If you stand at one end and look at yourself in the mirror at the other end, how far away would your reflection appear to be?

? meters total	
73	73

22. Writing to Explain How is a reflection different from a translation?

Lesson
19-3

Understand It!
The size and shape of a figure do not change when it is rotated.

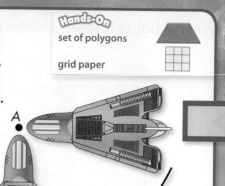

Rotations

Hands-On
set of polygons
grid paper

What is one way to move a figure?

A rotation moves a figure around a point.

In a computer game, you rotate a spaceship. It rotates as shown about point *A*.

A

Guided Practice*

Do you know HOW?

For **1** through **4**, tell if the figures are related by a rotation.

1.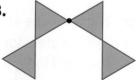

2.

3.

4.

Do you UNDERSTAND?

5. Does a rotation change a figure's size or shape?

6. Can every figure be rotated so that it lands on top of itself?

7. If you rotate the arrow below 180 degrees about point *X*, in which direction will the arrow be pointing?

Independent Practice

For **8** through **13**, tell if the figures are related by a rotation. You may use grid paper or pattern blocks to decide.

Tip *Another name for rotation is turn.*

8.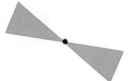

9.

10. (figure)

11. (figure)

12.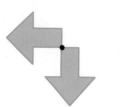

13.

DIGITAL
Animated Glossary, eTools
www.pearsonsuccessnet.com

*For another example, see Set A on page 464.

When a figure is rotated, the size and shape of the figure do not change.

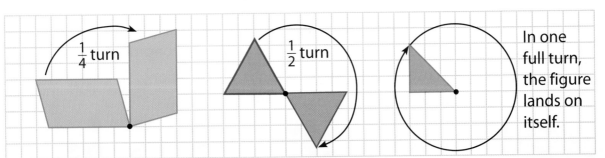

In one full turn, the figure lands on itself.

For **14** through **16**, copy each figure on grid paper. Then draw a rotation of the figure $\frac{1}{4}$ turn to the right.

14.
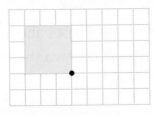

15.
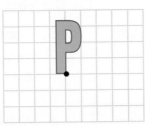

16.
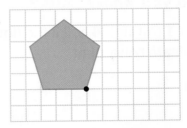

17. The sum of the angles of a pentagon is 540°. If every angle of the pentagon is the same measure, what is the measure of each of its angles?

18. What figure is formed when a triangle has rotated $\frac{1}{4}$ turn?

   A Circle   **C** Rectangle

   B Square   **D** Triangle

19. The shape to the right shows a pattern of translations, reflections and rotations. Describe each step.

For **20** through **22**, use the table at the right.

20. How much does one Tetra cost?

21. Cal bought 2 guppies and 4 tiger barbs. How much did he pay?

22. How much would it cost to buy 1 of each fish?

Fish	Price
Guppies	5 for $1.50
Tetras	3 for $6.00
Tiger Barbs	4 for $4.00

Lesson
19-4

Understand It!
Figures can be compared by their size and shape.

Congruent Figures
When are figures congruent?

Figures that are the same size and shape are congruent.

You can use translations, reflections, and rotations to test if two figures are congruent.

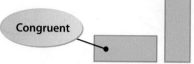

Guided Practice*

Do you know HOW?

For **1** through **4**, tell if the figures in each pair are congruent.

1.  2.

3.  4.

Do you UNDERSTAND?

5. If one of the house shapes above is rotated $\frac{1}{4}$ turn, will the two shapes still be congruent?

6. **Writing to Explain** Can a circle and a square ever be congruent? Why or why not?

Independent Practice

For **7** through **15**, tell if the figures in each pair are congruent.

7. 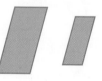 8.   9.

10. 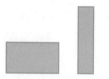 11.  12.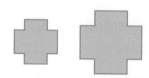

13.  14. 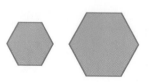 15.

*For another example, see Set B on page 464.

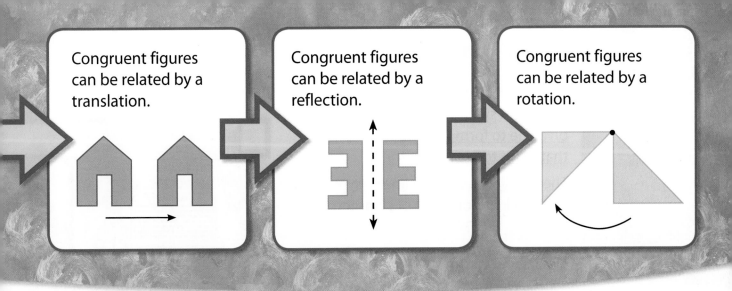

| Congruent figures can be related by a translation. | Congruent figures can be related by a reflection. | Congruent figures can be related by a rotation. |

Problem Solving

For **16** and **17**, describe everything that is the same and everything that is different about each pair of figures. Then tell if the figures are congruent.

16.

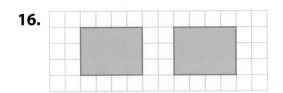

17.

18. Draw one line segment to connect the opposite corners of a square. What polygons have you created? Are these polygons congruent?

19. On a bus ride, Jasmine counted 24 taxis and 12 buses. How many buses and taxis did she count in all?

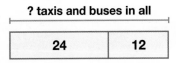

? taxis and buses in all

| 24 | 12 |

20. Reasoning Use the diagram below. Frida wrote a message on paper and held it up to a mirror. What does the message say?

21. Ozzie and Sam both travel 30 minutes to get to work each day. To get to work last week, Ozzie drove for three hours, and Sam drove for an hour and thirty minutes. How many more days did Ozzie work than Sam?

22. How many days are in 52 weeks?

   A 59 days   **C** 365 days

   B 364 days   **D** 366 days

DIGITAL
Animated Glossary
www.pearsonsuccessnet.com

Lesson

19-5

Understand It!
Some figures have two
halves that are congruent.

Line Symmetry

Hands-On
grid paper

What is a line of symmetry?

A figure is symmetric if it can be folded
on a line to form two congruent halves
that fit on top of each other.

The fold line is called a line of symmetry.
This truck has one line of symmetry.

Guided Practice*

Do you know HOW?

For **1** and **2**, tell if each line is a line
of symmetry.

1.  **2.**

For **3** and **4**, tell how many lines of
symmetry each figure has.

3.  **4.**

Do you UNDERSTAND?

5. Do some figures have no lines
of symmetry?

6. How many lines of symmetry does
the figure below have?

7. Writing to Explain How many
lines of symmetry does a bicycle
tire have?

Independent Practice

For **8** through **11**, tell if each line is a line of symmetry.

8.   **9.** 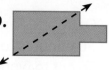 **10.**   **11.**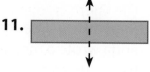

For **12** through **15**, tell how many lines of symmetry each figure has.

12.  **13.**   **14.**   **15.**

For another example, see Set C on page 464.

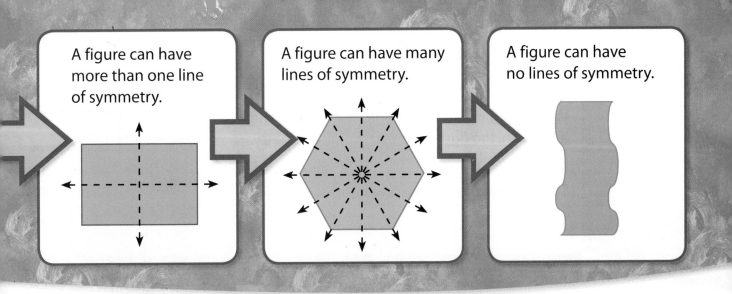

A figure can have more than one line of symmetry.

A figure can have many lines of symmetry.

A figure can have no lines of symmetry.

For **16** through **23**, trace each figure on grid paper, and draw lines of symmetry if you can.

16.

17.

18.

19.

20.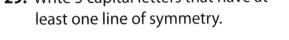

21.

22.

23.

24. How many lines of symmetry does a scalene triangle have?

25. How many lines of symmetry does an isosceles triangle have?

26. Reasoning Vanessa drew a figure and said that it had an infinite number of lines of symmetry. What figure did she draw?

27. Draw a quadrilateral that does not have a line of symmetry.

28. The Thomas Jefferson Memorial in Washington, D.C. has one line of symmetry. Use the picture at the right to describe where the line of symmetry is.

29. Write 5 capital letters that have at least one line of symmetry.

30. How many lines of symmetry does a square have?

    A None   **C** 4 lines

    B 2 lines   **D** 6 lines

DIGITAL   Animated Glossary, eTools
www.pearsonsuccessnet.com

Lesson
19-6

Understand It!
A figure can be rotated a
$\frac{1}{4}, \frac{1}{2}, \frac{3}{4}$, and full turn.

Rotational Symmetry

Hands-On
set of polygons

What is rotational symmetry?

When a figure can rotate onto itself in less than a full turn, the figure has rotational symmetry.

If you rotate this figure a $\frac{1}{4}$ turn, it has rotated 90°. This figure has rotational symmetry.

Guided Practice*

Do you know HOW?

Does the figure have rotational symmetry? Write yes or no.

1.   2.

3.   4.

Do you UNDERSTAND?

5. A figure that has been rotated a $\frac{1}{4}$ turn has been rotated ___ degrees.

6. A figure that has been rotated 180° has been rotated a ___ turn.

7. A figure that has been rotated a $\frac{3}{4}$ turn has been rotated ___ degrees.

Independent Practice

In 8 through 15, does the figure have rotational symmetry? Write yes or no. Give the least angle measure that will rotate the figure onto itself. You may use pattern blocks to help.

8. 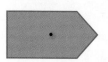   9.   10.   11.

12.   13.   14.   15.

DIGITAL
Animated Glossary, eTools
www.pearsonsuccessnet.com

*For another example, see Set D on page 465.

This figure has rotational symmetry. It must be rotated 180°, or a $\frac{1}{2}$ turn, to land on itself.

This figure has rotational symmetry. It can be rotated 90°, 180°, or 270°, or a $\frac{1}{4}$ turn, a $\frac{1}{2}$ turn, or a $\frac{3}{4}$ turn, to land on itself.

This figure does not have rotational symmetry. It must be rotated 360°, or a full turn, to land on itself.

Problem Solving

For **16** and **17**, fill in and use the table to the right.

16. Valerie has 16 yards of fencing material to build a dog run. She wants to put the fence around a rectangular area. Complete the table to the right for the possibilities of the fencing.

Side A Length	Side B Length	Area
1 yd		7 sq. yd
2 yd		
3 yd		
4 yd		

17. Which area is the largest? What is another name for this shape?

18. There are 48 boxes in a warehouse. If there are 22 packages of paper in each box, how many packages of paper are there in the warehouse?

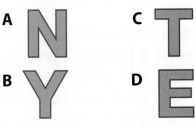

? packages of paper

| 22 | 22 | 22 |

Packages of paper in each box

19. Which capital letter below has rotational symmetry?

A N   C T

B Y   D E

20. Where would the parentheses have to go to make this equation true?

$$18 - 2 + 12 - 8 = 20$$

21. The Megaray Kite has an area of almost 1,500 square meters. Suppose the wind suddenly changes and the kite moves 25 meters east. Has the shape or size of the kite changed? Explain.

Lesson
19-7

Understand It!
Learning how and when
to draw a picture can
help solve problems.

Draw a Picture

Hands-On
grid paper

Lisa has been asked to draw a large arrow that is exactly the same shape as the one shown on the grid at the right.

Make a large arrow that is exactly the same shape. Explain how you know it is the same shape.

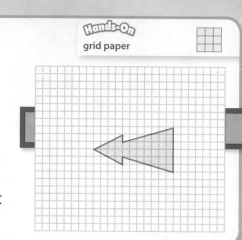

Guided Practice*

Do you know HOW?

For **1** and **2**, make a large figure that is exactly the same shape. Explain how you know it is the same shape.

1.   2.

Do you UNDERSTAND?

3. Suppose that you drew the arrow above so that it was pointing vertically. Would the shape of the arrow change?

4. Draw a picture of a shape. Then triple each side.

Independent Practice

Solve.

5. Draw a large figure. Then draw a smaller figure that is exactly the same shape.

6. If you were to cut out a hexagon to make a sign similar to the shape below, how would you draw it to make it twice the size?

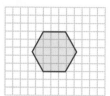

Stuck? Try this....

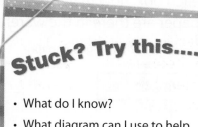

- What do I know?
- What diagram can I use to help understand the problem?
- Can I use addition, subtraction, multiplication, or division?
- Is all of my work correct?
- Did I answer the right question?
- Is my answer reasonable?

Plan

What do I know? I know the length of each side of the arrow. The arrow is 11 units long from left to right.

What am I asked to find? To make an arrow that is exactly the same shape

Solve

Double the length of each side.

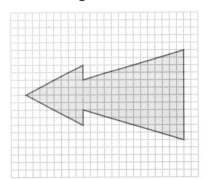

The shapes are the same because the length of each side was doubled.

7. Stephen is listening to a book on tape. The book has 17 chapters and each chapter is about 22 minutes long. How many minutes will it take to listen to the complete book?

8. Six people are taking part in a charity walk. Two people walked for 8 miles, three people walked for 6 miles, and one person walked for 10 miles. How many miles did they walk in all?

9. Which can be rotated less than one complete turn and look exactly the same?

A B   C H

B V   D R

10. Which of the following shapes has exactly four lines of symmetry?

A   C

B   D

11. Jackie and Kendall are part of their school's relay race team. Each member of the team has to run for one-half mile of a 3-mile race.

   a Draw a picture to help you find how many members are on the relay team.

   b How many other members are on the relay team besides Jackie and Kendall?

12. Lawrence's father said that he would put 12 dollars into Lawrence's savings account for every 20 dollars Lawrence put into it. If after a year his father had put 96 dollars into Lawrence's account, how much did Lawrence put into his account?

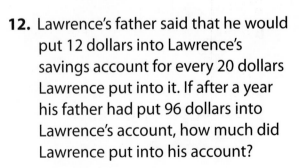

eTools
www.pearsonsuccessnet.com

1. Four of Mrs. Li's students decorated a bulletin board. Whose shape has 4 lines of symmetry? (19-5)

Ralph   Liza

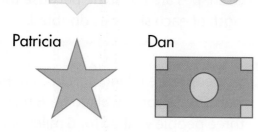

Patricia   Dan

A Ralph

B Liza

C Patricia

D Dan

2. Which figure below has rotational symmetry? (19-6)

A

B

C
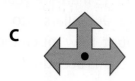

D

3. Which transformation can be used to show that the figures are congruent? (19-4)

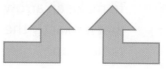

A Turn

B Translation

C Rotation

D Reflection

4. Corby made a pattern with geometric tiles. Which shows his pattern reflected over the line? (19-2)

A
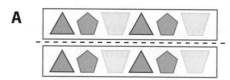

B
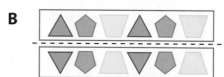

C
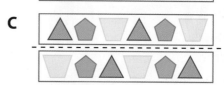

D
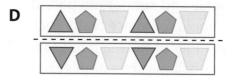

5. Which of the following represents a translation? (19-1)

A Turning over a pancake

B Seeing yourself in a mirror

C Moving a checker diagonally on a checker board

D A dog rolling over

6. Which letter of the alphabet is a reflection of the letter b? (19-2)

   A The letter d or the letter p

   B The letter d or the letter q

   C Only the letter p

   D Only the letter d

7. Which figures are related by translation? (19-1)

   A

   B

   C

   D

8. Cassidy made the shape to the right. Which shape below is the same shape? (19-7)

   A

   B

   C

   D

9. What is the new position of this shape after it makes a $\frac{1}{2}$-turn rotation? (19-3)

   A

   B

   C

   D

10. Which motion can be used to show that the two figures are congruent? (19-4)

   A Turn

   B Rotation

   C Reflection

   D Translation

11. Which of the following represents a rotation? (19-3)

   A Riding a sled down a hill

   B A fan blade on a moving fan

   C The image of a tree in a lake

   D Jumping straight up

Set A, pages 448–453

How can you move a shape on a plane?

A translation moves a figure in a straight direction.

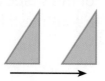

A reflection of a figure gives its mirror image.

A rotation of a figure moves it about a point.

A figure can be related by more than one manipulation.

Remember that two figures can be related by more than one manipulation.

Tell how the two figures are related to each other.

1.    2.

3.    4.

5.    6.

Set B, pages 454–455

Are the figures congruent? If so, tell if they are related by a reflection, translation, or rotation.

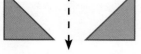 

The triangles are the same size and shape, so they are congruent. They are related by a reflection.

The circles are not the same size, so they are not congruent.

Remember that you can use translations, reflections, and rotations to test if two figures are congruent.

Are the figures in each pair congruent?

1.    2.

3. 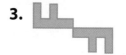   4.

Set C, pages 456–457

How many lines of symmetry does the figure have?

Fold the figure along the dashed line. The two halves are congruent and fit one on top of the other.

It has 1 line of symmetry.

Remember that figures can have many lines of symmetry.

Draw the lines of symmetry for each figure.

1.   2.   3.

Set D, pages 458–459

What kind of rotation does the figure make?

This figure can be rotated 90°, or a $\frac{1}{4}$ turn, to land on itself.

This figure can be rotated 180°, or a $\frac{1}{2}$ turn, to land on itself.

This figure can be rotated 90°, 180°, or 270°, or a $\frac{1}{4}$ turn, a $\frac{1}{2}$ turn, or a $\frac{3}{4}$ turn, to land on itself.

Remember, a figure has rotational symmetry if it can rotate onto itself in less than a full turn.

Tell what kind of rotational symmetry each figure has.

1.   2.

3.   4.

5.   6.

Set E, pages 460–461

Make a letter "T" that is exactly the same shape. Explain how you know it is the same shape.

What do I know?   The letter is 11 units in vertical height and spans 9 units horizontally.

What am I asked to find?   To make a letter T that is exactly the same shape.

Double the dimensions of the figure above.

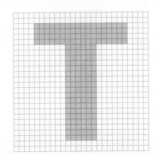

Remember to measure the figure before you draw it.

1. Draw a letter "L" that is exactly the same shape. Explain how you know it is the same shape.

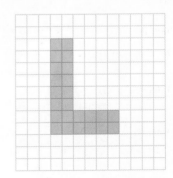

Topic 20 Probability

1 How many passengers can fit in each cabin of the London Eye Ferris Wheel? You will find out in Lesson 20-3.

Review What You Know!

Vocabulary

Choose the best term from the box.

> • likely   • outcome
> • probability • tree diagram

1. __?__ is the likelihood that an event will happen.

2. The possible result of a game or experiment is the __?__.

3. A __?__ event is one which will probably happen.

Chance

Give the chance of each outcome for the yellow part of the spinner.

4.
   ☐ out of ☐

5.
   ☐ out of ☐

6.
   ☐ out of ☐

7.
   ☐ out of ☐

Fractions

Write a fraction to describe the part of each region or set that is shaded.

8.

9.

10. **Writing to Explain** Would you eat more if you ate $\frac{1}{4}$ of a small pizza or $\frac{1}{4}$ of a medium pizza?

2

The curveball was a pitch that changed the game of baseball. Who threw the first curveball in a ballgame? You will find out in Lesson 20-2.

3

When people race model boats, each person uses a different radio signal to control their boat. How do the racers make sure they do not use the same radio signal? You will find out in Lesson 20-1.

Lesson

20-1

Understand It!
Use objects and pictures
to find the number of
possible combinations.

Finding Combinations

Hands-On
2-color counters and color tiles

How can you find all the possible combinations?

Jay's dentist is giving out dental floss and toothbrushes. Jay will get one toothbrush and one kind of floss. How many different combinations can Jay choose?

Floss

Toothbrushes

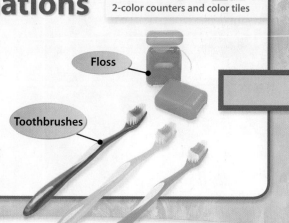

Guided Practice*

Do you know HOW?

For **1** and **2**, find the number of possible combinations. Use objects to help.

1. Choose one of the letters A or B and one of the numbers 1 or 2.

2. Choose one of the letters A, B, C, or D and one of the numbers 1 or 2.

Do you UNDERSTAND?

3. **Writing to Explain** In Exercises 1 and 2, does it matter whether you choose the letter first or the number first? Explain.

4. In the example above, if a third kind of dental floss is offered, how many combinations can Jay choose?

Independent Practice

For **5** and **6**, copy and complete the table to find the number of possible combinations. Use objects to help.

5. Choose one color counter and one color tile.

6. Choose a coin and a bill.

	Red Counter	Yellow Counter
Blue tile		
Green tile		

	Quarter	Dime	Nickel	Penny
1-Dollar bill				
5-Dollar bill				

eTools
www.pearsonsuccessnet.com

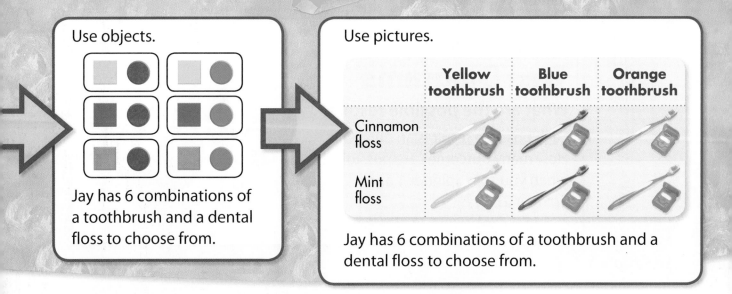

Use objects.

Jay has 6 combinations of a toothbrush and a dental floss to choose from.

Use pictures.

	Yellow toothbrush	Blue toothbrush	Orange toothbrush
Cinnamon floss			
Mint floss			

Jay has 6 combinations of a toothbrush and a dental floss to choose from.

For **7** and **8**, use objects or pictures to find the number of possible combinations.

7. Choose one pet dog, cat, or rabbit and one pet sitter Jill, Marta, or Dave.

8. Choose one of 3 books and one of 8 CDs to bring on a bus trip.

Problem Solving

9. In a model boat race, each person uses a different radio signal. The radio signal is changed using switches on the radio controller. Each switch can be "on" or "off." If there are 4 switches, how many combinations are possible?

 If there are 2 switches, there are 2 × 2, or 4 combinations. If there are 3 switches, there are 2 × 2 × 2 = 8 combinations.

10. Jane made 19 silver dollar pancakes. She took 7 and then gave an equal number to each of her two sisters. How many silver dollar pancakes did each sister get?

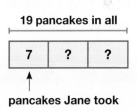

19 pancakes in all

| 7 | ? | ? |

pancakes Jane took

11. Reasoning Mr. Fines needed to buy numbers for an address plaque for his new store. He ordered the numbers 1, 3, and 5. If he could arrange the numbers in any order, what are the possible combinations for his store's address?

12. Tommy had a doctor's appointment at 4:45. He needs 15 minutes to get ready and 20 minutes to drive. At what time does Tommy need to start getting ready?

Understand It!
Make a tree diagram or multiply to find the number of possible outcomes.

Outcomes and Tree Diagrams

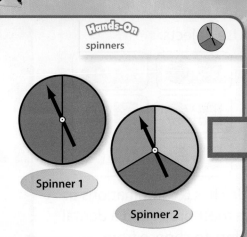

Hands-On
spinners

What are the possible results?

Each possible result is an outcome. How many outcomes are possible when you spin Spinner 1 and Spinner 2?

Spinner 1

Spinner 2

Guided Practice*

Do you know HOW?

For **1** and **2**, use the diagrams below.

Bag 1   1 3 5 7   Bag 2

1. List all the possible outcomes for picking one card from Bag 2.

2. Make a tree diagram to show all the possible outcomes for picking one card from Bag 1 followed by one card from Bag 2.

Do you UNDERSTAND?

3. What number sentence can you use to find the number of possible outcomes in Exercise 2?

4. **Writing to Explain** In the example at the top, why is Blue Blue an outcome but Red Red is not?

5. A board game uses Spinner 1 shown above. On each turn, Spinner 1 is spun twice. How many outcomes are possible for each turn?

Independent Practice

For **6** through **8**, make a tree diagram to list all the possible outcomes for each situation.

6. Spin Spinner 3 once and toss the number cube once.

7. Pick one card from Bag 3 and toss the number cube once.

8. Pick one card from Bag 3 and spin Spinner 3 once.

 When you make a tree diagram, you can list the outcomes in any order you like.

Bag 3

Number Cube

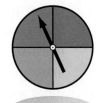

Spinner 3

DIGITAL

Animated Glossary, eTools
www.pearsonsuccessnet.com

For another example, see Set B on page 480.

Make a tree diagram. A tree diagram is a display that shows all possible outcomes.

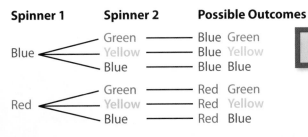

Spinner 1	Spinner 2	Possible Outcomes
	Green —— Blue	Green
Blue	Yellow —— Blue	Yellow
	Blue —— Blue	Blue
	Green —— Red	Green
Red	Yellow —— Red	Yellow
	Blue —— Red	Blue

There are 6 possible outcomes.

Multiply.

There are 2 outcomes for Spinner 1 and 3 outcomes for Spinner 2.

$$3 \times 2 = 6$$

There are 6 possible outcomes.

For **9** and **10**, multiply to find the number of possible outcomes.

9. Flip a coin and toss a number cube that is numbered 1 through 6.

10. Pick one card from each of two piles. One pile has the cards labeled F, I, T, P, N, C, and O. The other has the cards labeled A, R, S, and Q.

Problem Solving

For **11,** use the number cubes at the right.

11. How many outcomes are there for one toss of the octahedron and one toss of the dodecahedron?

12. Candy Cummings is credited with pitching the first curveball in a baseball game in 1867. Some pitchers know how to throw 2 types of curveballs, 2 types of fastballs, and 1 knuckleball. If a pitcher strikes out a batter on three pitches, how many different combinations of pitches can be thrown?

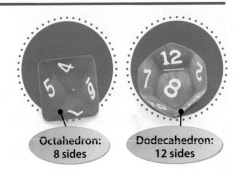

Octahedron: 8 sides   Dodecahedron: 12 sides

For **13** and **14**, use the drawing at the right.

13. Wearing a blindfold, you toss two rings. Both tosses land on a bottle. List all the possible outcomes.

14. Writing to Explain Would the number of possible outcomes change if there were more blue bottles than red and white bottles?

Lesson
20-3

Understand It!
Fractions can be used to describe the probability of an event.

Writing Probability as a Fraction

How can you find probability?

Katie is organizing T-shirts for 8 members of a team. She has 3 different colored shirts: blue, orange, and yellow. Without looking, what is the probability of Katie picking a yellow shirt?

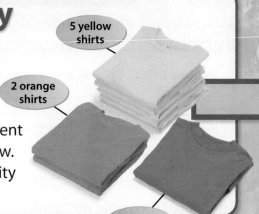

5 yellow shirts

2 orange shirts

1 blue shirt

Another Example **How can you describe probability?**

You have learned to use fractions to describe parts of sets, regions, and distances on number lines. In this lesson, you will learn how fractions can be used to describe probability.

An impossible event has a probability of 0. A certain event has a probability of 1. Any other event has a probability between 0 and 1.

Katie is **certain** to pick a shirt.

Katie is **likely** to pick a shirt that is yellow.

Katie is **unlikely** to pick a shirt that is blue.

It is **impossible** for Katie to pick a green shirt.

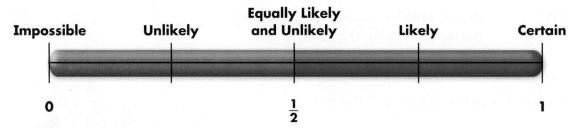

Impossible	Unlikely	Equally Likely and Unlikely	Likely	Certain
0		$\frac{1}{2}$		1

Explain It

1. What is the probability of picking a blue shirt?

2. How likely is it that Katie will pick an orange shirt? Explain.

You can use fractions to describe the probability of an event.

Probability <u>is the likelihood that an event will happen</u>.

$$\text{Probability} = \frac{\text{number of favorable outcomes}}{\text{number of possible outcomes}}$$

$$P(\text{yellow shirt}) = \frac{\text{number of yellow shirts}}{\text{number of shirts in all}}$$

$$P = \frac{5}{8}$$

The probability of picking a yellow shirt is $\frac{5}{8}$.

Guided Practice*

Do you know HOW?

For **1** through **4**, find the probability of selecting, without looking, a tile from the tiles shown below.

1. Crescent

2. Not a circle

3. Heart or crescent

4. Diamond

Do you UNDERSTAND?

5. In the example above, what is the probability of picking a blue or an orange shirt?

6. Describe an event that is impossible.

7. Describe an event that is certain.

Independent Practice

For **8** through **15**, write the probability of selecting, without looking, the card or letter described.

8. a consonant that is not M

9. the letter D, E, G, O, S, T, or U

10. a blue, orange or green card

11. a letter that is not G

12. a yellow card

13. the letter X

14. the letter Q

15. a vowel

Animated Glossary
www.pearsonsuccessnet.com

*For another example, see Set C on page 481.

Lesson 20-3

For **16** through **19**, write the probability and tell whether it is likely, unlikely, impossible, or certain to land on red when each spinner is spun once.

16.

17.

18.

19.

Problem Solving

20. Geometry Rectangle A is 4 feet by 6 feet. Rectangle B is 1 yard by 2 yards. Which rectangle has a greater perimeter?

21. How many windows are in a 9-story building if there are 28 windows per story?

22. Look at the problem below.

$$\triangle + 9 = \square$$

If $\triangle = 4$, what is $\square$?

23. Estimation Heather has read 393 pages of the latest "Girl Wizard" book. Irene has read 121 fewer pages than Heather. If there are 439 pages in the book, about how many pages does Irene have left to read?

For **24** through **26**, use the bags at the right.

24. From which bag would picking a red tile be a certain outcome?

25. What is the likelihood of picking a green tile out of Bag D?

26. What is the probability of picking a green tile out of Bag C?

For **27**, use the table at the right.

27. Each cabin of the London Eye Ferris wheel can hold up to 25 passengers. Jared is waiting for Samantha to get off the London Eye. He knows she will get out of Cabin 1 or Cabin 2. What is the probability that she is in Cabin 2? Write the probability as a fraction.

Cabin Number	Number of People
1	15
2	25

Tessellations

A **tessellation** is a repeating pattern of shapes that has
no gaps or overlaps.

Examples:

Some regular polygons make tessellations. The sides of regular polygons
have the same length.

square

equilateral triangle

hexagon

Two or more polygons can be
used to create tessellations.

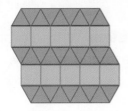

Some polygons cannot make a
tessellation. There are gaps.

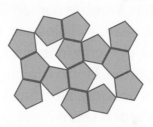

Practice

Solve.

1. Trace the shape shown below.
Does it tessellate?

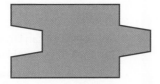

2. Trace the shape shown below.
Does it tessellate?

3. Draw a tessellation that uses
trapezoids and equilateral triangles.

4. Draw a tessellation that uses
octagons and squares.

Understand It!
Learning how and when to use reasoning can help you solve problems.

Use Reasoning

Mary, Kristen, Deborah, and Amy met on vacation. They are from New York, Georgia, Nevada, and Maine. Amy is from New York, and Kristen is not from Georgia. If Deborah is from Nevada, where is Mary from?

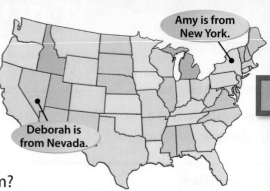

Amy is from New York.

Deborah is from Nevada.

Guided Practice*

Do you know HOW?

Make a chart and use reasoning to solve. Write the answer in a complete sentence.

1. Tony has 4 rabbits named Lenny, Emma, Beau, and Blossom. One is orange, one gray, one black, and one spotted. Emma is orange. Beau is not gray. Blossom is spotted. What color is Lenny?

Do you UNDERSTAND?

2. In the example above, when a "Y" is placed in a cell, why does an "N" get placed in the other cells in the same row and column?

3. Write a Problem Write a problem using the reasoning strategy.

Independent Practice

Solve each problem. Write the answer in a complete sentence.

4. There are 5 people in the Robinson family: Harry, Barb, Roger, Laurie, and Carrie. Their ages are 37, 36, 13, 10, and 5. Barb is the oldest and Carrie is the youngest. Laurie is 13. Harry is not 10. He is older than Roger. How old is Roger?

5. Six dancers want to form a triangle so that the same number of dancers is on each side. How should they stand? Draw a picture to solve.

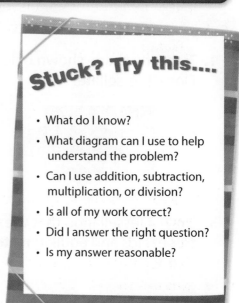

Stuck? Try this....

- What do I know?
- What diagram can I use to help understand the problem?
- Can I use addition, subtraction, multiplication, or division?
- Is all of my work correct?
- Did I answer the right question?
- Is my answer reasonable?

Make and fill in the table with the information you know.

	NY	GA	NV	ME
Mary				
Kristen		N		
Deborah			Y	
Amy	Y			

Each row and each column can have only one Yes because each girl can be from only one of the four states.

Fill in the row and column with No's (N) where there is one Yes (Y).

	NY	GA	NV	ME
Mary	N	**Y**	N	N
Kristen	N	N	N	**Y**
Deborah	N	N	Y	N
Amy	Y	N	N	N

Use reasoning to draw conclusions. There are 3 No's in Kristen's row. She must live in Maine. Put a Y in the Maine column. Complete the chart.

Mary is from Georgia.

6. What comes next in the pattern to the right?

7. Wendy, Chris, Lauren, and Santiago live on four different streets: Highland, East, Brook, and Elm. Wendy lives on Highland. Lauren lives on Elm. Chris does not live on East. What street does Santiago live on?

	Brook	East	Elm	Highland
Chris		No		
Lauren			Yes	
Santiago				
Wendy				Yes

8. Eric and his friends are playing volleyball. They made a total of 6 teams. If there are 4 players on each team, how many people are playing volleyball?

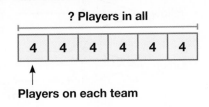

? Players in all

4	4	4	4	4	4

↑
Players on each team

9. Vicki has a bag with 6 blue marbles, 4 red marbles, 7 green marbles, and 8 yellow marbles all the same size. If she pulls out one marble without looking, which color is she most likely to choose?

A Blue   C Green

B Red   D Yellow

10. Weddell, Von Bellingshausen, Cook, Palmer, and Wilkes each explored Antarctica. Two were British, and one was Russian. The other two were from the United States. Palmer and Wilkes were from the same country. Cook was British. Weddell was from the same country as Cook. Which country was Von Bellingshausen from?

1. Newell and Mateo are playing a game. The spinner for the game is shown below.

If Mateo spins the spinner twice, what are all the possible outcomes? (20-2)

A 2 pinks or 2 yellows

B 2 yellows or 1 pink and 1 yellow

C 2 pinks or 1 pink and 1 yellow

D 2 pinks or 2 yellows or 1 pink and 1 yellow

2. Alyssa can buy one of 4 jewelry kits and one of 4 dolls. How many different combinations of kits and dolls can she buy? (20-1)

A 16

B 12

C 8

D 4

3. A fish tank has 2 black fish, 4 white fish, 12 orange fish, and 2 red fish. If one fish is pulled out randomly, which color is most likely to be picked? (20-3)

A Black

B White

C Orange

D Red

4. Which tree diagram shows the possible outcomes for spinning each spinner shown? (20-2)

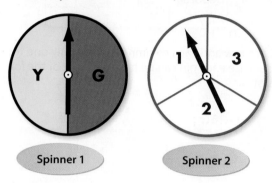

Spinner 1   Spinner 2

A

Spinner 1	Spinner 2	Outcome
Yellow	1	Y1
	2	Y2
Green	2	G2
	3	G3

B

Spinner 1	Spinner 2	Outcome
Yellow	1	Y1
	2	Y2
	3	Y3
Green	2	G2
	3	G3

C

Spinner 1	Spinner 2	Outcome
Yellow	1	Y1
	2	Y2
	3	Y3
Green	1	G1
	2	G2
	3	G3

D

Spinner 1	Spinner 2	Outcome
Yellow	1	Y1
	2	Y2
	3	Y3
Green	1	G1
	2	G2

5. The four children in the Wininger family are Ryan, Makena, Jackson, and Whitney. Each child attends Skyline Elementary. There is a child in Kindergarten, 1st grade, 3rd grade, and 5th grade. Makena is in 5th grade. Jackson is not in 1st grade. If Whitney is in 3rd grade, what grade is Ryan in? (20-4)

	K	1	3	5
Ryan				
Makena				
Jackson				
Whitney				

A Kindergarten

B 1st grade

C 3rd grade

D 5th grade

6. If Kinesha selects a balloon, without looking, from the ones below, what is the probability she will select a heart shaped balloon? (20-3)

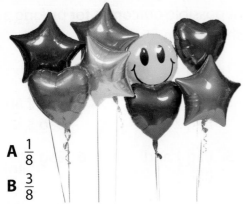

A $\frac{1}{8}$

B $\frac{3}{8}$

C $\frac{4}{8}$

D $\frac{3}{5}$

7. Ben, Gracie, Josh, and Avery each get to school in a different way. They come either by bus, walking, riding a bike, or in a car. Ben walks to school. Gracie does not come in a car. If Josh rides the bus, how does Avery get to school? (20-4)

A Bus **C** Riding a bike

B Walking **D** Car

8. There are 15 pieces of fruit in the fruit bowl. There are 8 bananas, 2 apples, 4 kiwi, and 1 peach. Which fruit would it be impossible for Regan to pick? (20-3)

A Pear

B Banana

C Peach

D Apple

9. Payton can choose steak, chicken, or pork, and one side of peas, corn, squash, green beans, potatoes, okra, or spinach for his main dish. How many different combinations can he choose? (20-1)

A 10 **C** 21

B 18 **D** 28

10. Describe the event below. (20-3)

The sun will orbit the Earth.

A Likely **C** Impossible

B Unlikely **D** Certain

Set A, pages 468–469

Choose one color and one shape.
Colors: Red or blue or green

Shapes: ☆ or ▢ or △

How many combinations are there?

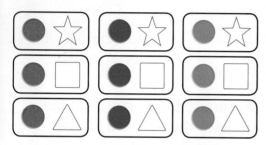

In all, there are 9 combinations.

Remember that the order does not matter when you count combinations.

Find the number of possible combinations.

1. Choose milk or juice plus a side of mashed potatoes, a baked potato, or green beans.

2. Choose a backpack, soft suitcase, or hard suitcase, and then choose one of 5 colors.

Set B, pages 470–471

List the outcomes for picking one item from Box 1 and Box 2. How many outcomes are possible?

You can make a tree diagram.

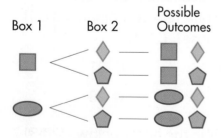

You can multiply.

There are **2** outcomes for Box 1 and **2** outcomes for Box 2.

$$2 \times 2 = 4$$

There are 4 possible outcomes.

Remember you can use a tree diagram or multiply to find the number of possible outcomes.

For **1** through **6**, find the number of possible outcomes for picking a shape from:

1. Bag 1
2. Bag 2
3. Bag 1 and Bag 2
4. Bag 2 and Bag 3
5. Bag 1 and Bag 3
6. Bag 3

7. Make a tree diagram to list the outcomes for picking the letters A, B, or C from Box 1 and the numbers 5 or 6 from Box 2.

Set C, pages 472–474

Beatrice wrote each letter of her name on a slip of paper and put the slips in a bag. If Beatrice draws one slip from the bag, what is the probability that she will draw a vowel?

The probability of drawing a vowel can be expressed as a fraction.

$$\frac{\text{number of vowels}}{\text{number of letters}} = \frac{4}{8}$$

The probability of drawing a vowel is $\frac{4}{8}$ or $\frac{1}{2}$ in simplest form.

Remember that fractions can be used to describe probability.

For **1** through **4**, write the probability of selecting a tile from the tiles below, without looking.

1. Diamond
2. Circle
3. Heart
4. Crescent
5. What is the likelihood of picking a star?

Set D, pages 476–477

Margaret put blue, green, yellow, and orange book covers on her math, science, spelling, and history books. She did not put green on her math book. She put blue on her science book and yellow on her history book. What color cover did she put on her spelling book? Use logical reasoning to solve.

	Math	Science	Spelling	History
Blue	No	Yes	No	No
Green	No	No	Yes	No
Yellow	No	No	No	Yes
Orange	Yes	No	No	No

Margaret put a green cover on her spelling book.

Remember you can use information from the problem to draw conclusions.

Use reasoning to solve. Copy and complete the table to help you.

	5	6	8	10
Larry				
Evelyn				
Terri				Y
Vivian				

1. Each person gets off an elevator on either the 5th, 6th, 8th, or 10th floor. Vivian gets off after Evelyn. When Larry gets off, he says bye to Terri, who is the last person to get off. Where does each person get off?

A.M. Time between midnight and noon.

acute angle An angle that is less than a right angle.

acute triangle A triangle with three acute angles.

addends The numbers that are added together to find a sum.
Example: 2 + 7 = 9

Addends

algebraic expression An expression with variables.

analog clock Shows time by pointing to numbers on a face.

angle A figure formed by two rays that have the same endpoint.

area The number of square units needed to cover a region.

array A way of displaying objects in rows and columns.

Associative Property of Addition Addends can be regrouped and the sum remains the same.

Associative Property of Multiplication Factors can be regrouped and the product remains the same.

average The mean, found by adding all numbers in a set and dividing by the number of values.

bar graph A graph using bars to show data.

benchmark fractions Fractions that are commonly used for estimation: $\frac{1}{4}$, $\frac{1}{3}$, $\frac{1}{2}$, $\frac{2}{3}$, and $\frac{3}{4}$.

breaking apart Mental math method used to rewrite a number as the sum of numbers to form an easier problem.

capacity The volume of a container measured in liquid units.

center A point within a circle that is the same distance from all points on a circle.

centimeter (cm) A metric unit of length. 100 centimeters = 1 meter

century A unit of time equal to 100 years.

certain (event) An event that is sure to occur.

chord Any line segment that connects any two points on the circle.

circle A closed plane figure in which all the points are the same distance from a point called the center.

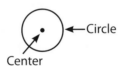
Circle
Center

circle graph A graph in the shape of a circle that shows how the whole is broken into parts.

circumference The distance around a circle.

common factor A factor that two or more numbers have in common.

Commutative Property of Addition Numbers can be added in any order and the sum remains the same.

Commutative Property of Multiplication Factors can be multiplied in any order and the product remains the same.

compatible numbers Numbers that are easy to compute mentally.

compensation Adding and subtracting the same number to make the sum or difference easier to find.

cone A solid figure with a base that is a circle and a curved surface that meets at a point.

congruent Figures that have the same shape and size.

coordinate grid A grid used to show ordered pairs.

counting on Counting up from the smaller number to find the difference of two numbers.

cube A solid figure with six congruent squares as its faces.

cup (c) A customary unit of capacity. 1 cup = 8 fluid ounces

customary units of measure Units of measure that are used in the United States.

cylinder A solid figure with two congruent circular bases.

data Pieces of collected information.

day A unit of time equal to 24 hours.

decade A unit of time equal to 10 years.

decimal point A dot used to separate dollars from cents or ones from tenths in a number.

decimeter (dm) A metric unit of length equal to 10 centimeters.

degree (°) A unit of measure for angles.

degrees Celsius (°C) A metric unit of temperature.

denominator The number below the fraction bar in a fraction. The total number of equal parts in all.

diameter A line segment that connects two points on a circle and passes through the center.

difference The answer when subtracting two numbers.

digital clock Shows time with numbers. Hours are separated from minutes with a colon.

digits The symbols used to write a number: 0, 1, 2, 3, 4, 5, 6, 7, 8, and 9.

Distributive Property Breaking apart problems into two simpler problems. *Example*: $(3 \times 21) = (3 \times 20) + (3 \times 1)$

divide An operation to find the number in each group or the number of equal groups.

dividend The number to be divided.

divisibility rules The rules that state when a number is divisible by another number.

divisible Can be divided by another number without leaving a remainder. *Example*: 10 is divisible by 2

divisor The number by which another number is divided. *Example*: $32 \div 4 = 8$

Divisor

edge A line segment where two faces of a solid figure meet.

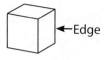
←Edge

elapsed time The amount of time between the beginning of an event and the end of the event.

equally likely (event) Just as likely to happen as not to happen.

equation A number sentence that uses the equal sign ($=$) to show that two expressions have the same value.

equilateral triangle A triangle in which all sides are the same length.

equivalent Numbers that name the same amount.

equivalent fractions Fractions that name the same region, part of a set, or part of a segment.

expanded form A number written as the sum of the values of its digits. *Example*: $2,000 + 400 + 70 + 6$

face A flat surface of a solid that does not roll.

←Face

fact family A group of related facts using the same set of numbers.

factors The numbers multiplied together to find a product.
Example: 3 × 6 = 18

Factor

fluid ounce (fl oz) A customary unit of capacity.
1 fluid ounce = 2 tablespoons

foot (ft) A customary unit of length.
1 foot = 12 inches

fraction A fraction is a symbol, such as $\frac{2}{3}$, $\frac{5}{1}$, or $\frac{8}{5}$, used to name a part of a whole, a part of a set, a location on a number line, or a division of whole numbers.

front-end estimation A way to estimate a sum by adding the first digit of each addend and adjusting the result based on the remaining digits.

gallon (gal) A customary unit of capacity. 1 gallon = 4 quarts

gram (g) A metric unit of mass. 1,000 grams = 1 kilogram

hexagon A polygon with 6 sides.

hour A unit of time equal to 60 minutes.

hundredth One part of 100 equal parts of a whole.

Identity Property of Addition The sum of any number and zero is that number.

Identity Property of Multiplication The product of any number and one is that number.

impossible (event) An event that cannot occur.

improper fractions A fraction in which the numerator is greater than or equal to the denominator.

inch (in.) A customary unit of length. 12 inches = 1 foot

inequality A number sentence that uses the greater than sign (>) or the less than sign (<) to show that two expressions do not have the same value.

intersecting lines Lines that cross at one point.

interval A number which is the difference between two consecutive numbers on the scale of a graph.

inverse operations Operations that undo each other.
Examples: Adding 6 and subtracting 6 are inverse operations. Multiplying by 4 and dividing by 4 are inverse operations.

isosceles triangle A triangle that has at least two equal sides.

key Part of a pictograph that tells what each symbol stands for.

kilogram (kg) A metric unit of mass. 1 kilogram = 1,000 grams

kilometer (km) A metric unit of length. 1 kilometer = 1,000 meters

leap year A unit of time equal to 366 days.

likely (event) An event that probably will happen.

line A straight path of points that goes on and on in two directions.

line graph A graph that connects points to show how data changes over time.

line of symmetry A line on which a figure can be folded so that both halves are congruent.

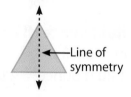

line plot A display of data along a number line.

line segment A part of a line that has two endpoints.

liter (L) A metric unit of capacity. 1 liter = 1,000 milliliters

mass The amount of matter that something contains.

mean An average, found by adding all numbers in a set and dividing by the number of values.

median The middle number in an ordered data set.

meter (m) A metric unit of length.
1 meter = 100 centimeters

mile (mi) A customary unit of length.
1 mile = 5,280 feet

millennium A unit for measuring time equal to 1,000 years.

milliliter (mL) A metric unit of capacity.
1,000 milliliters = 1 liter

millimeter (mm) A metric unit of length.
1,000 millimeters = 1 meter

minute A unit of time equal to 60 seconds.

mixed number A number that has a whole number and a fraction.

mode The number or numbers that occur most often in a data set.

month One of the 12 parts into which a year is divided.

multiple The product of any two whole numbers.

net A pattern used to make a solid.

Example:

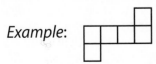

number expression An expression that contains numbers and at least one operation. A number expression is also called a numerical expression.

numerator The number above the fraction bar in a fraction.

obtuse angle An angle that is greater than a right angle.

obtuse triangle A triangle in which there is one obtuse angle.

octagon A polygon with 8 sides.

ordered pair A pair of numbers that names a point on a coordinate grid.

ounce (oz) A customary unit of weight.
16 ounces = 1 pound

outcome A possible result of a game or experiment.

outlier A number in a data set that is very different from the rest of the numbers.

overestimate An estimate that is greater than the exact answer.

P.M. Time between noon and midnight.

parallel lines In a plane, lines that never intersect. *Example*:

parallelogram A quadrilateral in which opposite sides are parallel.

partial products Products found by breaking one factor in a multiplication problem into ones, tens, hundreds, and so on and then multiplying each of these by the other factor.

pentagon A plane figure with 5 sides.

perimeter The distance around a figure.

period In a number, a group of three digits, separated by commas, starting from the right.

perpendicular lines Two intersecting lines that form right angles. *Example*:

pictograph A graph using pictures or symbols to show data.

pi (π) The ratio of the circumference of a circle to its diameter. Pi is approximately 3.14.

pint (pt) A customary unit of capacity. 1 pint = 2 cups

plane An endless flat surface.

plot To locate and mark a point named by an ordered pair on a grid.

point An exact location in space.

polygon A closed plane figure made up of line segments.

pound (lb) A customary unit of weight. 1 pound = 16 ounces

prediction An informed guess about what will happen.

probability A number telling the likelihood an event will happen.

product The answer to a multiplication problem.

protractor A tool used to measure and draw angles.

pyramid A solid figure whose base is a polygon and whose faces are triangles with a common vertex.

quadrilateral A polygon with 4 sides.

quart (qt) A customary unit of capacity. 1 quart = 2 pints

quotient The answer to a division problem.

radius Any line segment that connects the center to a point on the circle.

range The difference between the greatest value and the least value in a data set.

ray A part of a line that has one endpoint and continues endlessly in one direction.

rectangle A quadrilateral with 4 right angles.

rectangular prism A solid figure whose faces are all rectangles.

rectangular pyramid A solid figure with a rectangle for its base and triangles for all other faces.

reflection Gives its mirror image.

remainder The number that remains after the division is complete.

rhombus A quadrilateral in which opposite sides are parallel and all sides are the same length.

right angle An angle that forms a square corner.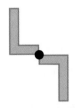

right triangle A triangle in which there is one right angle.

rotation Moves a figure about a point.

rounding Replacing a number with a number that tells about how many or how much.

S

scale Numbers that show the units used on a graph.

scalene triangle A triangle in which no sides are the same length.

second A unit of time. 60 seconds = 1 minute

side Each of the line segments of a polygon.

similar figures Figures that have the same shape and may or may not have the same size.

simplest form A fraction in which the numerator and denominator have no common factors other than 1.

solid figure A figure that has length, width, and height.

solution The value of the variable that makes an equation true.

solve Find a solution to an equation.

sphere A solid figure that includes all points the same distance from a center point.

square A quadrilateral with 4 right angles and all sides the same length.

square pyramid A solid figure with a square base and four faces that are triangles.

standard form A way to write a number showing only its digits. *Example*: 2,613

stem-and-leaf plot A display that shows data in order of place value.

straight angle An angle that forms a straight line.

sum The result of adding numbers together.

survey Collecting information by asking a number of people the same question and recording their answers.

symmetric A figure is symmetric if it can be folded into two congruent halves that fit on top of each other.

tablespoon (tbsp) A customary unit of capacity. 1 tablespoon = 3 teaspoons

teaspoon (tsp) A customary unit of capacity. 3 teaspoons = 1 tablespoon

tenth One of ten equal parts of a whole.

tesselation A repeating pattern that has no gaps or overlaps.

ton (T) A customary unit of weight. 1 ton = 2,000 pounds

translation A change in the position of a figure that moves it up, down, or sideways.

trapezoid A quadrilateral with only one pair of parallel sides.

tree diagram A display to show all possible outcomes.

trend A pattern in the data on a line graph, shown by an increase or decrease.

triangle A polygon with 3 sides.

triangular prism A solid figure with two bases that are triangles and the other three faces are rectangles.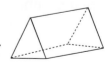

underestimate An estimate that is less than the exact answer.

unlikely (event) An event that probably will not happen.

variable A symbol or letter that stands for a number.

Venn diagram A diagram that uses circles to show the relationships between groups of data.
Example:

vertex (plural, vertices) The point where two rays meet to form an angle. The points where the sides of a polygon meet. The points where three or more edges meet in a solid figure that does not roll. The pointed part of a cone.

volume The number of cubic units needed to fill a solid figure.

week A unit of time equal to 7 days.

weight How heavy an object is.

word form A number written in words. *Example*: Four thousand, six hundred, thirty-two.

yard (yd) A customary unit of length. 1 yard = 3 feet

year A unit of time equal to 365 days or 52 weeks or 12 months.

Zero Property of Multiplication The product of any number and zero is zero.

Illustrations

Cover: Luciana Navarro Powell

Photographs

Every effort has been made to secure permission and provide appropriate credit for photographic material. The publisher deeply regrets any omission and pledges to correct errors called to its attention in subsequent editions.

Unless otherwise acknowledged, all photographs are the property of Scott Foresman, a division of Pearson Education.

Photo locators denoted as follows: Top (T), Center (C), Bottom (B), Left (L), Right (R), Background (Bkgd)

2 (CL) Bettmann/Corbis, (BC) Getty Images (CL) Russell Gordon/Danita Delimont, Agent (BR) Earth Imaging/Getty Images 7 (CR) Corbis 8 (BR) Getty Images 10 (TL) ©Rexford Lord/Photo Researchers, Inc. 26 (TL) ©Nicholas Veasey/Getty Images, (BL) NASA, (B) Getty Images 28 (TR) ©Nicholas Veasey/Getty Images 40 (BR) ©Ulrich Doering/Alamy Images 44 (TR) ©Mark Sykes/Alamy 52 (T) Marc Muench/Corbis (C) Jean-Pierre Courau, Private Collection/Bridgeman Art Library 53 (TL) Getty Images 54 (BR) ©Garold W. Sneegas 58 (L) ©Amos Nachoum/Corbis (CL) ©age fotostock/SuperStock 74 (L) ©Corbis (BC) J.M. Labat/Peter Arnold, Inc. 94 (TL) Roger Harris/Photo Researchers, Inc. (B) Purestock/Getty Images (TR) ©Nils Jorgensen/Rex USA (T) Roger Harris/Photo Researchers, Inc. 95 (TL) Getty Images 98 (BR) Richard Lewis/©DK Images 114 (All) ©Royalty-Free/Corbis 116 (BR) Tracy Morgan/©DK Images 126 (C) Pablo Martinez Monsivais/AP Images (TL) Mehau Kulyk /Photo Researchers, Inc. (BL) ©Chuck Pratt/Bruce Coleman Inc. (BC) ©Inga Spence/Getty Images 134 (TR) Jupiter Images 140 (C) Andy Holligan/DK Images (C) SSPL/The Image Works, Inc. (TL) ©Daniel Joubert/Reuters/Corbis 142 (BR) ©Daniel Joubert/Reuters/Corbis 144 (TR) GSFC/NASA 152 (BR) ©Daniel Joubert/Reuters/Corbis 162 (T) AP Images (B) ©Stefano Paltera/Reuters/Landov LLC (T) ©Richard D. Fisher (T) ©JSC/NASA 170 (BL) ©Panoramic Images/Getty Images 172 (BR) Getty Images 182 (BR) Jupiter Images 194 (TL) Getty Images (BL) 3D4Medical/Getty Images 195 (CC) Getty Images 196 (C) ©photolibrary/Index Open 199 Map Resources 202 (TL,BR) Getty Images 204 (BR) Netter medical illustration used with permission of Elsevier. All rights reserved. 214 (B) Momatiuk - Eastcott/Corbis (TL) Geosphere/Planetary Visions/Photo Researchers, Inc. (TR) Courtesy of New Bremen Giant Pumpkin Growers (TL) © Stockbyte 224 (C) ©Barbara Strnadova 234 (TR) ©VStock/Index Open 248 (B) ©Richard

Hamilton Smith/Corbis 249 (BL) Bettmann/Corbis 250 (B) ©Richard Hamilton Smith/Corbis 268 (TL) ©Charles E. Rotkin/Corbis (TL) The Granger Collection, NY (B) Getty Images (L) ©Ron Niebrugge/Alamy Images 270 (TR) ©VStock/Index Open 288 (CL) R. Harris/Photo Researchers, Inc. 290 (B) DK Images (TL) ©USGS/Photo Researchers, Inc. 296 (BC) Corbis (CLC,TC) ©photolibrary/Index Open (C) ©photolibrary/Index Open (TC) ©photolibrary/Index Open 306 (TCR) ©Jeff Rotman (Avi Klapfer)/Nature Picture Library (TR) Jupiter Images 308 (TR) Getty Images 314 (T) ©Susan Carlson/Getty Images (BL) ©Doug Pearson/Alamy Images (B) ©Rudy Sulgan/Corbis 327 (CR) Corbis 344 (TR) ©Robert F. Bukaty/AP Images 346 Getty Images 348 (TL) Getty Images (R) ©Goodshoot/Jupiter Images 349 ©Jeff Greenberg/Index Stock Imagery 352 (TR) Getty Images 354 (CR) ©Will & Deni McIntyre/Getty Images 364 (B) AP Images (CR) ©Jerry Cooke/Corbis (TR) Getty Images (TL) age fotostock /SuperStock (TL) ©Norman Tomalin/Alamy Images 366 (C) Jupiter Images (C) AP Images Photos 368 (TL) ©Royalty-Free/Corbis (TL) ©photolibrary/Index Open (CR) GK & Vicki Hart/Getty Images (BR) ©photolibrary/Index Open 370 (CLTC,BR) Getty Images (BC) Hemera Technologies (C) ©photolibrary/Index Open (TR) Jupiter Images 376 (C) ©Jonathan Blair/Corbis (TC) Jerry Young/DK Images 378 (CC) Getty Images (CL) Stockdisc 380 ©face to face Bildagentur GMBH/Alamy (C) Ingram Publishing (CR) Goodshoot/Jupiter Images (CR) ©DK Images (TR) Getty Images 388 (BR) ©Dean Fox/SuperStock 401 (BR) ©David R. Frazier Photolibrary, Inc/Alamy Images 402 (TL) DAJ/Getty Images (B) Keren Su/Corbis (C) ©Barbara Strnadova 408 (TR) Alaskan Express/Jupiter Images 432 (TL) ©Harold Sund/Getty Images (B) ©Don Klumpp/Getty Images (TC) NASA/ Science Faction/Getty Images (B) Getty Images 446 (B) ©James P. Blair/Corbis 448 (B) Max Alexander/©DK Images (TL) M. C. Escher's "Symmetry Drawing E78"/©The M. C. Escher Company, Baarn, Holland. All rights reserved. 450 (TB,TR) Getty Images (C) Hemera Technologies (TR) Jupiter Images (BR) M. C. Escher's "Symmetry Drawing E78"/©The M. C. Escher Company, Baarn, Holland. All rights reserved. 452 (TR) Jupiter Images 454 Jupiter Images 457 (BR) ©Asa Gauen/Alamy Images 458 (BR) ©Dean Fox/SuperStock 467 (TL) John Gress/Corbis 468 ©Alex Steedman/Corbis 478 Digital Wisdom, Inc.

Index